BIRDS IN MINNESOTA

The John K. Fesler Memorial Fund and David R. Fesler provided assistance in the publication of this volume, for which the University of Minnesota is grateful.

BIRDS IN MINNESOTA

ROBERT B. JANSSEN

Published by the
University of Minnesota Press, Minneapolis
for the
James Ford Bell Museum of Natural History

Second printing, 1988

Published by the University of Minnesota Press
2037 University Avenue Southeast, Minneapolis, MN 55414.
Published simultaneously in Canada
by Fitzhenry & Whiteside Limited, Markham.
Printed in the United States of America.

Library of Congress Cataloging-in-Publication Data

Janssen, Robert B.
    Birds in Minnesota.

    Includes index.
    1. Birds —Minnesota—Geographical distribution.
2. Bird populations—Minnesota. I. Title.
QL684.M6J36 1987   598.29776   87-5860
ISBN 0-8166-1568-3
ISBN 0-8166-1569-1 (pbk.)

Photographs courtesy of: **Steve Blanich** (Baird's Sparrow); **Marj Carr**
(Snowy Owl); **Betty D. Cottrile** (Yellow-bellied Flycatcher); **Robert O.
Ferguson** (Common Loon); **David B. Johnson** (Great Gray Owl); **James
P. Mattsson** (Ross's Gull, Northern Hawk-Owl); **Warren Nelson** (Greater
Prairie-Chicken, Sharp-tailed Grouse, Yellow Rail, Boreal Owl, Three-
toed Woodpecker, Black-backed Woodpecker, Bohemian Waxwing,
Henslow's Sparrow, Pine Grosbeak, Hoary Redpoll); **Karl Overman**
(Gyrfalcon); **Steve Wilson** (Spruce Grouse, Wilson's Warbler); **Ann Marie
Wyckoff** (Chestnut-collared Longspur).

The University of Minnesota
is an equal opportunity
educator and employer.

This book is dedicated to Brother Theodore Voelker
and Raymond Glassel, both of whom taught me that
"Birding is the Answer."

CONTENTS

Specialties of Minnesota — photographs between
pp. 160 and 161

Gyrfalcon
Common Loon
Spruce Grouse
Greater Prairie-Chicken
Sharp-tailed Grouse
Yellow Rail
Ross's Gull
Snowy Owl
Northern Hawk-Owl
Great Gray Owl
Boreal Owl

Three-toed Woodpecker
Black-backed Woodpecker
Yellow-bellied Flycatcher
Bohemian Waxwing
Wilson's Warbler
Baird's Sparrow
Henslow's Sparrow
Chestnut-collared Longspur
Pine Grosbeak
Hoary Redpoll

FOREWORD

One goal of a book on the distribution, seasonal occurrence, and abundance of birds in a state is to stimulate additional fieldwork. In time, the new information thus generated makes the original book obsolete. Janet Green and Robert Janssen wrote *Minnesota Birds: Where, When, and How Many* in 1975. Ten years later, obsolescence of this fine book prompted Bob Janssen to write the present volume.

What has happened? Does accumulation of new data come from real changes in distribution and numbers of birds? Or are we seeing the results of more people watching birds with better field guides and better binoculars? The answer is yes to both questions. One of my favorite birds, the American Woodcock, did not breed in Itasca State Park in the 1950s, when woodcock expert William Marshall spent each summer there directing the University's Biological Station. Now, after decades of steady, although unexplained, spread northwestward, woodcock breed so abundantly around Lake Itasca that I found seven broods there in two days in May 1984. The expansion of the breeding range has resulted in a big increase in migrant woodcock along the eastern Great Plains. It was a rare thing to see a migrant woodcock in western Minnesota in the 1950s. Today they occur regularly in migration and have begun to nest there.

Our short human lifespan makes it hard for us to appreciate the fluid ebb and flow of plants and animals, as their distributions constantly shift in response to long-term climatic changes. This is an important reason why we need to document the distribution of living things by preservation of specimens in research collections and by recording field observations in books such as this one. The details of distributions are always changing and precise published information is the resource that will allow people in the future to make sense of the changes.

But credit must also be given to the ever-growing army of birders, who today find and report rare birds with an efficiency much surpassing that of the relatively few birders of Dr. Thomas Roberts's day, 50 years ago. Have a small number of Varied Thrushes come to Minnesota each winter for decades and centuries, as they do today? Maybe. Probably. But if they did in the 1930s, no one knew about it. Today some are seen every year.

The spectacular growth in birding and the peculiar affliction called "listing" make it important to have yardsticks — authoritative sources that tell us what birds occur where, in what abundance, and when. Zoogeographers with Ph.D.s used to write most regional works. Today, modern birding has produced its own experts, amateurs mostly not trained in biology but fired with enthusiasm and with observational skills that are leading the way in field identification of birds. Bob Janssen is practically a type specimen of this new breed of experts.

Janssen has been editor of *The Loon,* the journal published by the Minnesota Ornithologists' Union, for 28 years, which probably makes him the senior editor of any bird journal in North America, or maybe even the world. He specializes in Minnesota birds, as did Dr. Roberts before him. Folklore has it that when Dr. Roberts's travels around the state took him briefly over the state line, his notebook was closed and his shotgun stowed away until the road led back into Minnesota. Bob Janssen is equally devoted to Minnesota birds and this volume is one result of his lifelong interest.

Harrison B. Tordoff
James Ford Bell Museum
of Natural History
University of Minnesota

PREFACE

It was in 1945 that I first saw Thomas Sadler Roberts's monumental volumes on *The Birds of Minnesota,* which had been published first in 1932 and then revised in 1936.

I well remember the purchase of the last set available in a large department store in downtown Minneapolis. The $15 purchase price seemed like a fortune to a 12-year-old, but it was probably one of the best investments I ever made.

Over the next year I read and devoured the information that Dr. Roberts had compiled on Minnesota birds starting with his account of his first trip to Grant County in 1879. Minnesota county names and locations of lakes, cities, towns, wildlife refuges, and other Minnesota geographical phenomena fascinated me.

Probably one of the most fascinating bits of information I ever came across on Dr. Roberts — I forget the source — was a statement made about his provincialism. It was stated that he stopped watching birds when he crossed into another state. There just wasn't the same fascination with observing birds in other states. I immediately related to this as I traveled back and forth as a youngster to my parents' childhood home in southern Wisconsin. When we crossed back into Minnesota, something was "different;" it was more "beautiful." I became more attentive, especially to the birds, as soon as the border was crossed. I didn't realize it at the time, but I was becoming or had become a provincial Minnesota birder.

Shortly after reading Dr. Roberts's volumes, I decided I wanted to visit all the areas in Minnesota he mentioned, and, more important, I vowed I would someday rewrite or, more accurately, keep up to date *The Birds of Minnesota.*

In 1947 I started my first Minnesota year list. Year lists became an obsession in the late '40s and into the '50s. At the same time, I began to visit many of the areas in the vicinity of the Twin Cities and some outstate areas that were well-known bird-watching haunts, the Bass Ponds, Cedar Avenue bridge, Theodore Wirth Park, Lake Harriet Refuge, Mother's Lake Marsh, and many other areas. My first trip to Frontenac, in Goodhue County, probably the favorite bird-watching spot in the state at the time, was a memorable occasion. We "hit" the warbler migration "head on."

On May 15, 1948 Blackburnian Warblers were dangling from the trees, and there were other warbler species all over the ground; my first introduction to a May wave.

It was in the late 1950s, after being away from the state for two years while serving in the army, that I became associated with the Avifaunal Club. It was at this time that I met the active field birders in the state, Bill Pieper, Ron and Hap Huber, Ray Glassel, and Brother Theodore Voelker. This group began "discovering" the now well-known spots for birding in Minnesota; the Felton Prairie, the Yellow Rail marshes of Mahnomen County, Swan Lake, Heron Lake, the Burrowing Owl nesting area in Traverse County, Lake Traverse, Salt Lake, Carlos Avery Refuge, Mille Lacs Lake, and, of course, the best place of all for birding, Duluth, with Minnesota Point and Hawk Ridge. During the 1960s and early '70s I was making 20 to 30 trips per year to Duluth to watch birds, visit friends, and hunt grouse.

Through these periods my records of birds were continually expanding: life lists and year lists were followed by month lists; migration dates, early and late, were kept on each species, maps of each species recorded were made. Daily field checklists and diaries of each weekend trip were kept.

It was in the 1950s that my interest in the Minnesota Ornithologists' Union (M.O.U.) began. I found out about the annual meetings, field trips, and, most important, their publication *The Flicker*. This publication really excited me, to actually find a place where Minnesota observations were recorded and a permanent record of Minnesota birdlife was printed.

It wasn't long after attending a few M.O.U. meetings that I found out they were looking for a new editor for *The Flicker*. (The name of the publication was changed to *The Loon* in 1964 when the Common Loon became the state bird.) At the December 1958 meeting I was offered the editorship. I readily accepted, not having the slightest idea what I was getting into, only knowing that I wanted to have something to do with the compiling of Minnesota bird records. My first issue came out in 1959 and quarterly issues have followed ever since.

In the 1960s I met Jan Green of Duluth, a fortunate occurrence for me. A person of like interests; she was particularly fascinated by the birds of the North Shore of Lake Superior in St. Louis, Lake, and Cook Counties. Her professionalism, her need for accuracy, and her enthusiasm for Minnesota birds were a great influence on me. We began a plan for the revision of Roberts's *Birds of Minnesota*. This was the beginning of my vow to keep up to date the written distribution of Minnesota birds, and a new state list was to be compiled with migration dates and distribution updated.

To make a long story very short, the result was the publication in 1975 of *Minnesota Birds: Where, When, and How Many* co-authored by Jan and myself. At the time of publication we committed to a ten-year revision of *Minnesota Birds*. I can well remember being questioned on the need for *Minnesota Birds* by a number of people. I was asked why do we need another state bird book when we have Roberts's *Birds of Minnesota?* Of course, the answer was obvious to me. When Dr. Roberts wrote his book, he reported a total state list of just over 320 species. By 1975 this total had grown to 374. The list as of December 31, 1986 has reached 400 species. We are adding one or two species per year, and distributions of all species are changing to some degree every year. The need to keep current on this information and create a continuous historical record of these changes is the reason this book was written.

The information collected herein tells the reader what species have been reported in Minnesota, in what parts of the state they are found, in what seasons they are present, and how abundant they are. Since it is intended that this book be used in conjunction with the standard field guides, no information on identification or habits is included. The basic purpose is to show the distribution, as far as we know it, of Minnesota bird species.

The information contained in this volume came primarily from records from individual birders published in *The Flicker/The Loon,* the official publication of the Minnesota Ornithologists Union. Hundreds of people from all parts of the state have contributed records and sightings that have been used in the seasonal report section of *The Flicker/The Loon.* Other journals, including *The Auk, The Wilson Bulletin,* and *American Birds,* have also contributed significant state records.

One of the problems to be confronted when compiling records for any region is verification. This was a significant problem when Jan Green and I wrote *Minnesota Birds: Where, When, and How Many.* We had to set ourselves up as "judge and jury" on all records because there wasn't any mechanism to handle the verification of records other than our own good judgment. A change in this procedure occurred in 1974 with the formation of the Minnesota Ornithological Records Committee (M.O.R.C.). This committee was formed to perform five principal functions: (1) to determine the acceptability of unusual bird sightings for inclusion in the permanent record of Minnesota birds; (2) to maintain the official list of Minnesota birds and to define the status of each species on that list; (3) to design the forms used in gathering the necessary information (e.g., the Seasonal Bird Observation Report form, the Request for Details form, the Daily Field Checklist of Minnesota birds; (4) to provide information on Minnesota birds as requested by other organizations for use in special projects; and (5) to educate birders in methods of keeping records and documenting rare species.

As of 1986 M.O.R.C. had considered and voted on over 750 individual bird sightings. The committee at present consists of the following individuals: Robert Janssen, chairman, Kim Eckert, Raymond Glassel, Janet Green, Richard Oehlenschlager, William Pieper, and Harrison Tordoff. Paul Egeland was an active member of the Committee during its formative years. In 1985 three alternate committee members were apponted by the chairman to vote on first state records, records where a second vote was required, and records involving committee members. These individuals are Renner Anderson, Donald Bolduc, and Terry Savaloja. M.O.R.C. keeps itself informed on data concerning identification and distribution by keeping up to date on current literature from ornithological journals and other available sources.

Minnesota has had a long tradition of documenting the distribution and status of the birdlife found within its boundaries. Beginning with the 1932 work of Dr. Roberts, the publication of *The Birds of Minnesota,* continuing through the journal *The Flicker* and now *The Loon,* and in 1975 the publication of *Minnesota Birds: Where, When, and How Many,* the tradition has been carried on. The publication of *Birds in Minnesota* continues this tradition, and it is my fervent hope and desire that this tradition will be carried on far into the future.

There are hundreds of people who have supplied information for this book. It would fill many, many pages to acknowledge every contribution. I would be remiss, however, if I did not acknowledge those people who have been most influential in my birding life. The first is Brother Theodore Voelker, who was a great inspiration to me in the 1960s. The many hours spent in the field with Brother Theodore, I will cherish for the rest of my life. It was a great loss to me and the whole Minnesota birding community when Brother Theodore passed away in 1972. It was fitting that he spent his last hours giving a lecture on bird identification to a group in Winona.

Janet Green and I collaborated for years in preparing the text for *Minnesota Birds: Where, When, and How Many.* Her professionalism and enthusiasm for Minnesota birds and the Minnesota environment have been a constant and continuing inspiration to me. Without her knowledge and help, this book would never have been published.

Kim Eckert's sharp eyes and ears, questioning mind, and caustic sense of humor have always kept me "on my toes." His publication of a *Birders Guide to Minnesota* has been a unique source of information not only to me, but to hundreds of birders in the state. My thanks to Kim for his many contributions to *The Loon* — he is certainly the largest single contributor to the magazine — and especially for his efforts as secretary of M.O.R.C. In 1975 when I autographed Kim's copy of *Minnesota Birds,* I stated: "Your enthusiasm, interest, and talent have been a joy, sometimes a frustration, but always a challenge. Thanks for your help." I still feel the same way.

Dr. Harrison "Bud" Tordoff has been my source of information and inspiration for years. His enthusiasm and professionalism have always been available whenever needed. His dedication to M.O.R.C. has been more than appreciated; it has been a guide to us all.

Last, and certainly not least, Ray Glassel, Minnesota's most enthusiastic birder, is the man who taught me the joys and tribulations of county listing. We have been in every nook and cranny of Minnesota together and have probably seen more sunrises than any living or dead Minnesotan after years of pre-dawn departures. (I can't prove this, but who really cares.) To Ray I say "thanks" and may we continue to learn more about Minnesota bird distribution.

R. B. J.

BIRDS IN MINNESOTA

MINNESOTA: UNIQUE GEOGRAPHY, DIVERSE HABITATS, RICH AVIFAUNA

Somewhere in a remote black spruce bog in Cook County, a June morning dawns cold. Although the temperature is not much above freezing, a virtually invisible Spruce Grouse comfortably broods her eggs, an equally hidden Boreal Owl roosts after a night of providing prey to its recently hatched young, a Black-backed Woodpecker drums on territory on a snag once occupied by a Three-toed Woodpecker family, and a wide array of flycatchers, thrushes, warblers, sparrows, and others harmonize in a dawn chorus. Also on territory in an adjacent alder swamp are pairs of Solitary Sandpipers, Wilson's Warblers, and Rusty Blackbirds — the sole representatives of their species nesting in the entire Great Lakes region of the United States.

On the same day in Rock County, the afternoon temperature approaches 100°. Still, the heat fails to daunt the activities of a pioneering family of Northern Bobwhites, an equally isolated Burrowing Owl stands guard over its burrow in a prairie pasture not far from an abandoned barn once occupied by a Common Barn-Owl, a Blue Grosbeak sings from the shade of the Sioux Quartzite escarpment where a pair of Say's Phoebes attempted to nest not too many years previously and where both a lost Curve-billed Thrasher and an off-course Brewer's Sparrow were discovered, while Dickcissels and a lone, unmated Lark Bunting line a nearby fence wire.

So dissimilar are the climates, habitats, and birds of these two locations, that it seems unlikely for both to be within the borders of the same state. Indeed, the distance separating the two places, which lie in the northeastern and southwestern corners of Minnesota, approaches 500 miles. Thus, the far corner of Rock County lies closer to the Oklahoma-Kansas border and to Cheyenne, Wyoming, than it does to Grand Portage in the eastern tip of Cook County. Meanwhile, Grand Portage is as close to the James Bay portion of cold Hudson Bay as it is to Rock County.

Equally remote from each other are the northwestern and southeastern corners of the state. Kittson County's croplands of the Red River Valley are less distant from such Canadian outposts as Saskatoon and Flin Flon than from the deciduous bottomlands of Houston County's Mississippi

3

River Valley. In turn, the turkeys, moorhens, Acadian Flycatchers, titmice, Prothonotary Warblers, and Henslow's Sparrows of Houston County are closer to the Ohio River Valley cities of Louisville and Cincinnati than they are to the magpies of Kittson County's aspen parklands, over 450 miles away.

Obviously, then, the birder is left with plenty of room to roam within the 84,000 + square miles of Minnesota, the twelfth largest state in area and, except for Texas, the largest east of the Rocky Mountains. In fact, just one of its counties, St. Louis, 6,700 plus square miles in area, seems vast enough to qualify for statehood—the county is, after all, larger than Connecticut, Delaware, Rhode Island, or Hawaii.

The population statistics are more modest. Although there are about four million Minnesotans, roughly half of them are concentrated in the Twin Cities metropolitan area, so that the state remains, for the most part, a land of wide-open spaces, small towns, and, as one beer used to advertise, Sky Blue Waters. Even Minneapolis and St. Paul (known to most Minnesotans, for whom these must be the only cities in their world, as simply "The Cities") have populations under a half million, both leaving plenty of space for birds and birders in the relatively undisturbed and impressive array of lakes, river valleys, woodlands, fields, and marshes found within their suburbs and their corporate limits.

Duluth, the next largest urban area, distributes its nearly 100,000 residents so thinly within its 23-mile length that there seems to be more wilderness than civilization within the city limits. Indeed, more birds have been recorded within Duluth's corporate limits than in any other entire county in the state. And Rochester, with nearly 60,000 residents, the only other Minnesota community resembling a true city, takes on the appearance of a national wildlife refuge each fall and winter as some 30,000 Canada Geese crowd into Silver Lake in the center of town.

But it is more than just Minnesota's sheer size and unobtrusive human populace that result in its impressive avifauna. Its range of varied and productive habitats, equaled by few other states, also plays an integral role. The coniferous bogs and forests of the North spill over the Canadian border, reach their southern extreme in Minnesota, and are characteristic of the northeastern quarter of the state. Deciduous riverbottom forests with their southern aura come north to include the Mississippi River watershed which includes much of the southeastern quarter of Minnesota. Western prairie-type habitats extend east into western Minnesota from the Dakotas in the form of extensive farmlands interrupted by frequent wetlands and an occasional remnant of native grasslands. And the Great Lakes, represented by Lake Superior, even introduce a pelagic flavor, a coastal element, into the state.

Speaking of lakes, wetlands of all kinds represent another important

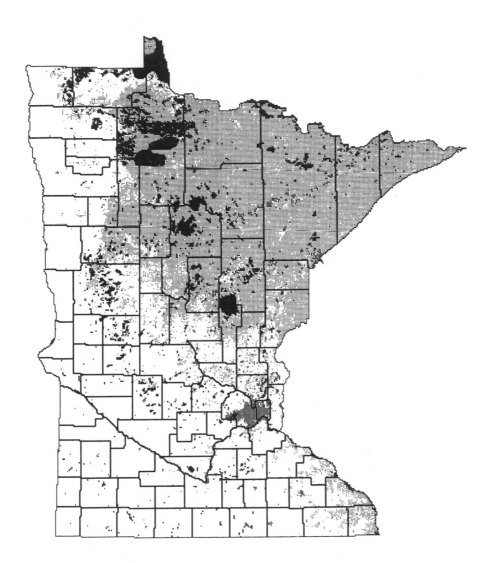

Land Use in Minnesota (1969). Courtesy of the Minnesota State Planning Agency.

□	cultivated, pasture, open	54.9%	46,653 square miles
⠿	forested	37.1	31,584
■	water	4.3	3,687
▪	marsh	2.3	1,997
▥	urban, developed	1.3	1,134

facet of the state's mosaic of habitats. Minnesota may be known as The Land of Ten Thousand Lakes, but in fact there are approximately 12,000 of them, so that no other state has as much surface water area. Shallower wetlands such as prairie potholes, sedge and cattail marshes, river backwater marshes, and the bogs, fens, and alder swamps of the boreal forest are even more numerous and also contribute to the diversity and abundance of Minnesota's breeding and migrating water birds. Major river systems such as the Mississippi (the world's largest drainage system has its source in Minnesota's Itasca State Park), Minnesota, St. Croix, and Red Rivers not only carve out valleys which serve as migration corridors for all varieties of land birds, but their backwaters and floodplains, especially in springs of high water levels, are also favored by flocks of migrant waterfowl.

Specialties

The richness of Minnesota's avifauna takes many forms and does not necessarily involve rarities highly sought by birders eager to compile a long life list. Several relatively common and widespread species ordinarily taken for granted assume special significance when found in concentrations that can border on the extraordinary.

Common Loons by the hundreds congregate each fall on Mille Lacs, and during the same season Canada Geese by the tens of thousands flock not only to Rochester but also to Lac Qui Parle Wildlife Management Area, where estimates approaching 100,000 geese have been made. November is the time for Tundra Swans to gather by the thousands at their Weaver backwaters staging area along the Mississippi River; at the same time other southbound waterfowl at Weaver and other locations in this valley from Lake Pepin downstream through Winona and Houston Counties can number into the hundreds of thousands. Equally impressive flocks of geese and ducks also swarm north in March and April through the prairie pothole country of western Minnesota and, in years of heavy snowmelt, through the backwaters and floodplains of the Minnesota and Mississippi River valleys. Also in spring during the brief smelt run in Duluth and along the North Shore of Lake Superior, thousands of loons, grebes, mergansers, and gulls gather. One can even be impressed by the lowly American Coot as flocks of 50,000 or more literally cover some lakes in fall.

The sheer number of waterbirds breeding in the state can be as impressive as the migrant flocks. Consider a concentration of perhaps 1,500 pelicans crowded into two small sites at Marsh Lake in Lac Qui Parle County. Or the vast island rookeries at places like Lake of the Woods (over 1,000 cormorant nests on Crowduck Island) and Long Lake in Kandiyohi County (2,300 nests of cormorants, herons, and egrets). Or the thousands of pairs of ducks nesting at Agassiz National Wildlife Refuge which are overshadowed by the refuge's huge colony of Franklin's Gulls — as many as 35,000 pairs have been censused. Meanwhile, some 1,000 pairs of Forster's Terns and 200+ pairs of Western Grebes concentrate on Lake Osakis in Todd County, and 12,000 adult Ring-billed Gulls at Duluth's Port Terminal (an amazing and alarming population explosion considering none bred here until 1973) compete for territory.

But more than just water birds concentrate in notable quantities in Minnesota. The fame of Duluth's Hawk Ridge is continent-wide because of the tens of thousands of hawks, and hundreds of owls, counted and banded here each fall — only two or three other sites average more hawks than Duluth each year. Nearly 75,000 hawks were recorded at Hawk Ridge in 1978; that same year on the single date of September 15, over 33,000 were seen — about 32,000 of these Broad-wingeds. (That same day, the banders had a record day by netting 348 hawks, all but a few of them Sharp-shinneds.) Other peaks of species of note: over 700 Turkey Vultures in a single day in 1983; a remarkable 1,229 Northern Goshawks (148 of these banded) on one day in 1982 when the season total for this species exceeded 5,800; no fewer than 17 Peregrine Falcons seen, including seven banded, in a single day in 1984; and the amazing night of October 20-21, 1984, when no fewer than 136 owls (131 of these saw-whets) were netted — the season totals for this record year approached 4,200 banded raptors, 741 of these Northern Saw-whet Owls.

Birds other than raptors also funnel south each fall in large numbers down the North Shore of Lake Superior and through Duluth. The movement of nighthawks, swallows, jays, crows, ravens, robins, waxwings, warblers, finches, and other passerines is often impressive: e.g., some 6,500 warblers censused during two successive mornings at Hawk Ridge in 1983, an early October count of at least 4,500 robins during a single morning (also at the ridge in 1983), a 1985 census at a nearby site tallied over 2,000 chickadees on one date and nearly 4,000 waxwings a few mornings later, and, on a single August day in 1986, a flight of 16,500 nighthawks passed over a North Shore yard. When the fog and drizzle settle onto Duluth's Park Point in May, August, or September, as many as 25 warbler species can be grounded into view. Speaking of warblers, no fewer than 30 species are known to have nested in the state (27 of these regularly); only the breeding ranges of the Orange-crowned and Blackpoll lie entirely north of Minnesota. Of final quantitative note are the thousands of Sandhill Cranes which crowd into their Norman County staging area each October, and the tremendous flocks of Horned Larks, Snow Buntings, and Lapland Longspurs that pour through the fields of western Minnesota during migration — a conservative estimate made by two awed birders once documented a flight of perhaps 200,000 longspurs overhead during one April day.

As impressive as such concentrations of the commonplace can be, it is the rarity that birders pursue with the most enthusiasm, and when trips are contemplated to places rich in potential life birds, the states of Alaska, Arizona, Texas, and Florida usually come first to mind. Recently, however, the American Birding Association polled its thousands of members to find out which birds were the most highly sought in the United States and Canada, and many of the species at the top of this survey are found in Minnesota. In fact, of the eight most-wanted birds, four are on Minnesota's regular list, as are 11 of the top 25 species. Certainly only two or three other states could claim to have as many species as high in the ranks of sought-after birds, and Minnesota clearly emerges as one of the prime birding states visited by birders from across the country.

The Minnesota species ranked in this survey among the top 25 include: Great Gray Owl (4th), a permanent resident which, during those winters when influxes occur, can become relatively easy to find (no fewer than 122 were counted during the winter of 1983-84); Gyrfalcon (6th), which has wintered in the Duluth harbor six consecutive years (four individuals were present in 1984-85); Boreal Owl (7th), which nests sparingly in northeastern Minnesota and, when calling on territory in spring, a relative certainty to locate (also, an unprecedented and incredible winter influx in 1977-78 produced no fewer than 66 individuals); Yellow Rail (8th), a widespread summer resident that has made the town of McGregor and its reliable rail marsh famous among birders everywhere; Snowy Owl (13th), the easiest of our "rarities" to see considering more of them winter in the Duluth-Superior harbor than anywhere else south of Canada; Northern Hawk-Owl (15th), another winter resident which typically and cooperatively remains in one area for weeks at a time; Northern Saw-whet Owl (19th), a surprisingly easy bird to observe when calling in the boreal forest each spring; Spruce Grouse (20th), normally a most elusive resident of the coniferous forest, which has become quite reliable in recent winters along Lake County Road 2; Three-toed Woodpecker (also 20th), granted, a most difficult resident to find unless found migrating in fall along the North Shore with the more numerous Black-backed Woodpecker (23rd), also a widespread breeding bird of the coniferous forest; and Connecticut Warbler (25th), anything but a rare summer resident, widespread and easily found once its song is heard.

Many other species found in Minnesota also attract birders from all over, and most of these are hardly rare, most relatively easy to find: Red-necked Grebe, Harlequin Duck, Northern Goshawk, Gray Partridge, Ruffed and Sharp-tailed Grouse, Greater Prairie-Chicken, American Woodcock, Thayer's Gull, Black-billed Cuckoo, Whip-poor-will, Olive-sided, Yellow-bellied, and Alder Flycatchers, Gray Jay, Boreal Chickadee, Sedge Wren, Bohemian Waxwing, Northern Shrike, Philadelphia Vireo,

Golden-winged, Cape May, and Mourning Warblers, Clay-colored, Grass-hopper, Henslow's, Le Conte's, Sharp-tailed, and Lincoln's Sparrows, Chestnut-collared Longspur, Snow Bunting, Pine Grosbeak, Red and White-winged Crossbills, Common and Hoary Redpolls. While all but a few of these are taken for granted by Minnesota's resident birders, all have been additions to the life lists of many birders visiting the state.

Finally, as previously mentioned, Minnesota's geography and its variety of habitats serve to provide the state with an abundance of birdlife. Specifically, since the western prairie, northern coniferous forest, and southern deciduous forest all reach their limits in this state, numerous birds are also found at the periphery of their ranges here. For example, several western species, regular in the grasslands and wetlands of western Minnesota, seldom or rarely occur east of the state: Eared and Western Grebes, Greater White-fronted Goose, Cinnamon Teal, Swainson's and Ferruginous Hawks, Prairie Falcon, Greater Prairie-Chicken, Franklin's Gull, Burrowing Owl, Black-billed Magpie, Mountain Bluebird, Sprague's Pipit, Lark Bunting, Smith's and Chestnut-collared Longspurs.

Another longer assortment of birds, typical of southern environs, also reaching the edge of their ranges in the state, are mostly absent from northern Minnesota: Snowy and Cattle Egrets, Little Blue Heron, Yellow-crowned Night-Heron, Wild Turkey, Northern Bobwhite, Common Moorhen, Yellow-billed Cuckoo, Eastern Screech-Owl, Red-bellied Woodpecker, Acadian and Willow Flycatchers, Tufted Titmouse, Blue-gray Gnatcatcher, Bell's Vireo, Blue-winged, Cerulean, Prothonotary, Kentucky, and Hooded Warblers, Louisiana Waterthrush, Yellow-breasted Chat, Northern Cardinal, Blue Grosbeak, Dickcissel, Field and Henslow's Sparrows, and Orchard Oriole.

In addition to numerous species that breed at their southern limit in the boreal forest, several winter and permanent residents of the northern part of the state disappear for the most part in southern Minnesota and beyond: Gyrfalcon, Spruce and Sharp-tailed Grouse, Snowy, Great Gray, and Boreal Owls, Northern Hawk-Owl, Three-toed and Black-backed Woodpeckers, Gray Jay, Common Raven, Boreal Chickadee, Bohemian Waxwing, Pine Grosbeak, White-winged Crossbill, and Hoary Redpoll.

And, not to mention countless casuals and accidentals, these Great Lakes species occur regularly on or along Lake Superior but are usually missing from the rest of the state: Red-throated Loon, Harlequin Duck, Oldsquaw, Black, Surf, and White-winged Scoters, Whimbrel, Red Knot, Parasitic Jaeger, Little, Thayer's, and Glaucous Gulls. In sum, the large assortment of peripheral species found in Minnesota not only results in a lengthy state list, but also provides the birder, whether a resident of the north or south, east or west, the opportunity and potential for finding new and unfamiliar birds in various corners of the state.

Seasons

When and where are there birds to be found in Minnesota? As already described, all times of the year and all parts of the state have something to offer, but there are some specifics worthy of note — some times and places are better than others.

It is the spring birding season that is probably anticipated more than any other, and, considering the extremes of Minnesota winters, such is especially true here. Long before winter has lost its grip — some would say its grip is firm even into June — the first "spring" migrants are welcomed back. Northbound Horned Larks appear along southern Minnesota roadsides as early as late January, while northern Minnesota's first harbingers are the flocks of crows moving north during February. But migration begins in earnest in mid-March (or as early as late February in milder years) as waterfowl, hawks, blackbirds, and the like return to southern parts of the state. Peak flights of waterfowl and hawks occur from late March into mid-April, shorebirds tend to pass through in earnest throughout most of May, while the peak of warblers is in mid- to late May. Our Big Day counts, generally run between May 20 and 25, average 180 species, with 192 our best effort — only six other states/Canadian provinces have ever done better. (A Big Day is defined as an effort by a single party of birders to see as many birds as possible within a calendar day.) Even into mid-June, several shorebirds and a few lingering passerines are still on the move. Spring is also the most favorable time for finding some sought-after permanent and summer residents: e.g., Ruffed and Sharp-tailed Grouse, Greater Prairie-Chicken, Wild Turkey, Northern Bobwhite, American Woodcock, Great Gray, Boreal, and Northern Saw-whet Owls, and Boreal Chickadee all vocalize more in spring than in summer.

Most visiting birders in search of additions to their life lists find the summer birding — and weather — most to their liking. Minnesota's winters may be infamous, but its summers are warm: July highs average in the '70s and '80s, with nighttime lows normally in the pleasant '50s and '60s. It may reach 100° a time or two each year, but the vicinity of Lake Superior is typically cool and wet well into June, and, even in mid-summer, an east wind off the big lake can hold North Shore highs in the '60s while the rest of Minnesota may be in the '80s or '90s. Summer birding is more predictable, with breeding species singing on territory and, thus, not difficult to locate. Although the nesting season begins in April for some birds (hawks and owls, for example) and extends into August for others, the best birding is in June and early July when most species vocalize. By mid-July many songbirds become relatively silent and more difficult to find, while the birder visiting the boreal forest in late May could arrive before some of the later migrants (e.g., Black-billed Cuckoo, Yellow-bellied and Alder Flycatchers, Connecticut and Mourning Warblers). However, as mentioned earlier, some nesting species are more vocal and more easily found in spring than in summer; there are also a few highly sought breeding birds (e.g., Northern Goshawk, Gray Partridge, Spruce Grouse, Red Crossbill) more easily found in fall or winter. Of final note in summer: visiting birders will find the boreal forests of the northeastern quarter of the state and, to a lesser extent, the prairies of northwestern Minnesota most worthwhile — only a few sought-after species are exclusive to the southern half of the state.

While many prefer spring migration over fall, it is during fall migration that most casuals, accidentals, and other rarities appear. (The weather, certainly, is better in fall: warm, clear days are more frequent in September and October than in April and May; consistently cold temperatures tend not to arrive until late October, while continuous snow cover is generally delayed until late November.) Probably the most unpredictable and exciting — and longest — season, fall actually starts in late June-early July as the first southbound shorebirds appear. In July the first warblers begin moving south from the boreal forest, with the peak warbler passage in mid-August through mid-September. Most other passerines peak during September, while in mid-month those impressive waves of Sharp-shinned and Broad-winged Hawks pass over Hawk Ridge in Duluth. October not only brings the first of the winter residents down from Canada, but other buteos, eagles, and goshawks peak in impressive numbers over Hawk Ridge in the last half of the month, and, while rarities can occur at any time and place during fall, it is clearly in October in Duluth and along the North Shore of Lake Superior that strays are most likely. November produces huge concentrations of waterfowl in the bays and marshes of the Mississippi River backwaters from Wabasha to Houston Counties, while in December, and even early January, the last few hardy migrants linger before moving farther south.

As mentioned earlier, a Minnesota winter is indeed infamous. Northern Minnesota, along with North Dakota and Montana, clearly has the coldest winters south of Canada: temperatures in the vicinity of -30° are not unusual, and recent years have had readings approaching -50°. Such extremes are rare, however, and January highs normally range in the teens and twenties, total snowfall averages only a surprisingly modest 40-60 inches per season (it is not unusual to find the ground free of snow into December or by late February), and a winter afternoon with average temperatures, sunshine, and minimal winds is actually quite pleasant. Not only have four million Minnesotans managed to survive these winters each year, but resident and visiting birders alike thrive in them. Of the state's eleven "most-wanted" species on the aforementioned survey, eight regularly occur in winter, and three — Gyrfalcon, Snowy Owl, and Northern Hawk-Owl — are exclusively winter residents. Other species such as Bohemian Waxwing, Northern Shrike, Snow Bunting, Pine Grosbeak, both crossbills, and both redpolls also enhance winter's reputation. Most winter residents arrive in late October or November and depart during March, but there are exceptions: waxwings and winter finches can appear, or disappear, at any time depending on berry and cone crops; stray ducks or gulls on Lake Superior are best searched for before late January (at which time the ice pack tends to move in); and late January, February, or even March provides the best hope for an influx of Great Gray or Boreal Owls along roadsides, desperate for prey after weeks of severe weather. And, as in summer, the best winter birding is found in northeastern Minnesota, especially the conifers, feeders, and harbors of Duluth and vicinity.

Sites

Several of the best birding areas in Minnesota have already been described — Rochester's Silver Lake, Lake Superior, the Mississippi, Minnesota, and St. Croix River Valleys, Mille Lacs, Lac Qui Parle Wildlife Management Area, Weaver's marsh, Marsh Lake, Lake of the Woods, Long Lake, Agassiz National Wildlife Refuge, Duluth's Park Point, harbor, and Hawk Ridge, the North Shore, McGregor's marsh, Lake County Road 2 — but there are many others.

Within the prairie-type landscape of western Minnesota, the extensive wetlands of Agassiz might be the premier area for migrant and breeding water birds. Such birds, however, also congregate at other favored locations like the string of border lakes, Mud, Traverse, and Big Stone — Mud Lake is also often shallow enough for fall shorebirds, while the hillsides and woods lining Traverse and Big Stone Lakes attract migrating hawks and passerines as well. Downstream from Big Stone Lake, the Minnesota River Valley begins in earnest with another set of three water impoundments. Two of these, Marsh and Lac Qui Parle Lakes, have already been mentioned, but the third reservoir and its surroundings within Big Stone National Wildlife Refuge are perhaps more interesting. A large heron rookery (which has hosted Little Blue Heron, Cattle and Snowy Egrets) and extensive marshes bordered by woodlands and native grasslands (disturbed only by outcroppings of rock and cactus) all result in a long refuge checklist. Farther downstream, the Minnesota River continues on to carve out a long, broad valley of riparian woods and prairie hillsides which serves as an important corridor for migrants of all kinds. The colonial water birds of Big Stone and Long Lakes have previously been highlighted, but other heron rookeries of western Minnesota, those at Pelican Lake in Grant County and at Pope County's Lake Johanna, are also impressive. One last oasis for water birds in the western part of the state, long a favorite among birders, especially for its shorebirds, is Salt Lake on the South Dakota border, Minnesota's only alkaline wetland.

But western Minnesota is more than just wetlands; its most valuable and unique habitat has to be the remnant tracts of native prairie grasslands. The best of these remnants lie along the beachline of glacial Lake Agassiz, which visibly extends from Rothsay Wildlife Management Area (a favored spot for booming prairie-chickens and migrant Prairie Falcons, Short-eared Owls, and Smith's Longspurs), through the Sandhill Crane staging area of southern Norman County, to the sandy Lark Sparrow haunts of the Agassiz Dunes tract, and north to the prairie-chicken and Sharp-tailed Grouse leks southeast of Crookston. Clearly, however, the most significant prairie tracts lie in the Felton prairie area of Clay County, not only the site of the state's sole Chestnut-collared Longspur population, but also the only location where Sprague's Pipit and, occasionally, Baird's Sparrow appear with any frequency. And of final note in western Minnesota, and a personal favorite, is Blue Mounds State Park, a unique blend of hundred-foot-high cliffs of Sioux Quartzite, extensive virgin prairie, and wooded streams — an outpost for Blue Grosbeaks as well as an oasis for strays from the south and west.

Farther east lie the river valleys of the southeastern quarter of Minnesota, haunts of birds more characteristic of the southeastern United States. As impressive as the backwaters and deciduous forests are within the valleys of the Minnesota and St. Croix Rivers, the most favored birding areas tend to lie within the influence of the Mississippi River Valley. Two particularly significant spots, both in Houston County, are the marshes and wooded backwaters near La Crescent and the extensive woodlands of Beaver Creek Valley State Park. The former spot is probably the most consistent in the state for Common Moorhen and Prothonotary Warbler, while the latter supports the state's only reliably nesting Acadian Flycatchers and is one of the few reliable areas for Tufted Titmouse and Louisiana Waterthrush. Farther upstream are Weaver's aforementioned Tundra Swan backwaters, and, just to the southwest, are the impressive wooded valleys of Whitewater Wildlife Management Area, one of only two Minnesota locations for Wild Turkeys. Just to the north is the Kellogg sand prairie area, which includes the state's most reliable thicket for Bell's Vireo, and farther upstream in Goodhue County lies the wooded community of Frontenac, a traditional favorite with Twin Cities birders for spring warbler migrations.

Birders in the Twin Cities, however, need not travel as far for warblers and other birds — again, there are many productive natural areas left intact in this metropolitan area. Spring warbler watching, for example, at places like T. S. Roberts Bird Sanctuary, Wood Lake Nature Center, or Theodore

Wirth Park is as good as — and often better than — anywhere in the entire state; also, the forests of Wolsfeld Woods and Murphy-Hanrehan Park are extensive enough to support healthy numbers of breeding birds like gnatcatchers, Louisiana Waterthrushes, Blue-winged and Cerulean Warblers (Hooded Warblers even nested at the latter location). Within the city limits of St. Paul, the Pigs Eye Lake rookery not only supports the largest Black-crowned Night-Heron colony in Minnesota but is also one of very few sites where Yellow-crowneds have nested in the state. Finally, the Black Dog Lake area is one of only a handful of places that is potentially good any time of year: in spring and fall for waterfowl, in summer in the thickets along the south shore where Bell's Vireos and chats appear with some frequency, and in winter when the power plant keeps the lake open for waterfowl (nowhere in the state has the Barrow's Goldeneye appeared more often) and gulls (Thayer's and Glaucous are regular only here and on Lake Superior).

So much has already been made of the birds of northeastern Minnesota that it's hard to know where to begin. Birders might first be tantalized by the Aitkin County specialties—not only McGregor marsh's Yellow Rails, Le Conte's and Sharp-tailed Sparrows, but also Rice Lake National Wildlife Refuge's reliable Sharp-tailed Grouse fields, and the Great Gray and Northern Hawk-Owl bogs along County Roads 1 and 18, and Highways 65 and 200. Or by the vastness of the so-called Big Bog country north of Red Lakes, its remoteness interrupted only by Highway 72 and a few other back roads. More accessible and popular is the Sax-Zim bog in St. Louis County, another good place to search for the likes of Great Grays and hawk-owls. Other birders might be more attracted by the scenic pines and spruce of Itasca and Scenic State Parks — the latter park a consistent nesting location for Spruce Grouse and Three-toed Woodpeckers in previous summers. Or intrigued by the possibility of rarities which frequently stray to larger lakes such as Mille Lacs and Lake of the Woods, especially in fall.

Of course, Lake Superior and its harbors — especially at Grand Marais and Duluth — comprise the premier area for unusual water birds, while its North Shore funnels large waves of fall migrants, including frequent casuals and accidentals, past vantage points such as Stoney Point, Hawk Ridge, and Park Point. The spring birding potential of Duluth's Park Point during periods of fog and drizzle is also worth reiterating, as are the winter raptor possibilities in the Duluth harbor. And, of final note, are the Gunflint Trail and Lake County Road 2, two roads that leave the North Shore to penetrate some of the state's best coniferous forests, where Boreal Owls (calling on territory along the Gunflint), Spruce Grouse (standing in the middle of County Road 2 at dawn during winter), and other specialties occur.

The possibilities seem endless — from cold black spruce bogs up north, to the arid open country of the southwest and the humid southeastern riverbottoms . . . from spectacular concentrations of the commonplace to highly sought and elusive specialties . . . from the abundance of migrants in passage, to the wide variety of nesting species, to the surprising assortment of winter visitants — it's all part of a phenomenon known as Minnesota. But where does one go from here to experience all this? Two suggestions come to mind. For complete information on, and directions to, Minnesota's birding areas, consult *A Birder's Guide to Minnesota* (published in cooperation with the Minnesota Ornithologists' Union, Bell Museum of Natural History, 10 Church St. S.E., Minneapolis), a county-by-county survey of more than 500 locations in the state. Or, better yet, put all the guidebooks aside, disregard the predictable security of what is already known of the status and distribution of the state's avifauna, find a map of your favorite county, and set out on your own. Much of Minnesota remains to be discovered: take some time to explore, to wander about independently — not only is what you find for yourself more rewarding than what someone else finds for you, but Minnesota ornithology benefits as well from your experience.

Kim R. Eckert

NOTES ON NOMENCLATURE, TERMINOLOGY, AND MAPS

The following comments on nomenclature, terminology, and maps will help the reader accurately interpret the information in the species accounts.

Nomenclature

The nomenclature, taxonomic sequence, and common names in this book follow those of *The A.O.U. Checklist of North American Birds* (Sixth Edition) published in 1983 by the American Ornithologists' Union.

Minnesota Status

The following definitions are used in assigning each species to a particular status:

1. *Regular.* Species for which there are records in at least nine (in some cases eight) of the past ten years. (A year is defined as the period from July 1 of one year through June of the following year; the current ten-year base period on which the status of each species is determined is from July 1, 1972 through June 30, 1982.) Normally occurs somewhere in the state every year. (304 species)

2. *Casual.* Species for which there are acceptable records in seven (and in some cases eight) six, five, or four (and in some cases three) of the past ten years. (28 species)

   An acceptable record is defined as a recognizable and preserved specimen, photograph, or tape recording, or a documented sight record accepted by the Minnesota Ornithological Records Committee (for an explanation of the voting procedure of the Records Committee, see *The Loon* 52:150–52 and 53:129–30).

   Species with records in eight of the last ten years are discussed by the Records Committee and by concensus are defined as either Regular or Casual; likewise, species with records in three of the last ten years are discussed and defined as either Casual or Accidental.

3. *Accidental.* Species for which there are acceptable records in two

17

(and in some cases three) or fewer of the past ten years. Accidental species fall into three categories:

A_a (49 species). Species for which there is a recognizable and preserved specimen, photograph, or tape recording taken in the state.

A_b (14 species). Species for which there is no specimen, photograph, or tape recording but for which there have been sight records substantiated by written documentation unanimously accepted by the Minnesota Ornithological Records Committee.

A_c (2 species). Species for which there is a question about the origin or wildness of the bird (does not include obviously escaped or released exotics).

4. Extirpated (2 species). Species that formerly occurred regularly in the state but have disappeared and are not expected to recur.

5. Extinct (1 species). Species that formerly occurred in the state, but no longer occur anywhere in the world.

The total state list as of December 31, 1986 is:

Regular	304
Casual	28
Accidental	65
Extirpated	2
Extinct	1
	400

Following is a list for each category:

Regular Species (304)

Red-throated Loon
Common Loon
Pied-billed Grebe
Horned Grebe
Red-necked Grebe
Eared Grebe
Western Grebe
American White Pelican
Double-crested Cormorant
American Bittern
Least Bittern
Great Blue Heron
Great Egret

Snowy Egret
Little Blue Heron
Cattle Egret
Green-backed Heron
Black-crowned Night-Heron
Yellow-crowned Night-Heron
Tundra Swan
Greater White-fronted Goose
Snow Goose
Canada Goose
Wood Duck
Green-winged Teal
American Black Duck

Mallard
Northern Pintail
Blue-winged Teal
Cinnamon Teal
Northern Shoveler
Gadwall
American Wigeon
Canvasback
Redhead
Ring-necked Duck
Greater Scaup
Lesser Scaup
Harlequin Duck
Oldsquaw
Black Scoter
Surf Scoter
White-winged Scoter
Common Goldeneye
Bufflehead
Hooded Merganser
Common Merganser
Red-breasted Merganser
Ruddy Duck
Turkey Vulture
Osprey
Bald Eagle
Northern Harrier
Sharp-shinned Hawk
Cooper's Hawk
Northern Goshawk
Red-shouldered Hawk
Broad-winged Hawk
Swainson's Hawk
Red-tailed Hawk
Ferruginous Hawk
Rough-legged Hawk
Golden Eagle
American Kestrel
Merlin
Peregrine Falcon
Gyrfalcon
Prairie Falcon
Gray Partridge

Ring-necked Pheasant
Spruce Grouse
Ruffed Grouse
Greater Prairie-Chicken
Sharp-tailed Grouse
Wild Turkey
Northern Bobwhite
Yellow Rail
Virginia Rail
Sora
Common Moorhen
American Coot
Sandhill Crane
Black-bellied Plover
Lesser Golden-Plover
Semipalmated Plover
Piping Plover
Killdeer
American Avocet
Greater Yellowlegs
Lesser Yellowlegs
Solitary Sandpiper
Willet
Spotted Sandpiper
Upland Sandpiper
Whimbrel
Hudsonian Godwit
Marbled Godwit
Ruddy Turnstone
Red Knot
Sanderling
Semipalmated Sandpiper
Western Sandpiper
Least Sandpiper
White-rumped Sandpiper
Baird's Sandpiper
Pectoral Sandpiper
Dunlin
Stilt Sandpiper
Buff-breasted Sandpiper
Short-billed Dowitcher
Long-billed Dowitcher
Common Snipe

American Woodcock
Wilson's Phalarope
Red-necked Phalarope
Parasitic Jaeger
Franklin's Gull
Little Gull
Bonaparte's Gull
Ring-billed Gull
Herring Gull
Thayer's Gull
Glaucous Gull
Caspian Tern
Common Tern
Forster's Tern
Black Tern
Rock Dove
Mourning Dove
Black-billed Cuckoo
Yellow-billed Cuckoo
Eastern Screech-Owl
Great Horned Owl
Snowy Owl
Northern Hawk-Owl
Burrowing Owl
Barred Owl
Great Gray Owl
Long-eared Owl
Short-eared Owl
Boreal Owl
Northern Saw-whet Owl
Common Nighthawk
Whip-poor-will
Chimney Swift
Ruby-throated Hummingbird
Belted Kingfisher
Red-headed Woodpecker
Red-bellied Woodpecker
Yellow-bellied Sapsucker
Downy Woodpecker
Hairy Woodpecker
Three-toed Woodpecker
Black-backed Woodpecker
Northern Flicker

Pileated Woodpecker
Olive-sided Flycatcher
Eastern Wood-Pewee
Yellow-bellied Flycatcher
Acadian Flycatcher
Alder Flycatcher
Willow Flycatcher
Least Flycatcher
Eastern Phoebe
Great Crested Flycatcher
Western Kingbird
Eastern Kingbird
Horned Lark
Purple Martin
Tree Swallow
Northern Rough-winged
Swallow
Bank Swallow
Cliff Swallow
Barn Swallow
Gray Jay
Blue Jay
Black-billed Magpie
American Crow
Common Raven
Black-capped Chickadee
Boreal Chickadee
Tufted Titmouse
Red-breasted Nuthatch
White-breasted Nuthatch
Brown Creeper
House Wren
Winter Wren
Sedge Wren
Marsh Wren
Golden-crowned Kinglet
Ruby-crowned Kinglet
Blue-gray Gnatcatcher
Eastern Bluebird
Mountain Bluebird
Townsend's Solitaire
Veery
Gray-cheeked Thrush

Swainson's Thrush
Hermit Thrush
Wood Thrush
American Robin
Varied Thrush
Gray Catbird
Northern Mockingbird
Brown Thrasher
Water Pipit
Sprague's Pipit
Bohemian Waxwing
Cedar Waxwing
Northern Shrike
Loggerhead Shrike
European Starling
Bell's Vireo
Solitary Vireo
Yellow-throated Vireo
Warbling Vireo
Philadelphia Vireo
Red-eyed Vireo
Blue-winged Warbler
Golden-winged Warbler
Tennessee Warbler
Orange-crowned Warbler
Nashville Warbler
Northern Parula
Yellow Warbler
Chestnut-sided Warbler
Magnolia Warbler
Cape May Warbler
Black-throated Blue Warbler
Yellow-rumped Warbler
Black-throated Green Warbler
Blackburnian Warbler
Pine Warbler
Palm Warbler
Bay-breasted Warbler
Blackpoll Warbler
Cerulean Warbler
Black-and-white Warbler
American Redstart
Prothonotary Warbler

Ovenbird
Northern Waterthrush
Louisiana Waterthrush
Kentucky Warbler
Connecticut Warbler
Mourning Warbler
Common Yellowthroat
Hooded Warbler
Wilson's Warbler
Canada Warbler
Yellow-breasted Chat
Summer Tanager
Scarlet Tanager
Northern Cardinal
Rose-breasted Grosbeak
Blue Grosbeak
Indigo Bunting
Dickcissel
Rufous-sided Towhee
American Tree Sparrow
Chipping Sparrow
Clay-colored Sparrow
Field Sparrow
Vesper Sparrow
Lark Sparrow
Lark Bunting
Savannah Sparrow
Grasshopper Sparrow
Henslow's Sparrow
Le Conte's Sparrow
Sharp-tailed Sparrow
Fox Sparrow
Song Sparrow
Lincoln's Sparrow
Swamp Sparrow
White-throated Sparrow
White-crowned Sparrow
Harris' Sparrow
Dark-eyed Junco
Lapland Longspur
Smith's Longspur
Chestnut-collared Longspur
Snow Bunting

Bobolink
Red-winged Blackbird
Eastern Meadowlark
Western Meadowlark
Yellow-headed Blackbird
Rusty Blackbird
Brewer's Blackbird
Common Grackle
Brown-headed Cowbird
Orchard Oriole
Northern Oriole
Pine Grosbeak
Purple Finch
Red Crossbill
White-winged Crossbill
Common Redpoll
Hoary Redpoll
Pine Siskin
American Goldfinch
Evening Grosbeak
House Sparrow

Casual Species (28)

Pacific Loon
Tricolored Heron
White-faced Ibis
Mute Swan
Brant
Barrow's Goldeneye
King Rail
Long-billed Curlew
Ruff
Red Phalarope
Pomarine Jaeger
Laughing Gull
California Gull
Iceland Gull
Black-legged Kittiwake
Sabine's Gull
Least Tern
Common Barn-Owl
Rufous Hummingbird
Say's Phoebe

Scissor-tailed Flycatcher
Carolina Wren
Bewick's Wren
White-eyed Vireo
Worm-eating Warbler
Western Tanager
Baird's Sparrow
Rosy Finch

Accidental Species (65)

Yellow-billed Loon A_a
Clark's Grebe A_b
Anhinga A_b
Fulvous Whistling-Duck A_c
Black-bellied Whistling-Duck A_c
Ross' Goose A_a
Eurasian Wigeon A_a
Common Eider A_a
King Eider A_a
American Swallow-tailed Kite A_a
Mississippi Kite A_b
Willow Ptarmigan A_a
Black Rail A_a
Purple Gallinule A_a
Whooping Crane A_a
Snowy Plover A_a
Wilson's Plover A_a
Mountain Plover A_b
Purple Sandpiper A_a
Long-tailed Jaeger A_a
Common Black-headed Gull A_a
Mew Gull A_b
Lesser Black-backed Gull A_a
Great Black-backed Gull A_a
Ross' Gull A_a
Ivory Gull A_a
Sandwich Tern A_a
Arctic Tern A_a
Dovekie A_a
Ancient Murrelet A_a
Band-tailed Pigeon A_a
White-winged Dove A_b
Groove-billed Ani A_a

Common Poorwill A_a
Chuck-will's-widow A_a
Lewis' Woodpecker A_a
Williamson's Sapsucker A_b
Western Wood-Pewee A_a
Black Phoebe A_b
Vermilion Flycatcher A_a
Violet-green Swallow A_b
Clark's Nutcracker A_a
Rock Wren A_a
American Dipper A_a
Northern Wheatear A_b
Sage Thrasher A_a
Curve-billed Thrasher A_b
Black-throated Gray Warbler A_a
Townsend's Warbler A_b
Hermit Warbler A_a
Yellow-throated Warbler A_a
Kirtland's Warbler A_a
Prairie Warbler A_b

MacGillivray's Warbler A_a
Black-headed Grosbeak A_a
Lazuli Bunting A_a
Painted Bunting A_a
Green-tailed Towhee A_a
Brewer's Sparrow A_b
Black-throated Sparrow A_a
McCown's Longspur A_a
Great-tailed Grackle A_b
Scott's Oriole A_a
Brambling A_a
House Finch A_a

Extirpated Species (2)

Trumpeter Swan
Eskimo Curlew

. Extinct Species (1)

Passenger Pigeon

When *Minnesota Birds* was published in 1975, the state list stood at 374 species. The changes that have occurred in the state list since that time are:

Deletions (5)

Chukar. The last of the introduced population died out in 1977.
Black Brant. Lumped with Brant.
Common Black-Hawk. The specimen found near Bemidji, Beltrami County, was found to be an escaped cage bird.
Gray-headed Junco. Lumped with Dark-eyed Junco.
European Goldfinch. The single record was determined to be of an escaped cage bird.

Additions (31)

Yellow-billed Loon
Clark's Grebe
Anhinga
Black-bellied Whistling-Duck
Mute Swan
Snowy Plover
Wilson's Plover
Mountain Plover
Laughing Gull
Common Black-headed Gull

Mew Gull
California Gull
Lesser Black-backed Gull
Ross' Gull
Sandwich Tern
White-winged Dove
Chuck-will's-widow
Rufous Hummingbird
Lewis' Woodpecker
Vermilion Flycatcher
Northern Wheatear

Sage Thrasher

Curve-billed Thrasher

Townsend's Warbler

Yellow-throated Warbler

MacGillivray's Warbler

Brewer's Sparrow

Black-throated Sparrow

Great-tailed Grackle

Scott's Oriole

Brambling

The discussion of the species accounts is usually divided into three sections: (1) Migration, including distribution, abundance, and early and late dates of arrival and departure. These dates are reported for north and south areas in the state as defined on the map (Figure 1) on page 25; (2) Summer Season, including breeding range, nesting records, and a map showing the general breeding range of each species found nesting in the state; and (3) Winter Season, including distribution and abundance during this season.

1. MIGRATION

The migration section under each species is written in the following manner: for summer residents and transient birds, the spring migration period is given first; for winter visitants, the fall migration period is given first. Since migration varies with the weather, normal and peak migration periods are described in terms of three ten-day segments for each month (for instance, early April, mid-April, and late April). Usually three dates are given to define the extreme ranges of the normal migration; if two dates appear, it means that there were multiple arrivals on one date. Those dates that are regarded as extraordinary are set in *italic type*. Extreme dates that are hyphenated refer to successive observations of the same bird. Since Minnesota extends for some 400 miles from Iowa to Canada, its latitudinal range affects the timing of migration, especially early in the spring and late in the fall. In recognition of this, dates are given for the northern and southern halves of the state. As shown in Figure 1, the state is further divided into nine regions (using county lines as boundaries) that are relatively homogeneous seasonally and vegetatively. By referrring to these regions we can discuss in greater detail the geographical variations and range for each species.

Abundance

The following abundance terms are used in discussing migration.

1. Abundant: Daily counts of as many as 50 birds; season counts of 250 or more birds.
2. Common: Daily counts of 6 to 50 birds; season counts of 25 to 250 birds by an active observer.

Counties and geographic regions in Minnesota.

3. Uncommon: Daily counts of 1 to 5 birds; season counts of 5 to 25 birds by an active observer.
4. Rare: Season counts of no more than 5 birds by an active observer.
5. Casual: Up to 3 birds seen in a decade by an active observer.
6. Accidental: Up to 3 birds seen in a lifetime by an active observer.

Obviously these terms are not absolute and are used only as general guides. The number of birds an observer sees depends a good deal on the amount of effort expended, the degree of skill possessed, and the kind of habitat covered. For our purposes, a very active observer is one who is afield for an average of one or more days every week.

2. SUMMER POPULATIONS

Species present during the summer are classified as residents if they nest in the state and as visitants if they do not. Species that do not nest in the state every year are termed casual summer residents. The abundance of birds during the nesting season is determined by the amount of their preferred habitat that is available and the location of it. Since abundance can vary considerably over relatively short distances, no absolute abundance figures are included on the range maps or in the text. The only available data on the absolute abundance of species during the nesting season is from the Breeding Bird Survey conducted by volunteers for the Branch of Surveys in the office of Migratory Bird Management of the United States Fish and Wildlife Service in Laurel, Maryland. Although information about many routes has been available since 1967 when the Minnesota surveys began, the coverage of the state is still incomplete. When more data from the surveys have accumulated, it will be possible to describe summer bird populations with greater precision.

Maps of Breeding Ranges

Breeding range maps are included for every species for which confirmed breeding data exists in the state since 1970. Confirmed breeding is defined as a nest with eggs, or adult sitting on a nest constantly, or eggshells near a nest; young in nest seen or heard; downy young or young still unable to fly seen away from the nest. The shading used on the maps gives an approximate breeding range for the most common species breeding in the state. The solid dots usually placed in the center of the county indicate a positive breeding record within the county indicated since 1970. A line with a question mark indicates the exact boundary is unknown. A few maps show dots outside the main breeding range, indicating isolated breeding in these areas. No attempt has been made to indicate a breeding range for rare breeders; these are indicated by single dots within the county of record. The shading on the range maps utilizes data on *observations* during the months of June and July only to avoid the possibility that nesting birds might be confused with migrants, but they include *nesting* data from any month. One of the purposes of presenting the maps is to stimulate fieldwork during the breeding season that will provide more data that can be used to correct any inaccuracies in the maps. There is much more to be learned about the breeding ranges of many Minnesota species.

3. WINTER POPULATIONS

Species that occur in the winter, either regularly or casually, are termed winter visitants if there are no data to prove that they breed locally. This term is also used for several species (for example, the Great Horned Owl and the American Robin) for which banding records or migration paths indicate that all or part of the winter population differs from the breeding population. If it is not known whether the winter population is different from the summer population, the phrase regular in winter is used. Species that are sedentary — that is, species in which most of the population remains in one area for the whole year — are classified as permanent residents. The terms used to describe the distribution and the abundance of each species in the winter are the same as those used for the migration seasons.

4. NOTES ON REFERENCES

MMNH in the Species Accounts refers to specimens and files at the James Ford Bell Museum of Natural History, formerly known as the Minnesota Museum of Natural History. MMNH was retained for purposes of continuity.

Editions of *The Flicker* and *The Loon* are on permanent file at the James Ford Bell Museum of Natural History.

SPECIES ACCOUNTS

RED-THROATED LOON *(Gavia stellata)*

Minnesota status. Regular. Migrant; accidental in summer (July and August) and winter.

Migration. Rare spring and casual fall migrant in the eastern part of the state (east of the Mississippi); casual or absent elsewhere. Almost all recent records are in spring. Usually seen as individuals or in pairs. Seven were seen on Mille Lacs Lake on November 9, 1972. *Spring migration period:* Late April through mid-June, with most birds seen from late May through early June on Lake Superior. Earliest dates: SOUTH, April 17, 22, 28; NORTH *March 31-April 7,* 29, 30, May 1. Latest dates: SOUTH; May 20 (only date); NORTH, June 17, 18, 22, *25* (two picked up dead at Duluth). *Fall migration period:* Mid-September through late November. Earliest dates: NORTH, September 16, 19, 26; SOUTH, October 30 (only date). Latest dates: NORTH, November 9, 13, 23; SOUTH, November 17, 26 (only dates).

Summer. Three midsummer observations, all from Lake Superior: July 3, 1981, Duluth; July 8, 1945, Duluth; July 3, 1952, Cook County.

Winter. Three records: January 1, 1954, Duluth; February 22, 1942, one bird in spring plumage, St. Cloud; March 9, 1952, two birds, Lake Superior, St. Louis County.

PACIFIC LOON *(Gavia pacifica)*

Minnesota status. Casual. Migrant; accidental in summer.

Records. There are two spring, three summer, and 12 fall records. The spring records are of a single bird seen on Lake Superior near Duluth on May 7, 1986 (winter plumage) and a spring-plumaged bird on May 24, 1986 *(The Loon* 58:128-29). The fall records range from an early date of September 10 to a late date of November 22. Fall records are from Lake Superior, St. Louis County (8), Mille Lacs Lake, Mille Lacs County (2), Leech Lake, Cass

County (1), and Lake Vadnais, Ramsey County (1). The summer records are: one bird remained on Lake Harriet, Minneapolis, Hennepin County, from June 13 to August 1, 1976 (*The Loon* 48:184); one bird was seen on Upper Rice Lake, Clearwater County, on June 5, 1982 (*The Loon* 54:178-79); one bird was seen in Jackson County on June 25, 1981 (*The Loon* 53:230).

COMMON LOON *(Gavia immer)*

Minnesota status. Regular. Migrant and summer resident; accidental in winter.

Migration. Common spring and fall immigrant in the eastern and central regions; uncommon in the western regions. Concentrations of several hundred, up to 750 birds, have been recorded, especially on Mille Lacs Lake in the fall (*Wilson Bulletin* 95:121-25). *Spring migration period:* Late March through late May, with the bulk of the migration from mid-April through early May. Earliest dates: SOUTH, March *12,* 18, 23, 25; NORTH, March 21, 25, 28. *Fall migration period:* Late August through early December, with a peak in mid-October. Latest dates: NORTH, December 15, 16, 19, *22*; SOUTH, December 7, 8, 9, *26, 30*.

Summer. Resident throughout the central and northern two-thirds of the state except in the Red River Valley; most numerous in the north-central and north-eastern regions. At present breeds as far south as Scott County in the east. Formerly nested as far south as the Iowa border; at present scattered individuals are reported on a number of lakes in the southern portions of the state each summer. Breeding may occur rarely in these areas.

Winter. There are six records of birds wintering or attempting to winter in the state. One bird was seen on the open Otter Tail River in Fergus Falls, Otter Tail County from January 29 to February 3, 1975; one bird was seen on the Mississippi River at Sartell, Stearns County on January 15, 1978; an injured bird spent the winter of 1973-74 at Pine River, Cass

Common Loon

County (*The Loon* 46:89); a single bird was seen on Silver Lake, Virginia, St. Louis County during January, February, and March 1976 (*The Loon* 49:101); an injured bird spent the winter of 1983-84 on the Otter Tail River, which flows out of Rush Lake, Otter Tail County. One bird was seen on Lake Superior at Stony Point, St. Louis County, on January 23 and 24, 1985.

YELLOW-BILLED LOON *(Gavia adamsii)*

Minnesota status. Accidental.
Records. One bird was seen on November 16, 1980 on Lake Winnibigoshish, Itasca County (*The Loon* 53:62). What could have been the same individual was seen on Lake Superior in St. Louis and Lake Counties on November 26, 27, and 28, 1980 (*The Loon* 53:62-63).

PIED-BILLED GREBE *(Podilymbus podiceps)*

Pied-billed Grebe

Minnesota status. Regular. Migrant and summer resident; casual in winter.
Migration. Common spring and fall migrant throughout the state; least numerous in the northeastern region in the fall. Concentrations of up to 200 birds occur during the fall migration. Some of the early and late dates could be confusion with wintering birds. *Spring migration period:* Early March through mid-May, with a peak in mid-April. Earliest dates: SOUTH, March 2, 3, 4; NORTH, March 10, 11, 15. *Fall migration period:* Mid-August through mid-December, with a peak in mid-October. Latest dates: NORTH, November 29, December 4, *26, 28;* SOUTH, December 15, 19, 20.
Summer. Common resident throughout the state with the exception of the northeast region in Cook, Lake, and northern St. Louis Counties where it is only a casual breeder.
Winter. Individual to two or three birds occasionally winter on open water areas of the

southeastern and east-central parts of the state. Single birds have been reported almost every winter at Black Dog Lake in Dakota County. Wintering birds have been reported as far north as Fergus Falls, Otter Tail County.

HORNED GREBE *(Podiceps auritus)*

Minnesota status. Regular. Migrant and summer resident; casual in winter on Lake Superior.
Migration. Common spring and fall migrant throughout the state. Peak concentrations of over 1,000 birds occur at Duluth at the time of the smelt run in late April and early May. *Spring migration period:* Mid-March through early June, with a peak in late April. Earliest dates: SOUTH, March *3,* 12, 19, 25; NORTH, March 26, 31, April 3. Latest dates (beyond breeding areas): SOUTH, May 14, 16, 24; NORTH, June 2, 6, 9. *Fall migration period:* Mid-August through mid-December, with the bulk of the migration from early October through mid-November. Earliest dates: SOUTH, September 5 (only date). Latest dates: NORTH (with the exception of Lake Superior), November 14, 17, 19; SOUTH, December 4, 6, 8.

Horned Grebe

Summer. Resident primarily in the northwestern region with recent breeding reported from Kittson (1966), Roseau (1971), Marshall (1984), Pennington (1984), and Mahnomen Counties (1958). Adults were seen at Tamarac National Wildlife Refuge, Becker County during the summer of 1978 and 1979, but no positive breeding was observed. In the west-central region several broods were seen during July 1977 on Lake Amelia, Pope County. Adults were also present on this lake in 1982 and 1983. Formerly more widespread with nesting documented for Jackson County (1885, 1900), McLeod County (1935), Wright County (1931), and Kandiyohi County (1944). There are a number of recent summer observations from the northeastern region (Cook County, one all summer 1985), but these probably represent postbreeding dispersal or nonbreeding birds.

Winter. Casual visitant on Lake Superior with late December, January, and February records from Cook, Lake, and St. Louis counties. One bird was seen on Black Dog Lake, Dakota County, from December 23, 1973 to January 19, 1974 for the only winter record away from Lake Superior.

RED-NECKED GREBE *(Podiceps grisegena)*

Red-necked Grebe

Minnesota status. Regular. Migrant and summer resident; casual in winter.

Migration. In the spring common only in the central part of the state, becoming abundant on Lake Superior at the migration peak. Uncommon in western and southern areas in spring. In the fall, uncommon throughout the state. Concentrations of up to 300 or more birds occur in the spring on Lake Superior during the late April and early May smelt run. *Spring migration period:* Early April through late May, with a peak in late April. There is one very unusual record of a single bird on Kelley Lake, Rice County, on February 27, 1985. This was probably an exceptionally early migrant. Earliest dates: SOUTH, *March 29,* April 5, 6, 7; NORTH, April 5, 7, 8. *Fall migration period:* Late August through early December; no peaks or concentrations noted. Latest dates: NORTH, November 20, 23, 30, December *2, 6, 21, 27;* SOUTH, December 1, 8, 13.

Summer. Resident primarily in the northwestern, central, west-central, and east-central regions; occurs sparingly in other parts of the state. One hundred nests were found at Agassiz National Wildlife Refuge, Marshall County, in June 1983. There are breeding records from as far east as Lake Kabotogama (1985), St. Louis County, and as far south as Swan Lake (1985), Nicollet County. In 1982 young were found at Oak Glen Lake, Steele County, in the south-central region. In 1986 a nest was found near Tracy, Lyon County, in the southwest region. There are previous records from Albert Lea, Freeborn County, and Heron Lake, Jackson County.

Winter. There are January and February records of up to five birds on Lake Superior in Cook, Lake, and St. Louis Counties.

EARED GREBE *(Podiceps nigricollis)*

Minnesota status. Regular. Migrant and summer resident; accidental in winter.
Migration. In the spring uncommon in the western regions; rare in the central, east-central, and south-central regions; casual in north-central and northeast regions. In the fall uncommon in the western regions, casual elsewhere. Concentrations of 30 to 75 birds can occur in spring and fall. *Spring migration period:* Early April through late May, with a peak in early May. Earliest dates: SOUTH, March *30,* April 5, 7, 8; NORTH, April 11, 14, 15. *Fall migration period:* The bulk of the population probably leaves the nesting areas in September; little information is available on fall movements. Latest dates: NORTH, October 31, November 11, 16, *29;* SOUTH, November 7, 8.

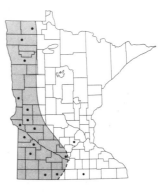

Eared Grebe

Summer. Resident primarily in the western regions and through the central part of the state as far east as Swan Lake, Nicollet County. Recent breeding has been reported from Swan Lake, Nicollet County, Alberta, Stevens County, Breckenridge, Wilkin County, Carver County (17 adults, 8 young, and 9 nests, 1986), Agassiz Refuge, Marshall County, Big Stone County, Lake Shibble, Swift County (53 nests, 1985), Yellow Medicine County, Lyon County, and Freeborn County (two adults, two young, 1985). May be expanding farther east and north with the increased use of sewage ponds as breeding sites. There are recent June records from Pelican Lake, Wright County, Moose Lake, Carlton County, and Lake Movil and Upper Red Lake, Beltrami County. Nests are in colonies; 100 nests were found at Agassiz Refuge, Marshall County, in June 1983, and 75 pair were present in June 1984.
Winter. There is one winter record of a single bird

in the Otter Tail River, Fergus Falls, Otter Tail County, from January 20 to March 19, 1979 (*The Loon* 51:99-100).

WESTERN GREBE *(Aechmophorus occidentalis)*

Western Grebe

Minnesota status. Regular. Migrant and summer resident; accidental in winter.

Migration. Common spring and fall migrant in the western region; locally abundant, especially in the fall. Casual elsewhere, except for breeding locations in the central regions during spring and fall. Concentrations of 100 or more birds have been recorded in the fall. The largest concentrations occur on Lake Osakis, Todd County: 500 were seen on August 11, 1983; 100 birds were recorded on Pomroy Lake, Kanabec County, in the eastern part of the state on October 30, 1971. *Spring migration period:* Mid-April through early June, with a peak in early May. Earliest dates: SOUTH, April *5,* 10, 15, 16; NORTH, April 18, 20, 24. Latest dates (beyond breeding areas): June 2, 6, 19, *26. Fall migration period:* Late August through mid-November. Latest dates: NORTH, November 9, 12, 29, *December 10, 22;* SOUTH, November 15, 17, December *2.*

Summer. Resident primarily in the western regions, eastward through the central region to Swan Lake, Nicollet County, and recently French Lake, Hennepin County, in the east-central region. Most common at Swan Lake, Nicollet County, Big Stone National Wildlife Refuge, Lac Qui Parle County, Lake Osakis, Todd County (300 pairs, June 1984), and Agassiz National Wildlife Refuge, Marshall County. The following records indicate the possible eastward expansion of breeding: June 2, 1979, Oak Lake, Pine County; June 12, 1984, Washington County; June 29, 1981, Rice Lake, Steele County; and July 9, 1977, Meeker County.

Winter. One bird remained on the open water of Big Stone Lake, Ortonville, Big Stone County, from mid-November 1977 to late March 1978.

CLARK'S GREBE *(Aechmophorus clarkii)*

Minnesota status. Accidental.
Records. The American Ornithologists' Union in
their *35th Supplement* (July 1985) to the *A.O.U.
Checklist* split the grebe genus *Aechmophorus* into
two species, the Western Grebe and the Clark's
Grebe, the latter being the newer species. The first
mention of the Clark's Grebe in Minnesota was a
bird seen on Marsh Lake, Lac Qui Parle county,
on April 24, 1983 (*The Loon* 57:134). On May 10,
1986 a Clark's Grebe was carefully identified and
documented on Ash Lake, Grant County *(The Loon*
58:110). On May 23, 1986 what probably was a
Clark's Grebe with abnormal coloration was seen
on Lake Osakis, Todd County *(The Loon*
58:110-11).

AMERICAN WHITE PELICAN
(Pelecanus erythrorhynchos)

Minnesota status. Regular. Migrant, summer resident, and summer visitant; accidental in winter.
Migration. Common migrant in the west central,
southwestern, and south-central regions and in
adjacent counties in the central region; locally
abundant (with concentrations of as many as 5,000
birds) in the southwestern region, mainly in the fall;
rare in the north-central and northeastern regions;
(one or two in Duluth every fall in September and
October, one at Grand Marais, Cook County, on
October 26 and 27, 1984), usually uncommon
elsewhere in the state. *Spring migration period:*
Early April through late May, with a peak during
the third week of April. Earliest dates: SOUTH,
March *20, 29, 30,* April *1, 2, 3;* NORTH, March *24,*
April *5, 7, 9.* (One bird was seen on Lake Superior,
Cook County, on May 24, 1977.) *Fall migration
period:* August through early November, with a
peak in the second half of September. Latest dates:
NORTH, November *5, 8, 12;* SOUTH, November *21,
28, 30, December 3, 8, 11* (one bird in Big Stone

American White Pelican

County, died), *19* (one on Cannon River, Rice County).

Summer. At present breeds at Marsh Lake, Lac Qui Parle County (1,450 nests June 1983), and on several small islets in Lake of the Woods, Lake of the Woods County. Flocks of nonbreeding birds occur frequently during June and July in south-central, west-central, and southwestern regions and occasionally farther east: Aitkin, St. Louis, Crow Wing, Rice, Houston (probably most are in Wisconsin waters), and Chisago Counties.

Winter. During the winters of 1978-79, 1979-80, 1982-83, 1983-84, and 1984-85, one or two birds wintered on the open water in downtown Albert Lea, Freeborn County. During 1979-80 four birds attempted to winter, but two of them died by mid-February.

DOUBLE-CRESTED CORMORANT
(Phalacrocorax auritus)

Double-crested Cormorant

Minnesota status. Regular. Migrant and summer resident; accidental in winter.

Migration. Common spring and fall migrant throughout most of the state, uncommon in the northeast but becoming common on Lake Superior in the spring. Until the early 1950s the species was abundant, and flocks of 1,000 to 5,000 birds were observed; peak flock size now is usually 200 to 500 birds, although 1,000 birds were seen in Nicollet County on October 7, 1983. Once again increasing in the 1980s. *Spring migration period:* Late March through mid-May, with a peak during the second half of April. Earliest dates: SOUTH, March *15, 19, 20,* 26, 28, 30; NORTH, April 3, 7, 8. *Fall migration period:* Mid-September through early December, with a peak during the third week of October; most birds have left by early November. Latest dates: NORTH, November 9, 16, 29, 30; SOUTH, November 24, 25, 28; December 2, 3, *5, 10, 12, 15, 19, 22.* One bird remained in Austin, Mower County, until January 6, 1985.

Summer. The species has bred in all regions of the state, but only sparingly in the north-central and northeast regions. At present there are active colonies in many counties, including Marshall, Pope, Lac Qui Parle, Le Sueur, Meeker, Big Stone, Lake of the Woods, Jackson, Grant, Aitkin, and Lake. Nonbreeding birds (or birds from undiscovered colonies) may be seen in any part of the state in summer. In recent years colonies have been increasing and the nesting range of the species has been expanding.

Winter. Single birds were seen on January 18, 1981 in St. Paul, Ramsey County; January 4, 1981, Hastings, Dakota County (possibly the same bird); January 1, 1980, Ortonville, Big Stone County; and February 18, 1981, Sherburne County. Two birds were seen at Prairie Island, Goodhue County, wintering on the Mississippi River, January 30 to February 15, 1983. One bird was seen on Silver Lake, Rochester, Omsted County, from December 3, 1983 to January 5, 1984. One bird remained on this same lake from November 1985 through February 1986.

ANHINGA *(Anhinga anhinga)*

Minnesota status. Accidental.
Records. One bird was seen high over Hawk Ridge, Duluth, St. Louis County, on September 20, 1982 (*The Loon* 55:28-29); the second record for the state occurred on May 26, 1984, when one bird was seen soaring over the Louisville Swamp area, Scott County (*The Loon* 56:203). On April 27, 1985 a single bird was seen and well documented near Hanover, Wright County (*The Loon* 58:46).

AMERICAN BITTERN *(Botaurus lentiginosus)*

Minnesota status. Regular. Migrant and summer resident.
Migration. Common only in the northwestern

American Bittern

region. Uncommon in all other regions of the state. Usually encountered as individuals. Recent declines have been noted in most parts of its range. *Spring migration period:* Late March through late May, with a peak in early May. Earliest dates: SOUTH, March 23, 25, 26; NORTH, April 7, 12, 15. *Fall migration period:* August through early November, with a peak in August in the north. Latest dates: NORTH, November 5, 14, 19, *December 28* (one bird in Carlton County, photographed); SOUTH, November 11, 13, 25, *December 20, 25* (latter date of one injured bird in Dakota County).

Summer. Best represented in the central, northeast, and northwestern regions. May breed very sparingly throughout the state wherever suitable marsh habitat exists. Numbers have declined drastically in recent years in southern and western regions.

LEAST BITTERN *(Ixobrychus exilis)*

Least Bittern

Minnesota status. Regular. Migrant and summer resident.

Migration. Uncommon spring and fall migrant in the southern half of the state; may be locally common in areas such as Big Stone National Wildlife Refuge in Lac Qui Parle and Big Stone Counties, casual to rare in the southwest. Casual to rare in the northwest and adjoining areas of the north-central regions, absent in the northeast, north of Duluth and adjacent Itasca and Koochiching Counties. Encountered as individuals. *Spring migration period:* Early May through early June, no peak period noted. Early dates: SOUTH, May 1, 5, 7; NORTH, May 1, 18, 29 (only dates). *Fall migration period:* Mid-September through early October; no peak period noted. Latest dates: NORTH, September 5, 16, 26 (only dates); SOUTH, October 5, 8, 12, *November 5, December 23* (one injured bird).

Summer. Resident in the south-central, southwest, northwest (except the Red River Valley), and portions of the north-central regions wherever suitable marsh habitat occurs. Absent from the

northeastern region north of Duluth and adjacent
Koochiching and Itasca counties in the north-central
region and over most of the southeast region.
Summer observations are increasing from a number
of areas, especially in the south; it is not known if
this is a factor of increased numbers of this species
or more coverage by observers in suitable habitat.

GREAT BLUE HERON *(Ardea herodias)*

Minnesota status. Regular. Migrant and summer
resident; casual in winter.

Migration. Common spring and fall migrant
throughout the state; least numerous in the heavily
wooded areas of northern regions. Concentrations
of 200-300 birds occur during peak fall migration
period. *Spring migration period:* Early March
through mid-May, with a peak in early April.
Earliest dates: SOUTH, because of wintering birds it
is sometimes difficult to determine exact early
spring migration dates, March 1, 4, 5; NORTH,
March *1,* 13, 17, 21. *Fall migration period:* Late July
through late December, with the bulk of the
migration in August and early September. Latest
dates: NORTH, November 21, 23, 26, December *1,*
15 (Cook County), *21* (Otter Tail County); SOUTH,
none can be given because of late-lingering birds
into mid-January (there are numerous December
dates); most birds have departed the state by late
November.

Great Blue Heron

Summer. Resident throughout most of the state
where suitable habitat for nesting colonies exists.
The colonies gradually decrease in size north-
eastward in the state. No colonies are known for
the southwestern region, although a large colony
exists on the Big Stone National Wildlife Refuge,
Lac Qui Parle County, in the adjacent west-central
region. The largest colonies (more than 300 nests)
occur in the southeastern, east-central, central, and
south-central regions. The largest colony known in
the north (300 + nests) is the Turtle River heronry
located near Bemidji, Beltrami County. There is

large fluctuation in colony size in any given area over a period of years.

Winter. Stragglers remain mainly in the southeastern part of the state (from the Twin Cities southward) around open water areas through late January. There is one record for Pine County in the northeast and one for Otter Tail County in the west-central region during January. Numbers diminish in February with records from Mower, Winona, and Dakota Counties. There are four records of birds in the north during February: February 13, 1967, Cotton, St. Louis County; February 17, 1977, Crow Wing County; one bird wintered at Fergus Falls, Otter Tail County, from December 13, 1980 to February 24, 1981; and one bird on February 22, 1984 at Mahnomen, Mahnomen County. This last bird could have been an extremely early migrant.

GREAT EGRET *(Casmerodius albus)*

Great Egret

Minnesota status. Regular. Migrant and summer resident.

Migration. Common spring and fall migrant in the southern part of the state (south of a line between southern Otter Tail and Anoka Counties); locally abundant in the fall, especially in the flood-plain lakes of the Minnesota River Valley. In the north the species is casual in the northwest in both spring and fall; accidental or absent over most of the north-central and northeastern regions. There is one record of two birds seen in Cook County in the extreme northeast part of the state on August 15, 1985 *(The Loon* 58:47). Has been gradually increasing in occurrence in the northern areas in recent years. Historically, the Great Egret was a casual late-summer visitant beginning in the early 1930s in the extreme southern part of the state (Freeborn and Martin Counties). By the 1940s the species had reached the Minnesota River Valley and the Twin City area, but still as a late-summer visitant. It was not until the 1950s that it became a regular spring and fall migrant in the southern part of the state. Concentrations of 100 and more birds occur during August and early September, mainly in the southern regions; but up to 40 + birds have been seen during late August in Aitkin County. The largest number on record is 504 seen at Carlos Avery Refuge, Anoka County on August 24, 1984 (*The Loon* 56:217). *Spring migration period:* Late March through late May, with a peak in mid-May. Earliest dates: SOUTH, March 23, 24, 27; NORTH, *March 9,* 29, April 2, 7, 10. *Fall migration period:* Late July through October, with some stragglers into November. Latest dates: NORTH, October 10, 12, 13, *November 14, 21,* (Duluth); SOUTH, November 8, 12, 13, *18, 20.*

Summer. Resident in the southern half of the state and in adjacent counties in the west-central region. Has been gradually spreading northward. It was seen all summer during 1974 in Clearwater County; up to 22 were seen at Agassiz National Wildlife Refuge on June 7, 1974, and they were seen there again during the summer of 1975. Nesting was first noted in 1980 when three nests were found. Ten nests were found at Sand Lake, Becker County, in 1983. Other recent summer occurrences have been recorded in the north from Pine, Clearwater, Norman, St. Louis (Duluth), and Lake (June 12, 1976) Counties. This species was casual in Minnesota until the 1930s; breeding was first recorded in Martin County (1938) and Winona County (1939). The largest colonies (from 50 to 100 nests) have been found in Washington, Dakota, Houston, Le Sueur, Pope, Grand, Lac Qui Parle, and Grant Counties.

SNOWY EGRET *(Egretta thula)*

Minnesota status. Regular. Migrant and summer resident. This species was first recorded in Minnesota on August 28, 1950 in Faribault County. Records slowly increased during the 1960s, and it was put on the regular state list by the late 1970s, when it was being recorded mainly in the southern

Snowy Egret

part of the state. Records began tapering off by the early 1980s and now (1987) the species status in the state may be changing to casual.

Migration. Uncommon to rare migrant with almost all records from the southern and western regions of the state as far north as Agassiz National Wildlife Refuge, Marshall County. There are two records from the northeast, April 22-27, 1985, Kinney, St. Louis County, and May 18, 1984, Silver Creek, Lake County. Concentrations of up to 14 birds have been recorded. *Spring migration period:* Mid-April to late May, no peak period noted. Earliest dates: SOUTH, April 10, 17, 24; NORTH, April 21, 25, May 3. *Fall migration period:* August to late September, peak period early September. Latest dates: NORTH, September 9, 22-25 (Otter Tail County) (only dates); SOUTH, September 9, 17, 25, *October 12.*

Summer. The only positive nesting for the species was at Big Stone National Wildlife Refuge, Lac Qui Parle County, during June and July 1977 (*The Loon* 49:185-86) and during June 1978 (*The Loon* 51:31). Ten nests were found in 1977 and 12 in 1978. Other summer records include June 19, 1977 near the Pelican Lake heron rookery, Grant County (*The Loon* 50:47); June 20, 1976, Lake Shakotan, Lincoln County *(The Loon* 49:102-3). Single birds were recorded at Agassiz National Wildlife Refuge, Marshall County, during the summer of 1965 and 1966, and one bird remained on the refuge from June 28 to September 9, 1976 (*The Loon* 48:177). During 1979 and 1980 birds were recorded in Lac Qui Parle County at Big Stone Refuge and in Grant County near the Pelican Lake rookery, but nesting was not confirmed. A single bird was present at the Lake Johanna rookery, Pope County, during June and July 1971 (*The Loon* 44:36-43). There are recent early June records from the Swan Lake area of Nicollet County: June 8, 1963 (*The Flicker* 35:99-100); June 6, 1979 (*The Loon* 51:154); and June 25, 1982 (*The Loon* 54:188). One bird was seen in western Hennepin County on July 31 and August 1 and 3, 1982. On June 1 and 2, 1984, a single bird was seen at Carlos Avery Refuge, Anoka County, and two birds were seen on June 24, 1984 at Long Lake, Kandiyohi County. In 1985 single birds were seen at Agassiz National Wildlife Refuge, Marshall County, on June 29 and July 2, and at Stacy, Chisago County, on June 2 and 3. There are also recent August records from Jackson and Traverse Counties. All of these records may indicate non-breeding or post breeding wanderers. It would appear that the nesting of this species in Minnesota was of very short duration, and it has now disappeared as a breeding bird, at least for the present.

LITTLE BLUE HERON (*Egretta caerulea*)

Minnesota status. Regular in 1970s, probably casual since early 1980s. Migrant and summer resident. **Migration.** Rare migrant in the southern regions south of a line from Grant County in the west to Chisago County in the east. There are three May records from the northeast, all from St. Louis County: May 27-29, 1972 at Virginia (*The Loon* 44:123); May 11, 1980, Duluth (*The Loon* 52:90); and May 23, 1985, Ely (*The Loon* 57:135). Usually encountered as single birds. Records of this species since 1980 have been decreasing. *Spring migration period:* Mid-April to mid-May, no peak noted. Earliest dates: SOUTH, April 10, 13, 15. *Fall migration period:* September, no peak period noted. Latest dates: SOUTH, September 9, 10, 14, *October 3.* **Summer.** During the summers of 1971 and 1972 this species established itself as a breeding species in the state at the heronry at Lake Johanna, Pope County; in 1971 one pair fledged two young (*The Loon* 44:36-43), and in 1972 eight nests produced 31 young (*The Loon* 44:107). During 1973 eight young were produced from three nests (*The Loon* 46:17). Two birds were seen at Lake Johanna during July 1974, but no nesting was noted. One nest was found at the Lake Johanna location on June 6, 1981 (*The Loon* 53:224). No nesting has been recorded since the breeding in 1981 at Lake Johanna. During June and July 1976 from four to seven birds were seen

Little Blue Heron

at big Stone National Wildlife Refuge, Lac Qui Parle County; the birds were possibly nesting, but no evidence was found (*The Loon* 49:48-49). The species nested at the Big Stone Refuge site during 1977. Nesting was suspected at Pelican Lake, Grant County, in 1972, and on July 10, 1976 three adults were found at Pelican Lake among the other herons in the rookery, but no evidence of nesting was found. Up to ten birds were seen at the same location during the summer of 1977, but, again, no nesting evidence was found. During the summer of 1979 birds were seen at the Pelican Lake and Big Stone Refuges, but once again no nesting was found. One nest was located on Pigs Eye Lake, Ramsey County, in 1979. A pair was seen in this area from May 1 to July 15. Nest building and incubation was observed. No nesting has been observed at this location since 1979. It would appear that the species has disappeared as a breeding species in the state at least for the present.

TRICOLORED HERON *(Egretta tricolor)*

Minnesota status. Casual. Spring migrant and summer visitant.
Records. A single bird was seen from May 10-24, 1963 at Agassiz National Wildlife Refuge, Marshall County (*The Loon* 36:106); another bird was seen on June 12, 1971 at Thief Lake, Marshall County (*The Loon* 49:93). The third record for the state did not occur until June 20, 1977 at Pelican Lake, Grant County, when up to four birds were seen until July 24, 1977 (*The Loon* 49:168 and 50:10). In 1981 a single bird was seen at Sherburne National Wildlife Refuge, Sherburne County on May 4, 5, 6, and 8 (*The Loon* 53:171). During 1982 there was a record of a single bird on May 20-23 at Osage, Becker County (*The Loon* 54:188-89), and in 1983 a single bird on July 7 at Alden, Freeborn County (*The Loon* 55:179-80). In 1984 a single bird was seen in Hennepin County on May 4 (*The Loon* 56:196). From June 24 to August 24, 1986 a single bird was

seen at Agassiz National Wildlife Refuge, Marshall
County (*The Loon* 59:49).

CATTLE EGRET *(Bubulcus ibis)*

Minnesota status. Regular. Migrant and summer
resident. First recorded in the state in 1959. Records
increased during the 1960s, with numerous reports
during the spring migration. Numbers peaked
during the 1970s, and breeding was recorded positively in one area and suspected in a number of
other areas. In the early 1980s records began to
decrease, and this species, like the Little Blue Heron
and Snowy Egret, may be reverting to a casual
migrant status in the state.

Cattle Egret

Migration. A rare spring and fall migrant mainly
in the southern half of the state and in adjacent
counties northward in the west-central region.
Casual in the north in spring and fall, recorded in
St. Louis, Itasca, Lake, Polk, Aitkin, Cook, and
Marshall Counties. Usually occurs as individuals or
in small groups of a few birds. Concentrations of
20 to 40 birds have been recorded near breeding
areas. *Spring migration period:* Mid-April through
late May, with a peak in mid-May. Earliest dates:
SOUTH, *March 30,* April 15, 17, 19; NORTH, April
11, 23, May 2, 7, 10 (only dates). *Fall migration
period:* Birds leave the breeding colonies by early
August; postbreeding congregations remain
throughout September. Individual stragglers are
recorded into October and November. Latest dates:
NORTH, November 4, 7, 8; SOUTH, November 3, 5,
7, *20.*

Summer. The first report of this species in Minnesota was on June 29, 1959 near Glenwood, Pope
County (*The Flicker* 31:103-4). In 1970 the number
of reports sharply increased and breeding was
suspected in Pope and Grant Counties. Nesting was
confirmed in 1971 at the heronry at Lake Johanna,
Pope County (*The Loon* 44:36-43). Thirty to forty
adults and immatures were present on August 14,
1971. Breeding was confirmed in 1972 at the

heronry at Pelican Lake, Grant County (*The Loon* 44:107). During June 1972, 20 adults and 20 young were present at the Lake Johanna site. No nesting was recorded at either site during the summers of 1973 and 1974, but adults were present in the area. During 1977 nesting was confirmed at Big Stone National Wildlife Refuge, Lac Qui Parle County, when 10 nests were found (*The Loon* 50:10). Nesting was also suspected at Pelican Lake during 1977 and at the Big Stone site during 1979, when up to 25 adults were present. Single birds have been recorded during June in the following other areas of the state: Larsmont, Lake County (June 1, 1977); Wabasha County (June 23, 1975); Freeborn County (June 30, 1975); Itasca County (June 18, 1982); and there is a July 27, 1982 record from Faribault County. During June and July 1983, birds were reported in Cottonwood (two-four), Washington, and Jackson Counties. In 1984 there was a resurgence of records when four nests were found at Lake Johanna, Pope County. Up to 13 birds were present at Long Lake in Kandiyohi County, and up to 24 birds were present at Pelican Lake, Grant County, both in June 1984. Birds were reported in Cottonwood (two), Ramsey, and Anoka Counties during June 1984.

GREEN-BACKED HERON *(Butorides striatus)*

Green-backed Heron

Minnesota status. Regular. Migrant and summer resident.
Migration. Common migrant in southern, east-central, central, and west-central regions. Becoming uncommon going northward into northwest, north-central, and northeastern regions; rare in the northern part of these regions; has never been recorded in Cook County. This species is increasing in northern and southwestern regions. Usually encountered as individuals, but occasionally five to ten birds may be found. *Spring migration period:* Early April through late May with a peak in the first week of May. Earliest dates: SOUTH, *March 28,* April 2, 4, 5; NORTH, April 27, 30, May 3. *Fall*

migration period: August through late October. Latest dates: NORTH, September 25, 26, 30, *October 14, 22, 31, November 6;* SOUTH, October 29, 30, 31, *November 9, 22, 25.*

Summer. Resident primarily in the southern half of the state with breeding confirmed as far north as Pine County (1979-80), Duluth (1979 and 1983), Aitkin and Crow Wing Counties (1972), Otter Tail County (1977), and Clearwater County (Itasca State Park). Summer records are increasing in northern regions with recent summer observations in Carlton, Cass, Itasca, Hubbard, Beltrami, Marshall, Polk, Kittson, and Lake Counties. Also increasing in southwestern regions with recent reports from Pipestone, Nobles, Murray, and Rock Counties. Nests in loose colonies of up to 10-15 nests (*The Loon* 52:99-101).

BLACK-CROWNED NIGHT-HERON
(Nycticorax nycticorax)

Minnesota status. Regular. Migrant and summer resident; casual in winter.

Migration. Common spring and fall migrant in the southern half of the state and in the west-central and northwestern regions as far north as Agassiz National Wildlife Refuge, Marshall County. The species is very unevenly spread over this range, in some areas common, in other areas absent. Usually encountered as individuals. *Spring migration period:* Late March through mid-May, with a peak in late April. Earliest dates: SOUTH, March *8, 9,* 15, 24, 25; NORTH, April 4, 9, 10. *Fall migration period:* Early September through late November, no peak period noted. Latest dates: NORTH, November 5, 17 (only dates); SOUTH, November 26, 28, 30.

Summer. Resident primarily in the southern part of the state, but absent over most of the south-eastern and portions of the south-central regions. The primary nesting colonies in the state are at Long Lake, Kandiyohi County (424 nests, 1979; 420 nests, 1980; 279 nests, 1981); Egret Island, Grant County

Black-crowned Night-Heron

(591 nests, 1981); Swan Lake, Nicollet County (126 nests. 1981); Lake of the Isles, Hennepin County (146 nests, 1981; 60 nests, 1983); Howard Lake, Anoka County (52 nests, 1981). There were 60 nests near Mountain Lake in Watonwan county in 1980, but none have been found since 1981. There are other colonies at Lake Johanna, Pope County, Big Stone National Wildlife Refuge, Big Stone County, and at Pigs Eye Lake, Ramsey County, but no current information is available on number of nests at these localities. The only known nesting colony north of Grant County is the one that was first discovered in 1963 at Agassiz National Wildlife Refuge, Marshall County. There are summer observations from Beltrami (1986), Clearwater (1972), Cook (1982), Lake (1982), and St. Louis (Duluth, 1979, 1984) Counties.

Winter. There are records of individual stragglers in December and January in the Twin Cities area and in Rice and McLeod Counties. One bird was present at Black Dog Lake, Dakota County, from December 1970 to January 23, 1971. The only February report is of a single bird in St. Paul on February 7, 1942.

YELLOW-CROWNED NIGHT-HERON
(Nycticorax violaceus)

Yellow-crowned Night-Heron

Minnesota status. Regular. Rare migrant and summer resident. This species was first observed in the state in 1955 as a breeding species in Houston County. Since that time numbers have spread up the Mississippi River Valley and adjoining Minnesota River Valley to the Twin City area. Expansion of the range has continued westward and northward; it reached Aitkin County in 1972, Otter Tail County by 1977, and was recorded on Agassiz National Wildlife Refuge, Marshall County, in 1980. One bird was recorded at Duluth on August 21, 1984. At the time that this range expansion was proceeding to the north and west, the population dwindled in the southeast, and the center of population appears to be in the Twin City area at present. Usually encountered as individuals.

Migration. Uncommon spring and fall migrant across the southern part of the state; casual in northern areas as far north as southern Aitkin, Cass, and Marshall Counties. Has been recorded in southern St. Louis (Duluth), Cook, and Koochiching Counties. *Spring migration period:* Early April through late May, with a peak the first half of May. Earliest dates: SOUTH, April 7, 9, 13; NORTH, April 24, 27 (only dates). *Fall migration period:* Probably from August to late September; most birds leave the breeding areas by mid-August. Latest dates: NORTH, September 14 (only date); SOUTH, September 24, 27, 28.

Summer. The first observations and first breeding record for the state occurred in the summer of 1955 near LaCrescent, Houston County *(The Flicker* 27:171-72); this small colony (two to five nests) remained active until the late 1970s. Confirmed nesting activity shifted northward into Dakota County (1964) and Ramsey County (1978) *(The Loon* 50:214-15), and an adult was observed on a nest in June 1984 at Pig's Eye Lake, Ramsey County. By 1981 the species was probably nesting in Aitkin County *(The Loon* 53:232 and 54:250-51). Nesting was confirmed in Aitkin County in June 1983. An immature bird was seen in Aitkin County as early as August 8, 1974, so breeding may have occurred in this area much earlier. There are June and July records from Crow Wing, Cass, Becker, Lac Qui Parle, Stearns, and Marshall Counties *(The Loon* 53:54 and 54:244-45), and Rock County (June 16, 1983).

WHITE-FACED IBIS *(Plegadis chihi)*

Minnesota status. Casual. Migrant and summer visitant. In 1895 a nest was found at Heron Lake, Jackson County, and there is a sight observation for the same locality in 1910. Most interesting was a flock of five Ibis (species?) at Heron Lake on June 2, 1986.

Records. On June 16, 1939 an Ibis was seen at Heron Lake, Jackson County (*Wilson Bulletin* 51:183). This bird was originally identified as a Glossy Ibis but has since been changed to Ibis (species?) (see appendix page 343). More recent is the one bird seen on October 6-7, 1956 near Weaver, Wabasha County. There were four records during the 1960s from Lac Qui Parle, Jackson (Heron Lake), and Goodhue Counties, and, most noteworthy, a record of two birds from Agassiz National Wildlife Refuge, Marshall County, on May 28, 1965. The last is the most northerly record for the state. These two birds were originally identified as Glossy Ibis (see *The Loon* 38:41), but the description does not rule out the more likely White-faced Ibis. During the 1970s there were 15 records for the species, with the majority of them in the spring (about two to one in favor of spring over fall) from the southern part of the state. Most noteworthy are the records from Cook County (ibis sp?) on May 20, 1978 (*The Loon* 50:171); Clearwater County (ibis sp?) May 8, 1975 (*The Loon* 48:179); Mahnomen County, May 25, 1977 (*The Loon* 49:181). In the 1980s there have been nine records thus far: three in April, four in May, one in June, and one in October. Records are from Cottonwood, Sherburne, Wilkin (*The Loon* 53:165), Polk (ibis sp?) (*The Loon* 55:128), Winona (October 3, 1983), Martin, (*The Loon* 58:138), Lac Qui Parle (*The Loon* 58:138), and Lyon Counties (*The Loon* 52-191). Migration dates range from an early date of April 13 in the spring to a late date of October 10 in the fall.

Note. A number of the above observations have been listed in the record as ibis species (?) because of the difficulty of separating White-faced and Glossy Ibis. It is presumed that most, if not all, recent Minnesota observations are of White-faced Ibis.

FULVOUS WHISTLING-DUCK
(Dendrocygna bicolor)

Minnesota status. Accidental.
Records. Two birds were seen on May 24, 1929, near Arco, Lincoln County (*Wilson Bulletin* 42:58), and one bird was shot from a flock of eight birds (species of other birds undetermined) on Lake Onamia, Mille Lacs County, on October 20, 1950 (photograph of specimen, *The Loon* 36:107).

BLACK-BELLIED WHISTLING-DUCK
(Dendrocygna autumnalis)

Minnesota status. Accidental.
Record. An adult was shot on October 19, 1984 at Rice Lake, Faribault County. The specimen was mounted and photographed (*The Loon* 58:97-98).

TUNDRA SWAN *(Cygnus columbianus)*

Minnesota status. Regular. Migrant; casual in summer and winter.
Migration. Common to abundant spring and fall migrant throughout the state; less common in the southwest. Concentrations of 1,000 to 5,000 birds may occur in the spring; however, groups of 20 to 100 are more commonplace. There are many traditional stopping places around the Twin Cities area and in outstate areas. Several of these include Mud Lake and Lake Traverse in Traverse County, the Weaver Marshes in Wabasha County, and the St. Louis River estuary at Duluth. In the fall flocks normally pass through the state quickly (*The Loon* 56:3-5), and large congregations do not usually appear except at the Weaver Marshes where concentrations of up to 10,000 birds have been recorded. Birds linger in this area until mid-December; there were 6,500 still there on December 3, 1985. *Spring migration period:* Early March through late May, with a peak in the first half of

April. Earliest dates: SOUTH, *February 20* (possible wintering bird?), March 1, 4, 5; NORTH, March *14* 25, 28, 29. Latest dates: SOUTH, May 15, 17, 18, *29*. *Fall migration period:* Late September through late December, with a peak from mid to late November. Earliest dates: NORTH, September 22, 24, 27; SOUTH, September *12, 25,* October 4, 6, 7. Latest dates: NORTH, November 23, 24, 25, *December 1, 3;* SOUTH, December 25, 26, 29.

Summer. There are a number of records of birds lingering into June and July in northern regions. Several of these birds are known to have been injured; in two instances in which one member of a pair was injured, the pairs remained and nested, in Mahnomen County (1932) and Otter Tail County (1956), respectively. Other locations include Agassiz National Wildlife Refuge, Marshall County, Lake Superior (Duluth and Cook County), Rice Lake National Wildlife Refuge, Aitkin County, St. Cloud, Stearns County, and Britt and Virginia, St. Louis County.

Winter. In January and February single wintering birds have been reported in the north from Otter Tail (Fergus Falls) and Aitkin Counties. In the south, single birds have been reported from Stearns (St. Cloud), Benton (Sauk Rapids), Carver (Carver Park), Olmsted (Silver Lake in Rochester), and Wabasha Counties. In the latter area, wintering birds have been reported with increasing frequency, which may account for the early spring migration dates from this region.

TRUMPETER SWAN *(Cygnus buccinator)*

Minnesota status. Extirpated. Formerly occurred as a migrant and summer resident. In 1966 a reintroduction program was started in Carver County (Carver Park Reserve, Hennepin Parks); birds have been raised in captivity and are beginning to disperse as free-flyers; the first documented migration from this flock occurred in December 1984 when 29 birds flew south, a number of which were observed in Missouri, Kansas, and Oklahoma; 16 of the 29 are known to have returned. In 1986 the first breeding in the wild took place from this captive flock. A pair nested and raised four young near Marcell, Itasca County. In 1986 the free-flying population was between 40 and 50 birds (*The Loon* 58:194). A family group of this species were seen and heard over Lake Traverse, Traverse County, on October 24, 1976 (*The Loon* 49:234–35). These birds were probably escapees from the Trumpeter Swan restoration project at LaCreek National Wildlife Refuge in South Dakota.

Former status. According to Roberts (1932), the species probably bred in many places throughout the prairie and the sparsely wooded parts of the state in the 1800s. No specimens are available from this era. Roberts listed nesting records for Nicollet County (1823); Pike Lake in central Minnesota, probably Hennepin County (1853); Heron Lake, Jackson County (1883); and Meeker County (1884 or 1885). A previously unpublished breeding record for northeastern Minnesota (possibly Aitkin County) in 1798 is mentioned in the *Wilson Bulletin* (76:331-32). Banko (1960) cited a field report of a pair of Trumpeter Swans that spent the summer of 1937 on a small marshy lake in Beltrami County. No details of identification were given in the original report, and the birds described may have been Tundra Swans. All summer observations of swans in the state should be very carefully checked for the possibility of this species reoccuring in the wild.

MUTE SWAN *(Cygnus olor)*

Minnesota status. Casual. Occurs as a spring and fall visitor on Lake Superior; accidental in winter. Records away from Lake Superior are probably of escaped or introduced birds.

Records. There are long established feral populations of this species in the northern Lower Peninsula of Michigan and in the Ashland, Wisconsin area.

As these populations have increased, a few birds have wandered across Lake Superior into Minnesota. The first record of these wandering birds was during late May and early June 1974 at Duluth. Three birds were seen in the harbor at Grand Marais, Cook County, on January 27, 1975 (*The Loon* 47:42-43). These birds remained in the area until March 16, 1975. During the spring of 1980 there was a flurry of sightings in the Duluth area, ranging from March 8 to May 31. Anywhere from two to seven birds were seen off and on Lake Superior near Duluth during this period (*The Loon* 52:116-17). Again in 1981 this species was reported along the shore of Lake Superior in the Duluth area, between the Lester and Talmadge Rivers; dates ranged from March 15 to early June of one to seven birds. In 1982 two Mute Swans were seen at Duluth from October 20 to November 11. In 1983 two were seen at Duluth from March 24 to 26, one in 1984 from April 24 to 26 and in 1986, one on April 1 and 2.

Note: Mute Swans occur in other areas of the state, for example, a released pair has raised young in Waseca, Waseca County, and these birds ranged to Sakatah State Park, Le Sueur County, and as far as Faribault, Rice County. Mute Swans have been observed at Fergus Falls, Otter Tail County, and at Carlos Avery Refuge in Chisago County. These birds and others reported in various parts of the state could be wild, but the odds favor released or escaped birds from captivity when seen away from Lake Superior.

GREATER WHITE-FRONTED GOOSE
(Anser albifrons)

Minnesota status. Regular. Migrant; accidental in winter.

Migration. Uncommon spring and rare to casual fall migrant in the western regions. Rare to casual in the spring and accidental in the fall in the central and eastern regions. Encountered in small groups of a few birds or up to 10-15, usually in company with other goose species; however, individual flocks of 50 to 75 birds are occasionally observed. *Spring migration period:* Mid-March through mid-May, with a peak in early April. Earliest dates: SOUTH, March *1, 3, 8,* 13, 15, 16; NORTH, March *8,* 21, 23, 26. Latest dates: SOUTH, May 11, 18, 21, *31;* NORTH, May 11, 19, *28. Fall migration period:* Late September through late November. Earliest dates: NORTH, September *9,* October 4, 11, 14; SOUTH, September 27, October 11 (only dates). Latest dates: NORTH, October 18, 22, 26, November 5, 25 (only dates); SOUTH, November 26, 27, 30, *December 2.*

Summer: Most unusual was the presence of a single bird at Agassiz National Wildlife Refuge, Marshall County, on July 11, 1984.

Winter. Single birds have been encountered with the wintering flock of Canada Geese at Silver Lake, Rochester, Olmsted County, December 2, 1968 to February 16, 1969, January 1970, January 1972, February 1974, December 1977, 1979, 1982, 1984. One bird was seen among Canada Geese at Lake Elmo, Washington County, on January 1, 1980. A single bird was seen at St. John's University, Stearns County, during the winter of 1963-64.

SNOW GOOSE *(Chen caerulescens)*

Minnesota status. Regular. Migrant, casual summer and winter visitant.

Migration. Usually a common spring migrant west and fall migrant throughout the state; at times abundant especially in western areas, at other times absent over large areas of the state. Large concentration of thousands of birds may be encountered at Lake Traverse and Mud Lake in Traverse County, especially in the spring, and at Big Stone National Wildlife Refuge (Lac Qui Parle County) and Agassiz National Wildlife Refuge (Marshall County) in the fall. Normal flock size varies from 50 to 100 birds. *Spring migration period:* Mid-March through late May, with the bulk of the migration in April. Earliest dates: SOUTH, February 24,

29, March *3*, 5, 10, 12; NORTH, March 11, 17, 18, 19. Latest dates: SOUTH, May 23, 28, 31, *June 2, 3;* NORTH, May 27, 29, 31. *Fall migration period:* Mid-September through early December, with a peak in Mid-October. Earliest dates: NORTH, September 5, 9, 11, 16; SOUTH, September 4, 7, 8, 15. Latest dates: NORTH, November 22, 25, 26, *December 3, 4;* SOUTH, November 28, December 1, 7, *16, 23.*

Summer. Single birds or pairs of nonbreeding birds (probably injured) occasionally spend the summer months in various parts of the state; there are mid to late June, July, and early August records for Lac Qui Parle, Olmsted, Traverse, and Stevens Counties in the south, and Aitkin, Otter Tail, Marshall, Becker, Lake of the Woods, and St. Louis (Duluth) Counties in the north.

Winter. Occasionally individuals or small groups of four to six birds remain with larger flocks of Canada Geese that are wintering in the state. This species has been recorded for several winters at Silver Lake, Rochester, Olmsted County. Individuals have also occurred in winter in Lac Qui Parle, Hennepin, Scott, Wright, Stearns, Washington, Otter Tail, and St. Louis (one at Virginia) Counties. On the Hutchinson, McLeod County, Christmas Bird Count, 20 were recorded on December 26, 1984.

ROSS' GOOSE *(Chen rossi)*

Minnesota status. Accidental.
Records. There are three records of single birds occurring with the flock of Canada Geese present at Silver Lake in Rochester, Olmsted County: October 20, 1964 to January 8, 1965 *(The Loon* 37:39); March 24 to April 1, 1983; and November 12-27, 1984. There are three other records of birds in the fall and early winter: November 18 to December 2, 1962, Jackson County *(The Flicker* 35:94-95); December 5, 1965 to early January 1966, Howard Lake, Wright County, two birds *(The Loon*

38:36-37); September 30, 1979, Twin Lakes, Kittson County. There are records in the file of probable intermediate or hybrid birds occurring in the state, the most recent being a bird studied carefully by many observers on Black Dog Lake, Dakota County, on December 13, 1981 (*The Loon* 54:105-11). The spring migration record is of a single bird at Sulheim's Slough, Watonwan County, on April 6, 1977 (*The Loon* 49:186-87). The most unusual record for this species is of a single bird that was reported to have occurred over a two-year period in a small pond in southern Washington County. The bird was "discovered" by birders in February 1983 and remained in the area until late June 1983 (*The Loon* 55:84-85).

BRANT *(Branta bernicla)*

Minnesota status. Casual. Migrant and summer visitant.
Records. There are a total of 11 records for the state. One bird was shot near Pierce Lake, Martin County, on November 23, 1956 (*The Flicker* 29:85, MMNH #12696). One bird was seen at Silver Lake, Rochester, Olmsted County, from October 7 to December 8, 1973 (*The Loon* 46:33). A flock of 18 Brant were seen at Buffalo Bay, Lake of the Woods, Lake of the Woods County, on November 2, 1963; a single bird was seen in with the large flock of Canada Geese at Fergus Falls, Otter Tail County, on October 28, 1984 (*The Loon* 56:270); one bird was seen at Agassiz National Wildlife Refuge, Marshall County, October 31, 1972 (*The Loon* 45:24); two birds were seen at Grand Marais, Cook County, on October 4, 1974 (*The Loon* 47:140-41); another bird was seen at Grand Marais, Cook County, on November 16, 1982 (*The Loon* 55:36). A single bird was shot by a hunter and identified by Department of Natural resource personnel on November 13, 1985 in Olmsted County. The spring records are of a single bird seen at Rice Lake National Wildlife Refuge, Aitkin County, May

17-31, 1966 (*The Loon* 38:105); a flock of five birds over Lake Superior near Grand Marais, Cook County, on April 21, 1984 (*The Loon* 56:194). The summer record is of two birds on Minnesota Point, Duluth, St. Louis County, from June 20, 1981 to July 1, 1981 (*The Loon* 53:174-75).

CANADA GOOSE *(Branta canadensis)*

Canada Goose

Minnesota status. Regular. Migrant, summer resident, and winter visitant. During the 1982 fall hunting season, 81,000 Canada Geese were harvested.
Migration. Common to abundant migrant throughout the state, especially in western regions. Least numerous in the northeast. Traditional congregating areas for flocks of 5,000 to 30,000 birds include Silver Lake in Rochester, Olmsted County (30,000 birds November 21, 1975 and December 1982); Lac Qui Parle Game Management area (75,000 birds October 30, 1978 and 70,000 on November 21, 1985), Lac Qui Parle County; and Agassiz National Wildlife Refuge, Marshall County. Normal flock size varies from 25 to 100 or more birds. *Spring migration period:* Late February through early May, with the bulk of the migration from late March through early April. Earliest dates: None can be given because of wintering birds; early arrivals in the south are from mid to late February, and those in the north are in mid to late March. *Fall migration period:* Early September through early December, with a peak in mid-October. Latest dates: None can be given because of the large numbers of wintering birds in many areas of the state.
Summer. The species formerly (in the nineteenth and early twentieth centuries) nested throughout Minnesota, with the probable exception of the northeastern region. During the 1930s and early '40s it disappeared as a breeding species. In the 1940s and 1950s the Fish and Wildlife Service instituted a breeding restoration program on the federal refuges (Agassiz, Tamarac, and Rice Lake) in the state. During the 1960s and '70s many state and

local agencies also introduced breeding flocks of birds in many areas of the state. As a result of these efforts, this species has returned as a breeding species to all regions of the state. It is only casual in the northeast at the present time. It is commonly found breeding on or around the National Wildlife Refuges and the major wildlife management areas in the state, but is increasing in all areas, especially in the metropolitan Twin Cities and other major metropolitan areas.

Winter. Regular winter resident wherever there is sufficient open water and food. Most numerous in the south, but flocks overwinter in Fergus Falls, Otter Tail County (3,000 on December 12, 1984), and a few have wintered as far north as Duluth, St. Louis County. One of the principal wintering locations for this species since 1947 has been on Silver Lake, Rochester, Olmsted County. The population increased from a few hundred wintering birds to over 5,000 in the early 1960s to as many as 30,000 at present. Also, large numbers congregate at the Lac Qui Parle Wildlife Management Area, Lac Qui Parle County; 60,500 were present on December 15, 1984. Small flocks of 10 to 50 birds winter where suitable water conditions exist across the southern part of the state.

WOOD DUCK *(Aix sponsa)*

Minnesota status. Regular. Migrant, summer resident, and winter visitant. The Wood Duck is number two in numbers taken during the fall hunting season, with 115,000 harvested in 1982.

Migration. Common to abundant spring and fall migrant throughout the state, with the exception of extreme northern and northwestern regions where it is uncommon. Peak numbers of 1,000 to 1,500 birds can be found along the Mississippi and Minnesota Rivers and at Rice Lake National Wildlife Refuge, Aitkin County. Usually encountered in pairs or up to 10 birds in one area. *Spring migration period:* early March through mid-May,

Wood Duck

with a peak in late April. Earliest dates: SOUTH, *February 28,* March 3, 4, 6; NORTH, March *11*, 22, 24, 25. *Fall migration period:* mid-August through early December, with the bulk of the migration in late September and early October. Latest dates: NORTH, November 3, 7, 11, *28, December 6, 12;* SOUTH, no dates can be given because of wintering birds—most birds have departed by early November, with stragglers into early December.

Summer. Resident throughout the state wherever there is suitable wooded habitat along streams and lakes. Has increased and expanded its range widely in the state over the past 30 years. Most common in the south, but is expanding northward and westward. Increasing in recent years in the Red River Valley and southwestern regions. Least numerous in the northeast. It reached Lake and Cook Counties in the extreme northeast as a breeder in the late '70s. This species is the fourth most numerous nesting duck in the state.

Winter. Regular but rare as an overwintering species in the southeastern quarter of the state. There are winter records as far north as Benton, Cass, Pope, and Otter Tail Counties in the central and western regions and as far north as Virginia, St. Louis County, in the northeast.

GREEN-WINGED TEAL *(Anas crecca)*

Minnesota status. Regular. Migrant and summer resident; casual in winter.

Migration. Common spring and fall migrant throughout the state except uncommon in the northeast during both seasons. During peak migration periods, gatherings of thousands of birds can be found on or near Rice Lake National Wildlife Refuge, Aitkin County, and Agassiz National Wildlife Refuge, Marshall County. During the 1982 fall hunting season, 46,000 Green-Winged Teal were harvested. *Spring migration period:* Early March through mid-May, with a peak in early April. Earliest dates: SOUTH, *February 28,* March 2, 3, 5;

Green-winged Teal

NORTH, March *11,* 29, 30, April 5. *Fall migration period:* Late August through early December; peak numbers occur in October. Latest dates: NORTH, November 14, 20, 21, *December 31;* SOUTH, December 13, 15, 19, *26.*

Summer. Scattered individuals or pairs can be found in almost any part of the state during the breeding season. This species is one of the rarest breeding ducks in the state. Broods have been seen at Waskish, Beltrami County, on August 4, 1978 (*The Loon* 50:206), Whitewater Park, Winona County, on July 2, 1976 (*The Loon* 48:186-87). Other counties with broods of young unable to fly are Roseau, Clearwater, Aitkin, Anoka, Wright, and Big Stone. There are summer records and breeding evidence from the following additional counties: SOUTH, Nobles, Wabasha, Rice, Hennepin, Washington, Pope, Chippewa, Meeker, Carver, Yellow Medicine, and Stevens; NORTH, Mille Lacs, Crow Wing, Itasca, Marshall, Polk, Otter Tail, Lake, and Cook.

Winter. Overwintering birds are occasionally seen in the southeastern and east-central regions of the state, with records from Hennepin, Ramsey, Dakota, Winona, Olmsted, and Freeborn Counties. There is one record from the northern part of the state, January 24, 1970, Virginia, St. Louis County.

AMERICAN BLACK DUCK *(Anas rubripes)*

Minnesota status. Regular. Migrant, summer resident, and winter visitant.

Migration. Uncommon spring and fall migrant in eastern and northern regions; uncommon to rare in other regions. During peak migration periods, flocks numbering 1,000 birds can be seen at Rice Lake National Wildlife Refuge, Aitkin County, and Agassiz National Wildlife Refuge, Marshall County. During the 1982 fall hunting season 4,000 American Black Ducks were harvested. *Spring migration period:* Mid-March through early May, with a peak in mid-April. Earliest dates: None can

American Black Duck

be given because of wintering birds; LATE SOUTH, May 15, 24, June 7. Early migrants in the north occur in late March. *Fall migration period:* Early September through early December; peak numbers occur in October. EARLY SOUTH, July 29, 30, 31. Latest dates: None can be given because of wintering birds. Most birds have left northern areas by late November or early December.

Summer. Resident primarily in the northeastern region and in Koochiching and Itasca Counties in the north-central region. Breeds occasionally as far south as Ramsey, Hennepin, and Wabasha Counties and as far west as Marshall, Clay, and Wilkin Counties. There are scattered summer observations of individuals in a few southern and western counties.

Winter. Uncommon to locally common winter visitant in the southeastern quarter of the state. Occurs with wintering flocks of Mallards and Canada Geese at such areas as Silver Lake in Rochester, Olmsted County, and Black Dog Lake, Dakota County. Occasionally individuals or a few birds winter as far north as Fergus Falls, Otter Tail County, Virginia, St. Louis County, and Grand Marais, Cook County.

MALLARD *(Anas platyrhynchos)*

Minnesota status. Regular. Migrant and summer resident; regular in winter.

Migration. Abundant spring and fall migrant throughout the state; most numerous in the western regions and least numerous in the northeastern region. Peak numbers (an estimated 30,000 to 60,000 birds) can be seen at Agassiz National Wildlife Refuge, Marshall County. The Mallard is #1 in numbers taken during the fall hunting seasons, with 236,000 harvested in 1982. *Spring migration period:* Early March through early May, with a peak in early April. Earliest dates: None can be given because of wintering birds; early arrivals in the north occur in late March. *Fall migration period:*

Mallard

Early September through late November, peak numbers depend on weather conditions but normally occur in late October and early November. Latest dates: None can be given because of wintering birds.
Summer. Resident throughout the state; most numerous in the western regions. This species is the most abundant breeding duck in the state.
Winter. Common in winter in the southern half of the state wherever there is sufficient open water on lakes and rivers. Up to 10,000 birds have been recorded in the winter in Wabasha and Dakota Counties. Usually uncommon or rare in the north but may be common where there is sufficient open water (usually near power plants). Common at Fergus Falls, Otter Tail County, and Grand Marais, Cook County.

NORTHERN PINTAIL *(Anas acuta)*

Minnesota status. Regular. Migrant and summer resident; casual in winter. During the 1982 fall hunting season, 13,000 Northern Pintails were harvested.
Migration. Common spring and fall migrant throughout most of the state; most numerous in western regions, uncommon in the spring and rare in the fall in the northeastern region. Peak concentrations of up to 5,000 birds or more occur in the lower Mississippi River Valley and also at Agassiz National Wildlife Refuge, Marshall County, and Tamarac National Wildlife Refuge, Becker County. *Spring migration period:* Late February through early May, with a peak in early April. Earliest dates: SOUTH, February 24, 26, 27; NORTH, *February 27,* March *8,* 18, 22, 24. *Fall migration period:* Early September through early December, an early peak occurs in late September and a late peak, depending on weather conditions, normally occurs in late October and early November. Latest dates: NORTH, November 7, 9, 11, *21, 26;* SOUTH, December 7, 10, 11.
Summer. Resident primarily in the western and

Northern Pintail

southern prairie regions where suitable marsh habitat exists. There are recent summer observations from the northeastern region and occasional breeding does take place in the north-central region. This species is not a common breeder in the state.
Winter. Occasionally birds will winter with concentrations of other waterfowl around large open water areas in the Twin Cities and southeastern and south-central regions. There are winter records of individuals from Cottonwood County in the southwest and Otter Tail and Cook Counties in the north.

BLUE-WINGED TEAL *(Anas discors)*

Blue-winged Teal

Minnesota status. Regular. Migrant and summer resident; accidental in winter. The Blue-winged Teal is #3 in numbers taken during the fall hunting season, with 111,000 harvested in 1982.
Migration. Common to locally abundant spring and fall migrant throughout the state, least numerous in the northeast. Concentrations in excess of 7,000 birds have been recorded (September 7, 1978, Tamarac National Wildlife Refuge, Becker County) and up to 20,000 were estimated on August 31, 1977 at Agassiz National Wildlife Refuge, Marshall County. *Spring migration period:* March through mid-May, peak numbers occurring in late April. Earliest dates: SOUTH, March *1,* 4, 6, 7; NORTH, March 24, 25, 28. *Fall migration period:* August through mid-November, with a peak in late August (north) to late September (south); most birds have left the state by mid-October. Latest dates: NORTH, November 11, 15, 19, *27;* SOUTH, November 27, 30, December 4, *18, 22, 28, 29.*
Summer. Resident throughout the state. This species is the second most abundant breeding duck in the state. Least numerous in the northeast.
Winter. There are two old records of wintering birds: February 3, 1940 in Hennepin County, and a flock of 15 birds spent the winter of 1941-42 at Morris, Stevens County, a most unusual record. An injured bird was seen along a small creek in Hennepin County on January 3, 1970.

CINNAMON TEAL *(Anas cyanoptera)*

Minnesota status. Regular. Migrant; accidental in summer. *Migration.* A rare spring and casual fall migrant mainly in western regions from Nobles to Marshall Counties, with a scattering of records in the central, south-central, and east-central regions. There is one record for Duluth, St. Louis County. Usually encountered as individuals, but two to three birds have been seen at one time. *Spring migration period:* Mid-April to early June. Earliest dates: March 31, April 5, 9. Latest dates: June 4, 8, 13. *Fall migration period:* The few fall records range from August 17 (Yellow Medicine County) to October 25 (Pope County) and October 29 (Cottonwood County).
Summer. There is a record of one bird seen from June 22 to July 6, 1980 in Lyon County (H. Kyllingstad, personal communication).

NORTHERN SHOVELER *(Anas clypeata)*

Minnesota status. Regular. Migrant and summer resident; accidental in winter. During the 1982 fall hunting season 7,000 Northern Shovelers were harvested.
Migration. Common spring and fall migrant throughout most of the state; uncommon in the spring and rare in the fall in the north-central and northeastern regions. Peak numbers of up to 9,000 birds have been estimated (August 1, 1976) at Agassiz National Wildlife refuge, Marshall County, but peak numbers of 100 to 200 birds are more commonplace. *Spring migration period:* Early March through mid-May, with a peak in early April. Earliest dates: SOUTH, *February 26,* March 1, 2, 3; NORTH, March 26, 28, April 3. *Fall migration period:* August through early December, with a peak in early October. Latest dates: NORTH, November 5, 6, 7, *23, 24;* SOUTH, December 10, 11, 15, *20.*
Summer. Resident primarily in the western regions

Northern Shoveler

and in the east-central, south-central, and southern portions of the central region. There are breeding records outside of this range from Cook, Itasca, and Aitkin Counties. Summer stragglers occur in southern portions of the central, north-central, and northeastern regions.

Winter. There are only five records of possible overwintering birds, two from the early 1940s in Hennepin County, a single bird in Ramsey County on January 10, 1972, and another single bird in Washington County on February 12, 1983. The only north record is of a single bird that overwintered at the Orwell Dam, near Fergus Falls, Otter Tail County, during 1983-84.

GADWALL *(Anas strepera)*

Gadwall

Minnesota status. Regular. Migrant and summer resident; casual in winter. During the 1982 fall hunting season 22,000 Gadwalls were harvested.

Migration. Common spring and fall migrant mainly in western and south-central regions; uncommon in east-central and southeastern regions; rare in the northeast and north-central regions. In the west, peak numbers of up to 10,000 to 30,000 birds have been recorded at Agassiz National Wildlife Refuge, Marshall County, in the fall. The incredible number of 42,600 were estimated there on October 14, 1976 and 39,000 on September 21, 1977. *Spring migration period:* Early March through mid-May, with a peak in early April. Earliest dates: SOUTH, February 28, March 1, 2; NORTH, March 16, 18, 21. *Fall migration period:* Mid-September through early December, with a peak in mid-October. Latest dates: NORTH, November 8, 12, 14, *30, December 18;* SOUTH, December 7, 8, 12, *17.*

Summer. Resident primarily in the west-central and northwestern regions, most numerous at Agassiz National Wildlife Refuge, Marshall County. Some breeding does occur in the central and south-central regions, and there are scattered breeding records from Cass, Crow Wing, and Aitkin Counties. There

are summer occurrences from the Duluth area.
Winter. Regularly overwinters at Shakopee, Scott
County. There are records of stragglers and overwintering birds from the Twin Cities, southeastward
to Winona and Olmsted Counties. The only northern record is of one that remained at Orwell Wildlife
Management Area, Otter Tail County, until January 29, 1978.

EURASIAN WIGEON *(Anas penelope)*

Minnesota status. Accidental.
Records. Before 1975 this species was considered
a casual spring migrant in the state. There had been
14 records ranging from an early date of March 26
to a late date of June 15. There are no specimens
for the state. The observations are scattered
throughout the state from the following counties:
Kittson, Hennepin, Stearns, Marshall, Goodhue,
St. Louis (Duluth), Aitkin, Jackson, Benton, Houston, and Mille Lacs. The last verified spring records
for this species were a bird photographed on June
5, 1973 at Big Sandy Lake, Aitkin County, and a
single bird identified during a waterfowl survey at
Blackduck Lake, Beltrami County, on May 14, 1976
(*The Loon* 54:43). On April 6, 1986 a single male
was seen among American Wigeons at Carlos Avery
Refuge, Anoka County (*The Loon* 58:99). There are
two fall records: a single bird remained at Wood
Lake Nature Center, Richfield, Hennepin County,
from October 18 to November 10, 1985 (*The Loon*
57:181-82), and what may have been the same bird
was seen in the same area during October and early
November 1986.

AMERICAN WIGEON *(Anas americana)*

Minnesota status. Regular. Migrant and summer
resident; casual in winter. During the 1982 fall
hunting season 40,000 American Wigeon were
harvested.

American Wigeon

Migration. Uncommon to common spring and fall migrant throughout most of the state; uncommon in the fall in the northeast. Peak numbers (of up to 15,000 birds) occur at the Weaver Marshes, Wabasha County, and at Agassiz National Wildlife Refuge, Marshall County. *Spring migration period:* Early March through early June, with a peak period in mid-April. Earliest dates: SOUTH, February 28, March 1, 2; NORTH, March *8*, 18, 22, 24. Latest dates: SOUTH, June 3, 4, 6. *Fall migration period:* Mid-August through mid-December, with a peak in late September and early October. Earliest dates: SOUTH, August 12, 16, 18. Latest dates: NORTH, November 9, 10, 11, *21, 25, 28, December 17;* SOUTH, December 18, 19, 20.

Summer. Resident primarily in the north-central region and adjacent counties in the northwestern and northeastern regions. Most numerous in Itasca and Beltrami Counties. The species occasionally breeds outside this area, with recent breeding reported in Stearns and Lac Qui Parle Counties.

Winter. Casual in winter from the Twin Cities area southeastward. There are two northern Minnesota records: January 25, 1975, Grand Marais, Cook County, and January 16, 1983, Hubbard County.

CANVASBACK *(Aythya valisineria)*

Minnesota status. Regular. Migrant and summer, accidental in winter. During the 1982 fall hunting season 7,000 Canvasbacks were harvested.

Migration. Common to sometimes abundant spring and fall migrant throughout most of the state except in the northeast where it is uncommon in the spring and rare in the fall. There are no records for Cook County in the extreme northeast. Large concentrations of this species can occur in the state, mainly in the Mississippi River Valley; on November 1, 1974, 70,000, and on November 1, 1983, 100,000 birds were recorded at Reno, Houston County. Concentrations of up to 5,000 birds occur in the spring on some of the lakes in the central part of

Canvasback

the state. *Spring migration period:* Early March through mid-May, with a peak in early April. Earliest dates: SOUTH, February 25, 26, 28; NORTH, *March 3, 6, 8, 11,* 26, 28, 29. *Fall migration period:* Late September through mid-December, with a peak from late October to early November. Latest dates: NORTH, November 18, 19, 24, *28, December 1;* SOUTH, December 15, 20, 23.

Summer. The primary breeding range of this species is in the northwestern region from Becker County north to eastern Kittson and Roseau Counties. It breeds sparingly as far south as Murray County in the west and Hennepin, Le Sueur, and Faribault Counties in the east.

Winter. A few stragglers remain until late December or early January in the southeastern and east-central parts of the state. Overwintering individuals have been recorded at French River, St. Louis County (January 3-23, 1971); Fergus Falls, Otter Tail County (December 16, 1972 to February 28, 1973); Hennepin County (December 31, 1972 to February 28, 1973); Wabasha County (January 27 to February 15, 1983); and Black Dog Lake, Dakota County (January 1 to February 3, 1962).

REDHEAD *(Aythya americana)*

Minnesota status. Regular. Migrant and summer resident; accidental in winter. During the fall 1982 hunting season 27,000 Redheads were harvested.
Migration. Common spring and fall migrant throughout most of the state except uncommon in the northeastern region. Most numerous in the western prairie regions. Peak concentrations of 7,000-8,000 birds occurred on September 16, 1976, Tamarac National Wildlife Refuge, Becker County. *Spring migration period;* Early March through mid-May; no peak period noted. Earliest dates: SOUTH, February *20,* 26, 28, March 1; NORTH, March 24, 27, 29. *Fall migration period:* Early September through early December, with peak numbers in late October. Latest dates: NORTH, November 24, 28

Redhead

29; SOUTH, December 18, 21, 23.
Summer. Resident primarily in the western prairie regions and in the central region as far east as the Twin Cities. Breeds sparingly in the south-central and southern portions of the north-central regions. **Winter.** There are records of stragglers into early January in Wright, Dakota, Scott, and Ramsey Counties. Overwintering birds have been recorded at Virginia, St. Louis County (1980-81), and in Scott County (1975, 1985-86).

RING-NECKED DUCK *(Aythya collaris)*

Ring-necked Duck

Minnesota status. Regular. Migrant and summer resident; accidental in winter. The Ring-necked Duck is #4 in numbers taken during the fall hunting season with 69,000 harvested in 1982.
Migration. Common to at times abundant spring and fall migrant throughout the state; most numerous in the eastern and central regions of the state. Large concentrations of these birds occur in the Mississippi River Valley during peak migration periods; on November 1, 1983 there were an estimated 250,000 birds at Reno, Houston County. Concentrations of 1,000-5,000 or more birds occur on a number of lakes in the northern region from St. Louis County to eastern Marshall County, especially in the fall. Over 44,000 were censused on October 13, 1977 at Tamarac National Wildlife Refuge, Becker County. *Spring migration period*: Early March through late May, with a peak in mid-April. Earliest dates: SOUTH, February *24*, 28, March 1, 3; NORTH, *February 26,* March *11,* 16, 21, 22. *Fall migration period*: Mid-September through early December, with a peak from late October to early November. Latest dates: NORTH, December 7, 9, 12, *15, 17, 18, 19*; SOUTH, December 9, 10, 11.
Summer. Resident primarily in the forested and forest prairie transition areas of the state; most numerous in the central, north-central, and northeastern regions. Scattered breeding occurs south to Hennepin, Waseca, and Nicollet Counties. This

species is the third most abundant breeding duck
in the state, ranking behind the Mallard and Blue-
winged Teal in abundance.

Winter. Stragglers are regularly observed from late
December to early January from the Twin Cities
and southeastward; there are also two records from
Lake Superior during this period. Possible over-
wintering birds have been reported only from
Dakota and Hennepin Counties in the south and
St. Louis County (Virginia) in the north.

GREATER SCAUP *(Aythya marila)*

Minnesota status. Regular. Migrant.
Migration. Common spring and fall migrant
primarily on larger lakes, especially on Lake Superior at Duluth; uncommon to rare spring and fall
migrant in all other regions of the state except along
the Mississippi River in the southeast region. During peak migration periods in the Mississippi River
Valley, this species may compose 30% or more of
the scaup flocks seen. *Spring migration period:* Late
March into early June, with the bulk of the migration in April. Earliest dates: SOUTH, March *1, 6, 11,*
17, 19, 20; NORTH, March *1, 3, 10, 18,* 28, 29, 30.
Latest dates: SOUTH, May 14, 21, 23; NORTH, June
2, 6, 8, *13. Fall migration period:* Early October
through early December, with a peak in late Oc-
tober and early November. Earliest dates: NORTH,
September *17, 20,* October 8, 15, 18; SOUTH,
September 26, October 8, 9, 10. Latest dates:
NORTH, November 10, *December 14* (only dates);
SOUTH, December 1, 2, 7, *13, 15, 16* (only dates).
Winter. There is a record of a single bird in Dakota
County on February 24, 1981. This could represent
a wintering bird or a very early spring migrant.
There is one well-documented record on January
1, 1984 at the Blue Lake Sewage Lagoons, Scott
County. There are reports of this species during late
December and early January but no substantiating
details are available for any of them; confusion with
the Lesser Scaup is likely.

Lesser Scaup

LESSER SCAUP *(Aythya affinis)*

Minnesota status. Regular. Migrant, summer resident, and summer visitant; casual in winter. The Lesser Scaup is #5 in numbers taken during the fall hunting season, with 50,000 harvested in 1982.

Migration. Abundant spring and fall throughout the state. Peak numbers are usually in the range of 15,000 to 25,000 birds, with up to 200,000 recorded at one time (November 1, 1983, Reno, Houston County). *Spring migration period:* Late February through late May, with the bulk of the migration in April. Earliest dates: SOUTH, February *15, 18,* 22, 23, 28 (dates earlier in February may be of wintering birds); NORTH, February *24,* March *3, 7, 9, 11,* 19, 23, 25. *Fall migration period:* Mid-September through mid-December, with the bulk of the migration from mid-October to mid-November. Latest dates: NORTH, December 18, 19, *28 29, 30; South,* December 19, 21, 23.

Summer. Resident only in the far northwest corner of the state. Very rare as a breeder in this area. There are former breeding records from Otter Tail (1893), Meeker (1903), and Kandiyohi (1942) Counties. Nonbreeding individuals or pairs may be present in all regions of the state.

Winter. Stragglers remain regularly into late December and early January, especially in the eastern part of the state; there are several early January dates for Duluth. In the north, birds have overwintered at Bemidji, Beltrami County, Fergus Falls, Otter Tail County, and Virginia, St. Louis County. In the south, late January and early February records have been recorded from Ramsey, Dakota, and Olmsted Counties. Mid-February dates may indicate very early migrants.

COMMON EIDER *(Somateria mollissima)*

Minnesota status. Accidental.
Records. The following specimens are in the Bell Museum of Natural History; MMNH #15812 and

#15813, October 25, 1959, Warroad, Roseau County; MMNH #22157 shot from a flock of four birds, November 5, 1966, Lake Reno, Pope County; MMNH #16400, November 7, 1959, Squaw Lake, Itasca County. One bird was carefully identified on November 7, 1953 at Grand Marais, Cook County (*The Flicker* 25:141-42). The only winter record is of a single bird seen on December 27, 1978 on Lake Superior, Stony Point, St. Louis County (*The Loon* 51:144). Another eider, either a female or immature, was seen on January 16, 1966 at Two Harbors, Lake County, but weather conditions made exact species identification impossible. On November 9, 1979 a single bird was seen on Battle Lake, Otter Tail County (*The Loon* 52:118). This bird was identifiable only as an eider. The exact species could not be determined.

KING EIDER *(Somateria spectabilis)*

Minnesota status. Accidental.
Records. On May 9, 1971, two pair were seen at Lower Red Lake, Beltrami County (*The Loon* 43:90-91). A female or immature bird was seen on Mille Lacs Lake on October 16, 1973 (*The Loon* 46:34). One bird was shot out of a flock of five or six birds on October 29, 1964 at Lost Lake, St.Louis County (*The Loon* 36:136). One bird was shot on November 3, 1976 at Lake Osakis, Todd County (*The Loon* 49:179). The two winter records are of one bird seen at Grand Marais, Cook County, on December 12, 1974 (*The Loon* 47:11-12) and a specimen (MMNH #18635) obtained at Knife River, Lake County, on January 13, 1963 (*The Flicker* 35:70).

HARLEQUIN DUCK *(Histrionicus histrionicus)*

Minnesota status. Regular. Migrant and winter visitant; accidental in summer.
Migration. A very rare spring and fall visitant, mainly on Lake Superior in the fall; accidental in

other parts of the state. There are a few records away from Lake Superior during migration; spring records include one in Goodhue County at Prairie Island along the Mississippi River on March 30, 1977 (*The Loon* 49:183); one at Lake Winnibigoshish, Kabekena River, Cass County; and a very late individual on June 5-7, 1956 on the St. Louis River near Eveleth, St. Louis County (*The Flicker* 32:35). In the fall there are three records away from Lake Superior: most unusual was one bird shot on the Minnesota River, Redwood County, on October 4, 1977; another bird was shot in Itasca County on October 27, 1973; another bird was seen at Bemidji, Beltrami County, on December 4-5, 1982 (*The Loon* 55:37). On Lake Superior birds have been seen beginning in late September, with most records from late October and early November. Earliest dates: September 30, October 4, 6. In spring, birds have been seen on Lake Superior until mid-April. Latest dates: April 10, 16, 18, *May 1*.

Winter. Individual birds have been recorded along the North Shore of Lake Superior in St. Louis, Lake, and Cook Counties from early December to late January. The latest date is January 29, 1978 at French River, St. Louis County. The only records of overwintering birds are of individuals seen at Silver Lake, Virginia, St. Louis County, during the winters of 1966-67 (subadult male) and 1967-68 (adult male). This was probably the same individual. The most unusual record is of a single bird seen on Dobbins Creek in Austin, Mower County. The bird was first seen on November 17, 1986, and observations continued all through December and into late January 1987 (*The Loon* 59:50).

Summer. A male was seen and photographed at Little Massacre Island, Lake of the Woods County, on July 11, 1985 (*The Loon* 57:135), and another male was seen at Grand Marais, Cook County, on July 8, 1985.

OLDSQUAW *(Changula hyemalis)*

Minnesota status. Regular. Migrant and winter visitant.

Migration. An uncommon to common spring and fall migrant on Lake Superior, primarily in Cook County, rare in northern and central regions. Casual to accidental in the southern regions. There are records along the Mississippi River in the southeast plus Mower (November 6-19, 1983, Austin), Freeborn, Faribault, Blue Earth, and Nicollet Counties in the south-central region and Jackson, Yellow Medicine, and Cottonwood Counties in the southwest. *Fall migration period:* Late October through early December. Earliest dates: NORTH, October *13,* 19, 21, 22; SOUTH, October 28, November 5, 24, 25 (only dates). *Spring migration period:* March and April, with stragglers present on Lake Superior during May and into early June. Latest dates: SOUTH, April 17, 25, 27; NORTH, May 29, June 1, 2.

Winter. Common winter visitant on Lake Superior. Most numerous in Cook County where normal flock size is 30 to 100 birds. There is a late December record from Cass County; one bird was seen on the Mississippi River, St. Paul, Ramsey County, on January 3, 1977; and one bird was seen from December 15, 1973 to January 18, 1974 in Big Stone County. These are the only winter records away from Lake Superior.

BLACK SCOTER *(Melanitta nigra)*

Minnesota status. Regular. Migrant; accidental in winter.

Migration. Rare spring migrant mainly on Lake Superior; in fall uncommon on Lake Superior and Mille Lacs Lake, rare elsewhere. As many as 50-60 birds have been seen on Lake Superior (Cook County) at one time. There are fall records away from Mille Lacs Lake and Lake Superior in Lyon, Pipestone, Houston, Wabasha, Clay, Beltrami, and

Aitkin Counties. There are three spring records away from Lake Superior; one in Hennepin County, one in Kandiyohi County, and another in Beltrami County. *Spring migration period:* Late April through early June. Earliest dates: SOUTH, April 17, 30 (only dates); NORTH, April *5,* 26, 28, 29. Latest dates: SOUTH, May 2 (only date); NORTH, May 25, 27, June 2, *8, 14. Fall migration period:* Early October through late November. Earliest dates: NORTH, *September 27,* October 6, 8, 10; SOUTH, October 18, November 6, 7. Latest dates: NORTH, November 21, 22, 25; SOUTH, November 14, 20, 25.

Winter. One bird was seen at Grand Marais, Cook County, on January 1, 1972.

SURF SCOTER *(Melanitta perspicillata)*

Minnesota status. Regular. Migrant; accidental in winter.

Migration. Rare spring migrant on Lake Superior; accidental elsewhere in spring. The only spring records away from Lake Superior are from Fisher Lake, Scott County, and Mille Lacs Lake. In the fall uncommon on Lake Superior and Mille Lacs Lake and rare elsewhere. There are recent (since 1970) fall records away from Lake Superior and Mille Lacs Lake in Traverse, Beltrami, Lyon, Cottonwood, Hennepin, Goodhue, Waseca, Mower, Murray, Marshall, and Otter Tail Counties. *Spring migration period:* Early May through early June. Earliest dates: SOUTH, April *14* (only date); NORTH, April 25, May 6, 7, 11. Latest dates: SOUTH, no data; NORTH, May 31, June 1, 3, *12, 16-23* (Grand Marais, Cook County, 1985). *Fall migration period:* Late September through mid-November, with a peak in late October (Lake Superior only). Earliest dates: NORTH, September 17, 23, 24; SOUTH, October *1,* 15, 16, 18. Latest dates: NORTH, November 12, 14 (three times), December *16, 24;* SOUTH, November 18, 19, 28, December *5.*

Winter. There are two winter records: one bird was seen on January 18 and 19, 1964 at Two Harbors,

Lake County; another bird, possibly injured, was seen in Ramsey County, on February 11, 1934.

WHITE-WINGED SCOTER *(Melanitta fusca)*

Minnesota status. Regular. Migrant. Casual in summer and winter.
Migration. Uncommon spring and fall migrant on Lake Superior and in the western regions of the state; rare to casual migrant elsewhere except on Mille Lacs Lake in the fall. Most birds are seen in the fall. Peak flocks of 30-50 birds are seen on Lake Superior. *Spring migration period:* Early April through early June with a peak in mid-May. Earliest dates: SOUTH, March *6, 21,* April 2, 4, 8; NORTH, April 11, 12, 13. Latest dates: SOUTH, April 23, May *11, 22, 24;* NORTH, June 6, 8, 10, *17. Fall migration period:* Mid-October through early December. Earliest dates: NORTH, *September 26,* October 6, 10, 12; SOUTH, October *1,* 10, 11, 13. Latest dates: NORTH, December 3, 6, 9, *21;* SOUTH, December 1, 4, 6, *15, 20.*
Summer. Casual summer visitant (no breeding evidence) in the northern regions. There are records of single birds and a small flock (once) from mid-June through late August in Lake, Cook, Cass, Clearwater, Beltrami, Marshall, Roseau, Polk, and Lake of the Woods Counties.
Winter. Casual winter visitant on Lake Superior, accidental elsewhere. There are records usually of one or two birds for late December, January, and February on Lake Superior in Cook, Lake, and St. Louis Counties. Birds are usually seen in early winter and numbers dwindle in February. The only winter record away from Lake Superior is from Grey Cloud Island, Ramsey County, where five birds were seen on January 16, 1943.

COMMON GOLDENEYE *(Bucephala clangula)*

Minnesota status. Regular. Migrant, summer resident, and winter visitant. During the 1982 fall

Common Goldeneye

hunting season 7,000 Common Goldeneyes were harvested.

Migration. Common spring and fall migrant in the eastern and central regions; uncommon in the western regions but common in the northwestern region. Flocks of up to 1,000 birds have been encountered (Houston County, February 25, 1984). *Spring migration period:* Late February through late May, with the bulk of the migration in late March and early April. Earliest dates: None can be given because of wintering birds. Latest dates: SOUTH, May 9, 16, 20, June 2 (Ramsey County); NORTH, none can be given because of breeding birds. *Fall migration period:* Early October through mid-December, with the bulk of the migration in November and early December. Earliest dates: NORTH, none can be given because of breeding birds; SOUTH, October 9, 10, 12. Latest dates: None can be given because of wintering birds.

Summer. Resident primarily in the northeastern and north-central regions (see map p. 25); highest breeding densities occur in Itasca and Beltrami Counties.

Winter. Common in winter in eastern, central, and north-central regions, especially along the Mississippi River and on Lake Superior, as far north as Beltrami and Cook Counties. Most numerous on Lake Superior and around the Twin Cities and along the Mississippi River in the eastern region. There is one record for Koochiching County on January 28, 1984.

BARROW'S GOLDENEYE *(Bucephala islandica)*

Minnesota status. Casual. Migrant and winter visitant.

Records. The majority of the records for this species in the state are from late fall, winter, and early spring on Lake Superior (Lake, Cook, and St. Louis Counties) and the Mississippi River in the Twin Cities area in Hennepin and Ramsey Counties, and especially in Dakota County where it has been seen at Black Dog Lake along the Minnesota River. On the Mississippi River it has been found as far north as Sherburne and Stearns Counties. It has occasionally been found away from the above areas: Rainy River, Lake of the Woods County; Otter Tail County; Mille Lacs Lake, Crow Wing County; Cass Lake, Cass County; and there are two records from the headwaters area of the Minnesota River in Big Stone and Lac Qui Parle Counties. There are also two records away from Lake Superior in the northeast: Chisholm, St. Louis County, and Nine Mile Lake, Lake County. Most unusual was the presence of a single male at Rochester, Olmsted County, in the southeast region from April 1 to April 11, 1986 (*The Loon* 58:141). Earliest dates: *October 15, November 9, 20, 30,* December 7, 8, 12. Latest dates: April 14, 22, 23, *May 7, 11.*

BUFFLEHEAD *(Bucephala albeola)*

Minnesota status. Regular. Migrant; rare summer resident and casual winter visitant. During the 1982 fall hunting season 15,000 Buffleheads were harvested.

Migration. Common spring and fall migrant throughout the state. Large concentrations contain anywhere from 20 to 60 birds, with peak counts at Agassiz National Wildlife Refuge, Marshall County, and Tamarac National Wildlife Refuge, Becker County, of 500 to 1,800 birds. *Spring migration period:* Early March through mid-May, with a peak in mid-April. Earliest dates: SOUTH, *February 25,* March *1,* 4, 6, 8; NORTH, March 10, 12, 13. Latest dates: SOUTH, May 16, 19, 24, *30;* NORTH, none can be given because of possible breeding birds. *Fall migration period:* Early October through early December, with a peak period in early November. A few birds may linger into early January. Earliest dates: NORTH, August 18, 24; SOUTH, September *20, 27,* October 2, 3, 6. Latest dates: NORTH, November 29, 30, December 3; SOUTH, December 9, 11, 12.

Bufflehead

Summer. The first brood of young reported in the state for this species was seen in July 1978 at East Park Wildlife Management Area, Marshall County (*The Loon* 50:213-14). Adults were present in June 1977 and July 1975 at the same location, so breeding may have taken place earlier. Another brood was seen in the same location on June 24, 1980, and adults were seen there during the summer of 1982. During the summer of 1984 this species was encountered at Agassiz National Wildlife Refuge, Marshall County. A brood of six young were seen on June 17, 1985 at Agassiz National Wildlife Refuge, Marshall County (*The Loon* 57:136). Most unusual was the sighting of a brood at Carver Park Reserve, Carver County, on June 5, 1983. Single birds have been seen during June and July in the following counties: Cook, St. Louis, Clearwater, Mahnomen, Cass, Douglas, Kittson, and Ramsey (July 13, 1975). These records indicate that this species may be a very rare breeder in the northern regions.

Winter. Rare in the winter on Lake Superior and in the southeastern part of the state from the Twin Cities area southeastward. Most records are from early winter, but the species has overwintered in both areas. There are recent overwintering records from the north in Crow Wing, Otter Tail, and Beltrami Counties.

HOODED MERGANSER *(Lophodytes cucullatus)*

Minnesota status. Regular. Migrant and summer resident; casual in winter.

Migration. Uncommon to at times common spring and fall migrant in the eastern and central regions of the state, uncommon in the western regions. Concentrations of up to 650 birds (Agassiz National Wildlife Refuge, Marshall County, on October 14, 1975). *Spring migration period:* Early March through mid-May, with a peak in early to mid-April. Earliest dates: SOUTH, *February 28,* March 2, 3, 4; NORTH, March 4, 6, 11. *Fall migration*

Hooded Merganser

period: Early September through mid-December with a peak in October. Latest dates: NORTH, November 28, 30, December 1, *15;* SOUTH, December 11, 17, 19.

Summer. Resident in all areas of the state except the southwestern region where there is no breeding evidence. It is very scarce over most of the west-central region. It has been reported in June and July in these counties in the southwest and west-central regions: Jackson, Lyon, Redwood, and Stevens. Most numerous in the southeast and north-central regions.

Winter. Stragglers stay regularly into late December and early January, and a few remain throughout the winter in the southeastern quarter of the state. In the north there are winter records for January and February from Lake, St. Louis (Duluth), Beltrami, and Otter Tail counties.

COMMON MERGANSER *(Mergus merganser)*

Minnesota status. Regular. Migrant, summer resident, and winter visitant.

Migration. Common spring and fall migrant throughout the state except in the northwest where it is uncommon. Large flock concentrations contain 100 to 200 birds, but huge concentrations can occur in the late fall along the Mississippi River, especially in Wabasha County. On December 3, 1979 an estimated 15,000 birds were present, and on December 13, 1981 the amazing total of 35,000 were seen near Read's Landing, Wabasha County. *Spring migration period:* Mid-February through mid-May, with a peak in late March and early April. Earliest dates: SOUTH, none can be given because of wintering birds, but early arrivals usually occur during the first two weeks in March; NORTH, none can be given because of wintering birds, but early arrivals usually occur in late March. Latest dates: SOUTH, April 28, 29, May 2, June *6, 15;* NORTH, none can be given because of breeding birds. *Fall migration period:* Mid-September (north) through mid-December,

Common Merganser

with a peak in late November and early December. Earliest dates: NORTH, none can be given because of breeding birds; SOUTH, *October 2* (Wabasha County), *30,* November 7, 8, 9. Latest dates: None can be given because of wintering birds.

Summer. Resident in the north-central and northeastern regions; usually around the larger lakes of this region. Most numerous in northen St. Louis, Lake, and Cook Counties.

Winter. Uncommon winter visitant in the southeastern region along the Mississippi River south of the Twin Cities and on Lake Superior; rare elsewhere in the northeastern region. Casual elsewhere in the state where open water occurs.

RED-BREASTED MERGANSER
(Mergus serrator)

Red-breasted Merganser

Minnesota status. Regular. Migrant and summer resident; casual in winter.

Migration. Common spring and fall migrant in the eastern and central regions, becoming abundant on Lake Superior in the spring. Uncommon migrant in the western regions. Large flock concentrations contain from 75 to 300 birds, with peak concentrations of 1,000 and more birds occurring on Lake Superior during the smelt run and in some southeastern and east-central areas. *Spring migration period:* Early March through late May, with a peak in early April (south) to late April (north). Earliest dates: SOUTH, March 5, 9, 10; NORTH, March *9, 18, 28,* 30, 31. Latest dates: SOUTH, May 14, 15, 16, June *6;* NORTH, none can be given because of breeding birds. *Fall migration period:* Early September through mid-December, with the bulk of the migration from late October through early December. Earliest dates: NORTH, none can be given because of breeding birds; SOUTH, October 1, 9, 20. Latest dates: NORTH, November 20, 25, December 2, *14, 18, 19;* SOUTH, December 9, 11.

Summer. Resident along the North Shore of Lake Superior in Cook, Lake, and St. Louis Counties.

There is documented breeding evidence from Mille Lacs Lake and Big Sandy Lake in Aitkin County and Leech Lake, Cass County (*The Loon* 50:122-23). There is also a record from Lake of the Woods on June 13, 1977, which was probably a late spring migrant. Other published breeding records away from Lake Superior are questionable and probably resulted from confusion with females of either Common or Hooded Mergansers.

Winter. Stragglers have been recorded on Lake Superior in late December, January, and an occasional bird into February, especially in Cook and Lake Counties. There are records of birds in early January and late February from Hennepin, Anoka, and Ramsey Counties; these could be records of late fall stragglers or very early spring migrants. A record from Stearns County on February 20, 1977 could also be of an extremely early spring migrant.

RUDDY DUCK *(Oxyura jamaicensis)*

Minnesota status. Regular. Migrant and summer resident; accidental in winter. During the 1982 fall hunting season 7,000 Ruddy Ducks were harvested.

Migration. Common spring and fall migrant throughout the state except in the north-central and northeastern regions where it is rare. Normal large flock size is 15 to 30 birds; peak concentrations of 1,500 to 4,000 birds (Silver Lake, McLeod County) have been recorded in the fall (Agassiz National Wildlife Refuge, Marshall County). *Spring migration period:* Early March through mid-May, with a peak in mid-April. Earliest dates: SOUTH, *February 22, 26, 29,* March 1, 3, 4; NORTH, *March 26,* April 1, 4, 7. *Fall migration period:* Early September through mid-December, with a peak in early October. Latest dates: NORTH, November 23, 30, December 5, *26-31* (Grand Marais, Cook County, *The Loon* 56:70); SOUTH, December 12, 14, 15, *January 3, 4, 9.*

Summer. Resident primarily in the western prairie regions and in the east-central and south-central

Ruddy Duck

regions as far east as the Twin Cities and Freeborn County. This species nested in 1982 and 1983 at Moose Lake, Carlton County, in the northeast, and there is nesting data from Cass and Clearwater Counties in the north-central region. These records indicate that it may be a rare breeder east of the prairies in the northern part of the state.

Winter. There is one winter record. A single bird was seen at Sherburn, Martin County, from January 24 to February 28, 1976.

TURKEY VULTURE *(Cathartes aura)*

Turkey Vulture

Minnesota status. Regular. Migrant and summer resident.

Migration. Uncommon spring and fall migrant throughout the state, becoming common at times at Duluth in the fall. More numerous in the east and central regions, least numerous in the western regions. High daily counts of over 700 birds have been made at Hawk Ridge, Duluth, in the fall; the record high season count is 1,446 in 1983. *Spring migration period:* Mid-March through mid-May, with the bulk of the migration in mid to late April. Earliest dates: SOUTH, *February 23* and *28, March 3,* 15, 16, 17; NORTH, March 19, 22, 23. *Fall migration period:* Early August through late October, with the bulk of the migration from early September to early October. Latest dates: NORTH, October 21, 26, 28, *November 6, 9*; SOUTH, October 26, 28, 31, *November 8, 26, 30, December 27* (specimen), *January 5.*

Summer. Resident throughout the forested part of the northern regions and along the St. Croix, lower Mississippi, and adjacent river valleys . In the nineteenth century there were breeding records from Traverse, Jackson, Becker, Nicollet, and Hennepin Counties. Now it is most numerous along the lower Mississippi River from Goodhue to Houston Counties, and in the north-central region. There are recent breeding records in Clearwater and Beltrami Counties. There are summer observations from

Renville, Nicollet, Redwood, Lac Qui Parle, Chippewa, Carver, Hennepin, Wright, Stearns, Kandiyohi, Washington, and Dakota Counties. There is a record from June 7, 1982 in Rock County, which probably represents a very late spring migrant.

OSPREY *(Pandion haliaetus)*

Minnesota status. Regular. Migrant and summer resident; accidental in winter.
Migration. Uncommon spring and fall migrant throughout the state. The record daily count of 45 birds was recorded at Hawk Ridge, Duluth, on September 6, 1978. The Hawk Ridge season high is 247 in 1984. *Spring migration period:* Late March through late May, with a peak in mid-April. Earliest dates: SOUTH, March 18, 19, 25; NORTH, March *10* 27, 28, 29. Latest dates: SOUTH, May 12, 15, 21, *June 11. Fall migration period:* Mid-August through late November, with the bulk of the migration in mid-September. Latest dates: NORTH, October 28, November 6, 7, *17;* SOUTH, November 23, 25, 27, *December 1, 15, 26.*
Summer. Resident in north-central and northeastern regions and in adjacent Becker, Mahnomen, Mille Lacs, and Pine Counties. In 1981, 160 nest sites on the Chippewa National Forest, Cass County, and 166 nest sites on the Superior National Forest, in Lake and Cook Counties. An estimated 102 nest sites were located in Crow Wing, Becker, Mahnomen, and Hubbard Counties. In 1979 there was a single nest at Lake Bronson State Park, Kittson County. There is a nest site on the Wisconsin side of the Mississippi River opposite Winona, Winona County; nesting may occur on the Minnesota side of the lower Mississippi River. During 1984 and 1985 attempts were made to reintroduce the Osprey as a breeding species in Hennepin County (*The Loon* 57:52-58).
Winter. The above late December dates indicate that stragglers remain about open water into early

Osprey

winter. The only known mid-winter dates are of a single bird seen on January 25 and February 7, 1976 along the open Mississippi River near Hastings, Dakota County (*The Loon* 48:73-74). A single bird was seen at Red Wing, Goodhue County, on February 19, 1979, and another at Black Dog Lake, Dakota County, on February 25, 1984 (*The Loon* 56:160). These latter two records could be of extremely early spring migrants.

AMERICAN SWALLOW-TAILED KITE
(Elanoides forficatus)

Minnesota status. Accidental. Summer resident in the nineteenth century.

Records. One bird was found dead in Washington County, April 29, 1966 (MMNH #23152, *The Loon* 39:67); another bird was shot near Spring Valley, Fillmore County, about August 18, 1949 (MMNH #9555, *The Flicker* 21:71-72). One bird was observed at the Cedar Creek Natural History Area on July 13, 1974 (*The Loon* 48:182); two observations were made in 1976, both near Itasca State Park, one in Hubbard County on April 22 and the other in Clearwater County on May 15 *(The Loon* 49:181).

Former status. In the nineteenth century the species was found breeding in the deciduous forest belt from the Twin Cities area at least as far north as Itasca State Park, Clearwater County. There are several nesting records from Becker and Hennepin Counties. Around the turn of the century the species decreased rapidly in numbers and was last reported during the breeding season in 1902 (Clearwater County), 1904 (Stearns County), and 1907 (Aitkin County). There are only a few additional reports: Cass County, September 14, 1914; Hennepin County, March 20, 1916; Sherburne County, May 18, 1921; McLeod County, July 29, 1923; Jackson County, August 22, 1902.

MISSISSIPPI KITE *(Ictinia mississippiensis)*

Minnesota status. Accidental.
Records. One bird was observed along the Root
River in Olmsted County on May 24, 1975 *(The
Loon* 47:130); another bird was observed near
Brown's Valley, Traverse County, on May 25, 1980
(The Loon 52:113); on August 31, 1973 a single bird
was seen near Arco, Lincoln County *(The Loon*
45:131); and most unusual because of the late date
was a single bird seen October 31, 1982 at Oxbow
Park, Olmsted County *(The Loon* 56:70-71). In
May 1986 there were three observations: May 14,
1986, Forestville Township, Fillmore County *(The
Loon* 58:134), May 20, 1986, North Oaks, Ramsey
County *(The Loon* 58:140), and August 19, 1986,
York Township, Fillmore County *(The Loon*
58:192-94).

BALD EAGLE *(Haliaeetus leucocephalus)*

Minnesota status. Regular. Migrant, summer
resident, and winter visitant.
Migration. Uncommon spring and fall migrant
throughout most of the state, least numerous in the
western prairies. Most often found along the major
rivers and larger lakes of the state. Peak fall daily
counts at Hawk Ridge in Duluth have reached
100+ birds in late November. The record is 105 on
November 25, 1983. The Hawk Ridge season high
is 384 in 1983. Concentrations occur along the lower
Mississippi River from Hastings, Dakota County,
to Houston County, during the late fall and early
spring; peak numbers of 50 to 100 birds have been
found in this area at that time. *Spring migration
period:* Mid-February through late April, with the
bulk of the migration in late March and early April.
Earliest dates: none can be given because of wintering birds. In both north and south areas of the state,
birds are seen in nonwintering areas by the end of
February and early March. *Fall migration period:*
Late August through late December, with the main

Bald Eagle

flight in late November and early December. Latest dates: None can be given because of wintering birds. South of the breeding range, the first stragglers migrating south can be seen by late August. The bulk of the population has left northern breeding areas by late November.

Summer. Resident in the northeast and north-central regions plus adjoining counties of the west-central (Otter Tail) and northwest (Mahnomen and Roseau) regions south to Mille Lacs and Pine County. The largest concentration of breeding birds is on the Chippewa National Forest in Cass and Itasca Counties, with 75 active nests (1981). A total of approximately 200 active nests are known from northern breeding areas (*The Loon* 54:85-86). Breeding territories continue to gradually increase across the main breeding range. Outside the main breeding range there are active nests at present in Houston County and on the Sherburne National Wildlife Refuge, Sherburne County. Historically there are nest records from Hennepin (1874), Stearns (1894), Jackson (late 1800s), and Marshall (1962) Counties.

Winter. There are mid-winter records of individuals from all regions of the state, especially around wildlife refuges where there is open water. The center of the wintering population in the state is in the Lower Mississippi River Valley, especially in Wabasha County (Reads Landing to Wabasha), with a scattering of birds in Dakota, Goodhue, Winona, and Houston Counties.

NORTHERN HARRIER *(Circus cyaneus)*

Minnesota status. Regular. Migrant and summer resident; casual in winter.

Migration. Common to uncommon spring and fall migrant throughout the state. Peak daily counts in the fall at Hawk Ridge, Duluth, number 100 to 150 birds; the highest was 169 on October 1, 1985. Numbers were decreasing at Hawk Ridge in the early 1980s; the total of 274 in 1983 was the lowest count since 1969, but in 1984 the count rebounded to 961.

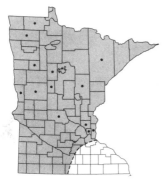

Northern Harrier

The Hawk Ridge season high was 1,207 in 1976.
Spring migration period: Early February through
mid-May, with the bulk of the migration from late
March to late April. Earliest dates: SOUTH, none can
be given because of wintering birds; NORTH, early
migration dates occur anywhere from February 10
to March 1. *Fall migration period:* Early August
through late November, with peaks from mid-
September to mid-October. Latest dates: NORTH,
none can be given because birds linger into
December and early January. Most birds have
departed the north by mid-November; SOUTH, none
can be given because of wintering birds.
Summer. Resident in central and northern regions,
formerly bred across southern regions of the state
but has disappeared from these areas since 1970.
Most numerous in northwest and north-central region. There has been a sharp decline in nesting
habitat for this species in recent years, and, as a
result, breeding numbers have been much reduced.
Winter. Casual in the southern half of the state and
some of the adjoining counties in the central
regions. Casual to accidental in the north, with
records from Polk, Wilkin, Otter Tail, Hubbard,
Clay, Aitkin, Wadena, and St. Louis Counties.
There are more records in December than during
January and early February, indicating a general
late migration exodus rather than overwintering
birds.

SHARP-SHINNED HAWK *(Accipiter striatus)*

Minnesota status. Regular. Migrant and summer
resident; casual in winter.
Migration. Uncommon to common spring and fall
migrant throughout the state. Abundant over Hawk
Ridge, Duluth, in the fall where peak daily counts
reach over 1,000 birds. The record daily high is
1,560 on September 15, 1978. The Hawk Ridge
season high is 21,974 in 1976. Migration data
suggest a population decline in the period from
1977-1983, and it is now (1986) showing signs of

Sharp-shinned Hawk

increase. *Spring migration period:* Early March through mid-May, with a peak in early and mid-April. Earliest dates: SOUTH, March 5, 12; NORTH, March *2, 3, 4,* 16, 17, 18. *Fall migration period:* Early August through mid-December, with the bulk of the migration in September. Latest dates: NORTH, November 22, 26, 28; SOUTH, December 10, 20.

Summer. Resident primarily in the northeast, north-central, and central regions. Rare to absent in southern areas and in the Red River Valley. There is one old (1921) nesting record from Murray County and an early summer observation (June 2, 1979) from Watonwan County.

Winter. Casual in the southeastern quarter of the state from the Twin Cities southward. Accidental in the north and west, with mid-winter records of individuals as far north as Itasca, Aitkin, St. Louis, and Cook Counties. These records probably represent very late fall migrants.

COOPER'S HAWK *(Accipiter cooperii)*

Cooper's Hawk

Minnesota status. Regular. Migrant and summer resident; casual in winter. Because of identification difficulties with the Sharp-shinned Hawk, the status of the Cooper's Hawk in migration and winter is poorly known.

Migration. Uncommon spring and fall migrant throughout the state; least numerous in western regions. Uncommon even at peak migration periods over Hawk Ridge, Duluth. The record daily high at Hawk Ridge is 12 on October 13, 1973. The Hawk Ridge season high is 117 in 1980. *Spring migration period:* Late March through mid-May, with the bulk of the migration in mid-April. Earliest dates: SOUTH, March 7, 15, 17, 23; NORTH, March *7, 17,* 23, 27, 30. *Fall migration period:* Mid-August through late November, with the bulk of the migration in late September and early October. Latest dates: NORTH, October 22, 23, 25, November *8, 30;* SOUTH, November 20, 24.

Summer. Resident throughout most of the state,

primarily in the southeast, east-central, and central regions. Absent in the northeast.

Winter. Casual in the southeastern quarter of the state, with mid-winter records from the Twin City areas south-eastward. Accidental in the north, with early winter (December and early January) records as far north as Aitkin, Becker, and Hubbard Counties. These probably represent very late fall migrants.

NORTHERN GOSHAWK *(Accipiter gentilis)*

Minnesota status. Regular. Winter visitant, migrant, and summer resident.

Migration. Rare to uncommon spring and fall migrant throughout the state; during invasion years this species can become common to abundant over Hawk Ridge, Duluth. In 1982, 5,819 individuals were counted at Hawk Ridge from September to December. In 1972 during the same period, 5,382 were counted. During invasion years there are peak daily counts of 200 to 800 birds, with a record high of an amazing 1,229 on October 15, 1982; in non-invasion years daily maximum counts of 50 birds have been made. *Fall migration period:* Early September through early December in noninvasion years and mid-August through late December in invasion years, with a peak in late October and early November. Earliest dates: NORTH, none can be given because of breeding birds; SOUTH, September *1, 9, 11,* 16, 21, 22. *Spring migration period:* Probably late February through early May, with the bulk of the migration from mid-March to early April. Latest dates: SOUTH, April 12, 14, 24, *28, 29, May 16:* NORTH, none can be given because of breeding birds.

Winter. Uncommon to rare visitant throughout the state, especially in the north, becoming common in eastern areas during invasion years. Recent invasion years appear to be at ten-year intervals: 1962-63, 1963-64, 1972-73, 1973-74, 1982-83, 1983-84. The invasions in the 1980s are the largest on record,

Northern Goshawk

and there were over 53 reports from 23 counties south to Mower, Martin, and Fillmore on the Iowa border and Pipestone, Cottonwood, and Jackson in south-western regions.

Summer. Local resident in the forested part of the state from northern Pine County and Crow Wing County to Roseau County.

RED-SHOULDERED HAWK *(Buteo lineatus)*

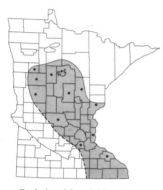

Red-shouldered Hawk

Minnesota status. Regular. Migrant and summer resident. Casual in winter.

Migration. Uncommon spring and fall migrant; formerly restricted to the southeastern region of the state. However, recent records show a definite northward and westward expansion of this species range into east-central and central regions, and the southern portions of the northeast and north-central regions. Casual to accidental in other regions of the state. There is a spring record from Swift and Cottonwood Counties and several fall dates from Duluth and Carlton County. *Spring migration period:* Probably mid-March through early May. Earliest dates: SOUTH, March 13, 14, 16 (it is difficult to give accurate spring arrival dates because of the presence of wintering birds); NORTH, March 12, 14, 16. *Fall migration period:* Early September through early November, with stragglers into December; most birds depart by late October. Latest dates: NORTH, October 15, 16, 23, *November 10, 12, 15;* SOUTH, none can be given because of wintering birds.

Summer. Resident primarily in the south-east, east-central, central, and southern portions of the north-central region. As mentioned under migration, this species is expanding northwestward in the state from its former range only in the southeast and east-central portions of the state. There are breeding records as far north as Becker (*The Loon* 56:274-75), Hubbard, Mahnomen, and Otter Tail Counties in the west and Aitkin and Pine Counties in the east. There are summer observations as far

north as Cass, Clearwater, Beltrami, and Clay
Counties and as far west as Lac Qui Parle County.
Winter. Formerly regular and uncommon in the
winter in the southeast region of the state on the
Mississippi River Valley and its tributary streams.
At present it is only casual in this area and is seldom
seen in the winter. It is unusual that as this species
has spread north-westward in the state, a few birds
have remained in the winter in east-central, central,
and north-central areas, indicating a complete shift
of the population northward. There are December,
January, and February dates from Crow Wing and
Sherburne Counties and January dates from Stearns
and Pine Counties in the north.

BROAD-WINGED HAWK *(Buteo playtypterus)*

Minnesota status. Regular. Migrant and summer
resident.
Migration. Common spring and fall migrant
throughout the state. Least numerous in western
regions, especially the southwest. Abundant at
Hawk Ridge, Duluth, in mid-September. Peak fall
daily counts at Duluth range anywhere from 8,000
to 10,000 birds, to a record high of *31,831* birds on
September 15, 1978. The Hawk Ridge season high
is 62,470 in 1970. *Spring migration period:* Late
March through mid-May, with a peak in late April.
This species has been reported many times in early
and mid-March, but most of these records are not
documented, and it is thought that they are the
result of confusion with the Red-shouldered Hawk
or Accipiters. Earliest dates: SOUTH, March *10* (one
acceptable record from Rochester, Olmsted County), 27, 28, 29; NORTH, April 1, 4, 6. *Fall migration period:* Mid-August through late October, with
a peak in mid-September. Latest dates: NORTH, October 28, 29, 31; SOUTH, October 28, 29, 30.
Summer. Summer resident in the heavier forested
portions of the state where there are upland openings and/or wetlands. Most common in northern
areas, excluding the Red River Valley. Rare to

Broad-winged Hawk

absent over much of the south, including the heavily forested regions of the southwest, and the west-central region.

SWAINSON'S HAWK *(Buteo swainsoni)*

Swainson's Hawk

Minnesota status. Regular. Migrant and summer resident.

Migration. Uncommon to rare spring and fall migrant in southeastern, south-central, south-western, and west-central regions. Casual elsewhere in the state, with records from Stearns, Pine, and Lake of the Woods Counties. In St. Louis County it is a rare regular at Hawk Ridge, Duluth, where from 1976 to 1984 at least one was recorded each fall. *Spring migration period:* Late March through mid-May, with a peak in late April. Earliest dates: SOUTH, March 19, 23, 27; NORTH, April 1, 3, 9. *Fall migration period:* Late August through early October, with a peak in mid to late September. Latest dates: NORTH, October 4, 5, 8, *16, 18, 20;* SOUTH, October 4, 5, 6, *22, November 2, 5, 7.*

Summer. Resident in west-central, southwest, and portions of south-central (Steele and Rice Counties) and southeast (Mower, Dodge, Olmsted, and Good-hue Counties) regions north to Dakota, southern Washington, and Wright Counties. In the west, north of Clay County, the breeding status of this species is unknown. There are summer observations from Clay, Becker, Polk, Pennington, Marshall, and Kittson Counties and an old breeding record from Polk County (1921). There are also summer observations from Nicollet and Renville Counties.

RED-TAILED HAWK *(Buteo jamaicensis)*

Minnesota status. Regular. Migrant and summer resident; regular winter visitant.

Migration. Common spring and fall migrant throughout the state, becoming abundant at Hawk Ridge, Duluth, in mid to late October. At Hawk

Ridge daily counts of 500 to 800 birds have been made, with a record 2,558 on October 28, 1984. The Hawk Ridge season high count is 11,665 in 1984. *Spring migration period: Mid-February* through early May, with a peak in early April. Earliest dates: SOUTH, none can be given because of wintering birds; resident birds return to their territories in March; NORTH, March 11, 15, 18. *Fall migration period:* Early August through late December, with a peak in October. Latest dates: None can be given because of wintering birds in the south and the presence of late fall and early winter stragglers in the north.

Summer. Resident throughout the state, except in the coniferous forests of the northeast and north-central regions. One of the most numerous breeding raptors in the state, second only to the American Kestrel in most areas of the state and the Broad-winged Hawk in the heavily forested (deciduous) areas of the state.

Winter. Uncommon in the southern half of the state; most numerous in the east-central and south-eastern regions. Rare in early winter and casual in late winter in the northern half of the state, except at Duluth where it is uncommon.

Taxonomic note. Three recognizable subspecies occur in the state: Harlan's Hawk (Buteo jamaicensis harlani), once considered a full species; western Red-tailed Hawk (B. j. calurus); and Krider's Hawk (B. j. kriderii). All are migrants throughout the state. At Duluth, in the fall, the black phase of the Western Red-tailed Hawk is regular, the Krider's Hawk is regular, and the Harlan's Hawk is accidental. Nothing is known about their relative abundance elsewhere in the state. The Eastern Red-tailed Hawk (B. j. borealis) is the breeding race in the state.

Red-tailed Hawk

FERRUGINOUS HAWK *(Buteo regalis)*

Minnesota status. Regular. Migrant. Casual in summer and accidental in winter.

Migration. A very rare spring and fall migrant mainly in western regions, with scattered records from north-central (Beltrami, Hubbard, Wadena, and Aitkin Counties), central (Morrison, Stearns, and Sherburne Counties), and east-central (Anoka, Hennepin, and Ramsey Counties) regions. In addition there is one fall record from Duluth (1984) and Blue Earth County (1980). Spring records outnumber fall records by about 2 to 1. *Spring migration period:* Probably mid-March through late April. Earliest dates: SOUTH, *March 10, 21,* 31, April 3, 7; NORTH, *March 18, 24,* April 7. Latest dates: SOUTH, May 6, 19, 25 (only dates); NORTH, May 24, 29, 31. *Fall migration period:* Late September through early November. Earliest dates: NORTH, *August 30,* September 28, 29, October 1, 15 (only dates); SOUTH, September 8, 23, 25. Latest dates: NORTH, October 21, 23 (only dates); SOUTH, October 24, 31, November 5.

Summer. There is no positive breeding evidence for this species in the state. There are June and/or July records along the western edge of the state from the following counties: Kittson (1895-96), Roseau (1948), Mahnomen (1964), Clay (1965), Wilkin (1980), Traverse (1966 and 1977), Lac Qui Parle (1891), Chippewa (1950), and Murray (1976).

Winter. There are two early winter records: December 12, 1981, Clay County, and January 2, 1972 Winona, Winona County (*The Loon* 48:121-22).

ROUGH-LEGGED HAWK *(Buteo lagopus)*

Minnesota status. Regular. Migrant and winter visitant; accidental in summer.

Migration. Uncommon to at times common spring and fall migrant throughout the state. May occasionally be very common along the North Shore of Lake Superior and at Hawk Ridge, Duluth. Peak daily counts of up to 200 birds have been recorded at Hawk Ridge; 204 on November 10, 1963. The Hawk Ridge season high is 739 in 1975. *Fall migration period:* Early September through early

December, with stragglers into late December; peak numbers occur from mid-October through mid-November. Earliest dates: NORTH, September 5, 6, 12; SOUTH, September 4, 6, 8. *Spring migration period:* Late February through mid-May, with the bulk of the migration from mid-March to early April. Latest dates: SOUTH, May 13, 15, 17, *21, 28;* NORTH, May 22, 23, 24, *30.*

Winter. Uncommon visitant mainly in the eastern half of the state, but in the Sax-Zim area of St. Louis County up to 40 birds have been seen in the early winter. Uncommon to rare in central and western regions.

Summer. There are June records from: Duluth; Lake Vermilion, St. Louis County; Aitkin County; Marshall County; and Lake of the Woods County. There is a record from Duluth on July 10, 1950 *(The Flicker* 22:127). An August 26, 1941 record from Waskish, Beltrami County, may represent a very early fall migrant.

GOLDEN EAGLE *(Aquila chrysaetos)*

Minnesota status. Regular. Migrant and winter visitant; accidental in summer.

Migration. Uncommon to rare fall migrant and very rare spring migrant anywhere in the state. Most frequently seen at Hawk Ridge, Duluth, and near the major wildlife management areas where there are waterfowl concentrations in the fall. The highest daily count at Hawk Ridge is eight on October 14, 1972. The Hawk Ridge season high is 37 in 1984. *Fall migration period:* October and November, with a few stragglers in September. Earliest dates: NORTH, September 13, 15, 16; SOUTH, October 12, 13, 14. *Spring migration period:* Probably from sometime in mid-February through mid-April. Latest dates: SOUTH, April 27, 28, 30, *May 17;* NORTH, May 4, 5, *20.*

Winter. Casual winter visitant anywhere in the state, except regular through the winter at the Whitewater Wildlife Management Area in Winona/Wabasha

Counties. In early winter (December) seen at Agassiz, Tamarac, Rice Lake, and Big Stone National Wildlife Refuges where there are concentrations of waterfowl.

Summer. An immature bird was seen on June 4, 1984 at Felton Prairie, Clay County (*The Loon* 56:196).

AMERICAN KESTREL *(Falco sparverius)*

American Kestrel

Minnesota status. Regular. Migrant, summer resident, and winter visitant.

Migration. Common to abundant spring and fall migrant throughout the state. Daily counts of 50 or more birds are common in the spring, and daily counts of 150 to 200 birds are recorded at Hawk Ridge, Duluth, in the fall. The record is 258 on September 19, 1954. The Hawk Ridge season high is 944 in 1979. *Spring migration period:* Early March through mid-May, with the bulk of the migration in late March and early April. Earliest dates: SOUTH, none can be given because of wintering birds; NORTH, March 6, 12, 14, 15. *Fall migration period:* Early August through late October, with a peak in September. Latest dates: NORTH, November 23, 25, 30; SOUTH, none can be given because of wintering birds.

Summer. Resident throughout the state. Least numerous in heavily wooded areas, especially in the northeast. Probably the state's most numerous breeding raptor.

Winter. Uncommon but regular in the southern half of the state, especially from Washington and Kandiyohi Counties southward. Casual in the northern half of the state. There are records from Clay, Clearwater, Marshall, Aitkin, Morrison, Itasca, Mille Lacs, Pine, Pennington, and southern St. Louis Counties.

MERLIN *(Falco columbarius)*

Minnesota status. Regular. Migrant and summer resident; casual in winter.

Migration. Rare spring and fall migrant throughout the state, becoming uncommon at peak migration periods over Hawk Ridge, Duluth. A total of 122 were recorded over Hawk Ridge in 1985; the highest daily count is 31 on September 14, 1957. *Spring migration period:* Late March through Mid-May, with a peak during mid-April. Earliest dates: SOUTH, March *15,* 21, 22, 23; NORTH, March *11,* 21, 28, 29. Latest dates: SOUTH, May 3, 5, 16; NORTH, none can be given because of breeding birds. *Fall migration period:* Mid-August through early November, with the bulk of the migration from late September to early October. Earliest dates: NORTH, none can be given because of breeding birds; SOUTH, August 5, 8, 13. Latest dates: NORTH, November 25, 26, 28; SOUTH, November 7, 14, 18.

Merlin

Summer. Resident in the northeastern and north-central regions and adjacent counties in the northwestern region. Very scarce throughout most of this area except possibly along the Canadian border in Lake, Cook, and St. Louis Counties. There are summer observations from Cass, Lake of the Woods, Kittson, Roseau, Morrison, Becker, Beltrami, Carlton, Itasca, Otter Tail, Marshall (possible nesting at Agassiz National Wildlife Refuge), Wadena in the north, and Hennepin and Stearns Counties in the south.

Winter. Since the late 1970s winter records for this species have increased dramatically. Before that it was considered to be accidental, with records from Fillmore, Hennepin, Cook, and St. Louis Counties. These records were from December and could represent late migrants. The only January and February dates were from Cook, Lake, and Stearns Counties, which seemed to represent wintering birds. During the winters of 1977-78 and 1979 observations were recorded from Mower, Stearns, Lac Qui Parle, Polk, and Sherburne Counties, and Duluth. During the winter of 1979-80 there were observations from Polk, Roseau, Big Stone, St. Louis, and Ramsey Counties. Continuing this increase in winter records, the winter of 1980-81 had observations from Clay, Hennepin, Dakota, and Mower Counties; 1981-82, Marshall, Hennepin, and Clay Counties: 1982-83, Marshall, Pennington, Pine, Wabasha, Dakota Counties, and Duluth; 1983-84, Blue Earth, Winona, Polk, Pennington, and Kittson (February 8) Counties. During the winter of 1984-85, there were reports from Brown, Wilkin, and St. Louis (Duluth) Counties, and there were three to five birds seen in Duluth. Whereas some of these records, those from early December and late February, may represent very late and very early migrants, respectively, most of the records (January and February dates) indicate a certain number of birds are wintering in the state.

PEREGRINE FALCON *(Falco peregrinus)*

Minnesota status. Regular. Migrant; accidental in winter. Regular summer resident until 1960.
Migration. A rare spring and fall migrant throughout the state. At Hawk Ridge, Duluth, the highest daily count reached was 17 birds on September 17, 1984. The highest annual total at Hawk Ridge was 34 birds in 1961. Annual totals at Hawk Ridge since 1980 are:

> 1980 – 15
> 1981 – 12
> 1982 – 23
> 1983 – 28
> 1984 – 33 (the highest since 1961)
> 1985 – 27

Spring migration period: Formerly early March to late May with no peak noted. Earliest dates: SOUTH, March 11, 12, 14; NORTH, March 17, April 4, 5, 6.
Fall migration period: Mid-August through late November, with a peak in mid-September. Earliest dates (beyond breeding areas): August 7, 13, 17. Latest dates: NORTH, November 3, 8, 13, *21,* December 1; SOUTH, November 19, 24, 26.

Summer. Formerly a resident along the bluffs of the Mississippi River south of Red Wing (nesting last reported in 1962); along the upper St. Croix River (nesting last reported in 1945); along the North Shore of Lake Superior (adults last observed near an eyrie in the summer of 1964); and in the Boundary Waters Canoe Area of Cook and Lake Counties (nesting last reported in 1964). In 1982 a reintroduction program was begun on a tract of The Nature Conservancy land in Wabasha County (*The Loon* 55:3-8) and also in Cook County in 1984. In 1985 the first nesting pair from these reintroductions was found on a cliff in Winona County. There are recent summer observations (June and July) in Dakota, St. Louis, and, most unusual, in Nobles County (*The Loon* 53:219).

Winter. The status of this species in winter is open to question; there are three dates from Hennepin County: December 13, 1941, January 10, 1957, and January 28, 1968. One bird, possibly a very late migrant, was seen at Duluth on December 23, 1969, and another overwintered in the Duluth harbor in 1985-86. This individual may have been from the release program of Peregrines begun along the North Shore of Lake Superior during 1985. There are unconfirmed reports in February from Hennepin, Sherburne, and Dakota (January 19, 1984) Counties. There were a number of reports of Peregrines in the Twin Cities area during December 1986. Again, these individuals were probably from the Peregrine release program carried out in Minneapolis during 1984 and 1985.

GYRFALCON *(Falco rusticolus)*

Minnesota status. Regular. Migrant and winter visitant. Status is poorly known because of frequent confusion with Northern Goshawks.

Migration. A very rare spring and fall migrant anywhere in the state. Most of the records are from Duluth and the Twin Cities, which probably reflects the distribution of observers more than the distribution of the species. All of the records are of individuals, and the vast majority are from the northern half of the state, although a few birds have been recorded as far south as the Iowa border. *Fall migration period:* Late October to late December. Earliest dates: NORTH, *September 16, 19, 21;* SOUTH, *September 22* (only date). *Spring migration period:* Probably occurs in February and March since all wintering birds have disappeared by mid-April. Latest dates: SOUTH, March 10, 26, *April 17* (only dates); NORTH, April 1, 3, 8, *13.*

Winter. A very rare winter visitant mainly in the Duluth area. Recently one or two individuals have wintered regularly in the Duluth harbor area where there is an abundant supply of Rock Doves and other food for this species. Four individuals were there during the winter of 1984-85. There are recent late December records from as far south as Wabasha, Hennepin, Washington, and Anoka Counties; recent January records from Aitkin and Stearns Counties; and recent February records from Roseau and Wadena Counties. Away from Duluth, overwintering birds have been recorded recently at Waskish, Beltrami County (1978-79), and Agassiz National Wildlife Refuge, Marshall County (1982-83).

PRAIRIE FALCON *(Falco mexicanus)*

Minnesota status. Regular. Migrant; casual in winter. The status of this species in Minnesota has been changing rapidly over the last few years, as it has done at intervals in the past. The species was considered a regular fall migrant in records from 1890-95; 1922-26; and 1930-37. From 1938 to the mid 1970s, the species became accidental in the state, with only summer observations in 1949 and 1959. Beginning in 1974 the species suddenly began reappearing and since that time has become regular in the state. The reason for this is unkown; there may have been an actual expansion of the population into the state or perhaps there has been better coverage where the bird has always occurred.

Migration. Rare fall migrant and casual spring migrant, mainly in the western third of the state, with a few stragglers farther east. There are fall migration records outside the west from McLeod, St. Louis (Duluth), Aitkin, Anoka, and Morrison Counties and one spring record from Lake County (April 19, 1980, *The Loon* 52:90). *Fall migration period:* Early August to late October, with most birds appearing in late September and early October. Earliest dates: August 5 (Otter Tail County); August 6 (St. Louis County); August 14 (Aitkin County); August 17 (Wilkin County). Latest dates: October 21, 24, 29, November 6, 7. *Spring migration period:* Mid-March through mid-May. Earliest dates: March 14, 21 (only dates). Latest dates: May 3, 14, 16.

Summer. A single bird was seen at Felton, Clay County, on June 23, 1984.

Winter. There are early December records from Aitkin (December 9, 1981) and Yellow Medicine (December 14, 1974) Counties. One bird wintered on the Rothsay Wildlife Management Area, Wilkin County, from January 5 to February 22, 1983 and again during the winters of 1983-84, 1984-85, and 1985-86. The species was reported to have over-wintered in the Fargo-Moorhead area of Clay County during the winter of 1980-81. There are February records from Cottonwood (February 6, 1983) and Rock (February 19, 1983) Counties.

GRAY PARTRIDGE *(Perdix perdix)*

Minnesota status. Regular. (Introduced.) Permanent resident.

Distribution. A permanent resident generally west of the Mississippi River. This species was not part of the native avifauna but entered the southwestern part of the state (Jackson and Nobles Counties) from Iowa, where it had been introduced. This

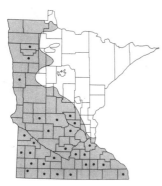

Gray Partridge

occurred sometime after 1914, and the species has been gradually extending its range northward and eastward. It also spread into the northwestern part of the state from North Dakota and Canada between 1926 and 1929. Birds were released by the Minnesota Department of Natural Resources in Martin County in 1926, in Hennepin County in 1927, and later in various parts of the southern and western regions. The first hunting season was in 1939. At present the species is a common resident mainly in western regions. Numbers fluctuate widely over a period of years and at times from year to year. There has been a general increase in numbers, and it was thought the species was becoming more abundant than the Ring-necked Pheasant (*The Loon* 49:205-10). Populations hit peak numbers in the late 1970s and early 1980s, but by 1984 the numbers appeared to have dwindled once again. The largest number harvested during a fall hunting season was 132,000 in 1978. An August roadside survey of Gray Partridge has been done by the Minnesota Department of Natural Resources each year since 1942. Numbers have ranged from a low of 1.7 birds per 100 miles in 1964 to a high of 45.3 birds per 100 miles in 1981. In spite of the fluctuations in numbers, the species continues to expand eastward in the state into areas where it was not regularly seen. The areas include Houston (nesting 1985), Fillmore, and Winona Counties in the southeast; Anoka and southern Mille Lacs Counties in the east-central and central regions; and Hubbard and Beltrami Counties in the north-central region.

RING-NECKED PHEASANT
(Phasianus colchicus)

Minnesota status. Regular. (Introduced.) Permanent resident.
Distribution. Common resident throughout most of the state with the exception of the northeast (except regular at Duluth) and north-central regions where it is absent and the northwest where it is rare. Most, if not all, records from the northern tier of counties

are probably game-farm releases. This species was not part of the native avifauna but was introduced into the state in 1905. Large-scale releases were begun in 1915, and the first hunting season was opened in 1924. Peak populations occurred in the early 1940s and the late 1950s. At present it is most numerous in and around the Twin Cities area and the area north of the Twin Cities in Anoka, Isanti, southern Kanabec, and south Mille Lacs Counties. "Clean farming" practices in the south and west-central portions of the state have resulted in drastic reductions in numbers from those found in these areas during the 1940s and 1950s. Also in these areas, numbers fluctuate from year to year depending on the severity of the winters in the region. Annual roadside counts of Ring-necked Pheasants have been conducted since 1941 by the Minnesota Department of Natural Resources. Counts have ranged from a high of 426 birds per 100 miles in 1958 to a low of 29 birds per 100 miles in 1975. In 1983 the count was 55 birds per 100 miles.

Ring-necked Pheasant

SPRUCE GROUSE *(Dendragapus canadensis)*

Minnesota status. Regular. Permanent resident.
Distribution. Permanent resident in the northeastern and north-central regions and in adjacent Roseau County. In June 1982, a female Spruce Grouse was recorded in Pine County in the east-central region (*The Loon* 54:200-202). This indicates a possible remnant population south of the present normal range of this species. In the nineteenth century the species was found regularly as far south as Mille Lacs Lake and Wadena and Carlton Counties (Roberts, 1932). At present it is best represented in the northern halves of Cook, Lake, and St. Louis Counties and in Koochiching and Lake of the Woods Counties. There was an extant population in the late 1960s and early 1970s in northern Hubbard County, but the present status is unknown. Usually encountered as singles or in pairs from early spring to early summer and in family groups of five

Spruce Grouse

or more birds in the summer. By fall these family groups gather into larger groups of 15 or more birds. Approximately 50 birds were seen near Faunce, Lake of the Woods County, during the winter of 1965-66. In November 1966, 118 were counted in one day near Norris Camp, Beltrami County. During 1984-85 16 to 20 birds were present all winter along County Road 2 near the junction with State Highway 1 in Lake County. In 1970 a statewide fall hunting season was established on the Spruce Grouse. An estimated 34,000 birds were harvested in 1980 and 14,000 in 1982. Like the Ruffed Grouse, the Spruce Grouse is probably subject to cycles of high and low populations.

WILLOW PTARMIGAN *(Lagopus lagopus)*

Minnesota status. Accidental.
Records. The records for this species occurred in three winters, though many years apart. One bird was collected on April 20, 1914, on Springsteel Island, Lake of the Woods County (MMNH #8479). During the winter of 1933-1934 an invasion occurred in Roseau, Lake of the Woods, and northern St. Louis Counties; three specimens were collected (MMNH #8024, #8030, #8031), and over 200 observations were reported between December 7 and April 25. The most recent observation, in 1964, was of two birds that came to a feeder at Graceton, Lake of the Woods County, between February 27 and March 12 *(The Loon* 36:66).

RUFFED GROUSE *(Bonasa umbellus)*

Minnesota status. Regular. Permanent resident throughout the forest portions of the southeast, east-central, central, north-central, and northeast regions, plus adjacent portions of the west-central (Glacial Ridge State Park) and northwest regions. Small populations exist as far west as eastern Steele and Rice (Nerstrand Woods State Park) Counties in the south-central region. A few birds were introduced into the Hennepin County Parks system in 1972, and this, plus the increase of remnant populations in these areas, resulted in birds being reported quite regularly in northern Hennepin County (*The Loon* 47:143 and 48:122). The Minnesota Department of Natural Resources has published a map showing Ruffed Grouse populatons existing in the Minnesota River Valley from the Twin Cities south to Mankato in Scott, Carver, LeSueur, Sibley, and Nicollet Counties. There is no evidence that a past or present population exists in these areas. The abundance of this species varies considerably, with peaks occurring in approximately ten-year cycles. Statistics have been kept since 1920 by the Minnesota Department of Natural Resources on numbers taken during each fall hunting season. Numbers have fluctuated widely as might be expected. The low was 59,000 in 1933 to a high of 1,400,000 in 1951; 940,000 were harvested in 1980; 580,000 in 1981; and 300,000 in 1982.

Ruffed Grouse

GREATER PRAIRIE-CHICKEN
(Tympanuchus cupido)

Minnesota status. Regular. Permanent resident; casual winter visitant.
Distribution. Resident on prairie tracts in the west-central and northwestern regions from Wilkin County north to Marshall County. A small population also exists in eastern Wadena, southern Hubbard, and western Cass Counties in the north-central region (*The Loon* 54:5-13). As of 1983 a census of this species indicated a population of approximately 1,500 males on booming grounds in the state (*The Loon* 55:121). This population has remained fairly stable over the past five years with some increases noted; this is probably due to more accurate censusing than to actual increase in birds. This is best represented by the recent discovery of small populations in Hubbard and Marshall Counties. The general population of this species declined

Greater Prairie-Chicken

rather sharply in the 1950s and 1960s. During this period extant populations in Morrison County disappeared (last seen in 1965). The population decline is a continuation of a trend that was first noted in the 1930s. Roberts (1932) described the Prairie-Chicken as breeding throughout the prairie and open woodlands of the state and also in areas where the forest had been cleared in the northeast. Resident flocks were present in Fillmore and Mower Counties until the late 1930s (*Wilson Bulletin* 51:242-43). Birds were last seen in the northeastern region (near Duluth) in 1952. This species was not an original native in the state but moved in from the south and southeast during the latter half of the nineteenth century, with the breaking up of the original prairie and the coming of farming to the state. Hunting seasons were held on the Greater Prairie-Chickens from the middle of the nineteenth century until 1942. Harvest statistics were kept only from 1921 to 1942, and for most of the period they were in aggregate with Sharp-tailed Grouse. The high number taken was 410,000 in 1925. In 1933, 29,000 Greater Prairie-Chickens were taken; 25,000 in 1934; and 36,000 in 1935. The season was closed from 1936 to 1939. In 1942, the last hunting season, 58,000 birds were harvested.

Migration. In former times large flocks of Prairie-Chickens would migrate south from northerly portions of their range in the state. These migrant birds would move to the cornfields of southern Minnesota and Iowa in the fall and return to northern areas in the spring. Movement to southern areas would begin in September and birds would return north during February and March. Present populations of birds in the state are for the most part sedentary, but occasionally birds have been reported away from the present ranges (Lincoln County, February 20, 1975; Renville County; and Big Stone County, December 4, 1983). Reintroduction attempts were made on the Chippewa Prairie in Chippewa County by the Department of Natural Resources in the early 1980s. Two birds were present and booming during the spring of 1983.

SHARP-TAILED GROUSE
(Tympanuchus phasianellus)

Minnesota status. Regular. Permanent resident.
Distribution. Permanent resident in the northern regions and adjacent Pine County in the east-central region. The species is most numerous in the northwestern part of the state in Roseau, Lake of the Woods, Koochiching, Polk, Kittson, Beltrami, Marshall, and Pennington Counties. Separated from this population is a smaller number of birds in Aitkin, Carlton, northern Pine, and central St. Louis (Floodwood to Zim) Counties. Vagrants have been recorded in Cook County (1968), probably individuals from the Thunder Bay, Ontario population. The species was formerly more widespread. A nest was recorded in Swift County in 1942. In presettlement times, this species was commonly termed "Prairie Chicken" (the species we now call by that name had not yet moved into the state). According to Roberts (1932), the Sharp-tailed Grouse was found on the prairies in the summer and retreated to the brushlands and open forests in the winter, and the early explorers and settlers found the species abundant in all regions of the state. When large portions of the prairie were plowed, the Greater Prairie-Chicken moved into the state, and the Sharp-tailed Grouse retreated to its present range in northern regions. Since 1948 harvest statistics from fall hunting seasons have been kept by the Minnesota Department of Natural Resources. Numbers have fluctuated widely from a high of 150,000 taken in 1949 to 50,000 in 1980. Numbers continued to decline in the early 1980s, with only 5,000 birds taken in 1984 and 1985. The main reason for the decline has been habitat loss.

Sharp-tailed Grouse

WILD TURKEY *(Meleagris gallopavo)*

Minnesota status. Regular. (Introduced.) Permanent resident.
Distribution. Permanent resident in the

Wild Turkey

southeastern region in Houston, Winona, Wabasha, Fillmore, and Olmsted Counties. These populations stem from releases made in the region of wild trapped birds in 1964, 1965, and 1968. The first releases of game-farm-reared birds were made in the region as far back as 1936. Populations have fluctuated from year to year but have maintained themselves, especially in Winona (Whitewater Wildlife Management Area) and Houston Counties. Releases were made in northeastern Olmsted County in 1970 and in other parts of the county (Root River Valley and Oxbow Park) in 1977. These releases have been successful and the birds are doing very well. Various sportsmen's clubs and other outdoor groups around the state have made attempts to introduce Wild Turkeys in many regions. "Wild" Turkeys are often encountered along roadsides in many areas of the state, but these birds usually disappear within a few years and none have established a permanent breeding population. Roberts (1932) considered that there was no positive evidence that this species had ever existed in Minnesota before settlement. Turkey gobbling counts had been conducted by the Minnesota Department of Natural Resources in southeastern Minnesota since 1975. The percentage of stops where turkeys were heard ranged from a high of 46% in 1977 to a low of 14% in 1983.

NORTHERN BOBWHITE *(Colinus virginianus)*

Minnesota status. Regular. Permanent resident.
Distribution. At present the only wild populations of this species occur in the southeastern region in Houston, Fillmore, Olmsted, and Winona Counties and the southwest in Rock County. It was formerly much more widespread in the southeastern and east-central regions. The species has been reported as far north as Pine, Morrison, Stearns, Pope, and Big Stone Counties, from a number of areas in the south-central region, and as far west as Pipestone and Lincoln Counties. This species is easily raised

Northern Bobwhite

in captivity by individuals and on game farms. The Department of Natural Resources released many birds up until 1952, but has not done so since. The peak period of abundance for this species was in the 1920s, and hunting seasons were held in the southeast until 1958. Harvests ranged from a high of 13,000 birds in 1927 to a low of only 600 birds in 1945. In 1958, the last year of hunting, 3,200 birds were harvested. Reports of this species away from the southeast or southwest corner of the state are of released or escaped birds.

YELLOW RAIL *(Coturnicops noveboracensis)*

Minnesota status. Regular. Migrant and summer resident.

Migration. A spring and fall migrant throughout the state. Little is known of the migratory habits of this secretive species, but there are records of its presence in all regions. *Spring migration period:* Probably late April through late May. Earliest dates: SOUTH, April 26, 30, May 3; NORTH, April 26, 28 (only dates). *Fall migration period:* Probably late August through early October. Latest dates: NORTH, October 2, 3, *16* (only dates); SOUTH, September 24, 26, 29, *October 26.*

Summer. The breeding distribution of this species is poorly known in the state. Roberts (1932) recorded nesting only from Lake Wilson, Murray County, in the southwest and breeding season records from Sherburne, Becker, Marshall, and Kittson Counties. On June 5, 1952 Nestor Hiemenz of St. Cloud found and photographed a nest of this species in a marsh just east of St. Cloud in Sherburne County. The nest contained ten eggs. Since the late 1950s much new data have been gathered on the summer distribution of this species. It was found to be common in a large grassy marsh along the Mahnomen-Becker County line near Waubun in 1959, and nesting was studied there in the 1970s. In the early 1970s the species was discovered to be common in a large marsh south

Yellow Rail

of MacGregor in Aitkin County. Birds have been seen and heard there regularly since that time (*The Loon* 56:68-69). In 1980 during a survey of prairie tracts in the western and northwestern regions, birds were heard in Wilkin and Pennington Counties (*The Loon* 52:170-76). There are also recent breeding records from Beltrami (Waskish), Cass (Swamper Lake), Polk, Norman, Marshall, Kittson, Clearwater, Traverse, and Crow Wing Counties. A single bird seen on June 10, 1976 in North Oaks, Ramsey County, was probably a very late migrant. From the above data it would appear that this species is well represented as a breeding species, especially in the northwest and north-central regions where suitable habitat exists. Once again, because of its secretive habits, it is often overlooked.

BLACK RAIL *(Laterallus jamaicensis)*

Minnesota status. Accidental.
Records. All records for this elusive species in Minnesota are sight observations. Those listed below are sufficiently detailed to be considered reliable. The spring observations are: May 1, 1951, Fox Lake, Rice County (one shot but specimen could not be found; a single feather was recovered, which compared favorably with existing specimens); May 12, 1962, Long Meadow Slough, Hennepin County (details on file MMNH); May 12, 1971, Frontenac, Goodhue County (*The Loon* 43:52); May 24, 1934, Little Rock Lake, Benton County (*The Loon* 37:52). From June 11 to 30, 1979 a single bird was seen and heard in a marsh in western Hennepin County near Mound (*The Loon* 51:142). There are two fall records, August 14, 1968, Martin Lake, Anoka County (*The Loon* 40:101); October 1, 1972, Girard Lake, Bloomington, Hennepin County (*The Loon* 44:121). A research study for a University of Minnesota Masters thesis on rails in the marshes of northern Ramsey County in 1950 listed this species as a migrant (*The Flicker* 26:4, Leo B. Pospichal, 1952), but no other data were given.

KING RAIL *(Rallus elegans)*

Minnesota status. Casual. Migrant and summer visitant.

Records. The present status of this species in Minnesota is generally unknown. There are few recent records, and what few birds were known to have been in the state seem to have disappeared from areas where they once occurred. Formerly the species was reported across the southern half of the state on a regular basis as far north as Stearns County. It was accidental in the north, with one record from Agassiz National Wildlife Refuge, Marshall County (May 25, 1968), and another from Hackensack, Cass County (August 5, 1936). This species was rarely if ever encountered in migration but was found on breeding territories. What scant records there are indicate birds returned in mid-April (April 10, 11, only dates) and left by September, with stragglers into October (September 16, 23, October 1, 21). Over the past 15 years the following are the only data recorded on the species in Minnesota: August 16 to September 11, 1971, Reiger Slough, Cottonwood County (four seen); summer 1972, was reported to have nested at Heron Lake, Jackson County; June 23, 1973, seen at LaCrescent, Houston County; May 3, 1974, Duluth, St. Louis County *(The Loon* 46:121-22); June 13, 1975, seen at Big Stone National Wildlife Refuge, Lac Qui Parle County; July to August 7, 1976, LaCrescent, Houston County (two adults and two young); June 2, 1977, Gabriel Lake, Lyon County; May 15, 1981 St. Paul, Ramsey County, one captured *(The Loon* 53:225-26); May 31, 1983, near St. Cloud, Stearns County, nesting attempted *(The Loon* 56:72). The most recent record is of a single individual seen and heard at Duluth, June 9-16, 1984 *(The Loon* 56: 190-91). This species is on the northern fringe of its range in Minnesota and has probably always been quite scarce in the state.

King Rail

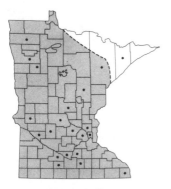

Virginia Rail

VIRGINIA RAIL *(rallus limicola)*

Minnesota status. Regular. Migrant and summer resident; accidental in winter.

Migration. Uncommon spring and fall migrant throughout most of the state; rare or absent over large parts of the north-central and northeastern regions. (There is one record for Cook County on September 28, 1984.) *Spring migration period:* Mid-April through late May, with a peak in early May. Earliest dates: south, April 15, 16, 17; north, April *15, 17, 20. Fall migration period:* A gradual exodus from breeding areas takes place in August and September. Latest dates: north, September 15, 28, October 2, *13, 16, 21;* south, October 19, 25, 30, *November 6, 11, 13.*

Summer. Resident throughout most of the state where suitable marsh habitat exists; best represented in the south, becoming scarce moving northward in the state. The species breeds as far north as Duluth and Virginia, St. Louis County, and was recorded at Hog Creek in northern Lake County during the summer of 1982. It is absent over large areas of the northern forested area in the north-central and northeastern regions.

Winter. There are six records: December 10, 1961, January 10 to February 7, 1959 (two birds), and February 21 to March 2, 1976, all in Hennepin County; December 30, 1978, Ramsey County; January 8, 1972, Winona, Winona County; and January 19, 1986, Bloomington, Hennepin County.

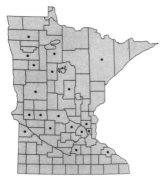

Sora

SORA *(Porzana carolina)*

Minnesota status. Regular. Migrant and summer resident; accidental in winter.

Migration. Common spring and fall migrant throughout most of the state except in the heavily wooded portions of northeast and north-central regions. *Spring migration period:* Mid-April through mid-May, with a peak in early May. Earliest dates: south, April *1, 4,* 9, 12, 13; north, April 4, 16,

17, 20. *Fall migration period:* Mid-August through mid-October, no peak period noted. Latest dates: NORTH, October 10, 15, *November 2;* SOUTH, October 24, 25, *November 18, 21.*

Summer. Resident throughout most of the state in suitable marsh habitat. Scarce to absent over heavily forested portions of north-central and northeastern regions.

Winter. In addition to the late November dates listed above, there are records from the southern part of the state on December 7 and 12, indicating possible wintering birds or very late migrants. There is one very old record of a wintering bird: November 30, 1893 to January 24, 1894, at Lanesboro, Fillmore County.

PURPLE GALLINULE *(Porphyrula martinica)*

Minnesota status. Accidental.
Records. Two specimens, both of adult birds that were found dead: June 11 or June 12, 1967, Sheldon Township, Houston County (MMNH #23021); November 11, 1963, near Toivola, St. Louis County (MMNH #19754). In addition, one immature bird was seen and photographed on September 5, 1970, at Oak Leaf Lake near St. Peter, Nicollet County (*The Loon* 42:119, photographs on file).

COMMON MOORHEN *(Gallinula chloropus)*

Minnesota status. Regular. Migrant and summer resident; accidental in winter.
Migration. Since the mid-1970s this species has become a rare spring and fall migrant in the southern part of the state. Casual in northwestern regions (Becker, Mahnomen, and Marshall [Agassiz National Wildlife Refuge, May 28, 1985 and May 27, 1986] Counties); accidental in Mille Lacs County (May 1, 1983) plus St. Louis (Duluth) and Lake Counties (October 14, 1973). A single juvenile bird was seen at the Northwoods Audubon Center, Pine

Common Moorhen

County, on September 18, 1981 (*The Loon* 56:269). *Spring migration period:* Late April through mid-May, no peak period noted. Earliest dates: SOUTH, April *2,* 21, 24, 28; NORTH, May 10, 1965 (Duluth), see above. *Fall migration period:* Probably from sometime in mid-August to mid-October. Latest dates: SOUTH, October 12, 13, 15, *25, 27.*

Summer. Resident but local in the southeastern and east-central regions of the state. Much reduced in numbers in recent years. Bred at Swan and Middle Lakes, Nicollet County, in the 1960s. Since the mid-1970s most of the breeding season records have been restricted to the Twin Cities area and southeastern regions along the Mississippi River (Goodhue and Houston Counties). Adults with small chicks were seen at Linden Lake, Brown County, during July 1985. There are also recent breeding season records from Stearns, Watonwan, Todd, and Kandiyohi Counties in the central part of the state. In the western portions of the state there is an old nesting record from Parkers Prairie, Otter Tail County (1903). During the summers of 1982 and 1985, the species was recorded at Agassiz National Wildlife Refuge, Marshall County, in the far northwest corner of the state. May and August records from Becker, Mahnomen, and Marshall Counties suggest that the species may breed rarely in these areas. The only other breeding season records from the north are from the Mud-Goose Wildlife Management Area, Cass County, on July 11, 1966 (*The Loon* 38:109) and one record from Rice Lake National Wildlife Refuge, Aitkin County, during 1982.

Winter. One old record: a single bird captured in Minneapolis on January 23, 1915.

AMERICAN COOT *(Fulica americana)*

Minnesota status. Regular. Migrant, summer resident, and winter visitant.

Migration. Abundant spring and fall migrant throughout the state except in the northeast where it is usually uncommon in the spring and common in the fall near Duluth, rare in Cook and Lake Counties. Large concentrations numbering in the thousands can be encountered in the fall, mainly in the western portions of the state: 36,000, September 6, 1978, at Agassiz National Wildlife Refuge, Marshall County; 50,000, October 16, 1971, in Douglas County; and 57,000, September 23, 1977, in Becker County. Hunting harvest statistics have been kept since 1919 by the Department of Natural Resources. Birds taken range from a high of 291,000 in 1919 to a low of 14,000 in 1961. In 1980, '81, and '82 numbers harvested are 58,000, 49,000, and 49,000, respectively. *Spring migration period:* Early March through late April, with the bulk of the migration in early to mid-April. Earliest dates: SOUTH, it is sometimes difficult to separate early migrants from wintering birds, March *1,* 5, 6, 11; NORTH, March *18,* 22, 26, 28. *Fall migration period:* Mid-September through early December, with a peak in mid to late October. Latest dates: NORTH, November 19, 20, 26; SOUTH, December 21, 13, 18.

American Coot

Summer. Resident throughout the state except in the northeastern region (one breeding record from Palo, St. Louis County) and adjoining counties in the north-central region (Koochiching, Itasca, and Aitkin). The main breeding range is west of the Mississippi River in the northern and central regions and west of Goodhue, Dodge, and Mower Counties in the south.

Winter. Stragglers remain in the east-central, central, southeast, and south-central regions regularly in December and early January. A few of these birds overwinter where there is suitable open water conditions and where other overwintering waterfowl are present, such as at Black Dog Lake, Dakota County, and Silver Lake, Rochester, Olmsted County. In the north the only place this species has been recorded in the winter is at Fergus Falls, Otter Tail County, along the open Otter Tail River.

SANDHILL CRANE *(Grus canadensis)*

Sandhill Crane

Minnesota status. Regular. Migrant and summer resident.

Migration. Common to abundant spring and fall migrant in local areas in the northwestern region and adjacent Wilkin County, uncommon to rare elsewhere in the state. Occurs in spring and fall in small flocks of up to 50 or 60 birds; concentrations of thousands of birds occur in the fall (10,000, October 17, 1982, east of Borup, Norman County). Staging areas in the fall are in eastern Kittson County and western Roseau County (Roseau Wildlife Management Area) near Borup, Norman County, and Rothsay Wildlife Management Area, Wilkin County. Occurs in eastern and central regions only as stragglers during spring and fall migration periods. *Spring migration period:* Late March through early May, with a peak in early and mid-April. Earliest dates: SOUTH, March 17, 19, 22; NORTH, March *19,* 27, 28, 31. *Fall migration period:* Early September through mid-November, with stragglers into December, peak numbers in mid-October. Latest dates: NORTH, November 11, 14, 15, *25;* December *2, 17;* SOUTH, November 20, 23, 27, *December 2.*

Summer. Best represented in the northwest (Kittson, Roseau, Marshall, and Pennington Counties) and north-central (Beltrami County) regions. An estimated 760-1,160 breeding pairs are found in these areas. Also found in the central and east-central regions in Todd, Morrison, Mille Lacs, Sherburne, Pine, Kanabec, Isanti, and Anoka Counties. There are also a few breeding pairs in the southern part of the north-central region in Cass, Crow Wing, and Aitkin Counties. In these areas there are an estimated 87 to 109 breeding pairs. The estimates of breeding pairs are based on observations by the Minnesota Department of Natural Resources personnel since 1980. There are summer observations in Koochiching County in the north-central area. A pair was present in the southeast region along the Root River near Hokah, Houston County, during the summer of 1983.

WHOOPING CRANE *(Grus americana)*

Minnesota status. Accidental. Migrant and summer resident in the nineteenth century.
Records. The only verified sightings since 1917 (see below) are of one bird seen on November 7, 1951 by the manager of the Rice Lake National Wildlife Refuge, Aitkin County (*The Loon* 40:21); and of two birds seen in Mahnomen County on October 12, 1985 (*The Loon* 58:45).

Several newspaper accounts in the 1960s and 1970s from northwestern regions indicate that the species may still pass over the western regions of the state in spring and fall. In May 1978 two reports of Whooping Cranes were made in Kittson County (*The Loon* 50:204). After careful consideration by the Minnesota Ornithological Records Committee of the details of these sight observations, it was decided that these birds were probably immature Sandhill Cranes and the reports were deleted from the record. Another published report of a possible Whooping Crane in Washington County on May 13, 1974 contains secondhand information and can only be considered a possible sighting (*The Loon* 46:127).
Former status. In the nineteenth century this species was a regular migrant and summer resident breeding throughout the prairie regions of the state. There are six specimens from the same era in the Bell Museum of Natural History. The last reported nesting in the state was in Grant County in 1876; the most recent regular sighting of birds was in Roseau County on April 23, 1917.

BLACK-BELLIED PLOVER
(Pluvialis squatarola)

Minnesota status. Regular. Migrant.
Migration. Uncommon to rare spring and fall migrant throughout the state; locally common mainly in the Duluth area in fall. Peak flock size at Duluth is usually 20 to 40 birds, but flocks of

up to 100 birds have been seen. *Spring migration period:* Late April through early June, with the bulk of the migration in mid to late May. Earliest dates: SOUTH, April *11,* 16, 19, 21; NORTH, May 6, 8, 9. Latest dates: SOUTH, June 4, 6, 9, *26;* NORTH, June 15, 16, 17, *25, 28, 30. Fall migration period:* Late July through mid-November, with the bulk of the migration from late September to late October. Earliest dates: NORTH, July *8,* 20, 27, 31; SOUTH, August 3, 4, 6. Latest dates: NORTH, November 5, 7, 11, *16, 22;* SOUTH, November 16, 17, 19.

LESSER GOLDEN-PLOVER
(Pluvialis dominica)

Minnesota status. Regular. Migrant.
Migration. Common spring and fall migrant in the central and western regions of the state. Rare in the spring and uncommon in the fall in the northeast and east-central regions, rare in the southeast at any season. The peak flock size is normally 20 to 50 birds, but occasionally peak migration flocks may contain 250 to 500 birds. Daily counts of 2,000 to 4,000 birds are possible at peak migration times in southwestern, south-central, northwest, and west-central regions. On October 8, 1983, 1,500 were seen in Pennington County and an estimated 1,000 were seen in eastern Traverse County on May 17, 1986. There appear to be two widely separated migration periods in the spring. A few birds enter the state in some years in late March, but in most years early migration dates are from mid to late April. *Spring migration period:* Late March through late June, with a peak in early and mid-May (3,000 + on May 15, 1978, Dodge County). Earliest dates: SOUTH, March *14,* 24, 27, 30; NORTH, April 20, 21, 23. Latest dates: SOUTH, June 6, 7, 8, *19, 26;* NORTH, June 10, 15, 18. *Fall migration period:* Late July through mid-November, with a peak from early to mid-October. There may be some overlap between spring and fall migrants; for example, birds were observed continuously from early June through

mid-July 1966 in one location in Stevens County. Two to eight birds were present during the period, and it was not known whether they were the same or different individuals. Earliest dates: NORTH, July *12,* 20, 29, 30; SOUTH, July *4, 5, 6, 17,* August 6, 7, 14. Latest dates: NORTH, November 6, 7, 9, *17, 18;* SOUTH, November 15, 16, 17.

SNOWY PLOVER *(Charadrius alexandrinus)*

Minnesota status. Accidental.
Records. The first acceptable record of this species in Minnesota was that of one bird seen at the Marshall sewage lagoons, Lyon County, on May 1, 1976 (*The Loon* 48:115). A single bird was seen and photographed at Big Stone, National Wildlife Refuge, Lac Qui Parle County, on April 24, 1981 (*The Loon* 53:220-21). July 11-18, 1982 a single bird was seen and photographed by many observers on Morris Point, Lake of the Woods County (*The Loon* 54:242). Another individual was seen at Zippel Bay, Lake of the Woods County, July 28, 1983 (*The Loon* 55:177). On June 30, 1986 a single bird was seen in Clay County (*The Loon* 58:142-43).

WILSON'S PLOVER *(Charadrius wilsonia)*

Minnesota status. Accidental.
Record. The two records for this species in the state are from Minnesota Point, Duluth, St. Louis County. The first individual was recorded on July 4, 1981 (*The Loon* 53:123-25) and the second (of possibly the same bird) was of an individual that remained May 15-20, 1982 (*The Loon* 52:243).

SEMIPALMATED PLOVER
(Charadrius semipalmatus)

Minnesota status. Regular. Migrant.
Migration. Uncommon spring and fall migrant

throughout the state. At times common, with peak flock size of 25 to 50 birds; occasionally larger concentrations occur (200+ seen, May 14, 1977, Oak Glen Lake, Steele County). *Spring migration period:* Mid-April through mid-June, with a peak in early to mid-May. Earliest dates: SOUTH, April *9*, 14, 16, 17; NORTH, April *16, 21, 28,* May 5, 6, 7. Latest dates: SOUTH, June 12, 15, 17; NORTH, June 19, 20, 21. *Fall migration period:* Mid-July through mid-October with the bulk of the migration from mid-August through early September. Earliest dates: NORTH, *June 29, 30,* July *1, 4,* 14, 16, 17; SOUTH, *June 26,* July *2,* 10, 14, 16. Latest dates: NORTH, October 13, 15, 19, *November 1;* SOUTH, October 7, 8, 12.

PIPING PLOVER *(Charadrius melodus)*

Piping Plover

Minnesota status. Regular. Migrant and summer resident. This species is endangered on both the Federal and State lists.

Migration. Rare spring and fall migrant anywhere in the state. Except at nesting locations, this species is seldom seen in the fall. *Spring migration period:* Mid-April through mid-May, no peak period noted. Earliest dates: SOUTH, April *10,* 17,22, 23; NORTH, April 21, 23, 24. Latest dates: SOUTH, May 27, 28, June 2, *10;* NORTH, none can be given because of breeding birds. *Fall migration period:* Late July through early September. Early dates: NORTH, none can be given because of breeding birds; SOUTH, no dates. Latest dates: NORTH, September 3, 6, 7, *12;* SOUTH, September 1, *28* (only dates).

Summer. At present known to breed at only two localities in the state: the Duluth harbor area, St. Louis County (*The Loon* 51:74-79), and the Pine Island and Currey Island area of Lake of the Woods County. Nests have been reported in the Duluth area since 1936, mainly from the Port Terminal. At present there are a few pairs restricted to the Port Terminal area (*The Loon* 56:100). Attempts are being made to create suitable habitat for breeding in the Duluth area. Only time will tell if the species will survive as a breeding bird in this area. Nesting was first reported at Pine and Currey Islands in 1932, but between 1941 and 1977 the area was never checked for breeding birds. Beginning in 1979 when the area was investigated, 20-30 nesting pairs were found (*The Loon* 51:144-45). A thorough study of this area was made during the 1982 and 1983 breeding seasons, and a population of 44 and 49 birds, respectively, was found (*The Loon* 56:110). There were 20 successful nests in 1983. The only other evidence of nesting in the state was during 1980. From June 18 to July 14 at least eight birds were present at Agassiz National Wildlife Refuge, Marshall County. Two nests and two broods were located during that period (personal communication with Jim Mattsson, Assistant Refuge Manager). One bird was seen from July 8 to 14, 1977 at Pelican Island, Leech Lake, Cass County. There are former breeding records and summer observations from the following counties: Otter Tail (1933), Douglas (1936, 1937), Crow Wing (1938), Becker, Lac Qui Parle, and Stevens.

KILLDEER *(Charadrius vociferus)*

Minnesota status. Regular. Migrant and summer resident; casual in winter.
Migration. Common spring and fall migrant throughout the state. Peak spring flocks number 25 to 30 birds, and peak fall gatherings number in excess of 100 birds. *Spring migration period:* Late February through late April, with a peak in early April. Earliest dates: SOUTH, February 22, 25, 26; NORTH, *February 25,* March 8, 11, 14. *Fall migration period:* Mid-August through early December, with the bulk of the migration from late September through October. Latest dates: NORTH, November 11, 12, 14; SOUTH, November 25, 28, December 3.
Summer. Resident throughout the state; widespread and numerous in all regions.
Winter. Probable late migrants have been record-

Killdeer

ed around open water areas into December and early January in the southern part of the state. Overwintering birds have been recorded in Winona (three, January 23, 1965), Scott (two, February 1967), Dakota, and Houston Counties. Individuals probably winter occasionally where suitable open springs exist from the St. Croix River Valley in Washington County southward along the Mississippi River Valley to the Iowa border.

MOUNTAIN PLOVER *(Charadrius montanus)*

Minnesota status. Accidental.
Records: Two birds were seen July 2-6, 1986 near Huntley, Faribault County *(The Loon* 58:154-58).

AMERICAN AVOCET *(Recurvirostra americana)*

American Avocet

Minnesota status. Regular. Migrant and summer resident.
Migration. A rare spring migrant anywhere in the state. Can be locally uncommon to common mainly in western regions during years of abundance and also in other local areas (35 on May 1, 1977, Rochester, Olmsted County [*The Loon* 49:182]). There are three records from the northeast: May 17, 1974; April 22, 1985 (Duluth); and May 23, 1980 (Lake County). In the fall, rare to casual in western regions. (There is one record of an exceptionally high count of 76 birds seen at Mud Lake, Traverse County, on July 9, 1977.) Five birds were seen on the early date of April 10, 1984 at Lake Calhoun in Minneapolis, Hennepin County. Accidental elsewhere. Normal flock size is five to 10 birds, with occasional peak counts of 30 to 35 or more birds. Before the 1950s this species was only a casual migrant in the state. *Spring migration period:* Mid-April through mid-May. Earliest dates: SOUTH, April *10,* 15, 17, 19; NORTH, April 19, 22, 29. *Fall migration period:* Very little is known; probably July through mid-October. Latest dates: NORTH,

August 9, 10, 16, *October 21, 23, 31;* SOUTH, October 10, 18, 19, *November 1.*

Summer. Between 1956 and 1964 this species was found nesting in several areas in the western part of the state; near Balaton, Lyon County (1956); near Alberta, Stevens County (1959); Orwell Refuge, Otter Tail County (1959); near Madison, Lac Qui Parle County (1959); Salt Lake, Lac Qui Parle County (1961, 1962, 1964). In 1973 downy young were found north of Ortonville, Big Stone County, and on June 13, 1984 one bird was present in Big Stone County. During the summer of 1977 this species was found nesting at Wells, Faribault County, in the south-central part of the state; two pair raised seven young. A single bird was seen at Waseca, Waseca County, on June 6, 1984. Nesting occurred at the Moorhead Sewage Lagoons, Clay County in 1977. Ten birds were present there on May 30 and eight on June 12. In 1980 an abandoned nest and one egg were found at Agassiz National Wildlife Refuge, Marshall County, on June 18, and an aggressive pair were found about one mile from the above nest site on June 21. Also during June 1980 four pair were present in the rice paddy area of Clearwater County north of Gonvick; two young were seen (R. Davids). During the summer of 1982 this species nested at the Crookston Sewage Lagoons, Polk County; four birds were seen there on June 17, 1983 and eight birds were present there from June 4 to July 23, 1984. The most recent nesting records are of a pair breeding in Traverse County; a nest with two eggs was discovered on July 13, 1984 (*The Loon* 56:204-5). A nest and young were seen during June and July 1985 near Cottonwood, Lyon County (*The Loon* 57:142). A pair attempted nesting at Lac Qui Parle County in May 1985 (*The Loon* 58:50). The only other evidence of nesting was from June 21 to July 8, 1887 at Brown's Valley, Traverse County, when several birds were collected and presumed to be nesting. Roberts (1932) states "although still a common bird in western North Dakota, the avocet has long been extinct in Minnesota. . . . There is reason to believe that during the early years of the settlement of the state it was a summer resident and nested on the prairies of the west, and probably to some extent in the sparsely wooded areas in the southeastern portion of the state."

GREATER YELLOWLEGS *(Tringa melanoleuca)*

Minnesota status. Regular. Migrant.
Migration. Uncommon spring and fall migrant throughout the state. Usually found in small groups of two to five birds, but occasionally concentrations of 25 to 35 birds are seen. *Spring migration period:* Late March through late May, with a peak in mid and late April. Earliest dates: SOUTH, March 19, 21, 22; NORTH, March 26, 28, 30. Latest dates: SOUTH, May 23, 27, 30, *June 6, 13, 18, 19, 20, 22;* NORTH, May 27, 28, 29. *Fall migration period:* There may be some overlap between spring and fall migrants. (The June dates listed above and below may represent late spring migrants, summering birds, or very early returning fall migrants.) The fall migration extends from late June through mid-November, with a peak in late October. Earliest dates: NORTH, *June 24,* July 1, 4, 5; SOUTH, June 23, 26, 27. Latest dates: NORTH, November 6, 7, 8, *14, 22;* SOUTH, November 17, 19, 22.

LESSER YELLOWLEGS *(Tringa flavipes)*

Minnesota status. Regular. Migrant.
Migration. Common to locally abundant spring and fall migrant throughout the state. Less common in the heavily wooded areas of the state in northeastern and north-central regions. This species is usually encountered in flocks of five to 25 birds, but larger aggregations of up to 600 birds are occasionally found, mainly in the fall, in areas of suitable habitat. *Spring migration period:* Late March through early June, with the bulk of the migration from mid-April to mid-May. Earliest dates: SOUTH,

March 17, 18, 19; NORTH, March 23, 28, 29. Latest dates: SOUTH, June 17, 18, 19; NORTH, June 9, 15, 17. *Fall migration period:* As with many species of shorebirds, there may be an overlap between late spring migrants and early returning fall birds. It is not known whether the mid to late June dates given above and below are very late spring migrants, summering nonbreeding birds, or very early returning fall migrants. Early June (1st to the 10th) dates are assumed to be late spring migrants; late June (20th to the 30th) are assumed to be early fall migrants. The fall migration period extends from late June to mid-November, with the bulk of the migration in August. Earliest dates: NORTH, June 24, 27, 30; SOUTH, June *21,* 26, 28, July 1. Latest dates: NORTH, October 23, 27, 29, *November 1, 12;* SOUTH, November 17, 18, 19.

SOLITARY SANDPIPER *(Tringa solitaria)*

Minnesota status. Regular. Migrant and summer resident.

Migration. Uncommon spring and fall migrant throughout the state; less frequently seen in western regions. Most records are of individual birds, but groups of two to six birds and peak aggregations of 10 to 20 birds (18 on August 29, 1974, Onamia, Mille Lacs County) are occasionally seen. *Spring migration period:* Mid-April through mid-May, with stragglers into mid-June. Peak numbers are reported in early and mid-May. Earliest dates: SOUTH, April *7, 8,* 12, 15, 16; NORTH, April 19, 20, 26. Latest dates: SOUTH, May 18, 20, 21, *June 2, 4, 15, 18;* NORTH, accurate late spring dates are difficult to give because of the possibility of nesting birds; most birds have left northern regions by late May or early June. *Fall migration period:* Very late June through mid-October, no peak period noted. Earliest dates: NORTH, because of the presence of possible breeding birds, it is difficult to give accurate return dates for this species; SOUTH, June 26, 28, 30. Latest dates: NORTH, October 13, 15, 17, *26;* SOUTH, October 9, 10, 18, *26.*

Solitary Sandpiper

Summer. The first nesting record for this species occurred July 11, 1973 when a pair and one half-grown young bird were found along the Mississippi River in Verdon Township, Aitkin County (*The Loon* 45:96). There is also a summer observation in this area on June 28, 1972. In 1980 and 1981 this species was found during the summer at two locations in Cook County. During the summer of 1982, breeding was confirmed in Cook County when adults and young were observed (*The Loon* 54:144-47). Nesting was also presumed in this area of Cook County in 1983 and 1984.

WILLET *(Catoptrophorus semipalmatus)*

Minnesota status. Regular. Migrant and summer visitant. Former summer resident.

Migration. Uncommon to rare spring migrant throughout the state; rare in the north-central and northeastern regions except at Duluth where it is uncommon. Rare fall migrant anywhere. Numbers vary from year to year; some years absent, some years well represented in the spring migration. Spring 1984 was an example of a year when it was well represented across most of the southern portions of the state. Peak flock size is usually six to eight birds, but there are a few records of up to 40 birds in a flock. *Spring migration period:* Mid-April to mid-May, with a peak in early May. Earliest dates: SOUTH, *March 21, April 2,* 10, 13, 15; NORTH, April 26, 28, 29. Latest dates: SOUTH, May 16, 17, 23, *June 1;* NORTH, May 24, 25, 26, *June 8, 24. Fall migration period:* Early August through late September, with no peak period noted. Earliest dates: NORTH, *July 20,* August 3, 11, 12; SOUTH, *July 25,* August 3, 8, 10. Latest dates: NORTH, September 25, 26, *October 7, 19* (only dates); SOUTH, September 13, 20, *October 11.*

Summer. Historically, little is known about the status of the Willet as a breeding species. The only information available for the nineteenth century is from Roberts (1932), who found that the species bred commonly in Grant and Traverse Counties in 1879 and that it was numerous in the breeding season in Lac Qui Parle County during 1889. It appears to have been only a casual resident since the beginning of the twentieth century. The only breeding evidence is from the Pomme de Terre River, Swift County, where broods were seen in 1931 and 1932. Recent summer observations, but no breeding evidence, include the following counties: Scott (July 1, 1961, three adults), Lac Qui Parle (several sightings, including a courting pair in 1962), Stevens (1964), Clay (1966), Traverse (two adults, 1970), McLeod (1971), Marshall (1971, June 29, 1975, and June 2, 1985), Jackson (four adults, June 27, 1976), Lyon (June 27, 1977 and July 22, 1985, a pair), Martin (June 20, 1982), and, most unusual, one at Knife River, Lake County, on July 6, 1982. Any one or all of these records may represent late spring or early fall migrant or nonbreeding summering birds.

SPOTTED SANDPIPER *(Actitis macularia)*

Minnesota status. Regular. Migrant and summer resident.
Migration. Common spring and fall migrant throughout the state. Normally encountered as individuals or in pairs, but occasionally congregations of 10 to 25 birds are seen, especially in the spring. *Spring migration period:* Mid-April through late May, with a peak in early May. Earliest dates: SOUTH, *March 22 (The Loon* 50:172), *April 4, 5,* 11, 13, 14; NORTH, *April 9, 11,* 14, 15, 20. *Fall migration period:* Mid-August through late October, no peak period noted. Most birds have left the state by late September. Latest dates: NORTH, October 16, 21, 22 *28;* SOUTH, October 22, 23, 25, *November 2.*
Summer. Resident, breeding throughout the state. Most numerous around lakes in northern regions and along the Mississippi River; well represented in all regions.

Spotted Sandpiper

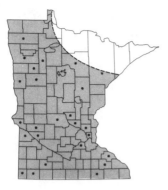

Upland Sandpiper

UPLAND SANDPIPER *(Bartramia longicauda)*

Minnesota status. Regular. Migrant and summer resident.

Migration. Uncommon spring and fall migrant throughout most of the state; rare to local in the north-central, northeastern, southeast, and most of the south-central regions. Usually seen as individuals or in small groups of two to five birds. Occasionally concentrations of up to 15 birds are seen in the early fall. *Spring migration period:* Mid-April through late May, with a peak in early May. Earliest dates: SOUTH, April 7, 15, 17, 18; NORTH, April 20, 25, 28. *Fall migration period:* Early July through late August; there is a gradual exodus from the state, with most birds departing by early August. Latest dates: NORTH, August 6, 10, 11, *24, 31, September 5, 23, October 19;* SOUTH, August 15, 21, 25, *September 11, 14, 30, October 4, 26.*

Summer. Resident throughout most of the state; best represented in western regions. Very scarce or absent over large portions of north-central and northeastern regions and in adjacent Pine and Kanabec Counties. Also local to absent over much of the southeast and south-central regions. In the north-central and northeastern regions, there are breeding records from Clearwater, Itasca (Grand Rapids), Aitkin, and St. Louis (Duluth and Hibbing) Counties. Recent observations indicate the species may be spreading northward and eastward where suitable grassy and open areas occur.

ESKIMO CURLEW *(Numenius borealis)*

Minnesota status. Extirpated. Regular migrant in the nineteenth century.

Former status. Roberts (1932) summarized all that is known about this species: "The Eskimo Curlew, now long since absent from Minnesota, formerly passed northward in the spring in great numbers through the western part of the Mississippi and Missouri valleys. . . . It is evident that it disappeared

from the western part of the state, where it was
without doubt once abundant as a spring migrant,
before that region was explored to any extent by
bird-students. No Minnesota specimens are
known.'' The few hearsay records that he cites are
from the 1880s.

WHIMBREL *(Numenius phaeopus)*

Minnesota status. Regular. Migrant.
Migration. Uncommon to locally common spring
migrant, and a very rare fall migrant in Duluth and
along the North Shore of Lake Superior. Normally
seen in small flocks of five to 25 birds, but occasionally much larger flocks are seen containing 200 to
300 birds (Cook County, May 31, 1983, *The Loon*
56:100). Casual to accidental elsewhere in the state
in both spring and fall, with records from Goodhue,
Olmsted, Wabasha, Lyon, Meeker, Renville,
Stearns, Aitkin, Cass, Traverse, Clay, and Marshall
Counties. *Spring migration period:* Mid-May
through mid-June, with a peak the last week of
May. Earliest dates: SOUTH, May 16, 17, only dates;
NORTH, *April 23, 26,* May 12, 16, 18. Latest dates:
NORTH (only), June 17, 19, 23, *29, July 1. Fall
migration period:* Poorly known, but probably early
July through late September. The species is too
scarce and infrequent in the fall to give accurate
migration information. As with many shorebird
species, late June or early July dates could be late
spring migrants, early returning fall birds, or nonbreeding summer wanderers. Earliest dates: NORTH
(only), July 7, 18, 21. Latest dates: NORTH,
September 24, 25, 27, *October 18.*

LONG-BILLED CURLEW *(Numenius americanus)*

Minnesota status. Casual. Migrant. Summer resident in nineteenth century.
Records. Twentieth-century records indicate that
this species is a casual migrant with spring records

from the following counties: St. Louis, Aitkin, Cass, Wilkin, Douglas, Lac Qui Parle, Kandiyohi, Meeker, McLeod, Hennepin, Lyon. These records range from an early date of April 10 to May 28. There are two fall dates, September 27 and October 28, both from Stearns County. There are no records since 1980.

Former status. In the nineteenth century this species was a numerous migrant, and it bred on the prairie south and west of the heavily forested portions of the state. Roberts (1932) cited breeding evidence from Jackson, Lac Qui Parle, and Polk Counties, and stated that the species was especially numerous on the western prairies from the Iowa line northward, preferring in the northwest region the sandy ridges or old beaches where prairie occurs on the eastern edge of the Red River Valley. There are three specimens in the Bell Museum of Natural History from this period.

HUDSONIAN GODWIT *(Limosa haemastica)*

Minnesota status. Regular. Migrant.
Migration. Uncommon spring migrant in western regions; rare spring migrant in central and eastern regions in most years. Casual to accidental throughout the state in fall. Spring flock size is usually ten birds or fewer, but occasionally concentrations of 25 to 30 birds are seen. The largest concentration on record of 300 birds occurred at the Crookston sewage lagoons, Polk County, on May 15, 1982. *Spring migration period:* Late April through early June, with a peak in mid-May. Earliest dates: SOUTH, April *10,* 13, 14, 15; NORTH, April *22, 25,* May 5, 8, 9. Latest dates: SOUTH, June 2, 6, 7; NORTH, June 6, 12, 13, *24. Fall migration period:* The dates listed are all on record in the state for the fall. Earliest dates: NORTH, July 17, August 8, 12, 26; SOUTH, July 4, 14 *(The Loon* 56:192), 21. Latest dates: NORTH, September 10, 15, 19, *October 4, November 5 (The Loon* 48:185); SOUTH, October 18, 28, 29, *November 1.*

MARBLED GODWIT *(Limosa fedoa)*

Minnesota status. Regular. Migrant and summer resident.

Migration. Common to occasionally locally abundant spring migrant in the prairie areas of west-central and northwestern regions; rare to uncommon elsewhere in the state. Uncommon fall migrant in western regions; accidental elsewhere. At the peak of spring migration in western regions, flocks of 50 to a maximum of 200 birds have been seen. *Spring migration period:* Mid-April through mid-May, with a peak in late April. Earliest dates: SOUTH, April 8, 9, 10; NORTH, March *26*, April 7, 9, 11. Latest dates (beyond breeding areas): NORTH, (northeast and north-central regions), May 24, 26, 27, *June 2, 20. Fall migration period:* Late June through late August, with the bulk of the migration in July; most birds have left the state by early August. Latest dates: NORTH, August 12, 13, 16, *September 9, 12*; SOUTH, August 21, 29, 30, *September 9, 26*.

Summer. Resident primarily on the prairie areas from Lac Qui Parle County in the west-central region northward to the Canadian border. Outside this area this species has been found breeding on two Wildlife Management Areas in Brown County (1978). During the summer of 1974, there were records from Stevens, Swift, and Yellow Medicine Counties in the west and Kandiyohi and Stearns Counties in the central region. These records indicate that a sparse breeding population exists in these regions where suitable habitat occurs. In the nineteenth and early twentieth centuries, the breeding territory of this species was more widespread in the state. Roberts (1932) indicated it was a summer resident throughout the prairie portions of the state, but there were no data from south of the Minnesota River. This makes the Brown County records listed above significant.

Marbled Godwit

RUDDY TURNSTONE *(Arenaria interpres)*

Minnesota status. Regular. Migrant.
Migration. Uncommon to rare spring and fall migrant throughout the state; common only at peak migration periods at Duluth and around the larger lakes in the central part of the state, such as Mille Lacs Lake and Leech Lake. Peak flock size in the Duluth area is usually 50 to 100 birds, but flocks of up to 300 birds have been recorded. Peak flocks of 10 to 30 birds have been recorded elsewhere. *Spring migration period:* Early May through mid-June, with a peak in late May. Earliest dates: SOUTH, May 4, 5, 12; NORTH, May *3,* 5, 9, 12. Latest dates: SOUTH, June 4, 6, 9, *21;* NORTH, June 13, 14, 16, *19, 22, 25. Fall migration period:* Late July through late September, with stragglers in October and early November. Earliest dates: NORTH, July *4, 11,* 21, 24, 25; SOUTH, July *6, 23* (only July dates), August 1, 16, 17. Latest dates: NORTH, October 23, 25, 27, *November 2, 3, 9;* SOUTH, September 25, 29, October 7.

RED KNOT *(Calidris canutus)*

Minnesota status. Regular. Migrant.
Migration. A casual to rare migrant throughout the state except uncommon in Duluth where the largest counts of up to 15 birds have been made. *Spring migration period:* Late May through mid-June. Earliest dates: SOUTH, May *9,* 20, 22; NORTH, May *5,* 16, 19, 21. Latest dates: SOUTH, May 30, June 6 (only dates); NORTH, June 11, 12, 14. *Fall migration period:* Late July through late September, with the bulk of the migration in Late August. Earliest dates: NORTH, July 19, 24, 28; SOUTH, July 27, August 24, 25, 28 (only dates). Latest dates: NORTH, September 18, 24, 28, *October 10-13* (Duluth), *21* (Lake of the Woods), *November 9* (Mille Lacs Lake, Mille Lacs County); SOUTH, September 14, 15, 26.

SANDERLING *(Calidris alba)*

Minnesota status. Regular. Migrant.
Migration. Uncommon to locally common spring and fall migrant in the eastern half of the state, especially at Duluth and around some of the larger lakes in the central region. Uncommon in spring and fall in western regions. Flocks frequently contain 10 to 100 birds, with peak daily counts at Duluth of 200 to 500 birds. *Spring migration period:* Late April through mid-June, with a peak in late May. Earliest dates: SOUTH, April *14,* 18, 24, 25; NORTH, April *30,* May 5, 6, 7. Latest dates: SOUTH, June 4, 5, 6, *13, 15;* NORTH, June 16, 18, 21. *Fall migration period:* Late June through early November, with the bulk of the migration in September. Earliest dates: NORTH, June 25, 28, 29; SOUTH, *June 28,* July 2, 3, 10. Latest dates: NORTH, November 2, 3, 7, *14;* SOUTH, October 28, 29, November 1, *9.*

SEMIPALMATED SANDPIPER
(Calidris pusilla)

Minnesota status. Regular. Migrant.
Migration. Common to locally abundant spring and fall migrant throughout the state. Normal peak flocks number 20 to 100 birds; occasionally larger concentrations of up to 500 birds are seen. *Spring migration period:* Mid-April through late June, with a peak in late May. Earliest dates: SOUTH, April *1, 8,* 12, 14, 15; NORTH, April *7, 14, 20,* 30, May 7, 8. Latest dates: SOUTH, June 14, 15, 19; NORTH, June 21, 23, 24. *Fall migration period:* Early July through late October, with the bulk of the migration from mid-August through mid-September. Earliest dates: NORTH, *June 25, 26, 28,* July 1, 2, 5; SOUTH, *June 28,* July 2, 3, 5. Latest dates: NORTH, October 11, 17, 19, *27;* SOUTH, October 27, 30, November 1. (The dates listed above between June 21 and 28 could be late spring migrants, early fall migrants, or nonbreeding summering birds.)

WESTERN SANDPIPER *(Calidris mauri)*

Minnesota status. Regular. Migrant. (Because it is difficult to separate this species from the Semipalmated Sandpiper, little is known about its status.)

Migration. Rare to uncommon spring and fall migrant throughout the state. Better represented in fall. The largest numbers (five to 25) of birds are reported in the southwestern region. This species was first added to the state list in 1960 (*The Flicker* 32:125), but it probably occurred before this date. *Spring migration period:* Late April through early June. Earliest dates: south, April *3,* 19, 23, 24; north, May 17, 23, 26 (only dates). Latest dates: south, June 1, 4, 6; north, June 1, 8 (only dates). *Fall migration period:* July through late September. Earliest dates: north, July 5, 8, 11; south, July 2, 3, 5. Latest dates: north, September 17, 19, 27, *October 13, 27;* south, September 10, 16, 25, *October 13.*

LEAST SANDPIPER *(Calidris minutilla)*

Minnesota status. Regular. Migrant.
Migration. Common spring and fall migrant throughout most of the state; uncommon in the spring in the north-central and northeastern regions. Peak flock size is five to 20 birds, but occasionally concentrations of 50 to 100 birds are seen. *Spring migration period:* Early April through early June, with a peak in mid-May. Earliest dates: south, *March 21, 30,* April 4, 5, 6; north, April 9, 14, 16. Latest dates: south, June 12, 13, 14; north, June 9, 11, 14. *Fall migration period:* Late June through mid-October. The June dates listed below may be very late spring migrants, nonbreeding summering birds, or very early fall migrants. Earliest dates: north, June 20, 21, 23; south, June 25, 26, 28. Latest dates: north, October 15, 16, 17, *25, 29;* south, October 21, 24, 29, *November 9.*

WHITE-RUMPED SANDPIPER
(Calidris fuscicollis)

Minnesota status. Regular. Migrant.
Migration. Uncommon spring migrant in eastern and central regions, locally common in western regions. Rare to casual fall migrant in all regions of the state. Peak flock size is three to 10 birds, but occasionally flocks of 20 to 50 birds are seen. At the peak of the spring migration in western regions of the state, daily counts of 200 to 400 birds have been made in such areas as Salt Lake, Lac Qui Parle County. *Spring migration period:* Late April through mid-June, with a peak in late May. Earliest dates: SOUTH, April 23, 24, 27; NORTH, *April 27* (only April date), May 13, 15, 16. Latest dates: SOUTH, June 14, 15, 17, *22*; NORTH, June 15, 16, 19, *21, 25, 27, 28*. *Fall migration period:* Mid-July to late October, no peak noted. There appears to be an overlap between late spring migrants and early returning fall birds. There are a number of late June dates (see above) and early July dates (see below), which could be either spring or fall migrants. Earliest dates: NORTH, July *5*, 10, 12, 14; SOUTH, July *1, 3, 6*, 16, 18, 23. Latest dates: NORTH (there are only a scattering of September dates), October 16, 17, 20, *30*; *November 1, 5*; SOUTH, October 9, 14, 16, *November 1, 4, 5*.

BAIRD'S SANDPIPER *(Calidris bairdii)*

Minnesota status. Regular. Migrant.
Migration. An uncommon spring and fall migrant throughout most of the state; rare in the spring and fall in the northeastern and north-central regions, except at Duluth where it is uncommon at both seasons. Normal flock size is three to 10 birds, with peak flock size of 25 to 100 birds seen occasionally. *Spring migration period:* Late March through mid-June, the bulk of the migration begins in late April and reaches a peak in mid-May. Earliest dates: SOUTH, March 20, 25, 26; NORTH, March 31, April

4, 8. Latest dates: SOUTH, June 6, 10, 12; NORTH, June 8, 11, 12, *19, 20. Fall migration period:* Mid-July to late October, with a peak in late August and early September. Earliest dates: NORTH, *June 28*, July 4, 9, 11; SOUTH, *June 28*, July *3, 6, 9*, 13, 16, 19. Latest dates: NORTH, October 17, 23, 25, November *6, 9*; SOUTH, October 31, November 1, 2, *6, 8, 11*.

PECTORAL SANDPIPER *(Calidris melanotos)*

Minnesota status. Regular. Migrant; accidental in winter.

Migration. Common spring and fall migrant throughout the state except in the northeast and north-central regions where it is uncommon in both seasons. Normal flock size varies from five to 10 birds up to 50 birds. At peak migration periods, concentrations of 100 to 500 birds may occasionally be seen. *Spring migration period:* Late March through mid-June, with a peak from late April to mid-May. Earliest dates: SOUTH, March 21, 23, 24; NORTH, March 25, 28, 31. Latest dates: SOUTH, June 6, 7, 9, *18*; NORTH, June 12, 17, 19. *Fall migration period:* Early July to mid-November, with a peak from mid-August to mid-September. Earliest dates: NORTH, *June 24, 27, 28*, July 1, 2, 5; SOUTH, *June 26, 28*, July 3, 4, 5. Latest dates: NORTH, October 31, November 5, 6, *17, 22*; SOUTH, November 12, 16, 17, *25*.

Winter. One bird was seen on December 24, 1974 at Cottonwood, Lyon County (*The Loon* 47:97).

PURPLE SANDPIPER *(Calidris maritima)*

Minnesota status. Accidental.

Records. A single bird was seen at Duluth on October 30, 1981 (*The Loon* 54:58-59); a single bird was seen at Big Sandy Lake, Aitkin County, from November 14 to November 17, 1977 (*The Loon* 50:47-48); a single bird was found at the harbor in

Grand Marais, Cook County, on December 17, 1966 and was collected on December 20, 1966, MMNH #22252 (*The Loon* 39:64).

DUNLIN *(Calidris alpina)*

Minnesota status. Regular. Migrant.
Migration. Uncommon to locally common spring migrant throughout the state, especially at Duluth during spring migration peak. Rare fall migrant throughout the state except at Duluth where it is uncommon to common. Normal flock size is 5 to 15 birds, with peak daily counts of 100 to 300 birds occasionally seen in the spring. *Spring migration period:* Mid-April through mid-June, with a peak in mid-May. Earliest dates: SOUTH, April 11, 12, 15; NORTH, April *17*, 25, 28, 29. Latest dates: SOUTH, June 11, 13, 14; NORTH, June 11, 12, 13, *17* (a single bird was seen at Duluth from June 13 to July 13, 1985). *Fall migration period:* Late July through early November; the main fall migration does not begin until late August. Earliest dates: NORTH, July *3*, 18, 19, 22; SOUTH, July *6*, 10, 19, 21. Latest dates: NORTH, November 5, 9, 11, *16, 17*; SOUTH, November 9, 10, 11, *17*.

STILT SANDPIPER *(Calidris himantopus)*

Minnesota status. Regular. Migrant.
Migration. Uncommon spring and fall migrant throughout the state; casual in the spring and rare in the fall in the north-central and northeastern regions. Better represented in the fall when it may be locally common in western and southern regions. Normal flock size ranges up to 20 birds, peak concentrations reach 100 birds. On August 22, 1971 an exceptionally large concentration of approximately 1,000 birds was seen in Lyon County. *Spring migration period:* Early May through early June, with a peak in mid to late May. Earliest dates: SOUTH, April *18, 24, 25*, May 1, 3, 4; NORTH, *April*

21, May 3, 5, 11. Latest dates: SOUTH, June 5, 6, 10, *13*; NORTH, June 12, 13, 15. *Fall migration period:* Early July through mid-October, with a peak in August. Earliest dates: NORTH, July 1, 2, 4; SOUTH, *June 28*, July 1, 4, 6. Latest dates: NORTH, September 25, 28, October 12, 14, *November 4*; SOUTH, October 15, 16, 17.

BUFF-BREASTED SANDPIPER
(Tryngites subruficollis)

Minnesota status. Regular. Migrant.
Migration. Rare spring migrant in western regions, casual to accidental elsewhere in the state in the spring. Uncommon to rare fall migrant throughout the state, best represented at Duluth. Normal flock size ranges up to 15 birds, occasionally at peak migration periods 25 to 50 birds may be encountered. *Spring migration period:* Early May to early June. Earliest dates: SOUTH, *April 26*, May 5, 6, 12; NORTH, May 2, 18 (only dates). Latest dates: SOUTH, June 6 (only date); NORTH, no data. *Fall migration period:* Late July through late September, with a peak in late August and early September. Earliest dates: NORTH, July 22, 23, 24; SOUTH, July *12*, 20, 23, 25.. Latest dates: NORTH, September 24, 25, 27, *October 1, 18* (Duluth); SOUTH, September 10, 11, 23, October *1, 22* (Rock County).

RUFF *(Philomachus pugnax)*

Minnesota status. Casual. Migrant.
Records. The first record for this European species in the state was one seen and photographed between May 23 and May 31, 1964 at Alberta, Stevens County (*The Loon* 32:44-45 and 53-55). Since that time, there have been 19 additional records in the state as follows. *Spring:* Sherburn, Martin County (April 19, 1986); Gaylord, Sibley County (April 26 to May 2, 1971); Island Lake, St. Louis County (April 29 to May 1, 1983); Aitkin, Aitkin County (May 9,

1982); Marshall, Lyon County (May 11, 1975 and
May 20, 1983); Lastrup, Morrison County (May 13,
1973); Albany and Sartell (two), Stearns County
(both on May 16, 1983); Moorhead, Clay County
(June 4, 1977). *Fall:* Marshall, Lyon County (July
9, 1979 and September 9 to 24, 1976); near Fergus
Falls, Otter Tail County (July 22, 1978 and *October
2,* 1976); Crookston Sewage Lagoons, Polk County (July 23, 1984). Another bird was seen in 1984 on
August 12 at Carlos Avery Refuge, Anoka County. During 1985 there were three records: May 10,
Agassiz National Wildlife Refuge, Marshall County; May 19, Goodhue County; July 18-19, Cottonwood, Lyon County.

SHORT-BILLED DOWITCHER
(Limnodromus griseus)

Minnesota status. Regular. Migrant.
Migration. As far as is known, this species is an uncommon to locally common spring and fall migrant
throughout the state except in the northeast (there
are a few records from Duluth and one on May 16,
1986 from Cook county) and north-central regions
where it is rare in both seasons. Only since the 1960s
when the genus Limnodromus was split into Long-
billed and Short-billed forms have birders differen-
tiated between the two species. The difficulty of
separating the two species in the field has made it
difficult to obtain information on this species'
distribution in the state. At present it would appear
that the Short-billed is possibly more widespread
than the Long-billed. It also appears (see below)
that the migration periods are different for the two
species. The Short-billed generally appears later in
the spring and earlier in the fall and does not linger
as late in the fall. This species is generally seen in
small flocks of up to 20 or 25 birds. There is one
report of a larger concentration: 250+ birds in
Jackson County on August 23, 1966. *Spring migration period:* Early May through early June. Earliest
dates: south, May 2, 3, 8 (there are a number of

late April dates for the south that are reported as the Short-billed species; however, there are no details on any observations to substantiate the records; NORTH, May 3, 5, 8. Latest dates: SOUTH, May 23, 24, 30, *June 4, 8, 10, 13*; NORTH, May 30, June 1, 2, *10. Fall migration period:* Early July through early September. Earliest dates: NORTH, *June 30,* July 2, 4, 5; SOUTH, *June 28,* July 2, 6, 8. Latest dates: NORTH, September 3, 4, *13, 15, 25, October 9* (only dates); SOUTH, September 2, 4, 9.

LONG-BILLED DOWITCHER
(Limnodromus scolopaceus)

Minnesota status. Regular. Migrant.
Migration. Uncommon spring and fall migrant throughout most of the state; rare especially in the spring in the north-central and northeastern regions. See the discussion under Short-billed Dowitchers about the range and occurrence of the two dowitcher species in Minnesota. This species is generally an earlier migrant in the spring and occurs much later in the fall. The difficulty in separating the two species is a problem when the migration overlaps in May and early fall (July and August) when the two species occur together. There is the possibility that some of the dates listed below and those listed under Short-billed Dowitcher may be for either species. Flock size in the Long-billed Dowitcher ranges from a few birds up to 30 or 50 birds, with peak concentrations of up to 200 birds. *Spring migration period:* Late April through late May. Earliest dates: SOUTH, April *13, 15, 16,* 23, 24, 25; NORTH, April 25, 29, May 2. Latest dates: SOUTH, May 22, 23, 28; NORTH, May 28, 29, June 2. *Fall migration period:* Early July through early November, with a peak in early and mid-October. Earliest dates: NORTH, July 7, 9, 10; SOUTH, *June 26, 28,* July 2, 3, 6. Latest dates: NORTH, October 12, *27, November 5* (only dates); SOUTH, November 8, 9, 11.

COMMON SNIPE *(Gallinago gallinago)*

Minnesota status. Regular. Migrant, summer resident, and winter visitant. Records have been kept
on the harvest of Common Snipe since 1919. From
the 1930s to the 1960s harvest figures were normally
less than 10,000 birds. In the 1970s and 1980s
numbers harvested have increased considerably:
36,000 were taken in 1971; 28,000 in 1976; 23,000
in 1980; and 14,000 in 1982.

Migration. A common spring and fall migrant
throughout the state. Spring concentrations of 10
to 15 birds are common; larger concentrations of
up to 50 or 60 birds are seen occasionally. Peak fall

Common Snipe

concentrations are usually 25 to 50 birds, rarely up
to 100 individuals. *Spring migration period:* Mid-
March through early May, with a peak in mid-
April. Earliest dates: SOUTH (it is difficult to determine exact migration dates because of wintering
birds), March 20, 22, 24; NORTH, March *15*, 25, 26,
28. *Fall migration period:* Postbreeding flocking
begins in mid-July, with migration from early September through late November; the bulk of the
migration is from late September through late October. Latest dates: NORTH, November 6, 8, 9, *17,
20*; SOUTH (because of wintering birds in some areas
of the south, it is difficult to give exact departure
dates), November 23, 24, 25.

Summer. Resident throughout the state. Most
numerous in the northern regions, becoming less
common in southern regions. Absent in many areas
in southwestern and southeastern regions.

Winter. Occurs regularly along open streams in east-
central and southeastern regions. Usually occur as
individuals, but up to four birds have been found
wintering in one location. In recent years a few birds
have been found in northern areas: December 21,
1974, Clifton, St. Louis County; January 3, 1983,
Fergus Falls, Otter Tail County; and January 29,
1980 near Walker, Cass County (*The Loon* 52:44).

AMERICAN WOODCOCK *(Scolopax minor)*

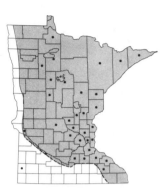

American Woodcock

Minnesota status. Regular. Migrant and summer resident. During fall hunting seasons the hunter harvest of American Woodcock has varied widely since the 1920s when only a few hundred birds were taken. In 1975, 65,000 birds were taken; in 1980, 67,000; and in 1982, 54,000.

Migration. Common spring and fall migrant in the southeast, east-central, central, north-central, and northeastern regions. Uncommon to rare in south-central, southwest, west-central, and northwestern regions during both migration seasons. In the early 1970s a definite pattern of westward range expansion took place in this species. Birds began to appear regularly in western and southern areas where they had previously been only infrequent. Birds were recorded in Pipestone, Lac Qui Parle, Clay, Becker, and Marshall Counties along the western margin of the state. During periods of peak migration in the fall, loose aggregations of up to 30 or 40 birds may occasionally be found in areas of good habitat. *Spring migration period:* Early March through early May, with a peak in mid-April. Earliest dates: south, March 2, 3, 4; north, March 16, 18, 20. *Fall migration period:* Early September through early November, with a peak in late September. Latest dates: north, November 5, 7, 9, *19*; south, November 7, 9, 19, *December 3, 29.*

Summer. Roberts (1932) listed this species as a "summer resident breeding throughout the state but best represented in counties bordering the Mississippi River south of Anoka." He made little or no mention of breeding in the northeast or north-central regions. At present this species is a resident from the southeast (along the Mississippi River) and east-central regions, increasing in numbers northward through the central, north-central, and northeastern regions. With the increase in birds seen during migration, mentioned above, birds are now breeding regularly in locations where they were previously infrequent. There are numerous recent June and July records from the western margin of the state, indicating that breeding is taking place in these areas. It nested in Becker County in 1973 (*The Loon* 47:101) and in Pipestone County in 1984 (*The Loon* 57:108).

WILSON'S PHALAROPE *(Phalaropus tricolor)*

Wilson's Phalarope

Minnesota status. Regular. Migrant and summer resident.

Migration. Common to locally abundant spring and fall migrant in western and central regions, uncommon in the east-central region, rare in the southeast and northeastern regions (casual in Cook and Lake Counties). Less common in the fall. This species is normally encountered in small groups of up to 10 birds, but larger concentrations are common at peak spring migration periods in western regions. Over 400 were seen at the Roseau River Wildlife Management Area, Roseau County on May 19, 1980. *Spring migration period:* Late April through late May, with a peak in mid-May. Earliest dates: SOUTH, April *15*, 20, 21, 22; NORTH, April *13*, 20, 27, 28. *Fall migration period:* Late July through late September. There is a gradual exodus from the state in July and August, with no noticeable peak as in the spring. Latest dates: NORTH, September 17, 24, 26; SOUTH, September 20, 25, 18, *October 9, 22.*

Summer. This species is a very local summer resident mainly in the northwestern and central regions. Scattered nesting pairs are found in west-central areas; in 1971 and 1972 it was found nesting in the rice paddies of Aitkin County, and it was found there on July 14, 1985. With the increase of rice paddies in the north-central part of the state, there has been an increase in summer occurrence of pairs in this type of habitat. The species has bred sporadically at Salt Lake, Lac Qui Parle County (1978), and in Lincoln County (1979), but this is the only recent breeding evidence south of the Minnesota River. Formerly (nineteenth century) the species was of regular summer occurrence in south-central and southwestern regions. There are recent June observations in Dakota, Washington, Rice, Faribault,

Chisago, and Rock Counties; thus some sporadic breeding may be occurring in these southern regions. There are early June records from the northeast (Duluth, Lake County), but these probably represent late migrants.

RED-NECKED PHALAROPE
(Phalaropus lobatus)

Minnesota status. Regular. Migrant.

Migration. Generally an uncommon to rare spring and fall migrant primarily in western regions; locally common in good habitat (e.g., sewage ponds) in western regions. Accidental or casual in north-central and northeastern regions. Occurs in flocks of up to 25 birds, with peak flock size of 50 birds. There are reports of concentrations of 100 or more birds in western areas at peak migration periods. *Spring migration period:* Early May through mid-June, with a peak in late May. Earliest dates: SOUTH, May 4, 5, 8; NORTH, May 10, 14, 15. Latest dates: SOUTH, June 6, 11, 12; NORTH, June 9, 12, 17. *Fall migration period:* Late July through early September, with a peak in late August and early September. Earliest dates: NORTH, July 16, 20, 25; SOUTH, *June 27, July 1, 13, 18*, 31, August 2, 3. Latest dates: NORTH, September 22, 28, 29, *October 8, 18*; SOUTH, October 1, 3, 6, *18, 28*.

RED PHALAROPE *(Phalaropus fulicaria)*

Minnesota status. Casual. Migrant.

Records. There are four records of this species in the fall and one in the spring. All are of individuals as follows: October 15, 1980, Minnesota Point, Duluth, St. Louis County (*The Loon* 53:60-61); October 29, 1976, Garrison, Crow Wing County (*The Loon* 49:44-45); November 12 to 19, 1977, Mille Lacs Lake, Mille Lacs County (*The Loon* 50:45-46); November 17, 1963, Knife River, Lake County (*The Loon* 36:25). The spring record is of a single bird seen at the Moorhead sewage lagoons, Clay County, from May 27 to 29, 1977 (*The Loon* 49:172-73).

POMARINE JAEGER *(Stercorarius pomarinus)*

Minnesota status. Casual. Migrant.
Records. There are approximately ten fall records and one spring record for this species; all are on Lake Superior in St. Louis County from Stony Point to Minnesota Point in the Duluth area. There may be more sightings of this species, but jaegers are extremely difficult to identify and observe (*The Loon* 54:46 48). The records for this species range from an early date of August 5 with other August dates on the 12th, 15th, and 17th. September observations were made on the 6th, 11th, and 16th. Late dates occur in October on the 11th, 14th, and 15th. The one spring record is for Minnesota Point, Duluth, on May 20, 1982 (*The Loon* 54:244).

PARASITIC JAEGER
(Stercorarius parasiticus)

Minnesota status. Regular. Migrant.
Migration. A rare fall migrant on Lake Superior, mainly in the Duluth area. Casual to accidental elsewhere in the state. There are fall records from the following counties: Jackson (specimen), Pipestone (specimen), Ramsey, Wabasha, Freeborn, Mille Lacs, Crow Wing, Aitkin, Clearwater, Lake of the Woods, and Cook. Single birds have been seen by fishermen on Lake of the Woods during September 1984 and 1985, indicating that the species may occur with the same frequency on this lake. In the Duluth area migration dates range from early August through late October, with the bulk of the observations in early to mid-September. Earliest dates: August 2, 3, 5. Latest dates: October 15, 16, 19, 27. Usually only single birds are observed, but occasionally two or three birds are seen together. There are five spring records, all from the Duluth

area: May 21, 1949; May 23, 1981; May 25, 1958; a specimen was picked up on Minnesota Point on June 1, 1969; and two birds were seen on June 2, 1983.

LONG-TAILED JAEGER
(Stercorarius longicaudus)

Minnesota status. Accidental.
Records. There are seven records for this species in the state. The only spring record is of an adult bird observed on April 12, 1962 on the Crow Wing River, Wadena County (*The Flicker* 34:54). Most unusual is the summer record: a single bird was collected near Warren, Marshall County, on July 1, 1898 (MMNH #8476). The five fall records are: August 24, 1981, two at Duluth (*The Loon* 54:64-65); September 16, 1961, Duluth (*The Flicker* 33:125-26); October 4, 1942, an immature female collected at Heron Lake, Jackson County (MMNH #8749); October 14, 15, 16, 1980, Duluth (*The Loon* 53:58-59); and an observation of an adult on November 16 or 17, 1934 at Dyers Lake, Cook County (Roberts, 1936).

LAUGHING GULL *(Larus atricilla)*

Minnesota status. Casual. Migrant.
Records. There are seven records of this species in the state, ranging from late May to early August. All of the records, with the two exceptions noted below, are from Lake Superior between Duluth and Stony Point in St. Louis County. The first record for the state was on August 16, 1975 when an immature bird was seen in a flock of Herring Gulls at Stony Point (*The Loon* 47:185-86). The first adults observed were two different individuals seen between May 20 and June 1, 1978 in the Duluth harbor area (*The Loon* 50:167-68). Also in 1978 an immature bird was seen by several observers at Stony Point on August 7 and again on August 26 (*The*

Loon 50:209-11). The next record was not until 1982, when an adult was seen by a number of observers at the Duluth harbor from May 18 to 22 (*The Loon* 54:241). On June 7, 1983 an adult was found on Sand Point, which extends into Lake Pepin at Frontenac, Goodhue County (*The Loon* 55:125). Subsequent observations in this area until June 15 revealed up to four adults and one sub-adult (*The Loon* 55:125-26). Most unusual was the observation of two birds on June 16, 1986 near Cherry Grove, Fillmore County (*The Loon* 58:137).

FRANKLIN'S GULL *(Larus pipixcan)*

Minnesota status. Regular. Migrant and summer resident.
Migration. A common spring and fall migrant in western and central regions and adjoining Nicollet County, becoming less common moving eastward. Rare to uncommon in the southeast and northeast and rare to absent over most of the north-central region except at Lake of the Woods, where it is seen in large numbers in the fall. Usually well represented in the east-central region in the fall. Casual or accidental in spring in the east. At peak migration it is not unusual to see thousands of birds in western and central parts of the state. Largest concentrations and migrating flocks are seen in the fall (12,000 Clay County, September 2, 1973; 5,000 Pine Curry Island, Lake of the Woods County, July 21, 1982; 5,000 Agassiz National Wildlife Refuge, Marshall County, September 30, 1984). Periodically large numbers move eastward in the state during the fall. *Spring migration period:* Mid-March through mid-May, with a few stragglers into June in nonbreeding areas. Peak numbers occur in late April. Earliest dates: SOUTH, March *5, 10,* 13, 14, 15; NORTH, March *2,* 29, April 5, 6; *Fall migration period:* Late July through late November, with the peak of migration in late September and early October. Latest dates: NORTH, November 4, 17, 21; SOUTH, November 23, 25, 27.

Franklin's Gull

Summer. Resident in western regions, breeding in large colonies that can fluctuate widely in numbers from year to year and over a period of years. At present the largest colony in the state is at Agassiz National Wildlife Refuge, Marshall County. Fluctuations in this colony can be seen from the following records: 1980, no nesting; 1981, 300 birds present, no nesting; 1982, 65,000 birds in the nesting colony; 1983, 35,000 birds in the nesting colony. In 1980 when the Agassiz Pool was dry and no nesting was reported on the refuge, portions of the colony moved to the nearby Thief Lake Wildlife Management Area, Marshall County. In May and June an estimated 5,000-10,000 pairs were present at Thief Lake. The only other presently known sporadic breeding location for this species is at Heron Lake, Jackson County. There were 100 nests found in 1985, and in 1986 this colony had increased to an estimated 2,000-3,000 nests. Large nesting concentrations have formerly been reported at Heron Lake: 50,000 in 1916 and 100,000 in 1937. Breeding has also been reported in Traverse (1942), Kandiyohi, Wilkin, and Clay Counties and at Lake Osakis, Todd County (five nests with eggs, May 27, 1981).

LITTLE GULL *(Larus minutus)*

Minnesota status. Regular. Migrant. Accidental in summer.
Migration. A very rare spring migrant on Lake Superior at Duluth, St. Louis County. There are two spring records away from Duluth: two adults were seen on Lake Pepin, Goodhue County, on the very early date of March 25, 1972. This was the first record for the state *(The Loon* 44:56). The other spring date is May 15, 1979 near Montrose, Wright County *(The Loon* 51:156). This species was recorded each spring in Duluth from 1973 through 1979 and again in 1981 and 1985. The species is accidental anywhere in the state in the fall: August 14 and 15, 1984, Worthington, Nobles County *(The Loon*

Little Gull

57:55); two records for Duluth, September 19, 1980 and September 29, 1981; Marshall, Lyon County, on October 19, 1975 (*The Loon* 48:38); Lake of the Woods, Lake of the Woods County, on October 24, 1984 (*The Loon* 56:265); and the latest date on record for the state, November 8, 1977 from Mille Lacs Lake, Mille Lacs County (*The Loon* 50:50). *Spring migration period* (at Duluth only): Earliest dates: May 9, 12, 18; Latest dates: June 6, 9, 17. Usually seen as individuals, but up to seven birds have been seen at one time in Duluth (May 27, 1973, three adults and four immatures).

Summer. A single bird was seen at Heron Lake, Jackson County, on July 2, 1985 (*The Loon* 57:177). In the latter part of May 1986 a single bird was seen by DNR personnel while investigating the Franklin's Gull colony at Heron Lake, Jackson County. In early June a pair was found and subsequently a nest containing three eggs was found and photographed. The nest was destroyed sometime in late June by high water (*The Loon* 58:166-70). The August 1984 dates listed for Worthington, Nobles County, and the July 1985 date may have been of birds that attempted to nest or succeeded in doing so at Heron Lake (*The Loon* 58:166-70).

COMMON BLACK-HEADED GULL
(Larus ridibundas)

Minnesota status. Accidental.
Records. A single adult bird was first seen on May 28, 1986 at North Heron Lake, Jackson County. The bird was seen in the large Franklin's Gull Colony present on the lake and was seen in close proximity to a pair of nesting Little Gulls. This individual was seen in the same area throughout June and July 1986 (*The Loon* 58:104-7).

BONAPARTE'S GULL *(Larus philadelphia)*

Minnesota status. Regular. Migrant and summer visitant.

Migration. Common migrant in central and portions of northern regions, occasionally abundant at Duluth and Mille Lacs Lake, rare in Cook and Lake Counties and the Red River Valley, uncommon to rare in southern regions. Concentrations occur regularly at Duluth in the spring (1,000 to 3,000 birds have been recorded), and at Mille Lacs Lake in the fall (200 to 500 birds are regularly seen; 1,000 on September 2, 1983, Crow Wing County). *Spring migration period:* Late March through early June, with a peak in early and mid-May. Earliest dates: SOUTH, March 26, 27, 30; NORTH, *March 27*, April *4, 6*, 13, 15, 18. Latest dates: SOUTH, May 13, 15, *31*; NORTH, none can be given because of summering birds. *Fall migration period:* Late July through late November, with the bulk of the migration in September. Earliest dates: NORTH, none can be given because of summering birds; SOUTH, July 22, 23, August 11 (only dates). Latest dates: NORTH, November 23, 24, 30, *December 2, 3, 6*; SOUTH, November 22, 27, 28.

Summer. There are midsummer (June 20 to July 20) records from Lake of the Woods, Leech Lake, and Duluth; these are of immature nonbreeding birds. By late July numbers increase in these areas as summering flocks are augmented by migrant birds. There are three records of immature birds in the southern part of the state: June 23, 1963, Grass Lake, Minneapolis, Hennepin County; June 29, 1975, Wright County; July 6, 1975, Split Rock Creek State Park, Pipestone County.

MEW GULL *(Larus canus)*

Minnesota status. Accidental.
Records. One adult bird was seen on September 19, 1982 at Knife Island, Lake County (*The Loon* 54:247-48).

RING-BILLED GULL *(Larus delawarensis)*

Minnesota status. Regular. Migrant and summer resident, and summer visitant; accidental in winter. **Migration.** Common to abundant spring and fall migrant throughout most of the state. Less common in some parts of the southeast and south-central regions in the southern portion of the state and north-central and northeast (Lake and Cook Counties) regions in the north. Normal peak flock counts during migration contain 300 to 800 birds, but peak daily counts can number up to several thousand birds (2,000, April 14, 1979, Cannon Lake, Rice County; 6,000, September 25, 1983, Lake of the Woods County). *Spring migration period:* Early March through late May, with the bulk of the migration in early April (adults) and in May (immature birds). Earliest dates: SOUTH, March 3, 4, 5; NORTH, March *10*, 25, 26, 28. *Fall migration period:* Mid-August through late December, with the bulk of the migration from mid-September through mid-October. Latest dates: NORTH, December 6, 12, 13, *January 1, 7*; SOUTH, December 13, 14, 18, *January 1, 2, 7.*

Summer. This species has been found breeding at five general locations in the state: Mille Lacs Lake, Mille Lacs County; Leech Lake, Cass County; the western tip of Lake Superior in the Duluth harbor area, St. Louis County; and Fourblock and Techout Islands, Lake of the Woods County. On June 16, 1984 three nests were found in Big Stone County at the Marsh Lake Pelican Colony. This may be the start of a new colony for this species. The colonies at Mille Lacs and Leech Lake are small, probably fewer than 100 nests at Mille Lacs and only a few nests on Leech Lake. There are no recent counts at either of these colonies. The colonies at Duluth and Lake of the Woods are very large. The colonies at Duluth started very modestly with one nest discovered in 1974 (*The Loon* 46:175-76) at the Port Terminal. Previous sporadic breeding had been reported in the area. Colonies are located at three points in the Duluth harbor, and a census taken in

Ring-billed Gull

1979 revealed 6,010 breeding adults in the area, phenomenal growth in a short period of time (*The Loon* 52:3-14). A survey done in 1971 in the Lake of the Woods area just east of the Northwest Angle located a total of 2,895 breeding pair on two different islands (*The Loon* 54:37-39). This species is also a summer visitant around many of the lakes in all parts of the state, but there is no breeding evidence other than that cited above.

Winter. The only winter records for this species are: one bird seen at Black Dog Lake, Dakota County, from December 1970 to February 1871; another bird in the same area from February 5 to 21, 1984; one bird at Duluth on February 12, 1984; a bird on February 16, 1984, Rochester, Olmsted County; and two in Wabasha County, February 21, 1984. The latter two records could be of extremely early spring migrants.

CALIFORNIA GULL *(Larus californicus)*

Minnesota status. Casual. Migrant.
Records. The first documented record for the state for this species was a single adult bird seen at Split Rock Creek State Park, Pipestone County, on May 30, 1975 (*The Loon* 47:130-31). In the fall the species has been documented at Mille Lacs Lake, Aitkin County, on September 9, 1976 (*The Loon* 49:56); Mille Lacs County on November 8-19, 1977 (*The Loon* 50:53-55); and in Crow Wing County on August 9, 1979. Other observations of this species in the state include three at Barnesville, Clay County, on April 10, 1978 (*The Loon* 50:123); one at Clinton, Big Stone County, on July 27, 1978 (*The Loon* 50:205). In 1984 one was seen at Agassiz National Wildlife Refuge, Marshall County, on April 12 (*The Loon* 56:194), and the first record for Duluth was of a single bird seen on November 25 and 27, 1984 (*The Loon* 57:60-61). The first record for the east-central area was a single first-year bird seen and later collected at Lake Harriet, Minneapolis, from November 5 to 15, 1985 (*The Loon* 58:16-18).

HERRING GULL *(Larus argentatus)*

Minnesota status. Regular. Migrant, summer resident, summer and winter visitant.

Migration. A common migrant in eastern and central regions, becoming locally abundant around large lakes and along the North Shore of Lake Superior. Uncommon in the western regions of the state, especially in the Red River Valley. Peak numbers occur in the northeast (western end of Lake Superior) in the fall and along the lower Mississippi River at the time of the fall freeze-up and spring thaw. Peak flocks can number anywhere from 1,000 to 5,000 birds in these areas, largest concentrations occurring in November. *Spring migration period:* Late February through late May, with the bulk of the migration from late March to mid-April. Earliest dates: SOUTH, February 19, 20, 24; NORTH (away from Lake Superior), *February 26, March 5*, 13, 14, 16. *Fall migration period:* Early September through early January, with the bulk of the migration in November. Latest dates: NORTH (away from Lake Superior), December 2, 5, 8, *16*; SOUTH, January 1, 2, 5.

Herring Gull

Summer. Summer resident on islands along the North Shore of Lake Superior and along the border lakes in the north-central region from Lake of the Woods to Cook County in the northeast, and also sparingly at Mille Lacs Lake. Nesting colonies along the North Shore number up to 1,400 nests or more. The largest colonies are at the Susie Islands and Taconite Harbor, Cook County, Silver Bay and Encampment Island, Lake County (*The Loon* 52:15-17). Around some of the larger lakes along the Canadian border there are colonies of up to 100 nests, but usually birds nest in isolated pairs or in small groups of up to 5 pairs. Small colonies of up to 200 birds have been found on the small islands in Lake of the Woods near the Northwest Angle (*The Loon* 54:37-39). A few nests were found in the Ring-billed Gull colony on Hennepin Island, Mille Lacs County, in 1968, 1969, and 1970, but there is no evidence of more recent nesting at this location.

This species is a summer visitant around many of the larger lakes throughout the state, usually non-breeding immature or subadult birds.

Winter. Common winter resident and winter visitant along the North Shore of Lake Superior during most years. Previously much more abundant in this area when there were open dumps near the shore of Lake Superior. Birds would number in the thousands at these locations during the winter. With the closing of these dumps, wintering numbers have dwindled. At present a few hundred winter in the Duluth and Grand Marais areas in most years, plus scattered smaller numbers at other locations along the North Shore. Can completely disappear from Lake Superior areas after severe cold. The species is accidental from January to mid-February away from Lake Superior, with records of one or two birds from Black Dog Lake, Dakota County (January 1 to February 20, 1971, January 1 to February 2, 1974, and January 19, 1980) and Rochester, Olmsted County (January 19, 1963).

THAYER'S GULL *(Larus thayeri)*

Minnesota status. Regular. Migrant and early winter visitant. This species, like the Iceland Gull, is very difficult to identify in the field. The Thayer's Gull was first identified in the state between Duluth, St. Louis County, and Two Harbors, Lake County, during the winter of 1970-71 and 1971-72 (*The Loon* 46:136-42). Over the last ten years this species has been recorded mainly as a migrant and winter visitant on Lake Superior and at Black Dog Lake, Dakota County.

Migration. A rare fall migrant along the North Shore of Lake Superior mainly in the Duluth area. In addition, there are a number of fall records from Black Dog Lake, Dakota County, where a large concentration of gulls occurs in November. There are also fall records in nearby Anoka, Hennepin, and Ramsey Counties. Rare in the spring along the North Shore of Lake Superior; most birds have left the area by late winter. Accidental to casual elsewhere in the state (little is known about movements in the spring), with records from Madison Lake, Blue Earth County, March 15, 1981; Boone Lake, Renville County, April 25, 1984; Wabasha, Wabasha County, April 30, 1986; Albert Lea Lake, Freeborn County, May 4, 1985; Lake Traverse, Traverse County, May 18, 1986; Heron Lake, Jackson County, May 28, 1986. *Fall migration period:* Late October to late November. Earliest dates: NORTH, October 15, 17, 19; SOUTH, November 14, 23 (only dates). *Spring migration period:* There are few data available on spring movements of this species. Most individuals have left the wintering areas by late February; however, there is a March 7 date for Duluth and a number of May dates mainly from Duluth, indicating a late-spring migration period originating from an unknown area. Latest dates: SOUTH, see above; NORTH, May 18, 20, 22 (only dates, all from Duluth).

Winter. An early winter visitant mainly on Lake Superior in December and January and at Black Dog Lake, Dakota County, in December. There are records at Black Dog Lake from December 2 to January 2; in Duluth there are records until February 1; and there is one record in Cook County until February 24.

ICELAND GULL *(Larus glaucoides)*

Minnesota status. Casual. Migrant and winter visitant.

Records. There are approximately 14 records in the state for this very difficult to identify species. A number of the early records are misidentifications of Thayer's Gulls. All but two of the records are from the North Shore of Lake Superior in St. Louis, Lake, and Cook Counties. They range from mid-November to mid-May: November 16, 1982, adult, Grand Marais, Cook County (*The Loon* 55:38); November 17, 1974, Gnesen Township, St. Louis County; December 2 and 9, 1986 an adult and immature, Grand Marais, Cook County (*The Loon*

59:54-55); what may have been the same individuals were seen at the Duluth dump in late December 1986; December 16-22, 1982, adult, Duluth (*The Loon* 55:33); January 2, 3, and 9, 1982, two adults, Duluth (*The Loon* 54:3-4); January 10, 1968, first winter, Knife River, Lake County (*The Loon* 41:26-27); January 15 and February 28, 1967, two immatures, Knife River, Lake County (*The Loon* 39:47-48); January 29, 1983, Duluth (*The Loon* 55:188-89); February 1 and March 14, 1976, first winter, Duluth; February 25, 1951, first winter, specimen (MMNH #10539), Duluth; February 28, 1967, second winter, Two Harbors, Lake County (*The Loon* 39:48); May 2, 5, and 18, 1978, second or third year, Duluth (*The Loon* 50:175-76). The only records away from Lake Superior are of an adult seen at Black Dog Lake, Dakota County, on November 18 and December 9, 1978 (*The Loon* 51:107-8), and one first winter bird seen on Lake Calhoun, Minneapolis, on December 8, 1986 (*The Loon* 59:55).

LESSER BLACK-BACKED GULL *(Larus fuscus)*

Minnesota status. Accidental.
Records. An adult was seen on Minnesota Point, Duluth, St. Louis County, on October 19 and 20, 1984 (*The Loon* 56:240-43).

GLAUCOUS GULL *(Larus hyperboreus)*

Minnesota status. Regular. Migrant and winter visitant.
Migration. An uncommon to rare spring and fall migrant in Duluth and along the North Shore of Lake Superior in Cook, Lake, and St. Louis Counties. Casual early winter (late November to early January) and spring migrant in the east-central region mainly in the Twin Cities area. There are records from Black Dog Lake, Dakota County, from an early date of November 21 and 26 to

Minnesota Specialties

No where else in North America for six consecutive winters (1979-80 to 1984-85) was the highly sought *Gyrfalcon* more easily found than in Duluth. Each winter different immatures were attracted to the harbor area by an abundance of prey (Rock Doves); as many as four Gyrs were present at one time or another in 1984-85.

Back in 1964 Minnesota had the environmental presence of mind to select a unique and thoroughly appropriate symbol of its Great North Woods and over 10,000 lakes—the *Common Loon.*

Probably the most elusive of all gallinaceous birds in the United States and Canada, *Spruce Grouse* have been uncharacteristically consistent at dawn in recent winters along the last four miles of Lake County, Road 2, as they pick at salt, gravel, and other grit in the road. In spite of its name, this species seems more closely associated with jack pines than with spruce.

Unlike the prairie-chicken, which typically is faithful to the same booming grounds year after year, *Sharp-tailed Grouse* are more elusive: their lek sites may change from year to year, even from day to day within a single season. Equally unpredictable is this species' habitat, some preferring the wide-open grasslands of the west, others at home in brushlands and tamaracks up north.

Decades ago agriculture was the ally of the *Greater Prairie-Chicken*; as the forests were cleared, this species spread into open country throughout most of the state. More recently, however, intensive farming practices have all but eliminated native prairie grasslands, and prairie-chickens are now confined to a few remnant tracts in northwestern Minnesota.

Yellow Rails may not be easy to see, but they are easily heard and surprisingly widespread in shallow marshes throughout much of northwestern and north-central Minnesota. Although this rail is sometimes heard by day, it is essentially nocturnal. Curiously, some nights when rails are known to be present in a marsh, its rhythmic ticking call is not heard.

Although not a characteristic Minnesota specialty, the *Ross' Gull* has wandered from the Arctic to be recorded in only five other states south of Canada. Apparently, this remote and little-known bird is attracted to ice on partially frozen lakes — once the ice is gone, so is the gull.

Grain spilled from elevators, railroad cars, and trucks in the Duluth harbor area attracts mice, rats, pigeons, and even a few pheasants. These, in turn, attract hawks and owls, most notably the *Snowy Owl*. In some years a dozen or more have wintered here; even in less productive years, this area typically hosts more Snowies than any other locale south of Canada.

Owls are typically elusive. However, the *Northern Hawk-Owl* couldn't be more cooperative; it hunts strictly by day, it prefers open country to concealing woodlands, it favors conspicuous perches in the manner of a kestrel or a shrike, and, once it appears somewhere in northern Minnesota (as happens most winters), the owl normally remains faithful to its locale for weeks at a time.

Although *Great Gray Owls* are usually thought of as a winter specialty of Minnesota, this species may be present at any season in the northern part of the state; nesting is recorded virtually every year. The Great Grays are more visible in winter, and every few years large incursions are noted. The largest was in 1983-84 when at least 122 individuals were counted.

This female *Boreal Owl* at her 1978 nest cavity along the Gunflint Trail in Cook County represents an ornithological event of historic proportions—the first documented breeding record of this species south of Canada. During that spring 15 territorial males were heard along the Gunflint; one or more Boreals have been heard there each spring since then. Winter sightings of this most elusive of all North American owls are rare, even during invasion years. During the amazing and unprecedented winter of 1977-78, however, they were hard to miss; 66 individuals were present.

Aside from the Boreal Owl, no permanent Minnesota resident is as difficult to find as the *Three-toed Woodpecker*. There are only a handful of nesting records, and it is usually impossible to find one of these birds on a given winter day. The best chance of seeing one is during a rare invasion winter, during fall migration along the North Shore of Lake Superior, or after a forest fire has left a burn in its wake.

Just as quiet and retiring as the Three-toed, the *Black-backed Woodpecker*, is, however, more widespread and easier to find in northern coniferous forests; chips of bark freshly scaled from a tree are often evidence that these woodpeckers are present. Migrants are also seen almost daily each October along the North Shore; as many as 14 individuals have been counted on a single day.

Perhaps no other species is as characteristic of the black spruce bog country of northern Minnesota as the *Yellow-bellied Flycatcher*. Yellow-throated or Yellow-breasted Flycatcher might have been more appropriate names, since other Empidonax species can also show some yellow on their bellies.

No other bird is as erratic in its wanderings as the *Bohemian Waxwing*. It is not unusual to see a flock feeding on buckthorn or mountain ash berries or crab apples one day and be gone the next once the food supply has been depleted. Bohemians are almost always in flocks, which often include hundreds of birds, and seldom in woods, since the fruit trees they rely on have been planted by humans.

Since the native grasslands of western Minnesota have been all but eliminated, the *Baird's Sparrow* can no longer be considered a regular Minnesota species. It is still occasionally seen, however, at the virgin prairies near Felton, although the individual in this record photo inexplicably turned up in Crow Wing County. Note the tail edged with white (field guides fail to mention this feature on Baird's and other grassland sparrows), the line emanating from the malar stripe streaks toward the spot on the ear coverts (only the Henslow's shares this facial pattern) the diagnostic tinge of pale orange on the crown spreading onto the nape, and the balanced proportions of the bill, head, and tail (unlike the Henslow's or Grasshopper Sparrows).

The *Wilson's Warbler* may not be a highly sought species, but it is a true Minnesota nesting specialty; no other state east of the Rockies and west of New England has a nesting record. (Similarly, the remote boreal forests of northeastern Minnesota host small breeding populations of two other species seen widely in migration: Solitary Sandpiper—only one other state south of Canada has recorded nesting—and Rusty Blackbird—only one other state south of Canada this side of New England has a nest record.)

Minnesota birders wishing to see a *Henslow's Sparrow* invariably head for O.L. Kipp State Park near Winona; no where else does this species occur consistently. Its range in the state remains unknown. Its song is easily overlooked, its habitat preferences defy easy explanation, and no one knows if the handful of records from west-central Minnesota are isolated from or contiguous with those far to the southeast.

There may be more elusive and more highly sought prairie species, but none enhance the beauty and mystique of native grasslands more than the *Chestnut-collared Longspur*. Its pattern of black, white, and chestnut is easily as handsome as the plumage of the most colorful warbler, and its skylarking song is as musical as any Horned Lark or Western Meadowlark.

Not only is the adult male *Pine Grosbeak* the most colorful of all winter residents (the White-winged Crossbill, also pink with black wings, is a close second, though lacking the grosbeak's counterpart of gray underparts), but it also has the most musical call—the loud, whistled notes can brighten even the coldest January day in the depths of winter.

It's often difficult, if not impossible, to separate Common from *Hoary Redpoll*; the two may prove to be conspecific. When in doubt about the identity of a marginally pale individual, it is safer to call it a Common, which generally outnumbers the Hoary in Minnesota by perhaps 50 or 100 to 1. It is better to wait for a classic and obvious Hoary: its upperparts are grayish rather than brown, its side streaks limited to nonexistent, its bill stubby, and both its rump and under-tail coverts pure white.

January 1 and 2, and spring dates of March 12, 17, and 30; Centerville Lake, Anoka County, November 19; Hennepin County, April 20 and 27; and additional records in Washington, Scott, and Ramsey Counties. Accidental elsewhere in the state, with fall records from Goodhue County (November 2, 1982) and Big Stone County (December 15, 1979). There are spring records from the following counties: Big Stone (March 15, 1973); Wabasha (March 30, 1981); Traverse (March 31, 1985); Roseau (April 9, 1927 [Roberts, 1932]); Freeborn (April 15, 1979); Goodhue (April 18, 1964); Houston (March 15, 1983); and Kandiyohi (April 22, 1966). Usually occur as individuals, but up to 15 birds have been found in concentrations of other gull species along the North Shore of Lake Superior. *Fall migration period:* (Lake Superior only): late October through mid-December, with a peak in late November. Immature and subadult birds appear first from late October to mid-November, followed by adults in late November. Earliest dates: October 26, 27, 31. *Spring migration period* (Lake Superior only): mid-March through late May, with no peak period noted. Adults depart first, most by mid-April; immatures and subadults linger into late May and early June. Latest dates: May 24, 27, 31, *June 1, 3, 6.*

Winter. Uncommon to rare winter visitant along the North Shore of Lake Superior in Cook, Lake, and St. Louis Counties. Found mainly at Duluth, where peak concentrations (mainly at the Duluth dump) of 10 to 15 (with one record count of 20) birds have occurred. Also found occasionally at Castle Danger, Lake County, and Grand Marais, Cook County, and where Herring Gull concentrations occur along the North Shore of Lake Superior. Disappears completely during some winters after very severe cold weather.

GREAT BLACK-BACKED GULL *(Larus marinus)*

Minnesota status. Accidental.
Records. There are nine records for the state, all from the Duluth area: September 3 through October

3, 1976 (*The Loon* 48:176); November 17, 1985 (*The Loon* 58:46); November 23, 1948 (*The Flicker* 21:63-64); December 16 to 22, 1982 (*The Loon* 55:32-33); January 3 to 9, 1982 (*The Loon* 54:66-67); January 20 and 21, 1983 (*The Loon* 55:85-86); March 15-29, 1986 (*The Loon* 58:93); April 30, 1962, photographed (*The Flicker* 34:99-100). During late December 1986 an adult bird was seen at the Duluth dump.

BLACK-LEGGED KITTIWAKE *(Rissa tridactyla)*

Minnesota status. Casual. Migrant.
Records. There are 11 records of individual birds in the state. Eight of the records are from early fall to early winter and two in late spring: August 11, 1984, Pipe Island, Leech Lake, Cass County (*The Loon* 56:271); September 11, 1983, Stony Point, St. Louis County (*The Loon* 55:179); September 12, 1978, Duluth (M. M. Carr, personal communication); October 26, 1984, Stony Point, St. Louis County (S. Wilson, personal communication); October 30,1976, Mille Lacs Lake, Crow Wing County (*The Loon* 48:189); November 20, 1980, Lakeside Township, Aitkin County, specimen (*The Loon* 53:55); November 20, 1983, Kettle River, Carlton County (*The Loon* 55:181); November 24, 1979, Grand Marais, Cook County (*The Loon* 53:52-53); December 15-16, 1964, Knife River, Lake County, photographed, first state record (*The Loon* 37:59-60); May 27-30, 1982, Duluth (*The Loon* 54:190). There is one summer record: June 11, 1982, Greenbush, Roseau County (*The Loon* 55:123).

ROSS' GULL *(Rhodostethia rosea)*

Minnesota status. Accidental.
Records. There is one record of this species, April 4-14, 1984 at Agassiz National Wildlife Refuge, Marshall County (*The Loon* 56:128).

SABINE'S GULL *(Xema sabini)*

Minnesota status. Casual. Migrant.
Records. There are ten records of individual birds in the state, nine of which are in the fall and one in the spring: August 30, 1975, Duluth *(The Loon* 47:186-87); on September 3, 17, and 18, 1985 a single bird was seen on Lake of the Woods, Lake of the Woods County *(The Loon* 57:180); September 9, 1984, Adams, Mower County *(The Loon* 56:265-66); September 12, 1978, Duluth *(The Loon* 50:221); September 24, 1984, Lake of the Woods, Lake of the Woods County *(The Loon* 56:266-67); October 1, 1944, Stillwater, Washington County *(Auk* 64:146-47); October 2, 1983, Lake Benton, Lincoln County *(The Loon* 55:178); October 12, 1980, Duluth *(The Loon* 51:142-44); October 17, 1982, Big Stone National Wildlife Refuge, Lac Qui Parle County *(The Loon* 55:30); May 26, 1979, Duluth *(The Loon* 51:142-44).

IVORY GULL *(Pagophila eburnea)*

Minnesota status. Accidental.
Records. There are approximately nine records of individual birds from Lake Superior in Cook, Lake, and St. Louis Counties from late October to mid-March: During the winter of 1970-71, there were three observations of possibly the same bird during February and March at three different locations along the North Shore of Lake Superior: October 28, 1970, north of the Onion River, Cook County; February 17, 1971, Duluth city dump; and March 14, 1971, Two Harbors, Lake County *(The Loon* 42:146). Other records are: December 1-21, 1976, Grand Marais, Cook County *(The Loon* 49:5-6); January 1, 1976, Duluth *(The Loon* 48:71); December 27, 1948, French River, St. Louis County *(The Flicker* 21:21); from late December 1966 to late January 1967, near Grand Portage, Cook County *(The Loon* 39:61); early January 1956, Two Harbors, Lake County (Mr. and Mrs. R. B. Evans,

notes in MMNH file); January 15, 1978, Duluth
(*The Loon* 50:49).

CASPIAN TERN *(Sterna caspia)*

Caspian Tern

Minnesota status. Regular. Migrant and summer
visitant; accidental summer breeder.
Migration. Common spring and fall migrant in
eastern regions and in central and north-central
regions. Uncommon at both seasons in south-central and all western regions. During peak migration
periods concentrations of over 200 birds (June 2,
1979, Duluth) have been recorded. *Spring migration period:* Late April through mid-June, with a
peak in late May and early June. Earliest dates:
SOUTH, April *16*, 21, 22, 23, 24; NORTH, April *11*,
30, May 2, 3. Latest dates: SOUTH, May 31, June
1, 2, *19, 22, 30*; NORTH, none can be given because
of summering birds. *Fall migration period:* Mid-July
through mid-October, no peak period noted; most
birds have left by mid-September. Earliest dates:
NORTH, none can be given because of summering
birds; SOUTH, July *8, 9*, 14, 24 (only dates in July).
Latest dates: NORTH, October 15, 16, 18, *25,
November 5*; SOUTH, October 11, 14, 17, *26, 27,
November 18*.
Summer. A few nonbreeding individuals remain
around the larger lakes, mainly in the north-central
region (especially Lake of the Woods) during June
and July. Occasionally seen around or near Mille
Lacs Lake. There is one breeding record for the
state: two nests were found in a Common Tern colony on Gull Island, Leech Lake, Cass County, on
July 9, 1969 (*The Loon* 41:83-84). During June 1985
there were 30 reports from 18 counties, mainly in
the northern half of the state, which may be an indication of future breeding on some of the larger
lakes in northern Minnesota.

SANDWICH TERN *(Sterna sandvicensis)*

Minnesota status. Accidental.
Records. On June 11, 1986 a single adult bird was
seen and photographed among the Common and
Caspian Terns at the Port Terminal, Duluth, St.
Louis County *(The Loon* 58:103-4).

COMMON TERN *(Sterna hirundo)*

Minnesota status. Regular. Migrant and summer
resident.
Migration. An uncommon spring migrant in eastern
and central regions; rare in Cook and Lake Counties and in western regions. Best represented in the
east; most often seen at or near breeding localities
in Duluth, Mille Lacs Lake, and other large lakes
in the north-central region. Uncommon to rare anywhere in the state in fall, seen mainly near breeding
localities. Because of the difficulty of separating this
species from the more widespread and common
Forster's Tern, a number of the migration dates
published for this species may be in error. The Common Tern is generally a later spring migrant than
the Forster's Tern. *Spring migration period:* Mid-
April (?) through early June, with a peak from mid
to late May. Earliest dates: south, April 16, 17, 18
(there are a number of published migration dates
between April 10 and 15, but these need verification); north, *April 27, 29,* May 1, 2, 3. *Fall migration period:* Early August through early October,
with the bulk of migration in early to mid-September. Latest dates: north, September 30, October
3, 6, *22, 23;* south, October 3, 11, 12, *21.*
Summer. At present, breeding occurs at four
general locations in the state; the Duluth harbor
area (three colonies, only 17 nests in 1985); Mille
Lacs Lake, Mille Lacs County (Hennepin and Spirit
Islands); Gull Island, Leech Lake, Cass County;
and Pine/Curry Islands and a number of smaller
islands in Lake of the Woods, Lake of the Woods
County. The colony at Gull Island numbered into

Common Tern

the 1,000s during the 1930s (Roberts 1932); its present status is unknown. From 1977 to 1984 pair counts at the Port Terminal area in Duluth varied from 146 (1983) to 227 (1981), with 100 in 1984. In 1963 this species bred in Becker County, and there may be small scattered nesting colonies on some of the large lakes in other areas in the northern part of the state. Scattered nonbreeding adults and immatures may also occur in northern areas. The presence of two birds on Sand Point, Frontenac, Goodhue County, on June 16, 1983, was an unusual occurrence.

ARCTIC TERN *(Sterna paradisaea)*

Minnesota status. Accidental.
Records. There are six spring records from late May to mid-June, all in the Duluth area: May 18, 1985 *(The Loon* 57:136); May 20-28, 1978, three different individuals *(The Loon* 50:173-75); May 27, 1973, three birds *(American Birds* 27:776); May 29 to June 2, 1983, four different individuals *(The Loon* 55:127); June 17, 1974 (personal communication, J. C. Green); June 6, 1985 (personal communication, N. Hiemenz).

FORSTER'S TERN *(Sterna forsteri)*

Forster's Tern

Minnesota status. Regular. Migrant and summer resident.
Migration. A common spring migrant west of the Mississippi River in southern, central, and western regions; uncommon in these areas in the fall. Rare to casual in spring in north-central and northeastern regions; casual in the fall in these areas. No peak concentrations noted. *Spring migration period:* Early April through mid-May, no peak period noted. Earliest dates: SOUTH, *March 31*, April 2, 4, 5; NORTH, April 14, 16, 17. *Fall migration period:* August through early October, no peak period

noted, with most birds departing by early September. Latest dates: NORTH, October 7, 8, 9, *14, 16, 18, 24;* SOUTH, October 9, 10, 14, *21.*

Summer. Local resident in western, south-central, east-central, and central regions. Small colonies are found in the Twin Cities area, the largest at Wood Lake in Richfield, Hennepin County. Up to 75 pair have nested in this area (1975). Large nesting colonies have also been reported at Heron Lake, Jackson County; Lake Osakis, Todd County (300 pair, 1984 and 1985); and at Agassiz National Wildlife Refuge, Marshall County. Rare to absent in southeast region; during a three-year study (1984-86) of the Mississippi River Valley on the Minnesota side from Goodhue to Houston Counties, only three nests of this species were found. The nests were found at the Weaver Marshes in Wabasha County, all in 1984.

LEAST TERN *(Sterna antillarum)*

Minnesota status. Casual. Migrant.
Records. Of the 11 records for the state, three have occurred in May, four in June, and four in August and September. Seven of the 11 records are in the southwest region (five in Lyon County!), two in the Twin Cities area: May 12 and 13, 1974, Marshall, Lyon County (*The Loon* 47:92); May 17, 1975, Marshall, Lyon County (*The Loon* 47:132-33); May 19-26, 1951, small flock at Mother Lake, Hennepin County (details on file); June 9, 1986, Duluth (*The Loon* 58:138); June 12 and 14, 1986, Rochester, Olmsted County, two different locations of what were probably the same bird (*The Loon* 58:129-30 and 144-45); June 14, 1975, near Adrian, Nobles County (*The Loon* 47:133); June 18, 1955, Moore Lake, Anoka County (details on file); August 10, 1978, Sham Lake, Lyon County (*The Loon* 50:220); August 11-14, 1985, Cottonwood, Lyon County (*The Loon* 58:48-49); September 11, 1965, Hendricks, Lincoln County (*The Loon* 38:40); September 26, 1970, Sham Lake, Lyon County (*The Loon* 43:25).

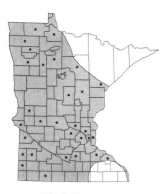

Black Tern

BLACK TERN *(Chlidonias niger)*

Minnesota status. Regular. Migrant and summer resident.

Migration. A common to abundant spring and fall migrant throughout the state, with the exception of Lake and Cook Counties in the northeast where it is casual to absent. It is a rare migrant in some parts of the southeast region (Olmsted, Fillmore, Dodge, and Mower Counties) away from the Mississippi River. Occurs in small loose flocks with migration peaks of 10 to 230 birds. Can be more abundant with hundreds of adults and immatures occurring at peak migration times, especially in the fall (August). *Spring migration period:* Late April through late May, with a peak in mid-May. Earliest dates: SOUTH, *March 22, 31, April 13*, 23, 24, 25; NORTH, April *19, 20*, 26, May 2, 5. *Fall migration period:* Mid-July through early October, with most birds leaving the state by mid-September. Latest dates: NORTH, September 27, October 1, 6, *28*; SOUTH, October 8, 10, 12, *27, November 7, 11.*

Summer. A resident throughout most of the state where suitable marsh habitat exists. The exceptions are the northeast where it is not known to breed in large portions of St. Louis and Koochiching Counties; it does not occur in Lake and Cook Counties, and it is rare to absent over the southeast region away from the Mississippi River. In the southeast it is decreasing as a breeding bird in the Mississippi River Valley.

DOVEKIE *(Alle alle)*

Minnesota status. Accidental.

Records. There are two November records (specimens) from the northern part of the state: November 5, 1962, near Grand Rapids, Itasca County (MMNH #18603); November 13, 1931, Lake of the Woods, Lake of the Woods County (MMNH #7820).

ANCIENT MURRELET
(Synthliboramphus antiquus)

Minnesota status. Accidental.
Records. There are six records for this species in the state, five in the fall in October and November, and one in winter in late February; October 1970, one bird was shot on Lake Kabetogama, St. Louis County (MMNH #27116); October 29, 1979, one bird was shot from a flock of Buffleheads on Lake Winnibegoshish, Cass County (*The Loon* 53:60); November 5, 1905, Lake Hook, McLeod County, specimen (MMNH #5947); November 14, 1961, Pelican Lake, Crow Wing County (MMNH #17658); November 22, 1950, Cutfoot Sioux Lake, Itasca County, specimen (MMNH #9639). The most unusual record is of a single bird found dead on Highway 371 at Ft. Ripley, Crow Wing County, on February 28, 1969 (*The Loon* 41:57).

ROCK DOVE *(Columba livia)*

Minnesota status. Regular. Introduced. Permanent resident.
Distribution. The original stock of this species consisted of domesticated birds introduced from Europe. Their wild and semi-wild descendants are found in cities and towns and around farm buildings throughout the state.

Rock Dove

BAND-TAILED PIGEON *(Columba fasciata)*

Minnesota status. Accidental.
Records. There are four records for the state, three in midsummer during June and July and one in the fall: June 12, 1971, Sand Dunes State Forest, Sherburne County (*The Loon* 43:57); June 23, 1975, St. Joseph, Stearns County (*The Loon* 47:186); July, 1969, near Morris, Stevens County (*The Loon* 41:68-69); September 18, 1982, Hawk Ridge, Duluth, St. Louis County (*The Loon* 54:249).

WHITE-WINGED DOVE *(Zenaida asiatica)*

Minnesota status. Accidental.
Records. A single bird was seen on October 13, 1985 at Duluth, St. Louis County (*The Loon* 58:92-93).

MOURNING DOVE *(Zenaida macroura)*

Mourning Dove

Minnesota status. Regular. Migrant and summer resident, regular in winter.
Migration. Common to abundant spring and fall migrant throughout the state except in the northeast and most of the north-central region, where it is uncommon. Usually seen as pairs or individuals in the spring, but flocking occurs in the fall when groups of ten to 20 or more are seen. Numbers appear to be reduced in recent years. *Spring migration period:* Early March through late April, with a peak in early April. Earliest dates: SOUTH, none can be given because of wintering birds, date of first arrivals being around March 10; NORTH, a few wintering birds occur in the north, making it difficult to give exact early arrival dates. They generally occur around March 20. *Fall migration period:* Fall flocking occurs in mid-July through August when birds are abundant in many areas of the state. The bulk of the population leaves the state in October. Latest dates: NORTH, a few birds winter in the northern regions, most migrants having left the area by mid-November, with a few stragglers into late December; SOUTH, none can be given because of wintering birds, the bulk of the population having left the state by late November.
Summer. A resident through the state except in the boreal forests of Cook, Lake, St. Louis, Koochiching, and Itasca Counties. The species reaches its greatest abundance in the wood lots and wind breaks of the southern and western regions.
Winter. A regular resident in suitable locations where food and water are available, mainly in southern localities. In recent years birds have begun to winter farther north with January and February

records as far north as Duluth in the east and Marshall and Polk Counties in the west. Usually winter as individuals around feeders in the south, but flocks of up to 30 or more birds have been recorded near farms in late December and early January. These numbers usually dwindle by late winter, indicating die-off or birds moving out of the area.

PASSENGER PIGEON *(Ectopistes migratorius)*

Minnesota status. Extinct.
Discussion. The demise of this species is too well known to need lengthy retelling here. The last bird died in the Cincinnati Zoological Gardens in 1914. Roberts (1932) summarized the Minnesota information: "An abundant summer resident throughout the state, breeding both irregularly in large colonies and regularly in isolated pairs in all wooded regions. The large spring flocks ceased arriving about 1880 and after that date (the species) diminished rapidly in numbers. There are no reliable records for the state since 1895." From existing records, it appears the species was most abundant in the deciduous woodlands of the southeast, central, and northwestern regions of the state. There are eight specimens from Minnesota in the Bell Museum of Natural History.

BLACK-BILLED CUCKOO
(Coccyzus erythropthalmus)

Minnesota status. Migrant and summer resident.
Migration. Uncommon spring and fall migrant throughout the state. Usually encountered as individuals. *Spring migration period:* Early May through early June, with a peak in late May. Earliest dates: SOUTH, *April 13, 22,* 29, May 1, 4; NORTH, May 9, 12, 13. *Fall migration period:* Early August through early October, no peak period noted. Latest dates: NORTH, October 3, 4, 5; SOUTH, October 3, 6, 10, *22.*

Black-billed Cuckoo

Summer. A widespread but never numerous resident throughout the state. Numbers vary from year to year, particularly in northern regions where it becomes numerous during outbreaks of tent caterpillars. There is one very late nesting record: young were found in a nest on September 8, 1974 in Sherburne County (*The Loon* 46:47).

YELLOW-BILLED CUCKOO
(Coccyzus americanus)

Yellow-billed Cuckoo

Minnesota status. Regular. Migrant and summer resident.

Migration. Uncommon spring and fall migrant in the southern half of the state and the northwestern region as far north as Marshall County. Rare to casual spring and fall migrant in the north-central and north-eastern regions. The population of this species appears to be spreading northward and eastward into the north-central and northeastern regions. Encountered as individuals. *Spring migration period:* Early May through early June, with a peak in late May. Earliest dates: SOUTH, May 6, 8, 11; NORTH, May *12, 18*, 28, 29, 30. *Fall migration period:* Early August through early October, no peak period noted. Latest dates: NORTH, September 18, 22, 24, *October 3, 4*; SOUTH, September 30, October 1, 2, *18, 21*.

Summer. Resident in the southern and central portions of the state and up the western edge of the state into the northwestern region and western edge of the north-central region, as far north as Marshall and Lake of the Woods Counties. Casual in the remainder of the north-central and east-central regions, and in all of the northeastern region. Best represented in the southeastern, south-central, and east-central regions.

GROOVE-BILLED ANI
(Crotogphaga sulcirostris)

Minnesota status. Accidental.
Records. There are nine records for the state, all but one in the fall for the months of September, October, and November. The one exception is a single bird seen on July 17, 1978 between Belgrade and Brooten, Stearns County (*The Loon* 52:185-86). The fall records are: September 17, 1959, near Ortonville, Big Stone County, specimen (MMNH #15765); October 5, 1973, Roseau River Wildlife Area, Roseau County (*The Loon* 46:34, 92-93); October 5, 1983, Lutsen, Cook County (*The Loon* 56:75); October 20, 1958, Nassau, Lac Qui Parle County, bird found dead (*The Flicker* 31:60); October 20, 1968, Woodbury Township, Washington County, one shot (*The Loon* 41:54); October 26, 1985, Avon, Stearns County, specimen (*The Loon* 57:178); October 27, 1975, Larsmont, Lake County (*The Loon* 48:73); November 7-12, 1983, Sleepy Eye, Brown County (*The Loon* 56:75). Roberts (1932) mentioned that one bird was collected (MMNH #8478) along the Mississippi River near Red Wing, Goodhue County, but it was subsequently discovered that the bird was shot on the Wisconsin side of the river (*Passenger Pigeon* 26:26-28). It is presumed that all of the above records are of the Groove-Billed Ani; however, the Stearns, Roseau, and Lake County records are considered ani (species?).

COMMON BARN-OWL *(Tyto alba)*

Minnesota status. Casual. This species has occurred at all seasons and has bred in the state; it formerly occurred more regularly.
Distribution and discussion. This species was formerly a rare to casual permanent resident in the southern part of the state. Roberts (1932) stated it "occurs irregularly and infrequently throughout the year." Since 1965 there have only been nine reliable

reports of the species in the state. In the early 1960s there were several reports from the southwestern (Cottonwood County), southeastern (Dodge County), and south-central (Steele and Watonwan Counties) regions, including a breeding record in Martin County, near Northrup, from September to November 1963 and a sight observation of one from Duluth in the northeast. The reports before 1960 are not continuous, making it difficult to determine the exact previous status of the species in the state. The majority of the records are from the southern half of the state. It is not certain whether the species has always been casual, with erratic periods of abundance, or whether it was a rare but regular permanent resident south of a line from Lac Qui Parle to Hennepin Counties. Earlier nesting records are from Martin (1923 and 1924) and Rice (1891) Counties. The species, it appears, has always been casual to accidental in the north; breeding-season observations include a family near Park Rapids, Hubbard County (1944), a pair near Lutsen, Cook County (1953), one in a barn near Waskish, Beltrami County, during the summer of 1980. All other previous northern reports are from the fall and winter, several in the late 1920s from Douglas to Roseau Counties; one in Duluth in 1960; again near Duluth (Hermantown) one was found dead in a barn in January 1984 (*The Loon* 56:195); and on August 20, 1986 an injured bird was turned over to a conservation officer in Crookston. The bird had gotten caught in a swather while a farmer was harvesting grain. The exact location was T151N R48W NW Section 5 Polk County (*The Loon* 59:47–48). Other recent records are September 3, 1973, near Blue Mounds State Park, Rock County (*The Loon* 46:37–39); October 20, 1975, Murray County (*The Loon* 48:40); March 14, 1978, Northfield, Rice County (*The Loon* 50:211–12); May 11, 1984, Wood Lake Nature Center, Richfield, Hennepin County (*The Loon* 56:159–60).

EASTERN SCREECH-OWL *(Otus asio)*

Minnesota status. Regular. Permanent resident.
Distribution. A permanent resident primarily in the
southern half of the state. There are records as far
north as southern St. Louis County (three old
records) in the northeastern region and southern
Itasca (Grand Rapids, one record) County in the
north-central region. In western regions the species
has been reported as far north as the Canadian
border in Roseau County; however, it is casual or
accidental anywhere north of Otter Tail, Aitkin,
Crow Wing, and Pine Counties. Breeding has been
confirmed from as far north as Washington and
Ramsey Counties in the east, Morrison County in
the central region, and in the west there is an old
(1921) breeding record from Crookston, Polk
County. Currently this species nests as far north as
Battle Lake in Otter Tail County. It is absent from
Cook, Lake, and St. Louis Counties in the northeast, from most of the north-central region except
for southern Aitkin and Crow Wing Counties and
the one record in Itasca County, as mentioned
above, and there are records from Clearwater
County. It was reported in Clay County during the
winter of 1984-85.

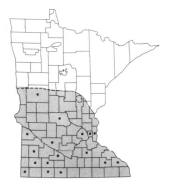

Eastern Screech-Owl

GREAT HORNED OWL *(Bubo virginianus)*

Minnesota status. Regular. Permanent resident.
Distribution. This species is found commonly in
every county in the state, with the exception of the
north-central region where it is uncommon, as it is
in the heavily forested portions of the northeast.
Most common in the southern half of the state.
Banding records indicate that birds in the northern

Great Horned Owl

third of the state are partially migratory, and many individuals may move away from this area during some winters. The Great Horned Owl is the most numerous breeding owl species in the state. The subspecies known as the Arctic Horned Owl is a casual winter visitant mainly in northern regions, but there are records as far south as the central region (Twin Cities area).

SNOWY OWL *(Nyctea scandiaca)*

Minnesota status. Regular. Migrant and winter visitant.

Migration. An uncommon fall migrant into the northern half of the state, numbers decreasing southward to the central part of the state where it is uncommon to rare and to the southern part of the state where it is casual to accidental. In spring rare to casual everywhere except in extreme northern areas. Birds gradually leave the state and head northward in late winter. This species invades the state periodically and numbers vary from year to year. During invasion years it usually arrives earlier in the fall and lingers later into the spring. Encountered as individuals. *Fall migration period:* Early October through mid-December. Earliest dates: NORTH, *September 13*, October 2, 4, 5; SOUTH (there is one early August date from 1927, exact date unknown, in Washington County published in Roberts [1932]), October 12, 16, 23. *Spring migration period:* Mid-February (possibly earlier in the south) through mid-April, with stragglers in May. Latest dates: SOUTH, April 11, 13, 14, *May 3, June 3* (this latter date is from 1890 in Meeker County and was published in Roberts [1932]); NORTH, May 9, 16, 18, *28*.

Winter. Rare to uncommon visitant mainly in the northern and central two-thirds of the state, casual in the southern one-third of the state. Best represented in the Duluth area, where 15 to 20 individuals may be found. A peak number of 23 were found there in mid-February 1982. Numbers vary from year to year and from place to place. Invasions may be localized or across wide areas of the state, mainly in the north, and occur two or three times a decade. A few individuals reach as far south as the Iowa border during invasion years.

NORTHERN HAWK-OWL *(Surnia ulula)*

Minnesota status. Regular. Migrant, winter visitant, and accidental summer resident.
Migration. A rare fall migrant into northern regions except in the northwest where it is casual; casual to accidental farther south. The most southerly record is one individual that was first seen in Wabasha County in mid-November 1962. In the west, it has been recorded as far south as Traverse County. In spring rare to casual across northern regions; birds gradually move northward out of the state by late winter. Numbers vary from year to year, with invasions occurring once to possibly twice per decade. Encountered as individuals. *Fall migration period:* Mid-October through late November, with earlier arrival dates during invasion years. Earliest dates: NORTH, *September 15, 23, 25*, October 6, 9, 10; SOUTH, October *12*, 20, 27, 31. *Spring migration period:* Mid-February through early April, with stragglers into May during invasion years. These stragglers in the north may represent breeding birds. Latest dates: SOUTH, March 12, 22, *May 21* (only dates); NORTH, May 2, 4, 6, *27*.
Winter. Rare visitant in the northern regions (casual in the northwest), especially in the Red Lake bog area of Lake of the Woods and Beltrami Counties, in the Sax-Zim area of St. Louis County, and in Aitkin County. Casual to accidental in central regions (Todd County, January 9, 1984) and accidental in southern regions. The species occurs in the central and south only during invasion years. The farthest south record is the above mentioned bird in Wabasha County, which remained in the area until late January 1963; it has been recorded as far south as Stevens County in the west. During

Northern Hawk-Owl

invasion years several birds may be found in areas of good habitat and abundant food supply. The most significant recent invasion occurred during the winter of 1962-63.

Summer. After major invasion years a few individuals remain in northern regions to breed. Breeding was reported in Norman County in 1885 and Roseau County in 1906 or 1907. Recent breeding has been recorded in St. Louis County in 1963 (*The Flicker* 35:129-34); in Lake of the Woods County in June 1980 (*The Loon* 54:182-85); and in Aitkin County in May 1980 (*The Loon* 53:138). Also in 1980 a single bird was seen near Waskish, Beltrami County, on July 13 (*The Loon* 53:53-54).

BURROWING OWL *(Athene cunicularia)*

Burrowing Owl

Minnesota status. Regular. Migrant and summer resident.

Migration. Rare migrant in the southwest and west-central regions. Casual in the northwest region, accidental elsewhere. There are recent accidental records from Duluth, St. Louis County (May 15, 1979), Blue Earth County (September 8, 1974), and Bay Lake, Crow Wing County (November 20, 1974), and Bay Lake, Crow Wing County (November 20, 1975). Most birds are observed on potential breeding areas but very few actually nest. This species was more common in the west-central and southwest regions in the 1920s and 1930s. It was especially well represented on the prairies of Lac Qui Parle County. However, because western Minnesota is on the eastern edge of the regular range of this species in the United States, numbers varied from year to year and period to period. With intensive agricultural practices and the heavy use of chemicals in agriculture, numbers of this species have been reduced over its whole range, including reduction in Minnesota. *Spring migration period:* Early April through late May, with most first arrivals in late April. Earliest dates: SOUTH, *March 26*, April 5, 7, 9; NORTH, April 10 (only date). *Fall migration period:* Most birds have left the breeding areas by late September. Latest dates: NORTH, no data; SOUTH, October 7, 14, 15, *December 14* (this latter date from 1893, Roberts [1932]). **Summer.** A very rare or casual resident in the southwest and west-central regions, as far north as Clay County in the northwest region. Since 1974 there have been only six documented nesting records: near Jeffers, Cottonwood County, 1974 (*The Loon* 46:171); Foster Township, Big Stone County, 1977; near Downer, Clay County, 1980 (*The Loon* 52:116); Hancock, Stevens County, 1981 (*The Loon* 53:227); near Hardwick, Rock County, 1982 and 1983 (*The Loon* 55:57, 56:56). Before the mid-1960s breeding had been recorded as far north as Mahnomen County and as far east as Jackson County in the southwest. A study done in the early 1960s in west-central Minnesota (*The Loon* 37:2-17) indicated that this species selects farmland habitats of short-cropped pastures populated by colonies of Richardson's Ground Squirrels.

BARRED OWL *(Strix varia)*

Minnesota status. Regular. Permanent resident.
Distribution. Resident throughout the more heavily wooded portions of the state; it is most often associated with mature bottomland, hardwood forests near lakes and rivers. Most numerous in southeast, east-central, central, and southern portions of the north-central regions. Least numerous and absent over wide areas in the western prairie regions and south-central region. Occasionally winter influxes occur, especially in the north, indicating that this species may be partially migratory in the state. During the winter of 1983-84 there were 63 individual reports of birds mainly in the east-central and southeastern regions. During the winter of 1984-85 individuals were recorded in Clay, Lac Qui Parle, Otter Tail, Lyon, and Cottonwood Counties, all in western regions.

Barred Owl

GREAT GRAY OWL *(Strix nebulosa)*

Great Gray Owl

Minnesota status. Regular. Migrant, winter visitant, and summer resident. A local permanent resident in the north.

Migration. A rare fall migrant across northern regions. The Great Gray Owl has no regular fall migration pattern. Irruptions, invasions, or just general southward movement can begin anytime from October through December. Numbers vary considerably from year to year, with invasions occurring at infrequent and irregular intervals. The largest invasions took place during 1968-1969, 1977-1978, and 1983-1984 (*The Loon* 56:143-47), beginning in October each year and concentrated mainly along the North Shore of Lake Superior. In spring little migrational movement is evident as most birds (nonresidents) leave the state gradually and are gone by mid-March. Birds seen in April or May are considered residents. This species is an accidental migrant in the central and east-central regions and in the eastern portions of the south-central region; there are records from Goodhue and Fillmore Counties in the southeast. It has been recorded in the southwest region and in most of the south-central and west-central regions. *Fall migration period:* Most migrant birds do not arrive until late October; August and September dates are probably resident birds. Earliest dates: NORTH, October 4, 10, 11, 15; SOUTH, no data. *Spring migration period:* A gradual exodus. Latest dates; SOUTH, March 5, 15, 23 (only dates); NORTH, difficult to determine because of resident birds.

Winter. Rare winter visitants in the north-central and northeast regions, becoming uncommon in localized areas during invasion years. Most regular within a hundred miles of the Canadian border. During years of major invasions individuals can be found as far south as the east-central region, mainly in the Twin Cities area. This occurred most recently during the winters of 1965-66, 1968-69, 1977-78, and 1983-84. There were 122 individuals recorded in March 1984. Accidental farther south. In the west, the species has been recorded as far south as Otter Tail County, February 1, 1976 (*The Loon* 49:101-2).

Summer. The first documented nest record for this species came in 1935 in Roseau County (*The Flicker* 7:17). Breeding has been recorded regularly in Roseau County since 1970. Breeding records have been documented in the north-central region in Lake of the Woods (six nests, 1984), Koochiching, Itasca, Cass, and Aitkin Counties; it is a regular summer resident in Aitkin County. In the northeast region there are breeding records from St. Louis County and summer sight observations from Cook, Lake (June 20, 1985, Whyte Road), and Carlton Counties. There are also summer sight observations in Clearwater (1966), Becker (1980), and, most unusual, one in Anoka County on June 11, 1981 (*The Loon* 53:173).

LONG-EARED OWL *(Asio otus)*

Minnesota status. Regular. Migrant, summer resident, and winter visitant.

Migration. As far as is known, a rare spring and fall migrant throughout the state except in the Duluth area in the fall. Banding records at Hawk Ridge, Duluth, during the fall (late August through late November) from 1972 to 1984 show 1,110 individuals banded (peak of 164 in 1978), an average of approximately 90 individuals per season. This indicates a regular migration through this area; whether this is true for the state as a whole is not known, but records certainly indicate Duluth is a focal point for this species' migration in the state. Because of the secretive habits of this species, it may be more common. *Spring migration period:* Probably early March through late April. Earliest dates: SOUTH, none can be given because of wintering birds; NORTH, *March 5, 20*, April 2, 11, 14. *Fall migration period:* Little is known other than records from Duluth, which indicate a migration period of mid-September to mid-November, with a peak in

Long-eared Owl

late October. Stragglers occur into December in both north and south regions. Latest dates: NORTH, December 3, 11, 12; SOUTH, none can be given because of wintering birds.

Summer. Local resident in the heavily wooded portions of east-central, central, north-central, and portions of the northwestern regions (known only from single nesting records at Ada, Norman County, Crookston, Polk County, and in Marshall County in the northwest). No records from the prairies in west-central, southwest, and south-central regions. There is one breeding record from 1978 in Watonwan County in the south-central region. Little is known about its presence in the southeast, but it is presumed to be a casual breeder. In the northeast there are nesting records from the Duluth area.

Winter. A rare but regular winter visitant in the southern part of the state, primarily in the east-central and southeast regions. In the northern half of the state it is a casual visitant, mainly in the Duluth area, where there are January and February records. There are also winter records from Moorhead, Clay County. Casual also in the southwest and west-central regions, with recent records in Redwood and Otter Tail Counties. Usually encountered as individuals but occasionally roosts of two to four birds can be found in pine plantations. It is not known whether these wintering birds are local residents or winter visitants from other areas; those seen on the prairie regions are most likely visitants.

Short-eared Owl

SHORT-EARED OWL *(Asio flammeus)*

Minnesota status. Regular. Migrant, summer resident, and winter visitant.

Migration. Primarily a rare to uncommon spring and fall migrant throughout the state, rare in the southeast, southwest, northeast, and north-central regions. Best represented in the northwestern and portions of the north-central regions, where it can be locally common at peak migration times. Normally encountered as individuals, but occasionally two to four are seen together. This species has declined dramatically in recent years all across the state. *Spring migration period:* Early March through late April; early spring dates for the south are difficult to give because of the presence of a few wintering birds, but generally they are early to mid-March. Earliest dates: SOUTH, March 7, 24, 25, 27; NORTH, March 2, 7, 12, 15, 16 (northwest). *Fall migration period:* Late September through early December, with the bulk of the migration in October. Latest dates: NORTH, November 23, 28, 30, December 4, 6; SOUTH, difficult to determine because of the presence of a few wintering birds. **Summer.** At present best represented in the northwestern and portions of the north-central region. Formerly more common. Recent breeding has been confirmed as far east as Hubbard and Aitkin Counties in the north-central region. In the west-central part of the state there is a recent (1978) nesting record for Chippewa County and old records from Meeker (1893) and Stearns (1940) Counties. In the southwest there are recent records from Rock County (1978) and an old record from Jackson County (1901). There are no breeding records in the eastern or south-central regions. There are breeding-season observations in St. Louis and Lake Counties in the northeast and Le Sueur and Martin Counties in the south-central region. There is much fluctuation in numbers of breeding birds from year to year, even in the main breeding range of this species. One year it may be well represented in an area, the next it may be absent. This is probably due to their need for a specific type of food, particularly voles (*The Loon* 54:98-99). **Winter.** An irregular and rare winter visitant. May be present in almost any region in the state when snow conditions and food supply conform to the species' needs. Most often seen in the southern part of the state, with recent December and February records in Dodge and Chippewa Counties, respectively. Occasionally birds are seen farther north, with January and February dates from Aitkin, Clearwater, southern St. Louis (Duluth), and Wilkin Counties.

BOREAL OWL *(Aegolius funereus)*

Boreal Owl

Minnesota status. Regular. Migrant, winter visitant, and summer resident.

Migration and winter. A regular but very rare migrant into northern regions, mainly the northeastern region in Cook, Lake, and St. Louis Counties. Casual farther south in the central region; accidental in the south and west. Like a number of other northern owl species, this species is subject to substantial variations in numbers from year to year. Winter invasions occur at irregular intervals into northern regions, with a few birds reaching into central and east-central regions. These invasions usually take place in late winter from mid-January through March, with many of the birds found dead or starving. The largest invasion on record occurred during the winter of 1977-78 when 66 individuals were recorded, mainly along the North Shore of Lake Superior in February and early March (*The Loon* 50:63-68). A large invasion also took place from November 1981 to April 1982 along the North Shore of Lake Superior, when 39 migrant and winter visitant observations were recorded (*The Loon* 54:176-77). There were other years of lesser invasions in the state. In 1963, nine were reported along the North Shore from February 15 to March 21. In 1966 there were 15 reports along the North Shore from January 9 to April 21. During the fall of 1976 eight Boreal Owls were trapped and banded at Hawk Ridge, Duluth, from October 22 to November 14. This was the first observation of a major fall migration of this species into the state. There were five records from the North Shore of Lake Superior and one from Agassiz National Wildlife Refuge, Marshall County, during the spring of 1977 (*The Loon* 49:166). The October 22 date was also the earliest fall date recorded for the species in the north. Migrations such as this had not been recorded in previous years, even though banding had been conducted at the Hawk Ridge site. The following indicate numbers banded since 1976: 1977 (5), 1978

(1), 1979 (2), 1980 (1), 1981 (2), 1984 (1). In all probability, these early migrations occur only at infrequent intervals; birds are usually not seen until mid-December. Most birds leave the state by late March, except in Cook County where breeding records exist (see Summer below). In central and southern regions there are records from the following counties: Isanti, Sherburne, Anoka, Hennepin, Ramsey, Carver, Renville, Nicollet, Le Sueur, Freeborn, and Fillmore. In the west from Kittson, Roseau, Marshall, Becker, and Mahnomen (February 14, 1985) Counties.

Summer. There are three positive breeding records for the state, all from Cook County; two of them occurred after major winter invasions. The first took place along the North Brule River during June and July 1978 (*The Loon* 51:20-27); another nest was found in June 1979 along a National Forest Service Road in Cook County (*The Loon* 51:198-99); and the third record came from north of Lutsen, Cook County, in May 1982 (*The Loon* 54:212-14). In recent years (the late '70s to the mid-'80s) Boreal Owls have been heard calling along the Gunflint Trail in Cook County. They are heard primarily from mid-April to early May but are occasionally heard in mid to late winter. As many as 15 were heard calling in this area in 1978 when one nest mentioned above was discovered. In early May 1986 birds were seen and heard in Lake County near Isabella. Numbers of calling birds vary from year to year, but a few can be heard every year during this period. A most unusual record is a bird heard calling in southern Itasca County on July 1, 1982. A singing male was heard July 12-29, 1985 nine miles north of Isabella, Lake County (*The Loon* 55:38-39) and in May 1983 in Roseau County. This was also after a major invasion in northern regions, so it is possible that this species is a rare nester or summer visitant in widely scattered areas of the northern regions.

NORTHERN SAW-WHET OWL
(Aegolius acadicus)

Northern Saw-whet Owl

Minnesota status. Regular. Migrant, summer resident, and winter visitant.

Migration. As far as is known, a rare spring and fall migrant throughout the state, except in the Duluth area in the fall. Banding records at Hawk Ridge, Duluth, during the fall (late August through late November) from 1972 to 1984 show 3,575 individuals banded, an average of approximately 275 individuals per season. A peak of 741 were banded in 1984, with a peak banding count of 131 occurring on October 20, 1984. This indicates that the species may be far more common than suspected in many areas of the state; however, Duluth is most likely a focal point for migration, as it is for many other birds of prey. Numbers vary from year to year, and, as for a number of owl species, there appear to be invasion years. But these seem to be less well defined in the Saw-whet Owl than in other owl species. *Spring migration period:* Late February (south and north) through early May (north), with a peak in April. Earliest dates: None can be given because of the presence of wintering birds throughout the state. *Fall migration period:* Mid-September through mid-November, with a peak in mid-October. Latest dates: None can be given because of wintering birds.

Summer. Resident throughout the more heavily wooded portions of the state from the southeast (very rare) to the northwest regions. Probably absent from most of the south-central, southwest, and west-central prairie regions where there are no nest records or breeding-season observations. The most recent (since 1980) breeding records have been in the following counties: Lake, Cook, Crow Wing, Norman, St. Louis, Lake of the Woods, and Beltrami, all in northern regions. Besides the counties where there is positive breeding information, breeding-season observations have been made in Hennepin, Winona, Aitkin, Hubbard, Cass, and

Lake of the Woods Counties.

Winter. A very rare winter visitant throughout the wooded portions of the state. There are records from both northern and southern areas. Casual to accidental in the southwest and west-central regions. It is presumed that the birds found in winter are visitants and not permanent residents, but that has not been fully confirmed. It is very difficult to determine the winter permanent resident range because of the species' silent and secretive habits in winter.

COMMON NIGHTHAWK *(Chordeiles minor)*

Minnesota status. Regular. Migrant and summer resident.

Migration. An abundant spring and fall migrant throughout the state. Largest migration flights occur in the fall, especially at Duluth and along the North Shore of Lake Superior where up to 1,000 birds per hour may be observed in late August. Extraordinary was a count of over 13,000 birds in one and one-half hours in Duluth on August 16, 1986 (*The Loon* 58:197). Concentrations do not occur in the spring. *Spring migration period:* Mid-April through late May, with the bulk of the migration in late May. Earliest dates: SOUTH, April *1, 10*, 15, 16, 20; NORTH, April *10, 16, 19, 30*, May 2, 3, 7. *Fall migration period:* Late July (north) through mid-October (south), with a peak in late August. Latest dates: NORTH, September 28, 29, 30, October *4, 12*; SOUTH, October 19, 20, 22.

Summer. Resident throughout the state. Most common around larger towns and cities where it nests on flat roofs of buildings. Also well represented in rural areas away from human habitation, where it nests in rocky openings in wooded areas.

Common Nighthawk

COMMON POORWILL *(Phalaenoptilus nuttallii)*

Minnesota status. Accidental.

Records. One bird was found almost dead on April

16, 1983 in Swift County (*The Flicker* 35:65-66) and subsequently was given to the Bell Museum of Natural History (MMNH #18903).

CHUCK-WILL'S WIDOW
(Caprimulgus carolinensis)

Minnesota status. Accidental.

Records. In July 1981 what was presumed to be an individual of this species was heard calling along County Road 11 in Sherburne County. The song was never positively identified. Positive identification was made at this same location during June and July 1982 when possibly two birds were heard and at least one of the individuals was seen by many observers (*The Loon* 54:139-41). One bird was back at the same location in June 1983 and June 1984. Another individual of this species was heard along the Minnesota River in Nicollet County on June 9, 1984 (*The Loon* 56:200).

WHIP-POOR-WILL *(Caprimulgus vociferus)*

Whip-poor-will

Minnesota status. Regular. Migrant and summer resident.

Migration. This very secretive species is seldom seen during migration. More often it is heard at or near breeding areas. Because it is seldom seen, it has been considered a rare spring and fall migrant throughout the wooded portions of the state, but numbers found in breeding areas would indicate that it is probably a more common migrant. Records indicate it is casual to rare in the southwest, west-central, and central regions. Quite local in occurrence. Little is known of its status in the fall because birds seldom sing at this season and thus are seldom reported. *Spring migration period:* Early April through late May, with a peak in early May. Earliest dates: south, April 9, 10, 12; north, April *12*, 22, 29, 30. *Fall migration period:* Early August through late September. Latest dates: north, September 26, 28, 29, *October 2*; south, September 28, October 2, 3.

Summer. A local resident throughout the more heavily wooded portions of the state (*The Loon* 57:6-7). Most numerous in the southeast along the Mississippi River and its major tributaries. Well represented on the Anoka Sand Plain area of Anoka and Isanti Counties and northward into the north-central and northwestern regions. Well represented but local in these areas. Absent to very rare and local in most of the northeast region. Not known to occur in most of the south-central and southwest regions or in the Red River Valley during the summer.

CHIMNEY SWIFT *(Chaetura pelagica)*

Minnesota status. Regular. Migrant and summer resident.

Migration. This species is a night migrant and is seldom seen as a migrant in the spring. In the fall roosting flocks and large gatherings are occasionally encountered. These flocks can consist of several hundred to 1,000 or more birds. Normally occurs around cities and towns where it appears after nocturnal migration flights. *Spring migration period:* Mid-April through late May, with a peak in early May. Earliest dates: SOUTH, April *8, 11*, 16, 17, 19; NORTH, April 25, 26, 29. *Fall migration period:* Mid-August through mid-October, with a peak in late September. Latest dates: NORTH, September 17, 20, 21, October *23, 26*; SOUTH, October 14, 17, 18, *26, 27, November 14*.

Chimney Swift

Summer. Abundant summer resident throughout most of the state; less common in the northwest corner of the state. Found in cities and towns where it nests near human habitations in chimneys and abandoned buildings. Also found in heavily wooded areas where it nests in hollow trees.

RUBY-THROATED HUMMINGBIRD
(Archilochus colubris)

Ruby-throated Hummingbird

Minnesota status. Regular. Migrant and summer resident.

Migration. A common spring and fall migrant throughout the state except in the southwestern region where it is uncommon in both seasons. Usually encountered as individuals in the spring. In the fall concentrations of ten or more birds may be found around feeding stations or where food is abundant. *Spring migration period:* Late April through early June, with a peak in late May. Earliest dates: SOUTH, April *12, 14*, 22, 23, 27; NORTH, *April 30*, May 4, 7, 8. *Fall migration period:* Early August through early October, with a peak in late August and early September. Latest dates: NORTH, October 6, 7, 9; SOUTH, October 6, 7, 8, *18, 28*.

Summer. A common resident in the northern part of the state. Numbers decrease southward in the state until it becomes rare to absent over much of the south-central and southwest regions. Seldom found in the Twin Cities area during the breeding season. Common around feeding stations in northern regions.

RUFOUS HUMMINGBIRD *(Selasphorus rufus)*

Minnesota status. Casual. Summer visitant and fall migrant.

Records. The first record of this species in the state was a single bird seen on August 4, 1974 at Grand Rapids, Itasca County (*The Loon* 46:167-68). The next records came in 1978 with birds being seen near Bemidji, Beltrami County, from September 6 through October 25 (specimen) and a single bird seen at a feeder in southern Washington County from late September to October 15 (*The Loon* 51:9-15). A single bird was seen in Alden Township, St. Louis County, on June 16, 1979 (*The Loon* 51:197). A single bird was seen at Cascade River State Park, Cook County, on July 30 and 31, 1985

(*The Loon* 57:177). The only record for the Twin
Cities area is a single bird seen in Bloomington,
Hennepin County, from October 13 to 25, 1980
(*The Loon* 52:187-88). The most recent observation
is of a single bird seen at a feeder, September 18-23,
1986 near Zumbro Falls, Wabasha County (*The
Loon* 58:200-201).

BELTED KINGFISHER *(Ceryle alcyon)*

Minnesota status. Regular. Migrant, summer resident, and winter visitant.
Migration. A common spring and fall migrant
throughout most of the state, uncommon in the
northwest. *Spring migration period:* Early March
through early May, with the bulk of the migration
in early to mid-April. Earliest dates: SOUTH, none
can be given because of wintering birds; NORTH,
March *19*, 25, 29, 30. *Fall migration period:*
September through late November. Latest dates:
NORTH, October 29, November 1, 8, *25, December
10* (Pennington County); SOUTH, none can be given
because of wintering birds.
Summer. Resident throughout the state wherever
there is suitable habitat, along small streams and
rivers; less common in the northwest region.
Winter. Overwinters from the Twin Cities area
southeastward to the Iowa border in the southeast
and south-central regions. Also seen in the southern
part of the central region and recently as far north
as Fergus Falls, Otter Tail County, in the west,
Stearns, Crow Wing, and Aitkin Counties in the
central portion of the state.

Belted Kingfisher

LEWIS' WOODPECKER *(Melanerpes lewis)*

Minnesota status. Accidental.
Records. A single bird was found in a small woods
just west of Santiago, Sherburne County, on December 28, 1974. This same individual remained in
the area all winter and into the spring. It was last
recorded on May 1, 1975 (*The Loon* 47:39-40).

RED-HEADED WOODPECKER
(Melanerpes erythrocephalus)

Red-headed Woodpecker

Minnesota status. Regular. Migrant, summer resident, and winter visitor.

Migration. A common spring and fall migrant in the southern half of the state and into the northwestern region. Decreasing in numbers northward into the north-central and northeastern regions where it is uncommon to rare. Absent over large areas of Koochiching, Itasca, and northern portions of St. Louis, Lake, and Cook Counties. Migrants in the northeast area are seen mainly along the North Shore of Lake Superior. *Spring migration period:* Late March (these could be wintering birds) through late May, with a peak in early May. Earliest dates: SOUTH, none can be given because of wintering birds; NORTH, April *10*, 20, 24, 26. *Fall migration period:* Early August through late October, with a peak in late August. Latest dates: NORTH, October 3, 4, 10, *16, November 17*; SOUTH, none can be given because of wintering birds.

Summer. A resident throughout the wooded portions of the state south and west of the northern boreal forests. In the northern forests it is occasionally present in less heavily wooded areas where openings have been created. Absent over large areas of the north-central region and most of the northeastern region.

Winter. Regular in winter in the southeast, south-central, east-central, and central regions as far north as Mille Lacs Lake (southern Crow Wing County) and as far west as Stearns County. The number of wintering birds varies from year to year, but occasionally it is common in oak woods in the southeast corner of the state. Casual as far north as Duluth in the east and Wadena County in the central part of the state. Generally it is unknown from western regions. There is one record on March 9, 1979 from Thief River Falls, Pennington County, indicating a wintering bird or an extremely early spring migrant. One bird was seen on February 24, 1984 at Lake Shetek, Murray County, indicating that a few birds may winter in the southwest region.

RED-BELLIED WOODPECKER
(Melanerpes carolinus)

Minnesota status. Regular. Permanent resident.
Distribution. Roberts (1932) stated that this species
had expanded its range into Minnesota in the early
part of the twentieth century; by 1930 it was found
breeding as far north as the Twin Cities area. In
the next 40 years this range had expanded as far
north as Mille Lacs Lake (Crow Wing County) and
as far west as the Des Moines River Drainage (Jackson County) but mainly as a visitant in fall, winter,
and spring, with little or no breeding evident in these
new areas of occurrence. Since the 1970s the range
of this species has continued to expand northward
and westward in the state, while remaining common
in areas of former expansion. At present it is a common resident in the southeast, south-central, east-
central, and central portions of the state as far north
as central Pine County, southern Aitkin and Crow
Wing Counties, westward to southern Todd and
Otter Tail Counties and up the Minnesota River
Valley to the western border of the state. In the
southwest it ranges to the western border of the state
in Rock (Rock River), Pipestone, and Lincoln
Counties primarily as a visitant in spring and fall.
In the spring and fall there are records for the
Duluth area and up the North Shore of Lake Super-
ior as far as Tofte and Grand Marais, Cook Coun-
ty. In the winter there are records as far north as
Warren, Marshall County (*The Loon* 47:192); Clay
County (December 7, 1981 to February 22, 1982;
January 1, 1985); Thief River Falls, Pennington
County (September 14, 1977 to January 2, 1978;
December 6, 1981; February 4 to 14, 1984; October
through November 1984; all during the winter of
1984-85); Duluth (December 20, 1981 and December 14, 1982). On January 12, 1985 one was seen
along the North Shore of Lake Superior in Lake
County, and two birds remained at a feeder in Her-
mantown, St. Louis County, until mid-December

Red-bellied Woodpecker

1984. There are no records for the northern portions of the north-central regions and many counties in the northwest region other than those mentioned above.

YELLOW-BELLIED SAPSUCKER
(Sphyrapicus varius)

Yellow-bellied Sapsucker

Minnesota status. Regular. Migrant and summer resident; casual in early winter.
Migration. Common spring and fall migrant throughout most of the state, less common in the southwest region. May be common anywhere in the state during peak migration periods. *Spring migration period:* Late March through early May, with a peak in mid-April. Earliest dates: SOUTH, February 29-March 1, March *3* (wintering birds?) *9,* 19, 20, 24; NORTH, *March 27*, April 3, 8, *9. Fall migration period:* late August through late October, with a peak in late September. Latest dates: NORTH, October 23, 24, 29 *November 10*; SOUTH, none can be given because of the many stragglers remaining into early winter; the majority of birds have left the state by late October.
Summer. Resident throughout the more heavily forested regions of the state; best represented in northern regions. Decreases rapidly south of the Minnesota River in south-central and southwest regions, although there are recent breeding records for Lyon (1975, 1984, 1985) and Cottonwood (1976) Counties and a sight record in Rock County (June 25, 1978).
Winter. There are early winter (December and early January) records for the Twin Cities area southward into the southeast and south-central regions and as far north as Stearns County: the latest dates are January 4, 1980, Mankato, Blue Earth County, and January 14, 1985, Roseville, Ramsey County. There is only one overwintering record: a pair at Pickwick, Winona County, during the winter of 1964-65. There is one late December record for Itasca State Park, Clearwater

County, in the north-central region, and one on January 1, 1972 at Windom, Cottonwood County, in the southwest region.

WILLIAMSON'S SAPSUCKER
(Sphyrapicus thyroideus)

Minnesota status. Accidental.
Records. There are two spring records for this western species in the state: April 22, 1972, Worthington, Nobles County (*The Loon* 44:52-53), and May 25, 1981, Winona, Winona County (*The Loon* 53:232-33).

DOWNY WOODPECKER *(Picoides pubescens)*

Minnesota status. Regular. Permanent resident.
Distribution. This species is a common resident throughout the state, breeding in all regions and occurring in winter. There is migrational movement of a northern race into the northern part of the state during the winter.

Downy Woodpecker

HAIRY WOODPECKER *(Picoides villosus)*

Minnesota status. Regular. Permanent resident.
Distribution. This species is a common resident throughout the state, breeding in all regions and occurring in winter in all regions. There is migrational movement of a northern race into the northern and central parts of the state from early October through late April.

Hairy Woodpecker

THREE-TOED WOODPECKER
(Picoides tridactylus)

Minnesota status. Regular. Winter visitant, casual summer visitant and resident.
Migration and winter. A very rare winter visitant

Three-toed Woodpecker

into the northeastern and north-central regions and casual as far south as Pine, Isanti, Washington, and Hennepin Counties in the east-central part of the state, Stearns County in the central region, and Becker County in the northwest region. The most southerly record is one at Carpenter Nature Center, Washington County, in late December 1981. Fall migrants usually enter the state in October, and most migrants have left by mid-April. During October 1985 there were records of 12 individuals at Hawk Ridge, Duluth, and Stony Point just northeast of Duluth along the North Shore of Lake Superior. Normally confined in winter to the northern parts of the northeast and north-central regions. Occasionally moves farther south—for example, from October 1974 to March 1975 up to seven individuals of this species were found near Platte Lake, Crow Wing County. During the winter of 1976-77 many individuals were reported in northern St. Louis County, and during the winter of 1982-83 many were reported in Cook, Lake, Itasca, and Beltrami Counties. A pair remained in a tamarack bog near Cuyuna, Crow Wing County, from November 1985 to February 1986, and a single individual was seen in a tamarack bog just north of Cambridge, Isanti County, during February 1986. **Summer.** Roberts (1932) reported a family group at Itasca State Park in 1902. It was not until June 1981 that the first nest of this species was found in the state, off the Gunflint Trail in Cook County (*The Loon* 53:221-22). This species is occasionally found in the summer in extreme northern areas from the Northwest Angle to Cook County along the Canadian border, with a few as far south as Itasca State Park. These records may indicate that it is an occasional breeder in extreme northern parts of the state.

BLACK-BACKED WOODPECKER
(Picoides arcticus)

Minnesota status. Regular. Permanent resident, migrant, and winter visitant.

Distribution. This species is a rare to locally uncommon resident in the coniferous forests of the northeast and north-central regions. Most numerous in the interior of Cook and Lake Counties. The breeding records are concentrated in this area plus northern St. Louis, Lake of the Woods, and Koochiching Counties, and Itasca State Park, Clearwater County. In these areas it is better represented during the winter months than during the summer, indicating migrational movement into the area during the fall and an exodus in the spring.

Black-backed Woodpecker

Migration and winter. An uncommon to rare spring and fall migrant mainly along the North Shore of Lake Superior as far south as Duluth. There is evidence of extensive migrational movement in the fall during some years. Most birds are seen from mid-October to early November. Fourteen were recorded at Hawk Ridge, Duluth, on October 16, 1982. During the fall of 1985 an unprecedented number were recorded moving south through Duluth in October (16 on October 16); there were a total of 71 individual records. When these large movements occur, the species is occasionally recorded south of the Coniferous Zone in the central and east-central regions in the fall and early winter. There are records as far south as the Twin Cities area of Anoka, Washington, Hennepin, Ramsey, and Dakota Counties. There are a few records of birds reaching even farther south and west: Rice County (November 25, 1981); Yellow Medicine County (December 12, 1888); most unusual, one bird at the Madelia Research Center, Watonwan County (February 8, 1968). In the spring there are two records from the southeast region: Goodhue County (April 20, 1935) and Winona County (May 4, 1957). In the central and west regions this species ranges to the edge of the prairie in winter to Stearns, Todd, Becker, Mahnomen, Marshall, and Roseau Counties. There are two records in Clay County in the Red River Valley: one in April 1938, the other in September 1950.

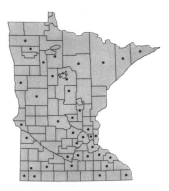

Northern Flicker

NORTHERN FLICKER *(Colaptes auratus)*

Minnesota status. Regular. Migrant, summer resident, and winter visitant.

Migration. Abundant spring and fall migrant throughout the state. Peak daily counts of 500 to 800 birds have been recorded, with a record high of 2,200+ in Duluth on September 20, 1985. *Spring migration period:* Late February through early May, with a peak in the second half of April. Earliest dates: SOUTH, none can be given because of wintering birds; NORTH, March 17, 22, 24. *Fall migration period:* Late August through late November, with a peak in late September and early October. Latest dates: None can be given because of stragglers and overwintering birds.

Summer. Resident throughout the state, widespread and rather evenly distributed everywhere.

Winter. Regular but uncommon throughout the southern half of the state; in the northern half rare from Duluth and Moorhead southward, casual to accidental farther north. One bird overwintered in Pennington County during the winter of 1984-85. The number of birds declines after mid-January, but the species has overwintered as far north as Cook County. It is not known whether the winter birds are lingering migrants or residents, but the former seems more likely.

Taxonomic note. There are numerous reports of flickers that have red or salmon-pink wing linings; most of these reports are from the western part of the state during migration or in the winter. A few of these reports give sufficient details for positive identification as Red-Shafted Flickers (C. a. cafer). One Red-Shafted Flicker wintered in Redwood County from October 1973 to mid-April, 1974 (*The Loon* 46:84-85).

PILEATED WOODPECKER *(Dryocopus pileatus)*

Minnesota status. Regular. Permanent resident.
Distribution. Uncommon to common permanent

resident in the eastern and central regions, decreasing in numbers moving westward in the state. Absent in most of the western tier of counties from Rock County in the southwest to Wilkin County in the west-central part of the state. Reaches close to the western edge of the state in the Minnesota River Valley in Lac Qui Parle County and in the northwest region from the eastern (forested) edge of Clay County to Kittson County. Best represented in the heavily forested river valleys and lake areas of the state.

Pileated Woodpecker

OLIVE-SIDED FLYCATCHER
(Contopus borealis)

Minnesota status. Regular. Migrant and summer resident.

Migration. An uncommon spring and fall migrant throughout the state. *Spring migration period:* Early May through mid-June, with stragglers even later in the south. Earliest dates: SOUTH, *April 30*, May 3, 5, 6; NORTH, May 6, 8, 10. Latest dates: SOUTH, June 11, 14, 18, *26, July 4*; NORTH, none can be given because of breeding birds. *Fall migration period:* Early August through very early October, with a peak in late August and early September. Earliest dates: NORTH, none can be given because of breeding birds; SOUTH, August 3, 6, 8. Latest dates: NORTH, September 18, 19, 21; SOUTH, October 1, 2, 5, *13, 20*.

Oliver-sided Flycatcher

Summer. Resident in the northeastern and north-central regions as far west as eastern Kittson, Marshall, and Becker Counties in the northwestern region. In the east there is breeding evidence as far south as Sturgeon Lake in northern Pine County.

WESTERN WOOD-PEWEE
(Contopus sordidulus)

Minnesota status. Accidental.
Records. There are five observations for the state,

Western Wood-Pewee

including one nesting record. The first record of this species in the state was of a single bird seen and heard on September 26, 1971 at Cottonwood, Lyon County (*The Loon* 44:115-16). On May 29, 1977 a nesting pair was found in Pelan Park in western Roseau County in the northwest corner of the state. The adults, nest, and young were seen by many observers until August 1, 1977 (*The Loon* 49:169-70). An individual was seen in this same area in June 1978, but nesting was not observed. On August 16, 1984 one bird was seen and heard near Duluth (*The Loon* 56:263-64). The most recent record is of a single bird seen and heard on August 25, 1985 in Clearwater County along the shore of Red Lake (*The Loon* 58:50).

EASTERN WOOD-PEWEE *(Contopus virens)*

Minnesota status. Regular. Migrant and summer resident.

Migration. Uncommon to common spring and fall migrant throughout the state; common only at migration peaks. Least common in western tier of counties in southwest and west-central regions. Encountered as individuals. *Spring migration period:* Late April through early June, with the bulk of the migration from mid to late May. (There are several early to mid-April dates assigned to this species, but these are probably the result of confusion with the Eastern Phoebe.) Earliest dates: SOUTH, April 21, 22, 25; NORTH, April *25, 29*, May 4, 5, 6. *Fall migration period:* Early August through early October. Latest dates: NORTH, September 26, 27, 28, *October 4*; SOUTH, October 5, 6, 8.

Summer. Resident throughout the wooded portions of the state, including groves in the prairie regions. Least common in the southwest region.

Eastern Wood-Pewee

YELLOW-BELLIED FLYCATCHER
(Empidonax flaviventris)

Minnesota status. Regular. Migrant and summer resident.

Migration. Uncommon spring and fall migrant throughout the state, occasionally common at migration peaks. Usually encountered as individuals, but loose groups of five to ten birds are seen at migration peaks. *Spring migration period:* Early May through early June, with a peak in late May. Earliest dates: SOUTH, April 30, May 2, 3; NORTH, May 6, 8, 10. Latest dates: SOUTH, June 8, 9, 10; NORTH, none can be given because of breeding birds. *Fall migration period:* Late July through late September, with the bulk of the migration from mid-August through early September. Earliest dates: NORTH, none can be given because of breeding birds; SOUTH, July *3, 9, 12,* 21, 29, 30. Latest dates: NORTH, September 15, 19, 20, *October 2;* SOUTH, September 26, 28, October 1, *11.* There is a record of an Empidonax Flycatcher, possibly this species, on November 24, 1973 in Minneapolis (see *The Loon* 46:39-40 and 47:48-49).

Summer. Resident in the coniferous forests of the northeast region as far south as Bruno, Pine County, and northern portions of the north-central region as far west as the Moose River in extreme eastern Marshall County. Best represented in northern Cook, Lake, St. Louis, Lake of the Woods, Koochiching, and Itasca Counties.

Yellow-bellied Flycatcher

ACADIAN FLYCATCHER *(Empidonax virescens)*

Minnesota status. Regular. Migrant and summer resident.

Migration. This species is seldom if ever recorded as a migrant. Individuals appear in breeding areas in late May or early June in the southeastern and east-central regions. It can be considered a very rare migrant in these regions. Earliest dates: May 16, 25, 31. Latest dates: August 20, 24, 27.

Acadian Flycatcher

Summer. In July 1967 a nesting pair was discovered in Beaver Creek Valley State Park, Houston County (*The Loon* 40:4-6). This record was not only the first breeding record for the state but the first confirmed record for the species in Minnesota, although there was a report of singing birds in 1940 along the Root River near Rushford, Houston County. This species has been regular during the breeding season at the Beaver Creek site from 1967 to the present (1986). In the 1970s this species began expanding its range northward and westward from the Houston County site. In June 1974 it was found nesting at Vasa, Goodhue County (*The Loon* 46:175) and was recorded in Nerstrand Woods State Park, Rice County. In 1975 birds were found at the Whitewater Wildlife Management Area, Winona County, and in 1976 they were found as far north as Franconia (Lawrence Creek), Chisago County, and as far west as Forestville State Park, Fillmore County. In June 1978 birds were found in Olmsted and Hennepin Counties. The species has been recorded on several occasions from 1982 to 1984 at Wolsfeld Woods, Hennepin County. In 1985 an individual was seen and heard throughout June and early July at Murphy-Hanrehan Park, Scott County, and in 1986 two nesting pair were found in the park during June and July. The above appears to be the present breeding range of this species in the state—Houston and Fillmore Counties in the south, north to Rice, Hennepin, and Chisago Counties; but it is regular only at Beaver Creek Park in Houston County.

ALDER FLYCATCHER *(Empidonax alnorum)*

Minnesota status. Regular. Migrant and summer resident. Because of the difficulty in separating this species from the Willow Flycatcher (E. traillii), the exact distribution of both species is rather poorly known in the state. A good summary of what was known of the ranges of both species up until 1981 is contained in an article by Robert M. Zink and Bruce A. Fall (*The Loon* 53:208-14). Little new information has been added since that time. Generally

Alder Flycatcher

the Willow Flycatcher is more southerly in distribution, the Alder more northerly, with a zone of overlap (sympatry) in the west-central and northwest regions.

Migration. An uncommon spring and fall migrant throughout the state. Migration appears to be from mid-May to early June. Early dates occur during the first week in May with two April dates (April 19, 1984, Aitkin County; April 29, 1975, Hennepin County) on record. There are two May 9 dates for the north (Otter Tail and Aitkin Counties). Records (by Janssen) from 1974 to 1983 indicate an early date of arrival of May 16, with an average arrival on May 23. There are late dates of June 9, 11, and 17 from the south. More data are needed to determine early arrival dates and peak migration periods in both the north and south. There are little or no data for the fall. Most birds have left breeding areas by late August. There is a late date of September 27, 1983 from Duluth.

Summer. Generally well represented in the northeastern, north-central, central, and east-central regions as far south as Chisago County and northern Anoka County in the east, Stearns County in the central region, and west to Otter Tail County in the west-central region. There is a zone of general overlap (sympatry) with the Willow Flycatcher along the southern and western edge of this range.

WILLOW FLYCATCHER *(Empidonax traillii)*

Minnesota status. Regular. Migrant and summer resident. See discussion under Alder Flycatcher.
Migration. An uncommon spring and fall migrant in the southern and western regions, rare in the far northwest. As in the Alder Flycatcher, migration appears to take place from early May to early June, with a peak in late May. This could be because the birds are more vocal at this time and more easily recorded. Early dates for this species occur during the last week in April and first week in May. Records (Janssen) from 1974 to 1983 indicate an

Willow Flycatcher

early arrival date of May 14, with an average arrival date of May 25. More data are needed to determine early arrival dates and peak migration periods. There are little or no data for the fall. There are two late dates in the southeast, Houston County, on October 4, 1983, and Fillmore County on October 2, 1985.

Summer. See *The Loon* 53:208-14 for breeding distribution data on this species. Generally well represented in the southern part of the state as far north as Chisago County in the east-central region, Stearns County in the central region, and in the west there are breeding records as far north as Marshall County in the northwest region. It has also been found as far north as Aitkin County in the north-central region. As mentioned under the Alder Flycatcher, there is a zone of overlap (sympatry) between the Willow and Alder Flycatcher. This occurs anywhere from Chisago County to Stearns County, west to Wilkin County, and north to Marshall County. It should be noted that there are records for the Willow Flycatcher as far north as southern St. Louis County in the east (probably strays) and Lake of the Woods, Roseau, and Kittson Counties in the central and western regions, respectively. However, breeding is not confirmed from these areas. Most birds have departed from breeding areas by late August.

LEAST FLYCATCHER *(Empidonax minimus)*

Minnesota status. Regular. Migrant and summer resident.

Migration. A common spring and fall migrant throughout the state. Usually encountered as individuals, but loose aggregations of five to ten birds are occasionally seen at peak migration periods. *Spring migration period:* Late April through late May, with a peak in mid-May. Earliest dates: SOUTH, April 20, 21, 22; NORTH, April *19*, 24, 28, 29. *Fall migration period:* Early August through early October, with the bulk of the migration from

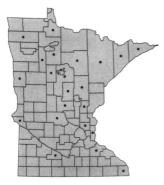

Least Flycatcher

late August through mid-September. Latest dates: NORTH, October 3, 6, 10; SOUTH, October 8, 10, 13.
Summer. Resident in the wooded portion of the state, including the groves on the prairies. Scarce to absent in many areas of the south-central and southwest regions.

BLACK PHOEBE *(Sayornis nigricans)*

Minnesota status. Accidental.
Records. There is one sight observation of this species in the state, September 13, 1952, Madison, Lac Qui Parle County (*The Flicker* 25:47-48).

EASTERN PHOEBE *(Sayornis phoebe)*

Minnesota status. Regular. Migrant and summer resident; accidental in early winter.
Migration. Uncommon spring and fall migrant throughout the state, least numerous in the south-west and west-central regions. Occasionally common at migration peaks in the eastern and central regions. Encountered as individuals, but loose aggregations of up to five birds may be seen at migration peaks. *Spring migration period:* Mid-March through very early May, with a peak in early April. Only in years of exceptionally early springs do birds arrive before late March. Earliest dates: SOUTH, March *3, 8*, 10, 11, 13; NORTH, March 28, 30, 31. *Fall migration period:* Late August through early November, with the bulk of the migration in September. Casual or accidental after late October. Latest dates: NORTH, October 2, 12, 13, *25*; SOUTH, November 9, 11, 13, *30* (*The Loon* 58:47).
Summer. A numerous summer resident, most common in northern regions. This species decreases in abundance southward in the state to where it is scarce to absent in large portions of the south-central and southwestern regions south of the Minnesota River.

Eastern Phoebe

SAY'S PHOEBE *(Sayornis saya)*

Minnesota status. Casual. Migrant. Accidental in summer.
Records. There are approximately ten records for this species during the spring (April and May) and fall (September) at widely scattered locations in the state. Seven of the records are from the far western tier of counties (Rock, Lac Qui Parle, Big Stone, Wilkin, and Clay) along the North and South Dakota border. The species has been recorded in three different years at Blue Mounds State Park in Rock County and nesting was suspected to have occurred in 1974. One or two birds were seen from April 13, 1974 to July 14, 1974 at the park *(The Loon* 47:13–15). One bird was seen on September 3, 1973 at Blue Mounds Park (K. Eckert). The records away from the western region are two from the North Shore of Lake Superior: French River, St. Louis County, on September 24, 1975 *(The Loon* 48:39) and Grand Marais, Cook County, on April 30, 1983 *(The Loon* 55:90). The first observation for the state occurred on September 3, 1963 at St. Charles, Winona County *(The Loon* 41:10-11).

VERMILION FLYCATCHER
(Pyrocephalus rubinus)

Minnesota status. Accidental.
Records. There is a single record of a bird seen and photographed at Elizabeth, Otter Tail County, on November 6 and 7, 1977 *(The Loon* 50:45).

GREAT CRESTED FLYCATCHER
(Myiarchus crinitus)

Minnesota status. Regular. Migrant and summer resident.
Migration. An uncommon to at times common spring and fall migrant throughout the state. Least numerous in the southwest (Rock and Pipestone

Counties) and northeast (Cook and Lake Counties) corners of the state. Normally encountered as individuals on breeding territories. Uncommon in the fall with a gradual exodus from breeding areas. *Spring migration period:* Late April to late May, with a peak in mid-May. Earliest dates: SOUTH, April *4*, 23, 25, 27; NORTH, *April 17*, May 4, 5, 7. *Fall migration period:* Early August through late September, with stragglers into late October. Latest dates: NORTH, October 5, 6, *16, 19, 22, 24, 26, 27* (all from the North Shore of Lake Superior); SOUTH, September 29, October 1, 2, *10, 16*.

Great Crested Flycatcher

Summer. Resident throughout the state except in the northeast (Cook and Lake Counties) and portions of the north-central region. Most numerous in the more heavily wooded regions near streams or lakes.

WESTERN KINGBIRD *(Tyrannus verticalis)*

Minnesota status. Regular. Migrant and summer resident.

Migration. An uncommon spring and fall migrant in western regions and eastward through the central and east-central regions. Casual over the northeastern and most of the north-central region except in Cass, Hubbard, and Wadena Counties. Absent or accidental over most of the southeast and south-central regions except in Brown and Le Sueur Counties. Usually encountered as individuals, but loose aggregations of five to 15 birds can be found at peak migration times in western areas. *Spring migration period:* Early May through early June, no peak period noted. Earliest dates: SOUTH, April *26, 30*, May 3, 4, 5; NORTH, May 3, 4, 6. *Fall migration period:* Early August through mid-September, with a peak in late August. Latest dates: NORTH, September 9, 12, 16, *24, 28, November 2-3*; SOUTH, September 12, 14, 17, *October 18 (banded)*.

Western Kingbird

Summer. A resident in western regions eastward through central and east-central regions. This species has a rather peculiar distribution in the state, and its absence from large areas which appear to be suitable for it are not easy to explain. Numbers fluctuate widely on the eastern edge of its range. There are breeding records and summer observations from the southwest corner of the state, Nobles County north to Chippewa County and eastward to Washington County on the Wisconsin border. It is represented in Anoka (Anoka Sand Plain) County northward through Morrison and Cass Counties to Roseau County. It is casual to accidental in summer over the remainder of the north-central region and all of the northeastern region. There is one record in Carlton County on June 7, 1983, probably a summer vagrant. Absent over the whole southeast and most of the south-central regions.

EASTERN KINGBIRD *(Tyrannus tyrannus)*

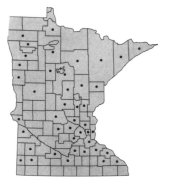

Eastern Kingbird

Minnesota status. Regular. Migrant and summer resident.
Migration. A common to occasionally abundant spring and fall migrant throughout the state. Usually encountered as individuals, but loose aggregations of ten to 20 birds may be seen at migration peaks. *Spring migration period:* Mid-April through late May, with the bulk of the migration in mid-May. Arrivals before late April are most unusual. Earliest dates: SOUTH, *March 30*, April *7*, 11, 15, 16; NORTH, April *10, 14, 17, 19*, 30, May 3, 4. *Fall migration period:* Early August through late September, with a peak in late August and early September. Latest dates: NORTH, September 21, 22, 26, *October 3, 9, 14, 15, 22, 24*; SOUTH, October 1, 4, 8, *15*.
Summer. Resident throughout the state, with breeding records from all regions in the state.

SCISSOR-TAILED FLYCATCHER
(Tyrannus forficatus)

Minnesota status. Casual. Spring and fall migrant; summer visitant.

Records. Spring and summer dates for this species range from late April through mid-July. Earliest date is April 27, 1983, Grand Portage, Cook County, and ranging to the only summer date of July 22, 1979, Moorhead, Clay County (*The Loon* 51:199). There are seven dates in the fall, ranging from August 10, 1963, Hennepin County (*The Flicker* 35:107) and August 18, 1984, Lake County (*The Loon* 57:35), with the rest of the dates in October: October 2, 1985, Grand Marais, Cook County; October 12, 1973, Duluth; October 23, 1958, Carlton County (specimen); October 23-26, 1982, Aitkin County; and October 24-28, 1975, Stony Point, St. Louis County. The majority of the spring records for the state are for northern regions, mainly in the northeast and north-central regions (Cook (2), Lake, St. Louis, Hubbard, Mille Lacs, Aitkin, Morrison, Becker, Norman, and Clay Counties); however, there are scattered records from many southern areas (Rock, Jackson, Olmsted, Winona, Hennepin, and Sibley Counties).

HORNED LARK *(Eremophila alpestris)*

Minnesota status. Regular. Migrant, summer resident, and winter visitant.
Migration. A common to abundant spring and fall migrant throughout the state except in the north-central region (Itasca and Koochiching Counties) and in the northeast away from Lake Superior where it is uncommon to rare. *Spring migration period:* Mid-January through mid-April, with the bulk of the migration from mid-February through late March. Earliest dates: SOUTH, none can be given because of wintering birds—first migrants usually arrive in early February; NORTH, *January 30,* February 10, 11, 12. *Fall migration period:* Mid-September through late November, with the bulk of the migration in October. Latest dates: NORTH, November 21, 25, 29, *December 16, 20*; SOUTH, none can be given because of wintering birds.
Summer. A resident throughout most of the state

Horned Lark

except in the heavily wooded portions of the north-east and north-central regions where it is absent. Most common on the western prairies and heavily cultivated regions in the south, central, and east-central regions.

Winter. Uncommon to occasionally common in winter in southern regions of the state as far north as Hennepin and Sherburne Counties in the east, Stearns County in the central region, and Big Stone County in the west. Does not occur north of these counties until after the first week in February nor after late November, except as noted above.

PURPLE MARTIN *(Progne subis)*

Purple Martin

Minnesota status. Regular. Migrant and summer resident.

Migration. A common to abundant spring and fall migrant throughout the state. Numbers have been decreasing in recent years. Large concentrations occur in the eastern part of the state during the fall premigration gatherings; 30,000 were estimated at Winona, Winona County, on August 14, 1981. Also, concentrations of thousands of birds occur at Duluth in the fall. *Spring migration period:* Late March through mid-May, with a peak in late April and early May. Earliest dates: SOUTH, *February 14 (specimen)*, March *8, 13*, 24, 27, 28; NORTH, April 7, 9, 10. *Fall migration period:* Late July through early October, with a peak in late August. Most birds are gone by mid-September. Latest dates: NORTH, September 12, 14, 17, *22, 26*; SOUTH, October 4, 6, 7, *15, 19, 21*.

Summer. Resident throughout the state. Most numerous in the Mississippi River Valley and in the central and western regions of the state, mainly in and around towns and cities.

TREE SWALLOW *(Tachycineta bicolor)*

Minnesota status. Regular. Migrant and summer resident.

Migration. An abundant spring and fall migrant throughout the state. Large premigration gatherings occur in the early fall in many parts of the state. These gatherings number in the thousands of birds: an estimated 20,000 were in Sherburne County on September 7, 1971; 2,000-3,000 were on Lake of the Woods on July 27, 1983. *Spring migration period:* Late March through early May, with a peak in mid to late April. Earliest dates: SOUTH, March *12*, 15, 17, 18; NORTH, March *22*, April 3, 4, 5. *Fall migration period:* Mid-July through carly November, with the bulk of the migration in August and September. Latest dates: NORTH, September 30, October 3, 9, *25, 26, 28, November 6*; SOUTH, November 3, 8, 9. **Summer.** Resident throughout the state; numerous in all regions.

Tree Swallow

VIOLET-GREEN SWALLOW
(Tachycineta thalassina)

Minnesota status. Accidental.
Records. There is one record for this western species; a pair was seen on October 25, 1942 at Rochester, Olmsted County (*The Auk* 60:455).

NORTHERN ROUGH-WINGED SWALLOW
(Stelgidopteryx serripennis)

Minnesota status. Regular. Migrant and summer resident.
Migration. A common spring and fall migrant in the southern, central, and northwestern regions; uncommon to rare in the spring and rare in the fall in the north-central and northeastern regions. Usually encountered in singles or in pairs. Occasionally large concentrations are seen in the fall migration: 200+ were seen at Monson Lake State Park, Swift County, on August 28, 1982. *Spring migration period:* Mid-April through mid-May, with a peak in late April. Earliest dates: SOUTH, *March 19*, April 4, 5, 9; NORTH, *April 8*, 14, 18, 19. *Fall migration period:* Mid-July through early October,

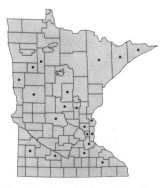

Northern Rough-winged Swallow

with a peak in early September. Latest dates: NORTH, September 18, 20, 29, *October 13, 19*; SOUTH, October 18, 20, 24.

Summer. Resident throughout the state. Numerous in the southern and central regions, and less numerous in the northern regions; scarce to absent over most of the northeastern region.

BANK SWALLOW *(Riparia riparia)*

Bank Swallow

Minnesota status. Regular. Migrant and summer resident.

Migration. A common spring and fall migrant throughout most of the state; uncommon in the north-central and northeastern regions. Large concentrations of up to 1,000 or more birds occur in the fall at peak migration periods. *Spring migration period:* Early April through mid-May, with a peak in late April. Earliest dates: SOUTH, April 5, 7, 8; NORTH, April 11, 16, 19. *Fall migration period:* Late July through early October, with the bulk of the migration in August. Latest dates: NORTH, September 27, 29, 30, October *3*; SOUTH, October 5, 8, 11.

Summer. Numerous resident throughout the state except in the heavily wooded portions of the northeast and north-central regions, though locally common around gravel and sand pits in these regions.

CLIFF SWALLOW *(Hirundo pyrrhonota)*

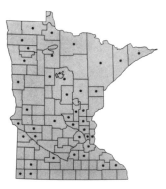

Cliff Swallow

Minnesota status. Regular. Migrant and summer resident.

Migration. Common to at times abundant spring and fall migrant throughout the state. Most numerous in the northwestern region, least numerous in the southwestern and south-central regions. Concentrations of up to several hundred birds occur during peak migration periods, especially in the fall. The amazing total of an estimated 2,000-3,000 were at Lake of the Woods on July 27, 1983. *Spring migration period:* Mid-April through late May, with a peak in early May. Earliest dates: south, April *6, 13*, 21, 22, 23; north, April *14*, 19, 20, 24. *Fall migration period:* Late July through early October, with a peak in early September. Latest dates: north, September 21, 27, 28; south, October 9, 10, 14.

Summer. A resident throughout the state. With the advent of the use of corrugated culverts as underpasses for streams in the western parts of the state, especially the northwestern region, the Cliff Swallow has increased tremendously in recent years as a breeding species in the state. Large nesting colonies numbering in the hundreds of pairs occur across the northern regions, especially in the northwest and north-central regions. They are especially abundant in Marshall and St. Louis Counties. Least numerous in the southwest and south-central regions.

BARN SWALLOW *(Hirundo rustica)*

Minnesota status. Regular. Migrant and summer resident.

Migration. A common to abundant spring and fall migrant throughout the state; especially abundant in the western regions. Concentrations of hundreds of birds occur at peak migration periods, especially in the fall. *Spring migration period:* Early April through late May, with a peak in late April. Earliest dates: south, *March 23, 31*, April 1, 3, 5; north, April 14, 17, 19. *Fall migration period:* Late July through late October, with the bulk of the migration in September. Latest dates: north, October 19, 25, 31, *November 2* (Paradise Beach, Cook County [*The Loon* 47:46]); south, October 29, 30, November 1, *12*.

Summer. Resident throughout the state. Most numerous in western and central regions; least numerous in the heavily wooded portions of north-central and northeastern regions.

Barn Swallow

GRAY JAY *(Perisoreus canadensis)*

Gray Jay

Minnesota status. Regular. Primarily a permanent resident; also an erratic fall migrant and early winter visitant.

Distribution. An uncommon to common permanent resident in the northeastern and north-central regions as far south as southern Carlton County in the east, southern Aitkin and northern Cass Counties in the central part of the state, to eastern Marshall and eastern Roseau Counties in the west. Most numerous in northern portions of this range. Usually encountered as individuals, but groups of six or more birds are occasionally seen.

Migration. Irregular fall irruptions are most noticeable along the North Shore of Lake Superior in St. Louis County. Roberts's *The Birds of Minnesota* mentions one invasion, that in the fall and winter of 1929-30 when a "considerable number wandered south" during the fall, with individuals "reported from many places" in the Twin Cities area throughout the winter. During fall and winter 1965-66 a southerly movement took place during October and November, with records as far south as Stillwater in November and St. Paul in January. These movements begin in mid-September, peak in October, and usually end by late November. During irruptions the species is common in the north-central and northeastern regions, and occasionally uncommon in the northern portions of the central and east-central regions. Birds reach as far south as the Twin Cities area in the eastern part of the state, Stearns County in the central region, and Clay County in the west. In 1974 birds were recorded as far south as Pine, Chisago, and Dakota Counties. A major southward invasion took place during the fall and early winter of 1976-77. Reports were received from Anoka, Hennepin, Ramsey, Washington, Sherburne, Stearns, Kanabec, Otter Tail, and Polk Counties; the most southerly sightings for the state were in Olmsted County in the east and Swift and Lac Qui Parle Counties in the west. A considerable westward movement was noted during November 1984 when there were numerous records in the Red River Valley in the northwest from Norman to Kittson Counties. In 1985 a single bird was recorded at a feeder in Shoreview, Ramsey County, from November 21 to December 21 (*The Loon* 58:49). No movement after mid-December has been noted. It would appear that irruptions occur in the fall, and birds return northward by mid-December. One bird wintered at Collegeville, Stearns County, during 1966-67, and another was seen there in late December 1981. The fall of 1986 produced the largest invasion on record, with no fewer than 452 individuals counted within the city limits of Duluth and along the North Shore as far as the Lake County line. The beginning of the flight became evident during mid-September (*The Loon* 59:41-44). By early October birds were as far south as Pine County, and one was recorded as far south as Murphy-Hanrehan Park, Scott County, on October 23. This was the southern-most record. During October and November 1986 birds were also recorded in Kanabec, Isanti, Mille Lacs, Chisago, Anoka, Hennepin, Ramsey, Wright, Washington, and Dakota Counties.

BLUE JAY *(Cyanactta cristata)*

Minnesota status. Regular. Permanent resident and migrant.
Distribution. A permanent resident throughout the state, breeding in all regions. In a study done in Anoka County in 1980, 121 nests were found in a one square-mile area (*The Loon* 52:146-49). Less numerous in northern regions in winter. It is not known conclusively whether the winter population in any area of the state is the same as the summer population.
Migration. A common to abundant spring and fall migrant throughout most of the state; most numerous as a migrant in northern regions in Duluth and along the North Shore of Lake Superior, especially in the fall. Studies done on this species in other areas suggest that many young birds of the year migrate

Blue Jay

out of areas where they were hatched. This movement of young birds probably takes place in northern regions; the majority of the adult population also moves out of northern areas in the fall and early winter, and birds return to these regions in the spring. The bulk of the migration in the fall is during September and October, and in the spring from early to mid-May.

CLARK'S NUTCRACKER
(Nucifraga columbiana)

Minnesota status. Accidental.

Records. All but one of the records are from September (earliest dates: September 8, 9, 12) through December (latest dates: December 6, 18, 24). Incursions from the west occur at infrequent intervals. Major incursions resulting in four or five individual records took place in 1894 (southwestern region), 1969 (northeastern region), and 1972 (in Cook, Itasca, Stearns, Hennepin, and Lyon Counties). In December 1973 one bird was seen at Tracy, Lyon County (*The Loon* 46:86), and in 1977 there were two records, one in Duluth on December 3 (*The Loon* 50:119) and the other in Minneapolis on December 24 (*The Loon* 50:120). There is one record of an individual overwintering at Christmas Lake, Hennepin County, from November 20, 1972 to April 8, 1973 (*The Loon* 45:20-21). The most recent record is of a single bird seen on September 13, 1986 at Austin in Mower County (*The Loon* 58: 199).

BLACK-BILLED MAGPIE (*Pica pica*)

Minnesota status. Regular. Permanent resident; migrant and winter visitant.

Distribution. During the past 25 to 30 years this species has become a permanent resident in the northwestern and north-central regions and into St. Louis County in the northeastern region. Breeding

has been recorded as far south as Clay and Norman Counties in the west and the Meadowlands
area in south-central St. Louis County and Tower-
Soudan State Park (June 1984) in northern St.
Louis County (*The Loon* 46:174-75). One bird was
seen on July 25, 1983 as far east as Cook County.
The primary resident range of this species is in the
northwest corner of the state in Kittson, Roseau,
Lake of the Woods, Marshall, Pennington, Red
Lake, and Polk Counties. There is one summer
record away from the breeding range, that of a
single bird seen July 9-13, 1979 at Big Stone National Wildlife Refuge, Lac Qui Parle County.

Black-billed Magpie

Migration and winter. Formerly this species was
considered to be a fall migrant and winter visitant
into the western regions of the state, primarily the
northwestern and southwestern regions. Invasions
occurred at infrequent intervals: those recorded in
the 1920s and 1930s came into the state from the
southwest; since the 1940s migrations and invasions
have come from the northwest. A major invasion
of this species occurred during the fall and winter
of 1972-1973. Over 200 reports of individuals were
recorded from late August to December 1972. Birds
reached the southwestern part of the state as far east
as Carver, Goodhue, Le Sueur, Dodge (December
30, 1972), and Steele (January 5, 1973) Counties.
During this invasion birds ranged as far east as
Cook and Aitkin Counties in the north and as far
south as Big Stone and Cottonwood Counties in the
west; hundreds of individuals were seen in the
northwest corner of the state during the same period
(*The Loon* 45:14). During the fall of 1973 another
minor invasion brought birds as far east as Morrison County. In 1974 birds were seen in the fall
and winter as far east as Hennepin County. Again,
in the fall of 1976 a major invasion occurred, but
this was mainly restricted to the northwest and adjacent counties in the north-central (Hubbard, Cass,
and Aitkin) and west-central (Otter Tail) regions.
However, a few birds did get as far south as Chippewa and Lac Qui Parle Counties. During these invasion years the first birds show up in late August,

with peak numbers in October. In the spring strag-glers remain until late May in nonbreeding areas.

AMERICAN CROW *(Corvus brachyrhynchos)*

American Crow

Minnesota status. Regular. Migrant and summer resident; regular in winter. Probably a permanent resident in most areas.

Migration. Abundant spring and fall migrant throughout the state. Least numerous in the boreal forests of the northeastern and north-central regions, but still abundant in these areas. Encountered in small groups of three to five birds or in larger flocks numbering into the hundreds. *Spring migration period:* Early February through mid-April, with the bulk of the migration in March. Earliest dates: None can be given becuase of wintering birds. *Fall migration period:* August through late November, with stragglers present into early winter in northern areas; the bulk of the migration is from mid-September through late October. Latest dates: None can be given because of wintering birds.

Summer. A resident throughout the state; numerous in all regions.

Winter. Common in winter in the southern half of the state; moving northward numbers decrease, but wintering numbers have been increasing along the North Shore of Lake Superior and across the whole northern part of the state. It would be considered uncommon to rare in the north-central and north-western regions. It is not known whether wintering flocks are local summer residents or are birds that have come from other areas.

COMMON RAVEN *(Corvus corax)*

Minnesota status. Regular. Permanent resident and migrant.

Distribution. A well-represented permanent resident primarily in the northeastern region as far south as northern Pine County in the east-central region and northern Mille Lacs County in the central region; becoming less common in the north-central regions as far south as central Aitkin and northern Cass and Wadena Counties. Uncommon in the northwestern region in eastern Polk (one on December 17, 1983 at Crookston), Red Lake, Pennington, Marshall, and Kittson Counties. Numbers of this species have been increasing across this range since the 1950s, and it appears to be expanding westward and very slowly southward. Concentrations of up to 50 or more birds are found in the winter at prime feeding areas (dumps), especially along the North Shore of Lake Superior.

Common Raven

Migration. A common fall migrant along the North Shore of Lake Superior. Many are seen at Hawk Ridge, Duluth, during the hawk-count period (September through November). However, it is not known where these birds are migrating to. There is no reported influx of birds into central regions of the state, although birds are found farther south in the winter along the southern and western edge of its range (Pine, Kanabec, Crow Wing, Becker, and Mahnomen Counties). There are a few scattered reports of migrant birds in the St. Croix River Valley (Chisago and Washington Counties, the latest and most unusual date being May 18, 1985 in Washington County) and the Mississippi River Valley (May 16, 1976, Frontenac State Park, Goodhue County [*The Loon* 48:80]; October 26, 1974, Hennepin County [*The Loon* 48:80]; one in Anoka County on April 4, 1985; two on March 8, 1986, Anoka County; and one bird was reported in Winona County on March 26, 1982). Some observers in LaCrosse, Wisconsin just across the Mississippi River from Houston County, Minnesota report this species as a regular but rare spring and fall migrant in the Mississippi River Valley. There is no evidence of this movement from Minnesota observers other than the records mentioned above.

BLACK-CAPPED CHICKADEE
(Parus atricapillus)

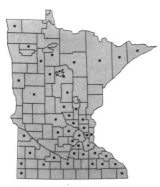

Black-capped Chickadee

Minnesota status. Regular. Permanent resident and migrant.

Distribution. A common to abundant permanent resident breeding throughout the state. Usually encountered in pairs or in small family groups of up to ten birds. In winter large groups of up to 30 or 40 birds are found around abundant food sources.

Migration. During spring and fall migration periods small groups of five to ten birds are often found with migrating groups of vireos, warblers, sparrows, and other passeriformes species. Migration is particularly noted in the fall, especially in areas such as the North Shore of Lake Superior; hundreds of birds can be counted on peak migration days. On September 12, 1985, 2,069 individuals were counted in three and a half hours in Duluth. This movement is noted from early September through late November, with a peak from mid-September through mid-October. These movements indicate birds leave breeding areas and move southward in the fall. Birds undoubtedly move in from Canada and then move northward in the spring.

BOREAL CHICKADEE *(Parus hudsonicus)*

Boreal Chickadee

Minnesota status. Regular. Permanent resident; migrant and casual winter visitant outside the regular range.

Distribution. An uncommon permanent resident throughout the northeastern and north-central regions as far west as eastern Marshall and Roseau Counties in the west-central region. Breeding has been reported as far south as Big Sandy Lake in northern Aitkin County and as far west as Hubbard County (*The Loon* 51:135-40). Usually encountered in pairs or in small family groups of five to eight birds, but occasionally larger groups are encountered, especially in the winter; on March 1, 1980, 75 were seen in the Sax-Zim area of central St. Louis

County. Numbers fluctuate widely over a number of years, but no specific period of population fluctuation has been determined. Most unusual is the record of a single bird in Lyon County in the southwestern region from July 7 to August 8, 1972.
Migration and winter. At infrequent intervals irruptions of this species occur in the fall starting in late September. Migrants are recorded every fall at Duluth and along the North Shore of Lake Superior. Birds move southward from the regular permanent resident range in northeastern and north-central regions, and numbers increase in these regions at the same time. These movements have taken birds as far south as Washington, Hennepin, Ramsey, Wabasha and Rice Counties in the east, Stearns County in the central region, and Lac Qui Parle, Cottonwood, and Yellow Medicine Counties in the west. Birds occur in these counties anywhere from early fall through the winter months and into early spring.

TUFTED TITMOUSE *(Parus bicolor)*

Minnesota status. Regular. Permanent resident. Casual visitant outside of resident range mainly in late fall, winter, and early spring.
Distribution. A permanent resident in the southeastern region (casual as far west as Mower County) and locally northward along the St. Croix, Minnesota, and Mississippi Rivers. Numbers vary markedly from year to year and breeding populations are very localized throughout this range. There are breeding records as far north as Washington, Hennepin, and Stearns Counties. There are breeding season observations from Deerwood, Crow Wing County: two birds on June 15, 1971; one bird seen in Otter Tail County on May 21 and 22, 1978; one bird in Nicollet County on June 4, 1974. Normally encountered as individuals or in pairs; however, in winter more may be found in loose association near abundant food sources. From the 1940s to the mid-1970s this species expanded its

Tufted Titmouse

breeding range northward in the state to where it was seen regularly in Hennepin County. Since the mid-1970s it has retreated southward from this area; no birds have been recorded at the Cedar Creek Natural History area, Anoka County, since 1975; the same is true for southern Hennepin County. At present most often seen in the southeast corner of the state (Houston and Fillmore Counties). However, one bird was observed in Washington County on June 8, 1983.

Migration and winter. Occasionally birds are found away from the resident range in the southeast region. There are records from Duluth and Virginia (two found dead on September 28, 1972), St. Louis County; Cook County along the North Shore of Lake Superior; Aitkin, Cass, Beltrami, and Hubbard Counties in the north-central region; Polk County in the northwest; and Douglas County in the west-central region. In the southwest there are records from Rock and Cottonwood Counties; in the central part of the state, as far west as Kandiyohi, McLeod, and Sibley Counties. Finally in the south-central region there is one record from Martin County along the Iowa border and there are records from Rice and Le Sueur Counties.

RED-BREASTED NUTHATCH
(Sitta canadensis)

Minnesota status. Regular. Permanent resident, migrant, and winter visitant.

Distribution. A permanent resident widely distributed but local across the northeastern and north-central regions. Nesting occasionally as far south as Washington, Ramsey, Hennepin, and Stearns Counties. One bird was seen in Houston County on June 28, 1984. Much more numerous and regular in the east-central region in winter. This species varies widely in numbers from year to year, especially in the winter. For example, in some winters it is common but in others it is uncommon or rare. The summer population in the north-central

Red-breasted Nuthatch

and northeastern regions does not appear to fluctuate as much.

Migration. An uncommon spring and fall migrant throughout most of the state. Common in the north-central and northeastern regions and occasionally common in the east-central region at peak migration periods. Least numerous in western regions. *Spring migration period:* Probably early April through late May, no peak period noted. Latest dates: SOUTH (beyond resident range), May 19, 21, 22, *29, June 3. Fall migration period:* Probably mid-August through early November, with the bulk of the migration in late August and September. Earliest dates (beyond resident range) in eastern and central regions: August 1, 3, 6.

Winter. A visitant most numerous in the northeastern and north-central regions but can occur anywhere in the state. Usually rare over most of the western regions. Numbers fluctuate widely from year to year, varying from rare to common.

WHITE-BREASTED NUTHATCH
(Sitta carolinensis)

Minnesota status. Regular. Permanent resident.
Distribution. A common permanent resident in all regions of the state except in the northeast. In the northeast this species has been reported (since the mid 1970s) occasionally in the summer. It is primarily a spring and fall migrant and winter visitant in St. Louis, Lake, and Cook Counties, although it did overwinter in 1983-84 in Cook County. The first nesting in St. Louis County was reported in 1974. Well represented (common to abundant) in all other regions and at all seasons.

White-breasted Nuthatch

BROWN CREEPER *(Certhia americana)*

Minnesota status. Regular. Migrant, summer resident, and winter visitant.
Migration. An uncommon to common spring and

Brown Creeper

fall migrant throughout the state. Least numerous in the northwestern region. Numbers fluctuate from year to year. Usually encountered as individuals. *Spring migration period:* Mid-March through late May, with a few stragglers into June in the south. Earliest dates: SOUTH, none can be given because of wintering birds; NORTH, difficult to determine because occasionally birds winter north to St. Louis, Beltrami, and Marshall Counties, early dates in normal years being in late March. Latest dates: SOUTH (away from breeding areas), June 9, 13. *Fall migration period*: Early September (north), mid-September (south), through early November (north), to probably late November (south). Latest dates: None can be given because of stragglers and overwintering birds.

Summer. Primarily a resident in the north-central (*The Loon* 47:108-13) and northeastern (*The Loon* 49:78-80) regions; south occasionally through the east-central region and probably into the whole southeast region along the Mississippi River. Nests have been reported in Hennepin, Goodhue, and Brown Counties, and there are summer observations along the Mississippi River in Winona and Houston Counties. A family group was seen at Cedar Creek Natural History Area, Anoka County, on July 7, 1979. Because of the secretive habits and nesting of this species, nests are seldom found or seen; it is possible it nests throughout the more heavily wooded regions of the state. There are summer records from Pope and Stearns Counties in the central region and, most unusual, one summer (July 15-19, 1972) record from Cottonwood County in the southwest region.

Winter. An uncommon to occasionally common winter visitant primarily in the southern half of the state. In some winters it is occasionally found in northern areas, north as far as southern St. Louis County in the east, southern Itasca and Clearwater Counties in the central part of the state, and Marshall County in the west. In late December 1983 there were records from Cook, Lake, St. Louis,

Itasca, Cass, and Otter Tail Counties. Overwintering birds are most numerous in east-central, southeast, and south-central regions.

ROCK WREN *(Salpinctes obsoletus)*

Minnesota status. Accidental.
Records. There are nine records of this western species in the state: April 18, 1948, Salt Lake, Lac Qui Parle County (*The Flicker* 20:111); April 22, 1979, Blue Mounds State Park, Rock County (*The Loon* 51:146); May 12, 1984, Gooseberry Falls State Park, Lake County (*The Loon* 56:270-71); May 13, 1922, Pipestone County, specimen MMNH #6269; August 23, 1974, Pipestone National Monument, Pipestone County (*The Loon* 47:94); October 28, 1962 near Dalton, Otter Tail County (*The Flicker* 34:130); October 29, 1966, Grand Marais, Cook County (*The Loon* 39:135); most unusual was the presence of a pair (which built a nest they later abandoned) at Bemidji, Beltrami County, from May 27 to June 17, 1984 (*The Loon* 56:190). The most recent record is of an individual seen on October 17, 1986, Duluth (*The Loon* 58:199-200).

CAROLINA WREN *(Thryothorus ludovicianus)*

Minnesota status. Casual. Migrant, summer visitant, and winter visitant.
Records. This species occurs very irregularly in the state. Most recent records are for the spring migration period in April and May. All records are for the eastern and central region except for one record in Pipestone County (May 23, 1976). Spring migration dates range from April 12 to May 25. There are fewer records in the fall, with most in October and November ranging from an early date of September 19 (Duluth, only September date) to late dates of November 28 (Deerwood, Crow Wing County), December 14 (Lutsen, Cook County), and December 13 (Swan Lake, Itasca County). There

are a number of records of birds showing up at feeding stations in October and November in the southern part of the state and remaining until late January. One bird remained into early February, another into March. These records are from Hennepin (photographed, *The Loon* 44:23-24), Ramsey, Dodge, Washington, Pope, and Martin Counties, all in the southern part of the state. In the summer there are former records of family groups or nests from Houston, Fillmore, Ramsey, and Washington Counties. There are no recent breeding records, although there are summer observations in Stearns, Hennepin, and Ramsey Counties. The most recent records for this species are May 25, 1981, Duluth (*The Loon* 53:173); November 28 to December 14, 1983, Lutsen, Cook County (*The Loon* 56:71-72); November 2-27, 1983, Merrifield, Crow Wing County (*The Loon* 56:72). Most unusual is the record of a pair seen in Rochester, Olmsted County, in July 1986 (*The Loon* 58:143-44). This pair was still in the same location during the fall of 1986. No nesting activity was noted.

BEWICK'S WREN *(Thryomanes bewickii)*

Minnesota status. Casual. Migrant and summer visitant.

Records. Like the Carolina Wren, this species occurs very irregularly in the state. Most records are from the spring migration period in April and May in the southeastern, south-central, and east-central regions as far north as Anoka County and west to Sibley, Rice, and Steele Counties. In addition, there are April records as far north as Aitkin and Crow Wing Counties (*The Loon* 48:79) and as far west as Lac Qui Parle County. Spring dates range from March 30 to one bird that remained in Winona, Winona County, from May 15 to 30 (*The Loon* 50:168-69). The most recent record is of a single bird seen in Olmsted County from April 27 to 30, 1986 (*The Loon* 58:137-38). There are very few fall dates, only a scattering in September and October ranging from September 6 to October 31. All records are from the east-central and southeastern region, with the exception of a bird at Duluth in September. There are former records of family groups or nests from Anoka, Ramsey, Hennepin, and Fillmore Counties. In addition, there are more recent summer observations from Houston, Washington, and Freeborn Counties (*The Loon* 54:245-46) and most interesting records from the early 1950s and again in 1983 at Sand Dunes State Forest, Sherburne County (*The Loon* 55:121).

HOUSE WREN *(Troglodytes aedon)*

Minnesota status. Regular. Migrant and summer resident.

Migration. A common spring and fall migrant throughout the state. Normally encountered as individuals or in pairs. *Spring migration period:* Mid-April through mid-May, with a peak in early May. Earliest dates: SOUTH, *March 30, April 1, 3, 8,* 13, 15, 16; NORTH, March *30,* April *6,* 22, 25, 26. *Fall migration period:* Mid-August through mid-October, with a peak in early September. Latest dates: NORTH, October 6, 7, 8, *15, 20, 21*; SOUTH, October 21, 24, 26, *November 17.*

Summer. A resident throughout the state; widely distributed and numerous in all regions.

House Wren

WINTER WREN *(Troglodytes troglodytes)*

Minnesota status. Regular. Migrant and summer resident; casual in winter.

Migration. Uncommon spring and fall migrant in the eastern and central regions; rare in spring and fall in western regions. Usually encountered as individuals. *Spring migration period:* Late March through late May, with a peak in late April. Earliest dates: SOUTH, March *4,* 15, 17, 23 (any dates in the first half of March could be wintering birds); NORTH, March 30, April 6, 7, 9. Latest dates: SOUTH

Winter Wren

(outside of breeding areas), May 19, 20, 21, *27, 28, 30*. NORTH, none can be given because of breeding birds. *Fall migration period:* Late August through mid-November, with the bulk of the migration in late September and early October. Earliest dates: SOUTH (away from breeding areas), August 20, 24 (only dates before mid-September). Latest dates: NORTH, October 24, 25, 26, *November 20*; SOUTH, November 11, 14, 16, *24, 25* (late November dates could indicate wintering birds).

Summer. A resident primarily in the coniferous forest of the northeastern and north-central regions as far west as Clearwater County. A family group has been reported as far south as Franconia, Chisago County (*The Loon* 48:187-88). There are June records in Hennepin, Houston, and Goodhue Counties, indicating that nesting may occasionally be attempted in the east-central and southeastern regions along or near the Mississippi River. July dates in Dakota (July 13, 1975) and Olmsted (July 25, 1976) Counties may be extremely early fall migrants or nonbreeding summer birds.

Winter. A casual or accidental winter visitant along open creeks in the east-central and southeastern regions. There are records as far north as Anoka and Hennepin Counties.

SEDGE WREN *(Cistothorus platensis)*

Sedge Wren

Minnesota status. Regular. Migrant and summer resident; accidental in winter.

Migration. This species is primarily a secretive night migrant and is seldom seen outside of its breeding habitat during migration. However, it is common in these areas across the state and is no doubt a common spring and fall migrant throughout most of the state except in the northeastern region where it is uncommon. *Spring migration period:* Late April through late May, with the bulk of the migration in mid to late May. Earliest dates: SOUTH, April *14, 16,* 20, 25, 26; NORTH, *April 20*, May 2, 5, 8. *Fall migration period:* Early August through mid-October, with the bulk of the migration in mid to late September. Latest dates: NORTH, September 24, 25, 30, *October 13, 23, November 9*, SOUTH, October 17, 22, 26, *November 2, 4*.

Summer. A well-represented and widely distributed resident throughout the state where grassy marshes and wet grassy uplands are present. Most numerous in western and central regions, least numerous in the northeastern region.

Winter. There is one record of this speices on January 25, 1981 near Lyle, Mower County, on the Iowa border (*The Loon* 53:110).

MARSH WREN *(Cistothorus palustris)*

Minnesota status: Regular. Migrant and summer resident; accidental in winter.

Migration. Like the Sedge Wren, this species is primarily a night migrant. It is quite secretive during migration and is usually encountered on its breeding territories. In suitable habitat (cattail marshes) this species is common in both spring and fall throughout most of the state except in the north-central region where it is uncommon and in the northeast where it is rare. *Spring migration period:* Late April through late May, with a peak in mid to late May. Earliest dates: SOUTH, *March 22, 26*, April *1*, 14, 16, 20; NORTH, April *23*, 29, 30, May 2. *Fall migration period:* Mid-August through late October. Latest dates: NORTH, October 18, 22, 24; SOUTH, October 27, 29, 31, *November 2, 26*.

Summer. A numerous resident throughout most of the state wherever suitable cattail marsh habitat exists. Decreasing in abundance northward, scarce to absent in the northeastern region and the eastern portions of the north-central region.

Winter. A single bird was seen at Gun Club Lake, Hennepin County, on January 27, 1953.

Marsh Wren

AMERICAN DIPPER *(Cinclus mexicanus)*

Minnesota status. Accidental.

Records. During the winter and spring of 1970 what

may have been a single bird was observed on several North Shore streams in Cook County from January 29 to April 4. This bird was first seen on the Temperance River on January 29, seen on the Cascade River (19 ½ miles northeast) on January 31, the Poplar River (halfway between the Temperance and Cascade) on February 1, and by many observers from February 8-22 and March 7 on the Temperance River. Then on April 4, 1970 a bird was seen on the Baptism River (21 miles southwest of the Temperance) (*The Loon* 42:136-37). There is a second-hand report of a probable individual seen in the spring of 1969 along the Manitou River, Lake County (*The Loon* 44:118-19). Another most interesting report of this species is of a bird seen June 8, 1971 at the outlet of Mink Lake, Cook County. This observer also reported that he had seen this species each year in late May from 1966 to the early 1970s at Trout Lake just east of Mink Lake (*The Loon* 50:213).

GOLDEN-CROWNED KINGLET
(Regulus satrapa)

Golden-crowned Kinglet

Minnesota status. Regular. Migrant, summer resident, and winter visitant.

Migration. An uncommon to common spring and fall migrant throughout the state. Least numerous in northwestern region. Common only at peak migration periods. *Spring migration period:* Mid-March through mid-May, with the bulk of the migration from early to mid-April. Earliest dates: SOUTH, none can be given because of wintering birds; NORTH, March 10, 14, 16. Latest dates: SOUTH, May 10, 14, 16; NORTH, none can be given because of breeding birds. *Fall migration period:* Early September through early December, with the bulk of the migration in October. Earliest dates: NORTH, none can be given because of breeding birds; SOUTH, *August 21*, September 10, 16, 19. Latest dates: NORTH, November 25, 27, 28; SOUTH, none can be given because of wintering birds.

Summer. Resident primarily in the boreal forests of the north-central and northeastern regions. There are summer observations in the north as far west as Agassiz National Wildlife Refuge, Marshall County, and Tamarac National Wildlife Refuge, Becker County, and former breeding records as far south as Onamia, Mille Lacs County, and Lake Vadnais, Ramsey County.

Winter. An uncommon winter visitant primarily in the east-central and southeastern regions of the state; rare to casual in the northern portion of the state especially in early winter as far north as Itasca State Park, Clearwater County, and Mahnomen and Becker Counties in the west and Duluth and southern St. Louis County in the east.

RUBY-CROWNED KINGLET *(Regulus calendula)*

Minnesota status. Regular. Migrant and summer resident; accidental in winter.
Migration: A common spring and fall migrant throughout the state; can be occasionally abundant for short periods at migration peaks. At peak migration times can be encountered in loose aggregations of ten or more birds. *Spring migration period:* Late March through late May, with the bulk of the migration from mid-April to early May. Earliest dates: SOUTH, March *3, 12,* 19, 20, 21; NORTH, *March 11, 18, 19,* 28, April 1, 3. Latest dates: SOUTH, May 23, 24, 29, *June 3, 6, 14*; NORTH, none can be given because of breeding birds. *Fall migration period:* Late August through early December, with a peak in late September and early October. Earliest dates: NORTH, none can be given because of breeding birds; SOUTH, August 20, 24, 26. Latest dates: NORTH, November 20, 22, 25; SOUTH, December 9, 10, 11, *16, 17.*

Ruby-crowned Kinglet

Summer. A regular but scarce summer resident in the northeastern and north-central regions. Best represented in the northeastern region. This species has been observed in the summer as far west as eastern Marshall County, and Itasca State Park,

Clearwater County. There is one former nesting record from St. Cloud, Stearns County, and summer observations from Anoka and Dakota County, indicating this species may breed occasionally outside the northeast and north-central regions. The first nest of this species was not found in the state until the 1940s.

Winter. There are three records from the northern part of the state: December 28, 1982 and February 27, 1974 (*The Loon* 46:86-87), both from Bemidji, Beltrami County, and late December 1974 to mid-February 1975, Proctor, St. Louis County. In the south there are occasional stragglers into late December (six records at the time of the Christmas counts) and very early January. One bird was seen at a feeder in Minnetonka, Hennepin County, from December 10, 1986, to January 24, 1987 (*The Loon* 59:54). The only overwintering record is of a single bird from December 28, 1974 to February 15, 1975 at Rochester, Olmsted County.

BLUE-GRAY GNATCATCHER
(Polioptila caerulea)

Blue-gray Gnatcatcher

Minnesota status. Regular. Migrant and summer resident.

Migration: Almost all birds seen during the migration season are on breeding territories. Rare to uncommon in the southeast, east-central, central, south-central, and eastern portions of the west-central regions. Found as far north as southern Chisago County along the St. Croix River, Mille Lacs County, along the Rum River, Morrison County, southern Crow Wing and Cass Counties along the Mississippi River, and Maplewood State Park in Otter Tail County, southward through Douglas, Pope, and Swift Counties. On May 18, 1986 a single bird was seen in Wilkin County in the west-central region. In the Minnesota River Valley, it is expanding westward and occurs in Nicollet, Blue Earth, Renville, and Brown Counties, with records as far as Granite Falls, Yellow Medicine

County, Marshall (*The Loon* 51:207) and Garvin Park, Lyon County, and Murray County in the southwest region. The most unusual records are of one bird in Duluth, St. Louis County, on October 27, 1982 (*The Loon* 55:31-32), the latest date on record for the state, and a single bird in Grand Marais, Cook County, on September 22, 1985 (*The Loon* 57:182). *Spring migration period:* Late April through late May. Earliest dates: SOUTH, April 17, 18, 19; NORTH, April 27, May 3, 9 (only dates). *Fall migration period:* Birds gradually depart from the state in August. Latest dates: NORTH, *October 27* (see above); SOUTH, September 16, 17, 20, *29*, *October 5*.

Summer. The migration distribution explained above is basically the breeding range of this species. Most numerous in the southeast region. In recent years it is expanding northward and westward along the major river valleys in the state—especially along the Minnesota River Valley in the central and south-central regions. It is at present well represented in Nicollet County and as far southwest as Lyon County (Garvin Park). The first nesting in Otter Tail County occurred in 1979 (*The Loon* 51:171-74) and in Rock County in 1981 (*The Loon* 53:167).

NORTHERN WHEATEAR *(Oenanthe oenanthe)*

Minnesota status. Accidental.
Records. There are two records for the state during the migration period in 1982: the first occurred on May 15, 1982 in Winona County (*The Loon* 55:151-53); the second, on September 27, 1982 at Roseville, Ramsey County (*The Loon* 55:27-28).

EASTERN BLUEBIRD *(Sialia sialis)*

Minnesota status. Regular. Migrant and summer resident; casual in winter.
Migration: A common spring and fall migrant throughout most of the state, may be locally abundant in the fall. Most numerous in central and

Eastern Bluebird

southern portions of the north-central region. Un-common in the northeastern and northern portions of the north-central region. Numbers fluctuate from year to year. Usually encountered in pairs in the spring; in fall loose aggregations of up to 40 or 50 birds may be seen. *Spring migration period:* Early March through mid-May, with the bulk of the migration in April. Earliest dates: SOUTH, *February 27,* March 1, 2, 3 (in the early part of the twentieth century when the species was more abundant in the state, early arrival dates were in late February); NORTH, March *6,* 14, 15, 19. *Fall migration period:* Early September through late November, with stragglers into late December. The peak of the migration is from late September through late October. Latest dates: NORTH, November 20, 23, *December 12*; SOUTH, none can be given because of stragglers seen throughout December.

Summer. A resident throughout the state, most numerous in the central region. The center of the breeding population is from Sherburne County northward to southern Cass County. Least numerous in the northern boreal forest and the open prairies of the west and south. With the advent of bluebird trails and the putting up of thousands of nest boxes for this species, the breeding population appears to be healthy and increasing in many areas in the state.

Winter. This species occurs casually most often in the southeastern region in early and mid-winter. Occasionally found as far north as St. Cloud, Stearns County, and sporadically occurs along the North Shore of Lake Superior. Most often reported in December and early January. Few birds overwinter; those that do occur mainly in the southeast. Mid to late February dates are most likely very early spring migrants. There are January records from Nicollet and Mower Counties in the south-central region. Usually seen as individuals or in pairs; 11 birds were recorded in Wabasha County on December 30, 1971, and four birds were seen from mid-December 1983 to mid-February 1984 along the Minnesota River in Nicollet County.

MOUNTAIN BLUEBIRD *(Sialia currucoides)*

Minnesota status. Regular. Migrant, accidental in summer and winter.

Migration: This species is a recent addition to the regular category of the state list, being casual before the early 1970s. Since that time, it has become a rare but regular spring migrant mainly in western regions from Rock County in the south to Marshall County in the north. The species becomes more casual moving eastward in the state. There is a scattering of spring records in the central regions from Brown, Le Sueur, Rice, Scott, Carver, Sherburne, Aitkin, Wadena, Beltrami, and Lake of the Woods Counties. In the east the species is accidental in the spring with records only from Wabasha, Carlton, and St. Louis Counties. *Spring migration period:* Early March through mid-April. Earliest dates: SOUTH, March 6, 17, 18, 23; NORTH, March 11, 15, 16. Latest dates: SOUTH, April 7, 9; NORTH, April 9, 11, 19. *Fall migration period:* Most unusual is the record of a single bird at Agassiz National Wildlife Refuge, Marshall County, on June 1, 1983, and another in Beltrami County on August 24, 1985. Accidental anywhere in the fall, with most records from the North Shore of Lake Superior in St. Louis County (October 12-13, 1984, Duluth, October 24, 1976, October 24, 1985, and November 21, 1977); Cook County (November 20, 1984) and Becker County (September), Chippewa County (October 13, 1985), and Anoka County (October 22, 1977).

Summer. A male Mountain Bluebird was found paired with a female Eastern Bluebird at a nesting box east of Aitkin, Aitkin County, during June and July 1986 *(The Loon* 58:194-96).

Winter: There are five winter records, two of them overwintering birds: three birds at Duluth, November 22, 1942 to March 16, 1943; one bird in Le Sueur County from January 14 to March 20, 1978 *(The Loon* 50:119-20); the other three records are of individual birds seen along the North Shore of Lake Superior in Cook County (January 20-24, 1971 and December 18, 1982) and at Duluth from early December to December 15, 1984.

TOWNSEND'S SOLITAIRE
(Myadestes townsendi)

Minnesota status. Regular. Migrant and winter visitant.

Migration: A very rare fall and spring migrant in the state. The records during migration are scattered across the state with no definite pattern or particular concentration in any one region. In the southwest there are records from Jackson and Lyon Counties; in the west-central region only in Lac Qui Parle County; in the north-central region in Beltrami, Itasca, and Crow Wing counties; in the central region from Stearns County only; in the south-central region from Nicollet, Rice, Blue Earth, Martin, and Freeborn Counties; in the southeast only from Houston County; in the east-central region from Hennepin, Ramsey, and Anoka Counties; and in the northeast from Cook, Lake, and St. Louis Counties. There are no records for the northwest. Encountered as individuals. Better represented in fall than in spring; fall records outnumber spring by approximately 2:1. Earliest dates: September 11 (Houston), 19 (Beltrami), 22 (Duluth). Latest dates: April 20, 26, 27, *May 4.*

Winter. Like the migration records, records of this species in the winter are scattered about the state. In the west-central region there are records from Lac Qui Parle and Otter Tail Counties; in the southwest from Redwood County; the only north-central region records are from Clearwater and Koochiching Counties; in the northeast there are again records from St. Louis, Lake, and Cook Counties; in the central region from Stearns and Carver Counties; in the east-central from Anoka, Ramsey, and Hennepin Counties; in the south-central region from Nicollet and Freeborn Counties; and finally in the southeast from Mower County. The majority of the winter records are from the month of December, with a few of these birds remaining into January and February. The only known February dates are from Austin, Mower County, December 23, 1978 to February 17, 1979 (*The Loon* 51:106-7);

Grand Marais, Cook County, February 4, 1978; Duluth, St. Louis County, February 20, 1978 (*The Loon* 50:221) and also in 1985 from January 14 to March 20; near Mankato, Nicollet County, February 8, 1980 (*The Loon* 52:42-43); and Ortonville, Big Stone County, on February 8, 1984 and also February 2, 1985.

VEERY *(Catharus fuscescens)*

Minnesota status. Regular. Migrant and summer resident.
Migration: An uncommon spring and fall migrant throughout the state. Least numerous in southwest and west-central regions. Usually encountered as individuals. *Spring migration period:* Late April through late May, with the bulk of the migration in mid-May. Earliest dates: SOUTH, April *12,* 17, 18, 19; NORTH, April 22, 25, 28. *Fall migration period:* Late July through late September. Birds gradually leave the state in August and are seldom seen in the fall. Latest dates: NORTH, September 28, 29, October 1, *12*; SOUTH, October 2, 4, 6, *14, 19, 22.*
Summer. A well-represented resident in the northern half of the state in the boreal forest as well as in the groves on the prairies of the northwest region south to Otter Tail and Pope Counties in the west-central region. In the southern half of the state this species is a resident as far south as Anoka, Ramsey, and Washington Counties in the east-central region and Stearns County in the central region. At present it is not known to breed in the southwest region, although there are observations from Lyon County. In the south-central region it is known from Nerstrand Woods State Park in Rice County. In the southeast it may breed sparingly along the Mississippi River and major tributary streams where there are heavy woods, in such areas as the Whitewater Wildlife Management Area in Wabasha and Winona Counties, Forestville State Park in Fillmore County; Beaver Creek Valley State Park in Houston County; and along the Zumbro River in eastern Olmsted County.

Veery

GRAY-CHEEKED THRUSH *(Catharus minimus)*

Minnesota status. Regular. Migrant; accidental in summer.

Migration: An uncommon to locally common spring and fall migrant throughout the state. Locally common only at peak migration periods in spring. Less often reported in fall. Usually encountered as individuals. *Spring migration period:* Early April through early June, with a peak in early to mid-May. Earliest dates: SOUTH, April 9, 10, 11; NORTH, April *18*, 26, 27, 28. Latest dates: SOUTH, June 1, 3, 4; NORTH, June 1, 5, 9. *Fall migration period:* Mid-August through mid-October, with the bulk of the migration in mid and late September. Earliest dates: NORTH, August *5*, 16, 17, 18; SOUTH, August 22, 28, 30. Latest dates: NORTH, October 10, 14, 18, *28, 29, November 5*; SOUTH, October 15, 17, 18.

Summer. There is one record of a bird from Eagan, Dakota County, on July 3, 1978 *(The Loon* 50:206).

Note. It is often difficult to identify species of thrush, especially during migration. The early spring dates given above may indicate confusion with Hermit Thrushes. My own personal records indicate an early south spring arrival date of May 1, with an average date of spring arrival based on 34 years of records, of May 8.

SWAINSON'S THRUSH *(Catharus ustulatus)*

Minnesota status. Regular. Migrant and summer resident; accidental in winter.

Migration: A common to occasionally abundant spring and fall migrant throughout the state. Locally abundant only at peak migration periods. Usually encountered as individuals. *Spring migration period:* Mid-April through early June, with a peak in mid-May. Earliest dates: SOUTH, April *4*, 7, 9, 10; NORTH, April 18, 22, 25. Latest dates: SOUTH, June 3, 4, 8, *11*; NORTH, none can be given because of breeding birds. *Fall migration period:* Late July

Swainson's Thrush

through early November, with the bulk of the migration from late August through late September. Earliest dates: NORTH, none can be given because of breeding birds; SOUTH, July 24, 27, August 8. Latest dates: NORTH, October 22, 25, 29, *November 5*; SOUTH, November 11, 13, *24, 25, 28.*

Summer. Resident in the northeastern and north-central regions as far south as southern St. Louis and Itasca Counties, west to Clearwater County and north to eastern Roseau County. May breed as far south as northern Pine County in the east.

Winter. One bird attempted to winter at a feeder in St. Paul during 1973. It was first seen on November 23 and was found dead on December 30 (*The Loon 46:42*).

Note: Thrush species are often difficult to identify, especially during migration. The early spring dates given above may indicate confusion with the Hermit Thrush. My own personal records show an early south spring arrival date of April 26, with an average date for spring arrival, based on 37 years of records, of May 7.

HERMIT THRUSH *(Catharus guttatus)*

Minnesota status. Regular. Migrant and summer resident; accidental in winter.

Migration: A common spring and fall migrant throughout the state. Locally abundant only at peak migration periods. Usually encountered as individuals, but loose aggregations of up to 20 birds can be found at peak periods. *Spring migration period:* Late March through mid-May, with the bulk of the migration in mid to late April. Earliest dates: SOUTH, March *17*, 24, 26, 27; NORTH, March *23, 31*, April 2, 6, 7. Latest dates: SOUTH, May 22, 23, 29, June *1, 11*; NORTH, none can be given because of breeding birds. *Fall migration period:* Early September through late November, with the bulk of the migration in mid-October. There are stragglers into December, especially in the southern part of the state (see Winter). Earliest dates: NORTH,

Hermit Thrush

none can be given because of breeding birds; SOUTH, August 29, September 1, 2, 3. Latest dates: NORTH, October 26, 27, 28, *November 7, 11, 21, 22, 24, 30*; SOUTH, November 24, 25, 30, *December 6.*

Summer. A resident throughout the northeastern and north-central regions south to northern Pine (Sturgeon Lake) County, northern Mille Lacs (Onamia) County, and west to eastern Marshall (Agassiz National Wildlife Refuge) and Roseau (Warroad) Counties.

Winter. There are a number of records of stragglers and birds attempting to overwinter in December and early January. These records are from Duluth (December 30, 1977 and January 1, 1978) and Fergus Falls, Otter Tail County (November 23, 1975 to January 6, 1976), in the north; December 10, 1983, Nicollet County; December 7-23, 1975, December 15-27, 1982, January 1-12, 1985, all in Hennepin County; January 1986 in Mower County; December 15, 1979, Rochester, Olmsted County; December 19, 1981 and December 17, 1983, St. Paul; January 1, 1981, Ramsey County; and December 19, 1983, Houston County in the south. There are overwintering records of four, possibly five birds in the state; one bird at a feeder in Duluth from December 17, 1972 to at least February 24, 1973; December 21, 1979 through February 1980, Mountain Lake, Cottonwood County; January 8, 1981 to February 28, 1981, Rochester, Olmsted County; one bird overwintered in Sherburne County during the winter of 1982-83, a single bird was seen on January 23, 1981 at Fairmont, Martin County, and a single bird was seen on January 31, 1986 in Washington County.

Note. Thrushes are often difficult to identify in the field, and many of the early and late dates listed under Gray-cheeked and Swainson's Thrush could be Hermit Thrushes, the much earlier and later migrant of the three species.

WOOD THRUSH *(Hylocichla mustelina)*

Minnesota status. Regular. Migrant and summer resident.

Migration: An uncommon spring migrant in eastern and central regions, rare spring migrant in the west. Almost all birds are encountered on breeding territories. Rare to absent in all regions in the fall as most birds have left breeding territories by late summer. This species reaches the northwestern limit of its range in the United States in Minnesota. Usually encountered as individuals. *Spring migration period:* Late April through late May. Earliest dates: SOUTH, April *7, 9,* 11, 13, 14; NORTH, *April 19, 29,* May 8, 9, 10. *Fall migration period:* Mid-August through early October; almost all birds have left by mid-September. Latest dates: NORTH, September 14, 18, 26, *October 14, November 6*; SOUTH, October 16, 17, 19.

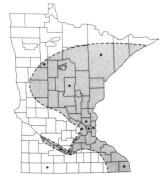

Wood Thrush

Summer. A resident primarily in the heavily forested hardwood areas of the state; prefers maple-basswood forests. Most numerous in the east-central and southeastern regions along the Mississippi River and its major tributaries. It is widespread but local in the maple basswood forests of the central and north-central regions as far north as Aitkin and Itasca Counties and into the northeastern region through Carlton, northern St. Louis (Lake Vermillion) County, to the hardwood forests in Cook County. In the west it is much less numerous but has been recorded as far north as Maple Lake, Polk County. There are recent June records from Lac Qui Parle County in the west-central region; Rock County, and a nest was found at Kilen Woods State Park, Jackson County, on June 21 and 29, 1976, both in the southwest region; and in Martin County in the south-central region. It ranges regularly up the Minnesota River Valley as far as Renville and Yellow Medicine Counties. These records indicate it may be expanding into areas of suitable habitat in the western part of the state.

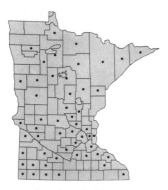

American Robin

AMERICAN ROBIN *(Turdus migratorius)*

Minnesota status. Regular. Migrant, summer resident, and winter visitant.

Migration. Abundant spring and fall migrant throughout the state. *Spring migration period:* Early March through early May, with the bulk of the migration from late March through late April. Earliest dates: SOUTH, early March to mid-March; NORTH, mid-March to late March; no exact dates can be given because of wintering birds. *Fall migration period:* Late August through late November, with the bulk of the migration from late September through late October. Latest dates: None can be given because of wintering birds.

Summer. Resident throughout the state from the prairie to the dense northern forests, nesting in heavily wooded areas as well as around human habitations.

Winter. Rare to uncommon winter visitant throughout most of the state but mainly in the south; occasionally common in the Twin Cities area and in the southeastern region; occasionally abundant along the North Shore of Lake Superior. In the Lake Superior area abundance is dependent on the berry crop of the Mountain Ash *(Scorbus americana).*

VARIED THRUSH *(Ixoreus naevius)*

Minnesota status. Regular. Migrant and winter visitant.

Migration and winter. A rare winter visitant from the west, mostly into north-central, northeastern, and east-central regions. This distribution pattern is probably related to the prevalence of feeders around heavily populated regions in the state to which the birds are attracted in the winter. The first record of this species was of a single bird that appeared at a feeder in February 1941 in Lake County along the North Shore of Lake Superior. From the 1940s to the 1960s this species occurred only accidentally in the state. From the 1960s to the present, it has become a regular winter visitant in the state, with a few records from scattered areas each fall and winter. There are few records for the southern part of the state except in the east-central region. The only counties of record in the south (outside the east-central region) are Stevens, Stearns, Kandiyohi, Sherburne, Rice, Winona, Olmsted, and Nobles. In the north-central and northeastern regions there are records from almost all counties in these regions (the only exceptions being Lake of the Woods and Wadena). During January and February 1984 birds were seen at feeders in Bemidji, Beltrami County, Hubbard County, Cass County, and Aitkin County. One bird was seen in Koochiching County on January 28, 1984, and another was picked up dead in Cook County on December 11, 1984. In the northwest region it has gone unrecorded except in Kittson, Marshall, and Clay Counties, and there is one record from Otter Tail County in the west-central region. Usually encountered as individuals, although two birds are occasionally recorded at feeding stations. *Fall migration period:* Late September through mid-December, with most early dates in mid to late November. Earliest dates: *September 20* (Duluth), *September 26* (Hennepin County), October 16, 22, 30. *Spring migration period:* Most birds have left the state by late March or early April, with a few stragglers into late April and into May. Latest dates: April 7, 14, 16, *May 7, 24.*

GRAY CATBIRD *(Dumetella carolinensis)*

Minnesota status. Migrant and summer resident; accidental in winter.
Migration: A common spring and fall migrant throughout the state except in the heavily forested areas near the Canadian border where it is rare to uncommon. During migration it is difficult to distinguish resident birds from migrants and no concentrations have been reported; usually encountered

Gray Catbird

as individuals. *Spring migration period:* Mid-April through late May, with a peak in mid-May. Earliest dates: SOUTH, April *8*, 15, 16, 19; NORTH, April *17*, 29, May 1, 2. *Fall migration period:* Probably from early August through early November, with the bulk of the migration in September. Latest dates: NORTH, October 26, 27, 29, *November 1, 5, 28*; SOUTH, October 28, 30, November 2, *9*. There are eight late November and early December dates for the southern part of the state, probably indicating birds attempting to overwinter.

Summer. A widespread and numerous resident throughout the state except in the heavy coniferous forests of the northeast where the species occurs only in brushy openings.

Winter. There are a number of mid to late December and January records of birds at feeders, most of them in the southern part of the state. There are two mid-December records for Duluth and Crookston, Polk County, and one in a January record from Little Marais, Lake County. These early winter birds are generally unsuccessful in wintering, and most have disappeared by early January. There are two records of overwintering birds; most amazing was a bird that showed up at a feeder in Warren, Marshall County, on December 14, 1975 and remained all winter. The other record is of a single bird that appeared at a feeder in Bloomington, Hennepin County, during November 1971 and remained until March 2, 1972 (*The Loon* 44:93-94).

NORTHERN MOCKINGBIRD
(Mimus polyglottos)

Minnesota status. Regular. Migrant, summer and winter visitant.

Migration: A rare spring and fall migrant anywhere in the state. It is difficult to describe the migration-period distribution for this species in the state, although it is regular especially in spring in Duluth and along the North Shore of Lake Superior. It has

Northern Mockingbird

occurred in scattered counties in every region of the state, probably best represented in eastern regions and least in western regions. Encountered as individuals or in pairs. *Spring migration period:* Mid-April through late May, with most observations in May. Earliest dates: SOUTH, April *6,* 14, 16, 19; NORTH, April 20, 30, May 2, 4 (only dates). *Fall migration period:* Late August through late November, with most dates in late October and November. Latest dates: Very difficult to determine because of wintering birds into December and January.

Summer. Until approximately 1950 this species was a casual summer visitant in the state. Since then it has become a rare but regular visitant into all regions of the state, with scattered records from approximately 20 counties. There are only two confirmed nestings in the state: Royalton, Morrison County (*The Loon* 41:128), in 1968 and 1969; Blue Mounds State Park, Rock County (*The Loon* 49:220-30), in 1977. There are summer sightings of this species along the North Shore of Lake Superior, most often in Cook County, but these are considered visitants.

Winter. A very rare visitant primarily in eastern and central regions in early winter (December and early January), casual in western regions, and accidental in the far south. There are winter records as far north as Cook, Lake, and St. Louis (Duluth) Counties in the east and Clearwater County (February 16, 1980) in the west. The only far south records are of a single bird in Rochester, Olmsted County, until January 16, 1985, and another individual seen in late December 1986 in Redwood County. Most overwintering attempts by this species are unsuccessful; the birds disappear by mid-January. There are two records of birds surviving until late February in Duluth, and there are four records of birds surviving until spring in the Twin Cities area.

SAGE THRASHER *(Oreoscoptes montanus)*

Minnesota status. Accidental.
Records: A bird was found dead on October 19, 1974 along a gravel road near Clarkfield, Yellow Medicine County, and was made into a specimen (*The Loon* 47:129). The first sight record is of a bird seen and photographed on May 13 and 14, 1985 at Agassiz National Wildlife Refuge, Marshall County (*The Loon* 57:115-17). On June 16, 1986 a single bird was seen at Carlos Avery Refuge, Anoka County (*The Loon* 58:139).

BROWN THRASHER *(Toxostoma rufum)*

Brown Thrasher

Minnesota status. Regular. Migrant and summer resident; casual in winter.
Migration: A common spring and fall migrant throughout the state, least numerous in the heavy coniferous forests of the northeastern and north-central regions. Less numerous in fall than in spring. Normally encountered as individuals or in pairs. *Spring migration period:* Early April through mid-May; most early arrival dates are in late April. Peak migration in early May. Earliest dates: SOUTH, March *21, 30*, April 2, 3, 4 (March dates may be of wintering birds); NORTH, April *7, 11,* 18, 20, 22. *Fall migration period:* August through October, with stragglers into early November. Latest dates: NORTH, October 24, 29, 31, *November 10*; SOUTH, November 3, 7, 10, *16, 17, 28, 30* (dates after November 10 may be of wintering birds).
Summer. A numerous and well-distributed resident throughout most of the state; absent from large areas of dense forest anywhere in the state. This species appears to occur in logged openings in forested regions, but not in natural openings.
Winter. There are numerous (over 50) records for this species from December through mid-March. Most of these records are in the eastern part of the state from Cook, Lake, and St. Louis Counties in the northeast southward through the east-central

and southeast region. One bird overwintered in Murray County in the southwest in 1983-84. Most of these records represent individual birds trying to overwinter at feeding stations. The majority of the birds disappear by early January, but a few survive into February and fewer make it through the entire winter. These overwintering birds usually show up at feeders during the first half of November; if they are successful in overwintering, they remain until mid-March or early April.

CURVE-BILLED THRASHER
(Toxostoma curvirostre)

Minnesota status. Accidental.
Records. There is one sight record of this species on September 9, 1976 at Blue Mounds State Park, Rock County (*The Loon* 48:179-80).

WATER PIPIT *(Anthus spinoletta)*

Minnesota status. Regular. Migrant; accidental in winter.
Migration: Uncommon spring migrant and common to occasionally abundant fall migrant throughout the state. Usually encountered in small groups of two to ten birds, but up to 20 or more are occasionally seen. *Spring migration period:* Very late March through late May, with the bulk of the migration in late April. Earliest dates: SOUTH, March 21, 23, 26; NORTH, March *14*, April *8, 9,* 19, 21, 23. Latest dates: SOUTH, May 22, 25, 28; NORTH, May 24, 27, 31, *June 7* (Cook County). *Fall migration period:* Mid-September through mid-November, with the bulk of the migration in October. Earliest dates: NORTH, September 3, 5, 7; SOUTH, September 12, 13, 16. Latest dates: NORTH, November 5, 6, 9, *18, 19, 20*; SOUTH, November 9, 14, 16, *29*.
Winter. There is one amazing record of a single bird at Duluth on January 19, 1978 (*The Loon* 50:56).

SPRAGUE'S PIPIT *(Anthus spragueii)*

Minnesota status. Regular. Migrant and casual summer resident.

Migration: A very rare spring and casual fall migrant in western regions from Rock County in the south to Kittson County in the north along the western margin of the state. Usually encountered in late spring on breeding territories mainly near Felton, Clay County. Accidental elsewhere in the state. The only recent records away from the western regions are from Wadena (May 1, 1971), Martin (October 3, 1975), Hennepin *(The Loon* 51:209), and St. Louis *(The Loon* 52:191-92) Counties. Usually encountered as individuals; however, three were seen on September 29, 1979 at Rothsay, Wilkin County. *Spring migration period:* Mid-April through early May. Because of the rarity of this species in the state, there are few migration dates. Earliest dates: April 11, 25, 27 (only April dates). *Fall migration period:* September and October. Latest dates: October 13, 15, 16.

Summer. A casual summer resident only on virgin prairie areas of the northwest region. Most recent summer records are from Clay County (Felton Prairie 1983-84), and there are isolated records from Norman (Rockwell Township, July 1980) and Polk (Tympanuchus Prairie) Counties. There are former nesting grounds from Kittson (1929), Pennington (1933), and Marshall (1937) Counties. Undoubtedly this species was more common in the nineteenth and early twentieth centuries when virgin prairie areas were prevalent in western regions. If the Nature Conservancy and the State Department of Natural Resources had not preserved prairie areas in the northwest region, this species would no doubt be extirpated in the state.

BOHEMIAN WAXWING *(Bombycilla garrulus)*

Minnesota status. Regular. Winter visitant; accidental in summer.

Migration and winter. Erratic in abundance and distribution from year to year. In some years rare, in others abundant. Present most often in northern and central regions; in years of abundance reaches the southern regions, but always casual to accidental in the southern one-quarter of the state, especially in the southwest region. Often seen in flocks of 50 to 100 birds, but flocks of 500 to 1,000 or more birds are occasionally encountered in northern regions, especially in Duluth (*The Loon* 57:59-60). Often encountered in southern regions in small numbers in association with Cedar Waxwings. In winter flocks of this species are most often encountered in the northern parts of the central region where there is an abundance of Mountain Ash or ornamental crab apple trees. Common around towns and cities where these trees are available. Flocks move about as food supplies are exhausted. *Fall migration period:* In years of abundance the first birds usually appear in late October in northern regions. Earliest dates: NORTH, *September 30*, October 11, 12, 16; SOUTH, October *2, 4, 9, 24* (only October dates), November 9, 10, 11. *Spring migration period:* Most birds have left the state by mid-April, although there are stragglers into May. Latest dates: SOUTH, May 8, 12, 16; NORTH, May 10, 16. **Summer.** There are two unusual records: June 20, 1972 a flock along State Highway 6 in Cass County; July 14, 1945, Many Point Lake, Becker County.

CEDAR WAXWING *(Bombycilla cedrorum)*

Minnesota status. Regular. Migrant, summer resident, and winter visitant.
Migration: A common to abundant spring and fall migrant throughout most of the state. Most numerous in eastern, central, and northwestern regions. Least numerous in west-central and southwest regions. Usually encountered in flocks during migration; the largest flocks occur in the fall (400 +, November 17, 1973, Duluth), although flocks of up

Cedar Waxwing

to 100 + birds are seen in early spring. On September 17, 1985, 3,396 were counted in three and a half hours in Duluth. *Spring migration period:* March through late May, with a peak in early April, south; and in late May, north. Early arrival dates and peak periods vary from year to year, and it is difficult to determine migrants from winter visitants, so no early dates can be given. *Fall migration period:* August through November, with a peak from mid-October to mid-November. Again, because of wintering birds, no late dates can be given.

Summer. A numerous resident in the wooded and semi-wooded portions of eastern, central, and northwestern regions. Most numerous in the northwest, east-central, and southwest regions. Scarce in the west-central and southeast regions. Flocks occur in these areas, but they appear to be non-breeding birds.

Winter. Common to occasionally abundant visitant especially in the south. Uncommon in the west-central and southwest regions, and absent in mid-winter during most winters in northern regions. It is not uncommon for flocks of 100 to 200 birds to occur in central regions where adequate food supplies of Mountain Ash and ornamental crab apples are available in the winter.

NORTHERN SHRIKE *(Lanius excubitor)*

Minnesota status. Regular. Migrant and winter visitant.

Migration and winter. An uncommon spring and fall migrant and winter visitant in the state. Most numerous in northern and eastern regions; least numerous in the southwest region. Numbers vary from year to year, from rare to locally common. For example, the winter of 1985-86 saw a major invasion of this species, with over 150 individuals seen in 61 counties, including 18 counties in the southern region. Usually encountered as individuals, but loose association of up to five birds may be found in winter in an area where food is abundant. *Fall migration period:* Early October through late November. Earliest dates: NORTH, September *14,* October 5, 7, 8; SOUTH, October 6, 8, 9. *Spring migration period:* Late February through late April. Most birds have departed by mid-March. Latest dates: SOUTH, April 15, 19, 21; NORTH, April 24, 25, 30.

LOGGERHEAD SHRIKE *(Lanius ludovicianus)*

Minnesota status. Regular. Migrant and summer resident; accidental in winter.
Migration. A rare to uncommon spring and fall migrant throughout most of the state; rare in the heavily forested portions of the north-central and northeastern regions. Numbers have decreased dramatically in recent years, and this species is probably rare anywhere in the state at present. Usually encountered as individuals; most birds are seen on breeding territories. *Spring migration period:* Early March through late April. Earliest dates: SOUTH, March 7, 8, 9; NORTH, *March 1, 6,* 18, 19, 23. *Fall migration period:* Probably from sometime in August through late October, with stragglers in November; almost all birds have left the state by late September. Latest dates: NORTH, October 26, 27, 30, November *6, 9, 14;* SOUTH, October 28, 29, *November 3, 24, 25, 27.*
Summer. A rare and very local resident in the state, absent over wide areas of heavily forested regions, especially in the north-central and northeastern regions. Recent breeding has been reported from Clay, Dakota, Anoka, Benton, Wright, and Morrison Counties. There are recent summer observations from counties in the northwest, central, and southwest regions. Formerly more common and widespread especially in southern and central regions. During a statewide nesting study done during June and July 1986, 27 nests were located in the state; six of the nests were found in Clay County, several others were found in Benton and Morrison

Loggerhead Shrike

Counties, two in Goodhue County, and single nests in Dakota, Fillmore, Sherburne, Lac Qui Parle, and Redwood Counties.

Winter. There are several December dates from as far north as Duluth, with one bird remaining through January until February 6, 1974 (*The Loon* 47:96). There are also December dates from Nobles (December 10, 1967), Lyon (December 18, 1976), Hennepin (December 17, 1977 and December 30, 1967) and Carver (one bird from December 13, 1974 to January 10, 1975; (*The Loon* 47:95) Counties.

EUROPEAN STARLING *(Sturnus vulgaris)*

European Starling

Minnesota status. Regular; introduced. Permanent resident; also regular migrant.

Distribution. Permanent resident throughout the state. This European species, which was introduced in the state of New York in 1890, made its first appearance in Minnesota in 1929 in Fillmore County. By the end of the 1930s it was widely distributed throughout the state, but it did not become abundant until the 1940s. Now it is found as a breeding species everywhere in the state, including wilderness areas like the Boundary Waters Canoe Area, but it reaches its greatest abundance in farming areas.

Migration. Most birds remain in the state all year round. During migration large flocks are seen, especially in the fall, but, unfortunately, people do not pay much attention to this pest species and as a result there are not enough data to describe the migration movements. It definitely migrates in fall in Duluth and along the North Shore of Lake Superior.

WHITE-EYED VIREO *(Vireo griseus)*

Minnesota status. Casual. Migrant.

Records. There are 11 records of this species in the state; six of them are from the month of May at the height of the spring migration period: May 3,

1977, Warner Nature Center, Washington County (*The Loon* 49:174); May 9, 1986, North Oaks, Ramsey County (*The Loon* 58:136); May 15-23, 1982, near Eitzen, Houston County (*The Loon* 54:184-86); May 23 and 24, 1965, Wacouta, Goodhue County (*The Loon* 37:149); May 23, 1980, Oxbow Park, Olmsted County (*The Loon* 52:112); May 24, 1977, Minnetonka, Hennepin County (*The Loon* 49:174-75). On June 4 and 5, 1983, there were at least two birds in Ramsey County (*The Loon* 55:90, 126-27). One bird remained at a Wildlife Management Area near Fairmont, Martin County, from June 6 to July 1, 1986 (*The Loon* 58:139). There is one other summer record: July 31, 1941, St. Cloud, Stearns County (*The Loon* 37:52), the first record in the state. There is one fall record from Dakota County on the very late date of October 21, 1980 (*The Loon* 53:59).

BELL'S VIREO *(Vireo bellii)*

Minnesota status. Regular. Migrant and summer resident.

Migration. All records are from the southern part of the state. A rare spring and fall migrant in the breeding range in the southeastern region, southern portion of the east-central region (Hennepin and Ramsey Counties) and casually in the far southwest corner of the state (Rock and Pipestone Counties). The few spring migration records from outside the known summer range may represent undiscovered or potential new breeding locations. These records are from the following counties: Stevens, Stearns, Carver, Wright, Le Sueur, Scott, Watonwan, Freeborn, and Lyon. *Spring migration period:* May. Earliest dates: May 5, 6, 7. *Fall migration period:* Birds gradually leave nesting areas in July and August. Latest dates: August 15, 21, 28, *September 15, 24* (both in Rock County).

Bell's Vireo

Summer: A very rare and local resident along the Mississippi River in the southeastern region from Houston to Goodhue Counties, occasionally northward into the east-central region (Black Dog Lake,

Dakota County). The most northerly nesting record is from Ft. Snelling, Hennepin County. On June 9, 1984 a nest with four eggs was found near Rochester, Olmsted County. There are summer observations (June and July) from Stearns, Ramsey, and Rice Counties. In the southwest there are June dates from Rock and Pipestone Counties. A singing male was collected in Rock County in June 1972 (MMNH #26035). Best represented as a breeding species in Wabasha County.

SOLITARY VIREO *(Vireo solitarius)*

Solitary Vireo

Minnesota status. Regular. Migrant and summer resident.
Migration. Uncommon to occasionally common spring and fall migrant throughout the state. Common only at peak migration periods. Usually encountered as individuals. *Spring migration period:* Late April through early June, with a peak in early May. Earliest dates: SOUTH, April 21, 22, 25; NORTH, April *19*, 26, 27, May 1. Latest dates: SOUTH, June 1, 2, 4; NORTH, none can be given because of breeding birds. *Fall migration period:* Probably early August through late October, with a peak in late August and early September. Earliest dates: NORTH, none can be given because of breeding birds; SOUTH, August *2*, 20, 21, 22. Latest dates: NORTH, October 3, 6, 11, *17, 19, 21, 22*; SOUTH, October 23, 27, 29, *November 1, 3, 15.*
Summer. Resident throughout most of the northeastern and north-central regions. There are breeding records as far south as Cromwell, Carlton County, and Emily, Crow Wing County, and there are summer observations west to Clearwater, Beltrami, and Roseau Counties. There is a most unusual record for July 8, 1983 in Houston County.

YELLOW-THROATED VIREO *(Vireo flavifrons)*

Minnesota status. Regular. Migrant and summer resident.

Migration: An uncommon spring and fall migrant throughout most of the state. Casual in the northeastern region (never recorded in Cook or Lake Counties) and portions of the adjacent north-central region. Also rare to casual in the southwest and portions of the west-central region. Numbers of this species have been increasing in recent years, and populations have been expanding northward and westward. Usually encountered as individuals or in pairs. *Spring migration period:* Late April through early June, with the bulk of the migration in early and mid-May. Earliest dates: SOUTH, April *20, 21,* 27, 29, 30; NORTH, May 5, 6, 9. *Fall migration period:* Late July through early October; the bulk of migration is in late August and early September. Latest dates: NORTH, September 26, 27, 28; SOUTH, October 4, 5, 9, *19, 26.*

Summer. A resident throughout most of the state except in the northeastern and portions of the north-central and the southwest regions. In the western part of the state it has been found nesting as far north as Pennington County, and there are summer observations as far north as the Canadian border in Kittson, Roseau, and Lake of the Woods Counties. In the central part of the state there is breeding evidence as far north as central Crow Wing County, with summer observations into northern Cass and southern Itasca Counties. In the east there is breeding evidence as far north as St. Croix State Park, Pine County, with summer observations into Carlton County and southern St. Louis County (Duluth).

Yellow-throated Vireo

WARBLING VIREO *(Vireo gilvus)*

Minnesota status. Regular. Migrant and summer resident.

Migration. A common spring migrant throughout most of the state; uncommon to rare in most of the northeastern region. Uncommon to rare over the whole state in fall, with a very gradual exodus from breeding territories. *Spring migration period:* Very

Warbling Vireo

late April through late May, with a peak in mid-May. Earliest dates: SOUTH, April 26, 29, 30; NORTH, *April 28,* May 5, 6, 7. *Fall migration period:* Late July through late September; most birds have left by late August or early September. Latest dates: NORTH, September 21, 22, 27; SOUTH, September 28, 30, October 2, *14.*

Summer. A resident throughout most of the deciduous woodlands of the state; least numerous in the northeast and north-central regions where it avoids the heavy continuous stands of coniferous forest and spruce bog country. Found in these areas where more open deciduous woodlands occur. Most numerous in the east-central and southeast regions.

PHILADELPHIA VIREO
(Vireo philadelphicus)

Philadelphia Vireo

Minnesota status. Regular. Migrant and summer resident.

Migration: An uncommon spring and fall migrant throughout the state. Common only at peak migration periods in local areas. Usually encountered as individuals. *Spring migration period:* Early May through early June, with a peak in mid-May. Earliest dates: SOUTH, May 4, 5, 6; NORTH, May *1,* 7, 8, 9. Latest dates: SOUTH, June 2, 3, 4; NORTH, none can be given because of breeding birds. *Fall migration period:* Mid-August through early October; the bulk of the migration is in early and mid-September. Earliest dates: NORTH, none can be given because of breeding birds; SOUTH, July *28, 30,* August *11,* 18, 19, 20. Latest dates: NORTH, October 11, 12, 14, *18;* SOUTH, October 6, 8, 9, *29.*

Summer. A resident primarily in the northwestern region in Cook, Lake, and northern St. Louis Counties and probably west through the coniferous forests of Koochiching and Lake of the Woods Counties. Even in this range the species is very scarce and local. There are two records outside this area: fledglings being fed by parents at Many Point Lake, Becker County, in 1961; one bird banded near Little Falls, Morrison County, on June 16, 1966—this could have been a very late spring migrant. Probably more common and widespread than suspected, it is overlooked because the song is so similar to that of the Red-eyed Vireo.

RED-EYED VIREO *(Vireo olivaceus)*

Minnesota status. Regular. Migrant and summer resident.

Migration. A common spring and fall migrant throughout the state. Occasionally abundant at peak migration periods. Usually encountered as individuals or pairs. *Spring migration period:* Very late April through early June, with a peak in mid and late May. Earliest dates: SOUTH, April *15, 18,* 27, 28, 30; NORTH, *April* 26, May 6, 7, 8. *Fall migration period:* Late July through mid-October. The bulk of the migration is in the first half of September. Latest dates: NORTH, October 13, 15, 16, *27*; SOUTH, October 20, 25, 26, *November 4, 6.*

Summer. A numerous resident throughout the heavily wooded areas of the state. Least numerous in the southwest region.

Red-eyed Vireo

BLUE-WINGED WARBLER *(Vermivora pinus)*

Minnesota status. Regular. Migrant and summer resident.

Migration. Most records are for the southern part of the state of birds on breeding territories. A rare spring and fall migrant mainly in the southeast region from Houston and Fillmore Counties north to Olmsted and Goodhue Counties. It is found regularly in the southern portions of the east-central region in Washington, Ramsey, Dakota, Hennepin (Wolsfeld Woods), Anoka (Carlos Avery Refuge), and Cedar Creek Counties. In the central region it has been found in Wright (Cokato), Sherburne (near St. Cloud), Stearns (St. Cloud), Kandiyohi (Sibley State Park), and Nicollet Counties. In the

Blue-winged Warbler

south-central region it is well represented in Scott County at Murphy-Hanrehan Park Reserve, and it has been observed in Rice (Northfield), Blue Earth (Cambria), Freeborn, and Brown Counties. In the southwest it has been seen in Lyon, Cottonwood, and Nobles Counties. In the north there are unconfirmed reports from St. Louis (Duluth), Otter Tail, and Hubbard Counties (see summer below). Usually encountered as individuals. *Spring migration period:* Late April through early June (south only). Earliest dates: April 27, 28, 30. *Fall migration period:* Probably late July through September. Latest dates: September 10, 13, 14, *20.*

Summer. A resident primarily in the southeastern region in Houston, Fillmore, Winona, Wabasha, and Goodhue Counties. A recent (1940s to 1960s) range expansion saw birds move northward into Washington, Hennepin, (Wolsfeld Woods), Anoka (Cedar Creek), and most recently into Scott County at Murphy-Hanrehan Park Reserve. There may be occasional breeding up the Mississippi River Valley as far as St. Cloud, Stearns County, and down the Minnesota River Valley as far as St. Peter, Nicollet County. A single bird was seen during the summer of 1985 in Flandreau State Park, Brown County. On June 3, 1984 a single bird was seen near Fergus Falls, Otter Tail County (*The Loon* 56:198). One bird, probably a spring vagrant, was recorded on June 11, 1977 in Lake County along the North Shore of Lake Superior, a long distance from the present breeding range of this species.

Taxonomic note. This species regularly hybridizes with the Golden-winged Warbler where the breeding ranges of the two species overlap. This occurs in Minnesota, at present mainly in Goodhue, Scott, and Anoka Counties. Both hybrids, the Lawrence's and Brewster's Warblers, have been reported from these areas (*The Loon* 49:171-72) and also during migration from the east-central and southeast regions.

GOLDEN-WINGED WARBLER
(Vermivora chrysoptera)

Minnesota status. Regular. Migrant and summer resident.

Golden-winged Warbler

Migration. An uncommon spring and a rare fall migrant in the eastern (casual in the southeast and over most of the northeast) and central regions of the state; casual to absent during both seasons in most areas of the western regions. This species appears to be expanding its range northward in the state with recent records in Lake, Cook, and central St. Louis Counties in the northeast and Koochiching County in the north-central region. It has not been recorded in most of the northwest region except in Clay and Becker Counties, and there is one record (August 21, 1974) from Agassiz National Wildlife Refuge in eastern Marshall County. It is also unrecorded over most of the west-central region except in eastern Otter Tail County. There are only a scattering of migration records from the southwest region. Usually encountered as individuals. *Spring migration period:* Early May through early June, with a peak about May 10. Earliest dates: SOUTH, April 30, May 1, 2; NORTH, *April 22, 30,* May 5, 8, 9. *Fall migration period:* Probably late July through late September. Latest dates: NORTH, September 12, 14, 15, *24, 28;* SOUTH, September 27, 30, October 2.

Summer. Resident primarily in the central part of the state, including portions of the east-central, central, and north-central regions. The primary breeding range appears to be from Chisago, Pine, and Carlton Counties in the east, westward through northern Anoka, Isanti, Kanabec, Aitkin, Cass, and Crow Wing Counties, and as far west as Hubbard and Clearwater Counties. It is expanding northward from this range into southern St. Louis and Lake (July 4, 1983) and Cook (July 1, 1983 and June 14, 1984) Counties in the northeast to Itasca and southern Koochiching, Beltrami, and Lake of the Woods Counties in the north-central region. There are also recent (1986) records from Cook County.

This species formerly bred in the southeast and as far north as Hennepin County (Roberts 1932); the only recent breeding evidence from this area was obtained in June 1985 when a male Golden-winged Warbler and a female Brewster's Warbler were found feeding young in Murphy-Hanrehan Park Reserve, Scott County.

Taxonomic note. See under Blue-winged Warbler for hybridization with that species.

TENNESSEE WARBLER *(Vermivora peregrina)*

Tennessee Warbler

Minnesota status. Regular. Migrant and summer resident.

Migration. An abundant spring and fall migrant throughout the state. Usually encountered as individuals, but during peak migration periods loose aggregations of a few birds up to ten individuals can be seen. *Spring migration period:* Late April through mid-June, with a peak in mid-May. Earliest dates: SOUTH, April 28, 29, May 3; NORTH, *April 29*, May 7, 8, 9. Latest dates: SOUTH, June 4, 5, 6, *11*; NORTH, none can be given because of breeding birds. A few birds remain in Duluth until mid-June, and there is a record on June 20, 1977 from Long Lake Township, Otter Tail County. *Fall migration period:* Mid-July through late October, with a peak in late August and early September. Earliest dates: NORTH (away from breeding areas), July 16, 17, 18; SOUTH, July *13*, 21, 23, 31. Latest dates: NORTH, October 24, 25, 31; SOUTH, October 26, 29, November 2, *7*.

Summer. Resident in the northeastern and north-central regions as far south as southern St. Louis County and Itasca State Park, Clearwater County. Throughout this range the species is very scarce except along the Canadian border in northern Cook, Lake, and St. Louis Counties.

ORANGE-CROWNED WARBLER *(Vermivora celata)*

Minnesota status. Regular. Migrant; accidental in summer and early winter.
Migration. A common to abundant spring and fall migrant throughout the state. Best represented in western regions. Abundant in local areas at peak migration periods. Usually encountered as individuals or in loose aggregations of a few to tens of birds. Over 100 were seen in a small area of Hole-in-the-Mountain County Park, Lincoln County, on October 2, 1983. *Spring migration period:* Mid-April through late May, with a peak in early May. Earliest dates: SOUTH, April *11*, 16, 18, 19; NORTH, April 17, 18, 21. Latest dates: SOUTH, May 23, 26, 27, June *1*; NORTH, May 27, 29, 31. *Fall migration period:* Mid-August through late October, with a peak in late September and early October. Earliest dates: NORTH, July *28, 31*, August *3*, 14, 16, 17; SOUTH, August 13, 15, 22. Latest dates: NORTH, October 17, 18, 21, *28, November 9*; SOUTH, October 27, 29, 30, *November 3, 5, 16.*
Summer. This species has not been found breeding in the state, although the regular breeding range reaches southern Manitoba along the Minnesota border in the northwest region. There are several old June dates, probably of very late migrants: June 11, 1915, singing male, Isanti County; June 10, 1935, singing male, Clearwater County; June 15 (2) and 23 (1), 1965, banded, near Hibbing, St. Louis County.
Winter. There is one record of a single individual December 4-13, 1968 in Ramsey County (*The Loon* 41:54-55).

NASHVILLE WARBLER *(Vermivora ruficapilla)*

Minnesota status. Regular. Migrant and summer resident.
Migration. A common to occasionally abundant spring and fall migrant throughout the state. Usually encountered as individuals but occasionally small

Nashville Warbler

groups of ten or more are seen in loose association at peak migration periods. *Spring migration period:* Late April through early June, with a peak in mid-May. Earliest dates: SOUTH, April *14*, 19, 23, 26; NORTH, April 28, 29, May 2. Latest dates: SOUTH, June 1, 3, 7; NORTH, none can be given because of breeding birds. *Fall migration period:* Late July through late October, with the bulk of the emigration in September. Earliest dates: NORTH, none can be given because of breeding birds; SOUTH, July *10*, 14, 15, 19 (Hennepin, Ramsey, and Winona Counties). Latest dates: NORTH, October 22, 23, 25; SOUTH, October 28, 29, 30, *November 7* (Nicollet County), *20-29* (*The Flicker* 14:15).

Summer. A numerous resident primarily in the northeastern and north-central regions, south to northern Washington and Anoka Counties in the east, Crow Wing and northern Mille Lacs County in the central part of the state, west to eastern Becker, Pennington, Marshall, and Roseau Counties. Most numerous in Cook, Lake, northern St. Louis Counties and northern portions of the north-central region. Most unusual was the presence of a male and female at Murphy-Hanrehan Park, Scott County, on July 14, 1984. These birds were probably very early fall migrants.

NORTHERN PARULA *(Parula americana)*

Minnesota status. Regular. Migrant and summer resident.

Migration. An uncommon spring and fall migrant in eastern and central regions; occasionally uncommon in eastern regions at peak migration periods. Rare to casual in western regions. Usually encountered as individuals. *Spring migration period:* Mid-April through early June, with a peak in mid-May. Earliest dates: SOUTH, April 12, 13, 15; NORTH, April *11*, 30, May 3, 6. Latest dates: SOUTH, June 2, 5; NORTH, none can be given because of breeding birds. *Fall migration period:* Late August through mid-October, with a peak in mid-September.

Northern Parula

Earliest dates: NORTH, none can be given because of breeding birds; SOUTH, August *1, 5*, 20, 23, 24. Latest dates: NORTH, October 6, 7, 8, *13*; SOUTH, October 14, 20, 22, *27, November 8, 9.*

Summer. A resident primarily in the northeastern and north-central regions as far south as southern St. Louis and Crow Wing Counties. Ranges as far west as eastern Becker and Polk Counties in the northwest region. The range in the northwest corner of the state is not well known. There is one record of a single bird in Hennepin County on July 1, 1971, probably a nonbreeding wanderer.

YELLOW WARBLER *(Dendroica petechia)*

Minnesota status. Regular. Migrant and summer resident.

Migration. A common spring and fall migrant throughout the state, mainly seen on breeding territories. Uncommon in the fall with a gradual exodus from breeding areas. Usually encountered as individuals. *Spring migration period:* Late April through late May, with a peak in mid-May. Earliest dates: SOUTH, April 21, 24, 25; NORTH, May 1, 3, 4. *Fall migration period:* Probably late July through late September; most birds have departed by early September. Latest dates: NORTH, September 21, 23, 29; SOUTH, September 28, 30, October 2, *8, 19, 24* (*The Loon* 48:188-89).

Summer. A numerous resident throughout most of the state, breeding in all regions but uncommon in the heavily forested areas of the northern regions where suitable habitat is limited.

Yellow Warbler

CHESTNUT-SIDED WARBLER
(Dendroica pensylvanica)

Minnesota status. Regular. Migrant and summer resident.

Migration. A common spring and fall migrant in eastern and central regions, uncommon in both

Chestnut-sided Warbler

spring and fall in western regions. Usually encountered as individuals. *Spring migration period:* Early May through early June, with a peak in mid-May. Earliest dates: SOUTH, May 1, 2, 3; NORTH, April *20, 25,* May 5, 6, 7. *Fall migration period:* Mid-August through early October, with a peak in early to mid-September. Latest dates: NORTH, September 27, 29, 30; SOUTH, October 4, 6, 7, *25, 31.*

Summer. A resident primarily in northern regions from Cook County in the east to eastern Marshall and Kittson Counties in the west. This range extends southward to northern Anoka County (Cedar Creek) in the east-central region, eastern Stearns County in the central region, Douglas (June 1983) and Clay Counties in the west. In the early twentieth century this species was fairly well represented in the southeastern region and in the area around the Twin Cities, but as this area was urbanized and the heavy forests cut, the species began to disappear. Roberts (1932) reported nests as far south as Houston County, but no nests have been reported for 45 years from the Twin Cities area southward. However, there are recent isolated summer observations in the southern part of the state from Winona, Rice, Dakota, and Cottonwood Counties, indicating possible infrequent nesting in this part of the state. A significant indication that breeding may once again be taking place in the Twin Cities was the presence of 15-20 individuals at Murphy-Hanrehan Park in Scott County during June 1986.

MAGNOLIA WARBLER *(Dendroica magnolia)*

Minnesota status. Regular. Migrant and summer resident.

Migration. An uncommon to occasionally common spring and fall migrant throughout the state. Most numerous in eastern regions where it is common at peak migration periods. Encountered as individuals. *Spring migration period:* Early May through early June, with a peak in mid-May. Earliest dates:

Magnolia Warbler

SOUTH, *April 22, 26*, May 1, 3, 4; NORTH, *April 23*, May 3, 6, 7. Latest dates: SOUTH, June 3, 4, 7, *26* (Minneapolis); NORTH, none can be given because of breeding birds. *Fall migration period:* Early August through mid-October, with the bulk of the migration in early and mid-September. Earliest dates: NORTH, none can be given because of breeding birds; SOUTH, August 12, 18, 19. Latest dates: NORTH, October 10, 13, 18; SOUTH, October 10, 13, 14, *November 1, 10*.

Summer. A resident in the northeastern and north-central regions as far south as central Carlton County, southern Crow Wing County, and Hubbard County west to central Roseau County. Most numerous in Cook, Lake, and St. Louis Counties.

CAPE MAY WARBLER *(Dendroica tigrina)*

Minnesota status. Regular. Migrant and summer resident; accidental in early winter.

Migration. An uncommon spring and fall migrant in the eastern regions, rare to casual at both seasons elsewhere in the state. Can occasionally be common in the east during the peak spring migration period. Normally encountered as individuals. *Spring migration period:* Early May to late May, with a peak in mid-May. Earliest dates: SOUTH, May 3, 4, 5; NORTH, May 2, 5, 7. Latest dates: SOUTH, May 31, June 2; NORTH, none can be given because of breeding birds. *Fall migration period:* Early August through late October, with stragglers into November. Earliest dates: NORTH, (nonbreeding areas), July 29, August 7; SOUTH, August 2, 9, 10. Latest dates: NORTH, October 23, 26, 27, *November 2, 13, 18*; SOUTH, October 14, 15, 19.

Cape May Warbler

Summer. A resident primarily in the northern part of the northeastern region in normal years. Summer resident numbers can fluctuate widely and appear to be tied to the outbreaks of spruce bud-worm infestations. At these times this species may be found in widely scattered localities in the northeastern and north-central regions. There are summer observations as far west as Hubbard and Clearwater Counties near Itasca State Park. The summer range in the northwest is unknown.

Winter. There are five late November and December records for this species; four of the individuals were coming to feeding stations: December 1, 1976 (road kill), Wabasha County; December 2, 1980, Stony Point, St. Louis County; November 28 to December 8, 1982, near Kellogg, Wabasha County; November 16 to December 21, 1975, Castle Danger, Lake County; and the latest date, December 22-27, 1982, Hutchinson, McLeod County.

BLACK-THROATED BLUE WARBLER
(Dendroica caerulescens)

Black-throated Blue Warbler

Minnesota status. Regular. Migrant and summer resident.

Migration. A rare spring and fall migrant anywhere in the state. Most birds seen are on breeding territories in the northeast region. It would appear that most spring migrants coming into the state enter from the east, possibly across Lake Superior, as few birds are seen in migration in other areas of the state. The same may happen in reverse in the fall. Of the few migrants seen, most are in eastern regions, mainly in Duluth and the Twin Cities. *Spring migration period:* Early to late May. Earliest dates: SOUTH, May 2, 3, 4; NORTH, May *1*, 16, 20, 21. Latest dates: SOUTH, May 23, 25, 28; NORTH (away from breeding areas), June 11, Mille Lacs County. *Fall migration period:* Mid-August through late October, with two stragglers into November. Earliest dates: NORTH, none can be given because of breeding birds; SOUTH, August 13, 14, 28. Latest dates: NORTH, September 25, 30, October 2; SOUTH, October 21, 23, 24, *31-November 1, 12-December 2* (*The Loon* 56:65).

Summer. Resident primarily in the northeastern region, especially in Cook and eastern Lake Counties where it is local in the stands of deciduous woods found in the coniferous forest. Also found casual in the north-central region of Cass, Beltrami, and Clearwater Counties. There are breeding season observations from Mille Lacs, Aitkin, and northern Pine Counties.

YELLOW-RUMPED WARBLER
(Dendroica coronata)

Minnesota status. Regular. Migrant and summer resident; accidental in winter.
Migration. An abundant spring and fall migrant throughout the state, the earliest and most abundant spring migrant warbler. Encountered in loose flocks that can number into the hundreds of birds; on September 21, 1980 over 1,000 birds were estimated in a small area along the shore of Lake Bemidji, Beltrami County, and at Hawk Ridge, Duluth, daily counts of over 1,000 are often made. *Spring migration period:* Very late March through early June, with the bulk of the migration from mid-April to early May. This species is usually not seen before April 10 in the south and April 15 in the north. Earliest dates: SOUTH, March 26, 30, 31; NORTH, April 1, 4, 6. Latest dates: SOUTH, May 28, 31, June 2; NORTH, none can be given because of breeding birds. *Fall migration period:* Although some birds begin to wander away from the breeding areas in mid-July, migration usually starts in the north in early August and in the south in late August, and continues through early November, with stragglers remaining until early winter; the bulk of the migration takes place from mid-September through late October. Earliest dates: NORTH, none can be given because of breeding birds; SOUTH, August 13, 15, 21. Latest dates: NORTH, November 24, 25, 26, *30*; SOUTH, November 18, 21, 28.
Summer. A well-represented summer resident in northeastern and north-central regions as far west as eastern Marshall and Roseau Counties. Most numerous in northern portions of these regions. During the summer of 1973 pairs were found as far

Yellow-rumped Warbler

south as Anoka and Sherburne Counties in the eastern and central regions. This may indicate occasional breeding south of the normal breeding range.

Winter. There are late November and December records from Cook County and Duluth in the north, and Hennepin, Ramsey, Dakota, and Houston Counties in the south. Birds have attempted to overwinter (surviving into January) at feeding stations in Cass County and Duluth in the north, and in Hennepin, Ramsey, Goodhue, and Wabasha Counties in the south. Two birds survived the entire winter, one in Bloomington, Hennepin County, and the other in Wabasha County (*The Loon* 53:114-15).

Taxonomic note. The Audubon's Warbler (*D.c. auduboni*) has been observed three times during the spring migration and once in the winter (*The Loon* 54:133) in the Twin Cities area. Also, one bird was seen in Grand Marais, Cook County, on November 21, 1985 (*The Loon* 57:184).

BLACK-THROATED GRAY WARBLER
(Dendroica nigrescens)

Minnesota status. Accidental.
Records. There are two spring records: April 24, 1938, Minneapolis (L. M. Aler, description in MMNH files); May 14, 1956, Madison, Lac Qui Parle County (specimen, MMNH #12245).

TOWNSEND'S WARBLER *(Dendroica townsendi)*

Minnesota status. Accidental.
Records. There is one spring sight record: May 22, 1979, Rice Lake, Scott County (*The Loon* 51:141-42).

HERMIT WARBLER *(Dendroica occidentalis)*

Minnesota status. Accidental.
Records. There are two spring records: May 3, Cambridge, Isanti County (specimen, MMNH #7735, *Auk* 48:435); May 14, 1983, one seen, Lac Qui Parle County (*The Loon* 55:88).

BLACK-THROATED GREEN WARBLER
(Dendroica virens)

Minnesota status. Regular. Migrant and summer resident.
Migration. An uncommon spring and fall migrant in the eastern and central regions, least numerous in the southeast region. Uncommon to rare in spring and fall in western regions. May be locally common in the east-central and northeast regions at peak migration periods. Usually encountered as individuals. *Spring migration period:* Late April through early June, with a peak in early and mid-May. Earliest dates: SOUTH, April 25, 26, 28; NORTH, *April 25, 28, 30*, May 1, 3. Latest dates: SOUTH, June 2, 8, 12; NORTH, none can be given because of breeding birds. *Fall migration period:* Mid-August through mid-October, with a peak in early September. Earliest dates: NORTH, none can be given because of breeding birds; SOUTH, August 17, 18, 19. Latest dates: NORTH, October 3, 7, 8, *12*; SOUTH, October 15, 17, 22, *November 1, 2, 3*.
Summer. A widespread but local resident in the northeast and north-central regions, with observations as far south as northern Pine County and northern Anoka (Cedar Creek) County in the east-central region and breeding to northern Mille Lacs County in the central region, and as far west as Tamarac National Wildlife Refuge, Becker County. The western boundary of the breeding range in the northwest is unclear. This species formerly bred in the Big Woods of Hennepin-Wright and adjacent counties, but there are no recent reports from this area other than the observations at Cedar Creek, Anoka County.

Black-throated Green Warbler

Blackburnian Warbler

BLACKBURNIAN WARBLER *(Dendroica fusca)*

Minnesota status. Regular. Migrant and summer resident.
Migration. An uncommon to occasionally common spring migrant in eastern and central regions, uncommon during both seasons in western regions. Common only locally at peak migration periods. Usually encountered as individuals. *Spring migration period:* Early May through early June, with a peak in mid-May; very seldom seen before May 8. Earliest dates: SOUTH, April 29, 30, May 1; NORTH, May 1, 4, 5. Latest dates: SOUTH, May 26, June 1, 2; NORTH, none can be given because of breeding birds. *Fall migration period:* Mid-August through early October, with a peak in early September. Earliest dates: NORTH, none can be given because of breeding birds; SOUTH, *July 31*, August 9, 10, 17. Latest dates: NORTH, September 24, 25, 26, *October 13, 17, 22*: SOUTH, October 6, 10, 12.
Summer. A resident primarily in the north-central regions. From these regions it is found sparingly south into Pine County and northern Anoka (Cedar Creek) County in the east and along the eastern margin of the northwest region in the west.

YELLOW-THROATED WARBLER
(Dendroica dominica)

Minnesota status. Accidental.
Records. There are five spring records of adult males in April and early May: April 21, 1985, Murphy-Hanrehan Park, Scott County (*The Loon* 57:111); May 6-8, 1980, Roseville, Ramsey County (*The Loon* 52:111-12); May 4-6, 1982, Wood Lake Nature Center, Richfield, Hennepin County (*The Loon* 54:180); May 4, 1986, Freeborn County (*The Loon* 58:130); May 8-9, 1984, Lake Elmo, Washington County, photographed (*The Loon* 56:188). There is one fall record: September 22, 1984, Moorhead, Clay County (*The Loon* 57:105-6).

PINE WARBLER *(Dendroica pinus)*

Minnesota status. Regular. Migrant and summer resident.

Migration. A rare spring migrant and a rare to uncommon fall migrant in east-central, central, northeast, north-central, and eastern portions of the northwestern regions. Rare to casual across all southern regions and the west-central region. Usually encountered as individuals. *Spring migration period:* Mid-April through late May, with most birds seen in early May. Earliest dates: SOUTH, April 15, 16, 17; NORTH, April 14, 17, 18. Latest dates: SOUTH (beyond breeding areas), May 25, 26, June 8; NORTH, none can be given because of breeding birds. *Fall migration period:* Mid-August through mid-October. Earliest dates: NORTH, none can be given because of breeding birds; SOUTH (beyond breeding areas), August *3*, 14, 15, 17. Latest dates: NORTH, October 7, 8, 10, *25, 31, November 11*; SOUTH, October 13, 14, 15, *November 1*. One very late migrant was seen near Buffalo, Wright County, from November 20 to 24, 1985 *(The Loon 57:183)*.

Pine Warbler

Summer. A local resident in the north-central, northern portions of the central and east-central regions as far south as northern Washington and Ramsey (Lake Vadnais) Counties in the east and northern Morrison and Todd Counties in the central region. Most frequently found in large stands of White Pine. Sparsely represented or absent in the northeast region in St. Louis, Lake, and Cook Counties.

Winter. One bird was seen at a feeder in Austin, Mower County, from November 17, 1985 to February 4, 1986 *(The Loon 58:48)*.

KIRTLAND'S WARBLER *(Dendroica kirtlandii)*

Minnesota status. Accidental.
Records. There are two records for this very rare species in the state, both in May: May 13, 1982,

Hennepin County (specimen, MMNH #5724); May 22, 1944, St. Cloud, Stearns County (*The Loon* 52:112).

PRAIRIE WARBLER *(Dendroica discolor)*

Minnesota status. Accidental.
Records. There are three records for the state: May 12, 1961, Bloomington, Hennepin County (*The Flicker* 33:92); May 30, 1968, Minnetonka, Hennepin County (*The Loon* 40:59-60); June 10, 1975, Spring Grove, Houston County (*The Loon* 48:70).

PALM WARBLER *(Dendroica palmarum)*

Palm Warbler

Minnesota status. Regular. Migrant and summer resident.
Migration. A common to abundant spring and fall migrant in the eastern and central regions: uncommon in western regions. Most common along the North Shore of Lake Superior in the fall, usually encountered as individuals, but loose aggregations numbering in the tens of birds can be seen at peak migration periods. *Spring migration period:* Mid-April through late May, with a peak in early May. Earliest dates: SOUTH, April 10, 11, 13; NORTH, April *15, 23, 24, 26.* Latest dates: SOUTH, May 25, 27, 31, *June 4, 9, 17*; NORTH, none can be given because of breeding birds. *Fall migration period:* Mid-August through early November, with the bulk of the migration from late September through mid-October. Earliest dates: NORTH, none can be given because of breeding birds; SOUTH, August 15, 17, 20. Latest dates: NORTH, October 27, 28, 31, *November 9, 11, 19*; SOUTH, November 3, 7, 10, *16*.
Summer. A scarce resident in the northeast and north-central regions west to eastern Roseau County in the northwest. Most often found in St. Louis County in areas of open or parklike tamarack and black spruce bogs.

BAY-BREASTED WARBLER
(Dendroica castanea)

Minnesota status. Regular. Migrant and summer resident.
Migration. An uncommon to rare spring and fall migrant in eastern and central regions. More often seen in fall than in spring. Usually encountered as individuals, but tens of birds can be seen at peak migration periods in the fall. *Spring migration period:* Early May through early June, with a peak from May 15 to 20. Earliest dates: SOUTH, April *30*, May 4, 5, 8; NORTH, May 9, 10, 11. Latest dates: SOUTH, June 1, 4, *14*; NORTH (away from breeding areas), June 6, 9. *Fall migration period:* Late July (north), late August (south) through late October; rarely seen after late September. Earliest dates: NORTH (away from breeding areas), July 17, 26; SOUTH, August 3, 9, 13. Latest dates: NORTH, October 2, 4, 6, *12, 25*; SOUTH, October 19, 20, 25.
Summer. A regular resident only in the northern portion of Cook, Lake, and St. Louis Counties in the northeast and Koochiching, Beltrami, and Lake of the Woods Counties in the north-central region; west to central Roseau County in the northwest. There are summer observations as far south and west as Itasca State Park in Clearwater County, but there is no positive breeding evidence from this area.

Bay-breasted Warbler

BLACKPOLL WARBLER *(Dendroica striata)*

Minnesota status. Regular. Migrant; accidental in summer.
Migration. An uncommon to occasionally common spring and fall migrant throughout the state; common at peak migration periods in many areas of the state. Usually encountered as individuals, but loose aggregations of tens of birds are occasionally found. *Spring migration period:* Late April through early June, with the bulk of the migration in mid-May. Earliest dates: SOUTH, April *20*, 25, 26, 27; NORTH, *April 30*, May 4, 5, 7. Latest dates: SOUTH, June

3, 4, 6; NORTH, June 8, 9, 10, *14. Fall migration period:* Early August through early October. Earliest dates: NORTH, *July 30*, August 8, 14, 15; SOUTH, August *5*, 14, 16, 20. Latest dates: NORTH, October 8, 9, 10, *13, 19, 24*; SOUTH, October 5, 8, 9, *25*.

Summer. There are three records of summer vagrants: June 20 and 21, 1974, Duluth; July 3, 1976, Duluth; July 18, 1981, Aitkin County (*The Loon* 53:175).

CERULEAN WARBLER *(Dendroica cerulea)*

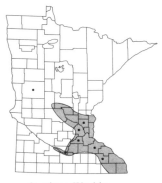

Cerulean Warbler

Minnesota status. Regular. Migrant and summer resident.

Migration. A rare spring and fall migrant in southeastern, east-central, and central regions with records from Aitkin and Crow Wing Counties in the north-central region, Otter Tail, Douglas, and Pope Counties in the west-central region, and Becker and Mahnomen Counties in the northwest. *Spring migration period:* May. Earliest dates: SOUTH, *April 24, 30*, May 3, 4, 6; NORTH, May 14, 18, 20. *Fall migration period:* A gradual exodus from breeding areas takes place in August with no distinct migration movements noted. Latest dates: SOUTH, August 23, 30, September 1; NORTH, no data.

Summer. Resident along the Mississippi River from Houston County in the southeast, northwestward into Goodhue, Scott, and Hennepin Counties, continuing northwestward into Stearns and Todd Counties and possibly as far north as Mahnomen County (*The Loon* 39:108-9). It nested at Maplewood State Park, Otter Tail County, in 1978. In the Minnesota River Valley it ranges upstream as far as St. Peter, Nicollet County, and during June 1985 a female and singing male were seen in Flandrau State Park, Brown County.

BLACK-AND-WHITE WARBLER
(Mniotilta varia)

Minnesota status. Regular. Migrant and summer resident; accidental in winter.
Migration. A common spring and fall migrant throughout the state. Usually encountered as individuals. *Spring migration period:* Mid-April through late May, with a peak in early May. Earliest dates: SOUTH, April *4, 10*, 13, 15, 17; NORTH, April *20*, 26, 27, 30. *Fall migration period:* Early August through mid-October, with the bulk of the migration from late August through late September. Latest dates: NORTH, October 11, 15, 19, *November 10*; SOUTH, October 23, 26, 29, *November 13*.

Black-and-white Warbler

Summer. A resident primarily in the northeastern and north-central regions southward to the northern portions of the east-central region (Cedar Creek, Anoka County, and possibly northern Hennepin County) and Mille Lacs County in the central region. Scarce in the central region south and west of Mille Lacs Lake. In the west this species ranges to the edge of the northwest region except in the far northwest corner of the state where there are observations from Roseau and Kittson Counties. This species formerly bred in the southeastern region along the Mississippi River, but there are no recent records for this area. There is one recent record from Le Sueur County along the Minnesota River on June 22, 1974.
Winter. There is one amazing record of this species from Duluth, February 15 to March 21, 1975 (*The Loon* 47:96-97).

AMERICAN REDSTART *(Setophaga ruticilla)*

Minnesota status. Regular. Migrant and summer resident.
Migration. A common spring and fall migrant throughout the state; least numerous in the southwest region. Occasionally abundant at peak migration periods; 1,000 were estimated on Minnesota

American Redstart

Point, Duluth, on August 28, 1978 (*The Loon* 51:50). *Spring migration period:* Late April through late May, with a peak in mid-May. Earliest dates: SOUTH, April 25, 27, 30; NORTH, *April 30,* May 6, 7. *Fall migration period:* Late July through late October, with the bulk of the migration from late August through mid-September. Latest dates: NORTH, October 24, 26, 28, November *13* (*The Loon* 48:36-37); SOUTH, October 22, 26, 29.

Summer. A well-represented and numerous resident throughout most of the state. Scarce or absent over the western half of the south-central region and all of the southwest region.

PROTHONOTARY WARBLER
(Protonotaria citrea)

Prothonotary Warbler

Minnesota status. Regular. Migrant and summer resident.

Migration. A very rare spring migrant in the southeast and east-central regions. Most records are from breeding areas. There are vagrant records as far north as Duluth (May 17, 1966) in the northeast; Agassiz National Wildlife Refuge (May 13, 1966), Marshall County, and Moorhead (May 19, 1982), Clay County, in the northwest; Swift County (May 17, 1969) in the west-central region; Murray County (May 29, 1978) in the southwest; and there are May records from the south-central region in Nicollet, Blue Earth, Le Sueur, Rice, and Mower Counties. In the central region there are May records from Stearns and Mille Lac Counties. In the fall, observations are mainly from breeding areas, and most birds have departed by late August. Encountered as individuals or in pairs. *Spring migration period:* May. Earliest dates: *April 11*, May 1, 2, 3. *Fall migration period:* A gradual exodus from breeding areas from late July through late August. Latest dates: August 23, 27, 30, September *3, 4, 23* (Pope County, *The Loon* 46:69) and Olmsted County, 1986.

Summer. A resident in the southeastern and east-central regions along the Mississippi, Rum, Minnesota, and St. Croix Rivers, as far north as central Chisago County and formerly Isanti County (1927) and southwest into Scott County. The majority of the summer records are from along the Mississippi River from Goodhue to Houston Counties. In 1984 nests were found in Ramsey County and in the Minnesota River Valley as far south as Brown County. The Brown County record indicates an expansion of the breeding range into the upper Minnesota River Valley. Most unusual is a record on July 2, 1973 from Spider Lake, Itasca County, in the north-central region.

WORM-EATING WARBLER
(Helmitheros vermivorus)

Minnesota status. Casual. Migrant.
Records. There are approximately 28 records for the state, all but four of which are for the spring migration from late April to late May. The earliest date is April 27, 1974 from Richfield, Hennepin County (*The Loon* 46:122), and there is one specimen from this period, April 30, 1962, Hennepin County (MMNH #17835). The majority of the records (14) are from the Twin Cities area and the southern part of the state. Outside the Twin Cities there are observations from Lac Qui Parle, Mower (3), Fillmore (2), Cottonwood, Brown, Blue Earth, Olmsted, and Waseca Counties. In the north there is one spring record from Otter Tail County on May 20, 1979 (*The Loon* 51:155); this is also the latest spring date. The fall records are from Minneapolis on August 26, 1973 (*The Loon* 46:172-73), and the other three records are from the north, all during the month of November: November 11, 1976, Hawk Ridge, Duluth (*The Loon* 49:45); November 15, 1975, Cass County (*The Loon* 48:38); November 18, 1973, Garrison, Crow Wing County (*The Loon* 46:35-36). Could these observations indicate that some type of reverse migration is occurring in this species?

OVENBIRD *(Seiurus aurocapillus)*

Ovenbird

Minnesota status. Regular. Migrant and summer resident; accidental in winter.
Migration. A common spring and fall migrant throughout the state. *Spring migration period:* Late April through early June, with a peak in mid-May. Usually encountered as individuals. Earliest dates: SOUTH, April *15*, 25, 26, 27; NORTH, May 2, 3, 4. *Fall migration period:* Mid-August through late October, with a peak in early and mid-September. Latest dates: NORTH, October 16, 17, 19; SOUTH, October 18, 20, 28, *November 2, 3, 15, 21, December 2.*
Summer. Resident throughout the wooded portions of the state, mainly in the northern, east-central, and southeastern regions. Scarce to absent over most of the south-central, southwest, and west-central regions. There are a few observations from the Minnesota River Valley in Nicollet and Brown Counties and from Nerstrand Woods State Park, Rice County. In the summer of 1979 there were June observations in Camden State Park, Lyon County, and in Chippewa County. These scattered records indicate casual breeding in some southern areas.
Winter. One bird in Minneapolis from December 27, 1974 to January 9, 1975 (*The Loon* 47:97-98).

NORTHERN WATERTHRUSH
(Seiurus noveboracensis)

Northern Waterthrush

Minnesota status. Regular. Migrant and summer resident.
Migration. An uncommon to common spring and fall migrant throughout most of the state. Common at peak migration periods in eastern regions. Least numerous in western regions and some portions of the north-central region. Usually encountered as individuals. *Spring migration period:* Mid-April through early June, with a peak in early and mid-May. Earliest dates: SOUTH, April *8*, 14, 16, 18; NORTH, April 30, May 2, 3. Latest dates: SOUTH,

May 30, June 1, 2; NORTH, none can be given because of breeding birds. *Fall migration period:* Late July through mid-October, with the bulk of the migration in late August through September. Earliest dates: NORTH, none can be given because of breeding birds; SOUTH, August 2, 4, 9. Latest dates: NORTH, October 3, 6, 8, *23, 26*; SOUTH, October 15, 19, 21.

Summer. Resident primarily in the northern portions of the northeastern region and the north-central region west to Beltrami County (Turtle Lake). Southward from this region this species has been recorded in northern Mille Lacs County and most interesting is its presence each summer in the Cedar Creek area of northern Anoka County. In this area it has been observed carrying food and no doubt it breeds here.

LOUISIANA WATERTHRUSH
(Seiurus motacilla)

Minnesota status. Regular. Migrant and summer resident.

Migration. A rare spring migrant in the breeding range in the southeastern and west-central regions as far north as central Pine County. There is one spring record from the northeast at Crooked Lake, Lake County, on May 28, 1977 (*The Loon* 50:206--7). There are scattered records from the central region in Stearns and Carver Counties and the south-central region in Blue Earth (Minneopa State Park), Rice, and Martin Counties. Seldom seen in the fall. Usually encountered as individuals on breeding areas. *Spring migration period:* Mid-April to mid-May, no peak period noted. Earliest dates: April *1, 4*, 17, 18 (south only). *Fall migration period:* A gradual exodus in August. Latest dates: September 8, 14, 20 (south only).

Summer. A local resident in the southeast and east-central regions along the Mississippi and St. Croix River Valleys and also up the Minnesota River Valley as far as Blue Earth County (Minneopa State

Louisiana Waterthrush

Park). Most often seen in Houston County (Beaver Creek Valley State Park). This species has recently been recorded in Chisago (Lawrence Creek) County and in central Pine County along the Lower Tamarack River. These birds may have been in this area previously since Roberts (1932) assigned this species to the area but Surber (1918-19) believed them to be Northern Waterthrushes. It is possible both species occur in the area. This species was formerly found around the small streams bordering the Minnesota River Valley in Hennepin County, but these birds disappeared in the early 1950s.

KENTUCKY WARBLER *(Oporornis formosus)*

Minnesota status. Regular. Migrant and summer visitant.
Migration. A very rare spring migrant in scattered localities, mainly in the southern part of the state during the month of May. During the last ten years there have been eight spring migration records ranging from an early date of May 7, 1975 in Hennepin County and May 8, 1984 in Redwood County to a late date of May 22, 1979 in Hennepin County. The other spring records are from Goodhue (May 12, 1965) and Olmsted (May 29, 1963) Counties in the southeast; Lyon (May 8, 1975) and Pipestone (May 9, 1973) Counties in the southwest; Clay (May 19, 1982, specimen) County in the northwest; and Washington (May 13-19, 1986) County in the east-central region. There is only one record that can be considered a fall record: August 19, 1963 in Anoka County. This species over a long period of time may be only of casual occurrence in the state.
Summer. There are summer records from Afton State Park, Washington County (*The Loon* 50:169-70); Nerstrand Woods State Park, Rice County (*The Loon* 52:185) and also June 17, 1983, Rice County; Big Stone National Wildlife Refuge, Big Stone County (*The Loon* 51:45); June 1964 and 1965 in Coon Rapids, Anoka County, and June 9,

1984, Bunker Hills Park, Anoka County. Most unusual was a single bird found aboard a ship in Minnesota waters on western Lake Superior near Duluth on July 24, 1964. All records are of males, but these records indicate the possibility of very rare breeding in the state even though no females or broods have been found.

CONNECTICUT WARBLER *(Oporornis agilis)*

Minnesota status. Regular. Migrant and summer resident.

Migration. A rare spring and fall migrant in eastern regions, casual to rare in most of the central and western regions. Encountered as individuals. *Spring migration period:* Early May to early June, with most records in late May. Earliest dates: SOUTH, May 5, 7, 8; NORTH, May 6, 7. Latest dates: SOUTH, June 9, 10, 11, *19*; NORTH, none can be given because of breeding birds. *Fall migration period:* Mid-August through early October. Earliest dates: NORTH, none can be given because of breeding birds; SOUTH, August 17, 18. Latest dates: NORTH, September 22, 23, 24, *October 1*; SOUTH, October 3, 5, 11, *27* (two records in Olmsted and Washington Counties).

Summer. Best represented as a resident in the north-central region from Koochiching, Aitkin, Hubbard, and Beltrami Counties westward into eastern Marshall and Roseau Counties in the northwest region. Also a local resident in the northeastern region in St. Louis, Lake, and Cook Counties and as far south as northern Pine County. In the early twentieth century, this species ranged as far south as the tamarack bogs of Isanti County, but it has not been reported there in 65 years! There is one record from Clay County on July 21, 1977, but this could have been a very early fall migrant.

Connecticut Warbler

MOURNING WARBLER *(Oporornis philadelphia)*

Mourning Warbler

Minnesota status. Regular. Migrant and summer resident.

Migration. An uncommon spring and fall migrant throughout the state. May occasionally be common at peak migration periods. Usually encountered as individuals. *Spring migration period:* Early May through early June, with the bulk of the migration in late May. Earliest dates: SOUTH, May 2, 5; NORTH, May 9, 10, 11. Latest dates: SOUTH (southern and west-central regions only), June 5, 8, 10; NORTH, none can be given because of breeding birds. *Fall migration period:* Probably late August through early October, no peak period noted. Earliest dates: NORTH, none can be given because of breeding birds; SOUTH, August *18*, 24, 28, 29. Latest dates: NORTH, September 20, 21, 23, *30*; SOUTH, October 8, 11, 14.

Summer. A common and well-represented resident throughout most of the wooded portions of the state from the east-central region (Washington, Ramsey, and Anoka Counties [*The Loon* 52:39-40]) northwestward through the central region (Stearns, Morrison, and Todd Counties), west-central region (eastern Otter Tail County), northward through the northwest region in eastern Marshall County to Roseau and Kittson Counties. During June 1983 and 1984 there were records from Brown County in the Minnesota River Valley.

MACGILLIVRAY'S WARBLER
(Oporornis tolmiei)

Minnesota status. Accidental.
Records. The only confirmed record is a specimen taken on May 11, 1958 at Madison, Lac Qui Parle County (*The Loon* 53:109-11).

COMMON YELLOWTHROAT
(Geothlypis trichas)

Minnesota status. Regular. Migrant and summer resident; accidental in early winter.
Migration. A common spring and fall migrant throughout the state. Usually encountered as individuals. *Spring migration period:* Late April through late May, with a peak in mid-May. Earliest dates: SOUTH, April *19*, 23, 24, 27; NORTH, *April 22*, May 1, 3. *Fall migration period:* Mid-August through late October, with a few stragglers into November; seldom seen after October 15. Latest dates: NORTH, October 9, 12, 13, *November 10*; SOUTH, October 31, November 1, 2, *15, 25*.
Summer. A very widespread and numerous resident throughout the state. Best-represented breeding warbler species and probably one of the most evenly distributed breeding species in the state.
Winter. There are four December records: December 15, 1962, Winona County; December 25, 1934, December 25, 1957, both from Hennepin County; and one on December 28, 1982 at Buffalo, Wright County (*The Loon* 55:33).

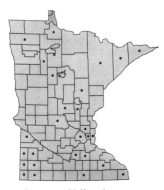
Common Yellowthroat

HOODED WARBLER *(Wilsonia citrina)*

Minnesota status. Regular. Migrant and summer resident.
Migration. A very rare spring migrant since the early 1970s, mainly in the east-central, south-central, and southeast regions of the state. Before this time there was a record in Minneapolis on May 17, 1942 and another in 1962 (see Summer below). Records predominate in the Twin Cities area where there is a concentration of observers. There are spring records from the north in Otter Tail County on May 31, 1976 (*The Loon* 48:116); Crow Wing County on May 17, 1984 and May 24, 1983 (*The Loon* 55:124-25); and Clearwater County on May 13, 1977 (*The Loon* 49:232-33). In addition to the Twin Cities area, there are spring records from Rice and

Hooded Warbler

Le Sueur Counties. The earliest dates in spring are April 22 (Rice County) and April 30 (Minneapolis). There are only three fall migration records: August 25, 1983, Houston County; September 10, 1969, Ramsey County (*The Loon* 42:36); and, most unusual, October 3, 1982, Rochester, Olmsted County (*The Loon* 55:30).

Summer. There are three early June dates: one bird was banded and photographed on June 2, 1962, Washington County (*The Flicker* 34:130); one bird banded June 2, 1973 at Isle, Mille Lacs County (*The Loon* 45:65); one bird June 7, 1979, Sherburne County (*The Loon* 51:156). These birds could have been late migrants. Indications of nesting are a singing male from June 14-22, 1975 at Itasca State Park, Clearwater County (*The Loon* 57:143), and a singing male near Prior Lake, Scott County, from May 19 to July 1, 1980 (*The Loon* 52:195-96). In 1984 the first nesting for the state was recorded when a pair at a nest were found during June at Murphy-Hanrehan Park Reserve, Scott County (*The Loon* 57:9-11). During late June 1986, two singing males were seen at Murphy-Hanrehan Park, but no nesting evidence was found.

WILSON'S WARBLER *(Wilsonia pusilla)*

Minnesota status. Regular. Migrant and summer resident.

Migration. An uncommon to occasionally common spring and fall migrant throughout most of the state. Usually encountered as individuals. *Spring migration period:* Late April through early June, with the bulk of the migration in late May. Earliest dates: SOUTH, April *21-22*, 28, 30; NORTH, May 3, 7, 8. Latest dates: SOUTH, June 11, 13, 15; NORTH, none can be given because of possible breeding birds. *Fall migration period:* Early August through late October. Earliest dates: NORTH, none can be given because of possible breeding birds; SOUTH, August 1, 7, 11. Latest dates: NORTH, September 28, 29, October 1, *8, 15, 19*; SOUTH, October 18, 20, 22, *November 4, 9*.

Wilson's Warbler

Summer. Roberts (1932) reported this species during the summer in Marshall County in 1901 and 1902. No further mention was made of this species in summer until 1975 when one was seen along Blesner Creek in Northern Lake County. In 1976 it was observed in late June in Cook County. In 1977 there were sightings on June 30 at Babbitt, St. Louis County, and on July 13 at Itasca State Park, Clearwater County; in 1978 there were late June sightings in Cook County. During May and June 1980 breeding was confirmed for the state when adults feeding just fledged young were found along Hog Creek in northern Lake County. Several other singing males were found in the same area (*The Loon* 52:182-83). During the summer of 1982 singing males were observed in northern Lake and Cook Counties. On June 20, 1985 three singing males were found along the Whyte Road in Lake County. Because of the difficulty in finding the nest of this species (see *The Loon* 52:182-83) and the remoteness of the breeding area, it seems reasonable to assume that this species breeds sparingly in the northern portions of Cook, Lake, and St. Louis Counties, and probably in suitable habitat areas in northern portions of the north-central and northwestern regions.

CANADA WARBLER *(Wilsonia canadensis)*

Minnesota status. Regular. Migrant and summer resident.
Migration. An uncommon spring and fall migrant throughout most of the state; least numerous in the western region, especially in the southwest. Usually encountered as individuals. *Spring migration period:* Early May through early June, with the bulk of the migration in late May. Earliest dates: SOUTH, May 1, 4, 6; NORTH, May 5, 9, 12, 13. Latest dates: SOUTH, June 6, 9, 11, *22*; NORTH, none can be given because of breeding birds. *Fall migration period:* Mid-August through early October, with very few birds seen after mid-September. Earliest dates: NORTH, none can be given because of breeding

Canada Warbler

birds; SOUTH, August 9, 11, 12. Latest dates: NORTH, September 22, 25, 26; SOUTH, October 2, 10, 13.
Summer. Resident primarily in the northeastern and north-central regions. More numerous in the northeastern region. Nesting activity has been reported as far west as Itasca State Park, Clearwater County, and as far south as Onamia, Mille Lacs County. There are observations in late June 1978 and 1980 at Cedar Creek Natural History Area, Anoka County. These records may indicate casual breeding in the northern portion of the east-central region.

YELLOW-BREASTED CHAT *(Icteria virens)*

Yellow-breasted Chat

Minnesota status. Regular (?). Migrant and summer resident.
Migration. A very rare to casual spring migrant in the southeastern, east-central, south-central, and southwestern regions. Some years entirely absent. There are four spring records from the north: two from Duluth on May 29, 1974 (*The Loon* 47:92) and May 18, 1982 (*The Loon* 54:188-90); one record from Old Mill State Park, Marshall County, on May 13, 1978 (*The Loon* 50:176-77); and the fourth from Fosston, Polk County, on May 11, 1921. There is also one spring record from Stearns County. A casual migrant in the fall, with most records from the southwest. The most unusual record is from Grand Marais, Cook County, from September 20-23, 1983 (*The Loon* 56:65-66). Encountered as individuals. *Spring migration period:* May. Earliest dates: SOUTH (only), May 2, 5, 6. *Fall migration period:* August and September. Latest dates: SOUTH (only), September 4, 16, *October 15.*
Summer. A casual resident in the southeastern and southwestern regions. There are nesting records as far north as Winona County in the east and Big Stone County in the west. Some years entirely absent as a breeder; at other times fluctuates from year to year. Years of noticeable presence include 1948 and 1953-55 along the lower Mississippi River in Winona and Houston Counties; in 1950-52 along

the Cannon River in Goodhue County; and in 1939 and 1944 along the Minnesota River in Lac Qui Parle and Big Stone Counties. There are recent June records from Scott County (*The Loon* 52:114); Dakota County (*The Loon* 47:92) and also June 9-19, 1984 and again in June and July 1985; and in Hennepin, Ramsey, and Le Sueur Counties. There is one record from Clay County in the northwest on July 21, 1984. This is probably a summer vagrant. The most recent nesting record is one from Whitewater Wildlife Management Area, Winona County, in 1976.

SUMMER TANAGER *(Piranga rubra)*

Minnesota status. Regular. Migrant and summer visitant.

Migration. A very rare spring and fall migrant mainly in the southern part of the state and at Duluth and along the North Shore of Lake Superior. There are records from all southern regions. Counties of record in the south in spring are Goodhue, Olmsted, Fillmore, Hennepin, Ramsey, Washington, Mower, LeSueur, Martin, Kandiyohi, Lac Qui Parle, Lyon, and Pipestone. In the north there are four May records from Duluth and one from Becker County. Accidental in the fall, there are single August and September records and four October records from Duluth, one from Cook County on October 30, 1982, and one from Hubbard County on September 13, 1983. Encountered as individuals. *Spring migration period:* Late April through late May. The earliest date in the south is April 27, 1978 from Marshall, Lyon County, and the earliest date north is May 12. *Fall migration period:* August through October. The earliest date north is August 24, 1980 in Duluth; the latest date is one bird in Duluth from October 19 to November 7, 1981 and another on October 20, 1984 (*The Loon* 56:269-70). The only southern Minnesota fall date is one in Steele County on September 1, 1975.

Summer. There are June dates from Goodhue (June

1952), Winona (June 14, 1963), Anoka (June 1, 1984), Otter Tail (June 18, 1983), and Crow Wing (June 18, 1981) Counties.

SCARLET TANAGER *(Piranga olivacea)*

Scarlet Tanager

Minnesota status. Regular. Migrant and summer resident.

Migration. An uncommon spring and fall migrant in eastern, central, and northwestern regions; rare to uncommon in the west-central region and rare in the southwest region. Usually encountered as individuals. *Spring migration period:* Late April through early June, with a peak in late May. Earliest dates: SOUTH, April *12, 18*, 29, 30, May 1; NORTH, May *1*, 9, 10, 11. *Fall migration period:* Mid-August through late October, with the bulk of the migration in late September. Latest dates: NORTH, October 6, 20, 21, *November 26* (Grant County); SOUTH, October 19, 26, 27.

Summer. A well-represented resident in the more heavily wooded portions of the state. Most numerous in the central, east-central, and southeast regions. Least numerous and absent over wide areas in the south-central, southwest, and in the Red River Valley of the northwest region.

WESTERN TANAGER *(Piranga ludoviciana)*

Minnesota status. Casual. Spring migrant; accidental in summer.

Records. There are approximately 25 records for this species in the state. The vast majority of the records (22) are for the spring migration from very late April to very early June. The dates range from an early date of April 29, 1981 (North Oaks, Ramsey County [*The Loon* 53:169]) to a late spring date of June 1, 1983 at Agassiz National Wildlife Refuge, Marshall County (*The Loon* 55:92). Other county records during May are Hennepin, Ramsey, Washington, Mower, Stevens, Lac Qui Parle, and

Martin in the south, and St. Louis, Cook, Beltrami, Clay, Becker, Morrison, and Mille Lacs in the north. There are two records for the summer: June 28, 1971 from Agassiz National Wildlife Refuge, Marshall County, and August 9, 1977, Chaska, Carver County (*The Loon* 49:239). In addition, a specimen of a Western X Scarlet Tanager hybrid was collected on August 17, 1950 in Anoka County (MMNH #9481).

NORTHERN CARDINAL *(Cardinalis cardinalis)*

Minnesota status. Regular. Permanent resident. **Distribution.** This species entered the state from the southeast in the late nineteenth century. From that time onward it has expanded its range in the state northward and westward. By the mid-1930s it was an established resident from the Twin Cities area southward. By the 1960s it had extended its range northward to Morrison County and westward to Lac Qui Parle County. The expansion has slowly continued northward, westward, and along the North Shore of Lake Superior. This expansion usually begins with visitants occurring in late fall, winter, and spring into new territory. Some of these

Northern Cardinal

individuals, it appears, retreat southward to breeding areas, but a few remain and establish resident populations. The northernmost records at present are from the North Shore of Lake Superior in Cook (Grand Portage) and Lake Counties, Koochiching County in the north-central region, and Roseau, Pennington, and Kittson (winter 1985) Counties in the northwest. These records indicate it is still expanding northward (most records are from early winter), but the species is very scarce to absent over wide areas north of a line from Duluth in the east and Fergus Falls, Otter Tail County, in the west. In December 1983 there were records at Crosby, Crow Wing County, Walker, Cass County, Duluth and Hibbing, St. Louis County. The species is a very numerous breeder in the southeast, east-central, south-central, and central regions. Northward from here numbers of breeders decline, but there are recent breeding records from Duluth and in southern Aitkin, Crow Wing, and Cass Counties. In 1984 there were June records from Benedict, Hubbard County, Aurora, St. Louis County, and Bagley, Clearwater County. In the southwest the species is very scarce, but records are increasing since the late 1970s in Rock, Pipestone, and Lincoln Counties. There are no breeding records in the southwest. This species is best represented in the east-central and southeast regions in the Mississippi River Valley and its tributaries, where it is abundant to common at all seasons.

ROSE-BREASTED GROSBEAK
(Pheucticus ludovicianus)

Rose-breasted Grosbeak

Minnesota status. Regular. Migrant and summer resident; accidental in winter.

Migration. A common spring and fall migrant throughout most of the state. Usually encountered as individuals or in pairs. *Spring migration period:* Late April through early June, with a peak in mid-May. Earliest dates: SOUTH, April *14, 15,* 20, 23, 24; NORTH, April *11*, 30, May 1, 2. *Fall migration period:* Mid-August through late October, with a few stragglers into November and a peak in early September; the majority of birds have left the north by mid-September and the south by early October. Latest dates: NORTH, November 5, 8, 11, *20, 30*; SOUTH, November 14, 21, 22, *December 2, 17.*

Summer. A resident throughout the wooded portions of the state. Most numerous in the deciduous forests of the central and southern regions, especially in the Mississippi and Minnesota River Valleys and adjacent areas.

Winter. There are a number of late December and January records of individuals attempting to winter at feeders in both northern and southern regions. Only two of these birds remained all winter: one from December 1982 to February 1982 at a feeder in Eagan, Dakota County (*The Loon* 55:86), and one from early December 1984 to February 24, 1985 at Rochester, Olmsted County. Records from the north include one bird at Tofte, Cook County, on January 24, 1975 (*The Loon* 47:97); one at a feeder all during December 1982 at Crookston, Polk County; and one in Crow Wing County on January 21, 1980. In the south one bird remained at a feeder in south Minneapolis until February 1, 1980; another at a feeder in Bloomington, Hennepin County, until December 27, 1975; one at Eastman Nature Center, Hennepin County, until January 18, 1983; and another in Winona, Winona County, until January 4, 1973.

BLACK-HEADED GROSBEAK
(Pheucticus melanocephalus)

Minnesota status. Accidental.

Records. The first record for this species in the state was a male reported on June 6, 1940 at Minnesota Point, Duluth (Mrs. W. C. Olin). The next record was not until 1967, when a male was seen from mid-July to August 9 at Mendota Heights, Dakota County. This bird was seen feeding a juvenile at a feeder on August 6 (*The Loon* 39:130). In 1972 a second-year male was seen again in Mendota Heights (not the same location as above), Dakota County, on April 19 and 26 (*The Loon* 44:121-22). There was another report in the same general area in Ramsey County, possibly of the same bird, on August 4, 1972. On June 10, 1975 another male was seen at Blue Mounds State Park, Rock County (*The Loon* 47:139). On August 19, 1979 what could possibly have been a female or juvenile individual of this species was reported from Minneapolis. This bird may have been a hybrid (*The Loon* 51:164-69). Most interesting was the record of a first-year male in Grand Marais, Cook County, October 18-25, 1981 (*The Loon* 54:61-62). In 1982 there was a report of a male seen near Encampment Forest, Lake County, on October 10. On May 5, 1983 another male was seen near Chanhassen, Carver

County (*The Loon* 55:93). On May 24, 1984 a male
was seen in St. Paul, Ramsey County (*The Loon*
56:96). On May 24, 1986 a single male was seen at
Blue Mounds State Park, Rock County (*The Loon*
58:140).

Note. Because of the difficulty of separating some
juvenile grosbreaks in August, Rose-breasted and
Black-headed birds seen at this time of year must
be carefully identified. There are other records of
possible hybrids between the two species.

BLUE GROSBEAK *(Guiraca caerulea)*

Blue Grosbeak

Minnesota status. Regular. Migrant and summer
resident.

Migration. A very rare spring and fall migrant in
the southwest region in Rock, Pipestone, Murray,
Nobles, and Redwood (one record, September 15,
1984) Counties. The first record for the state was
in 1961. Most birds seen are on breeding territories.
There are four records away from the southwest
corner of the state, all at the height of the spring
migration in May: two are from Dakota County,
May 17, 1972 (*The Loon* 59:192) and May 27, 1980
(*The Loon* 52:116); another individual was seen near
Judson, Blue Earth County, May 10-21, 1974; and
one male was seen near Byron, Olmsted County,
on May 27, 1984 (*The Loon* 56:197). Encountered
as individuals or in pairs. *Spring migration period:*
Mid to late May. Earliest dates: May 10, 15, 16.
Fall migration period: September to early October.
Latest dates: October 2, 3, 5.

Summer. Occurs only in the southwest corner of
the state. This area of Minnesota is the northeast
fringe of the normal range of this species in the
United States. Actual nesting has been documented
only for Rock County: two adults and three immatures were seen near Beaver Creek, Rock County, on September 4, 1972; nesting was first suspected
at Blue Mounds Park, Rock County, during the
summer of 1974 (*The Loon* 47:47-48); and two nests
were found in the same area on July 16, 1976. This

species has been observed during June and July in Pipestone (Cazenovia), Murray (southwest of Chandler), and Nobles (Leota, Worthington, Adrian, and Kinbrae) Counties. Young being fed by adults were found near Leota, Nobles County, during August 1985.

LAZULI BUNTING *(Passerina amoena)*

Minnesota status. Accidental.
Records. There are approximately 13 records for the state, all in April, May, and June. These records, all of adult males unless otherwise noted, are: the earliest date is of one seen on the very early date of April 17, 1985 at White Bear Lake, Ramsey County (*The Loon* 57:110-11); May 8-10, 1930, Lakefield, Jackson County (Roberts 1932); May 18-19, 1964, Moorhead, Clay County (*The Loon* 36:105); May 18, 1984, Duluth (*The Loon* 56:262); May 22, 1984, immature male, Duluth (*The Loon* 56:262); May 22, 1974, Moorhead, Clay County (*The Loon* 46:115-16); May 24, 1981, Lutsen, Cook County and May 26, 1981, Grand Marais, Cook County, possibly the same bird (*The Loon* 53:162-63); May 26, 1956 (banded), Lac Qui Parle County; May 27, 1979 specimen, Minneapolis; June 4, 1935, Madison, Lac Qui Parle County; June 26, 1983, North Branch, Chisago County (*The Loon* 55:120); and May 5-11, 1986, Clearwater, Stearns County (*The Loon* 58:192).

In addition to the above records, there are three records of birds described as hybrids with the Indigo Bunting. Two of these are specimens taken in Marshall County (June 26, 1929, MMNH #7493) and Rock County (May 16, 1964, MMNH #19922). The other observation of a hybrid was on June 24, 1943 in Sherburne County (*The Loon* 37:53). There is another hybrid specimen (MMNH #19921) taken in Rock County on July 4, 1964 that shows 25 percent plumage characteristics of the Lazuli Bunting (*The Loon* 37:47).

INDIGO BUNTING *(Passerina cyanea)*

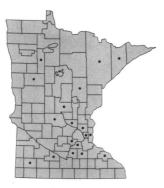

Indigo Bunting

Minnesota status. Regular. Migrant and summer resident.

Migration. A common spring and fall migrant in the eastern and central regions; uncommon in the western regions and in the heavily forested portions of the northern regions in both spring and fall. Encountered as individuals. *Spring migration period:* Late April through early June, with a peak in mid-May. Earliest dates: SOUTH, April 24, 26, 27, 28; NORTH, May 9, 10, 12. *Fall migration period:* Late July through mid-October, with the bulk of the migration in early September. Latest dates: NORTH, October 5, 7, 12, *23, 25, 28*; SOUTH, October 13, 15, 17, *25*.

Summer. A resident throughout the state; most numerous in the southeastern, south-central, east-central, and central regions. Becomes less common northward, especially in the heavily forested portions of the northeast and north-central regions and also in the prairie areas of the northwest region. Also less numerous in the southwest region.

PAINTED BUNTING *(Passerina ciris)*

Minnesota status. Accidental.

Records. There are four records, all in spring during the month of May: May 2, 1893, specimen (MMNH #4724) Madison, Lac Qui Parle County, probably an escaped bird (Roberts, 1932); May 12-15, 1965, Schroeder, Cook County (photographed, (*The Loon* 37:150); May 27-28, 1969, specimen (MMNH #25661), Mountain Lake, Cottonwood County. On May 18, 1986 a male was seen near Lismore, Nobles County (*The Loon* 58:129).

DICKCISSEL *(Spiza americana)*

Minnesota status. Regular. Migrant and summer resident.

Migration. Numbers fluctuate dramatically from one year to another. Some years abundant, some years uncommon. Numbers also vary from south to north; in years of abundance ranges farther north. For example, in 1983, a year of abundance, birds were recorded as far north as Cook County in the east, May 7-9 (*The Loon* 55:172-73), and in the west as far north as Pennington County. In 1976 and 1977, years of invasion, it reached the Canadian border in Kittson County. In years of normal abundance it is usually found in the southern part of the state as a common to uncommon spring migrant. In the north it is an uncommon migrant during any year; in the northern half of the state in years of abundance, it is uncommon to rare in the northwest and rare to casual in the north-central and northeast regions. In other years it is absent over all the northern regions. Usually encountered as individuals, but loose aggregations of ten to 20 birds may be found. *Spring migration period:* Early May to early June, with a peak in late May. Earliest dates: SOUTH, *April 23, 24, 27*, May 1, 4, 5; NORTH, May 2, 4, 7. *Fall migration period:* A gradual exodus from the state during August and September. Latest dates: NORTH, August 3, October *21-23,* Duluth (only dates); SOUTH, September 29, October 3, 4.

Dickcissel

Summer. A resident in the southern half of the state in years of normal abundance as far north as Chisago, Stearns, Stevens, and Traverse Counties. In years of peak abundance the range extends northward, especially in the western part of the state, and occasionally extends as far north as Kittson County in the northwest corner of the state. During the summer of 1983 up to 50 birds were seen in Polk County, and it was recorded as far north as Pennington County. In the northeast, even in years of abundance, it seldom extends its range beyond southern Crow Wing and Pine Counties, although there are summer observations mostly from the 1930s from Lake (Two Harbors), St. Louis (Virginia), and Itasca (Lake Pokegama) Counties.

GREEN-TAILED TOWHEE *(Pipilo chlorurus)*

Minnesota status. Accidental.
Records. There is one record for this species: a single bird remained at a feeder in Duluth from early December 1966 to mid-January 1967 (photographed, *The Loon* 39:135).

RUFOUS-SIDED TOWHEE
(Pipilo erythrophthalmus)

Rufous-sided Towhee

Minnesota status. Regular. Migrant and summer resident; casual in winter.
Migration. An uncommon spring and fall migrant primarily in the southeast, east-central, and north-central regions. Sporadic and local in occurrence, absent over wide areas. Casual to rare in all other regions of the state. Usually encountered as individuals. *Spring migration period:* Mid-April through late May, with a peak in late April. Earliest dates: SOUTH, *March 21, 23, 30,* April 10, 11, 12; NORTH, April 5, 26, 27, 28. *Fall migration period:* Early September through late November; the bulk of the birds have left by mid-October. Latest dates: NORTH, October 20, 25, November 4, 13, *15, 21, 25, December 2*; SOUTH, November 21, 25, 26. Late November and early December dates indicate possible wintering birds or birds attempting to overwinter.
Summer. A local resident primarily in the southeast, east-central, and western portion of the north-central regions. Absent in the prairie areas of the southwest and west-central regions and in boreal forest areas of the north-central and northeastern regions. There is one record for Lake County on July 7, 1975. It is occasionally present on the eastern edge of the northwest region from Becker County to eastern Kittson County. It is not found in the Red River Valley. In the southwest there is one summer vagrant record: a single bird was seen on July 5, 1985 at Blue Mounds State Park, Rock County.
Winter. There are approximately 15 records of birds

attempting to overwinter, usually at feeders in the Twin Cities area or in the southeastern part of the state. Most of these attempts are unsuccsssful, but individuals have been recorded into February in Ramsey, Anoka, Hennepin, Olmsted, Fillmore (from December 14, 1984 to the first week in April 1985), and Lac Qui Parle Counties. One bird was at a feeder in Austin, Mower County, during December 1982. Most unusual was a single bird that overwintered at Lutsen, Cook County, along the North Shore of Lake Superior during the winter of 1979-80 and also a bird recorded in Duluth on January 9, 1982. A bird was seen at Dassel, Meeker County, on January 1 and 2, 1984, and one was at Rochester, Olmsted County, on December 27, 1983.

AMERICAN TREE SPARROW *(Spizella arborea)*

Minnesota status. Regular. Migrant and winter visitant.
Migration. Abundant spring and fall migrant throughout the state. Usually encountered in flocks numbering from a few individuals to hundreds at peak migration periods. *Fall migration period:* Mid-September through late November, with a peak during October. Earliest dates: NORTH, September *10*, 13, 18, 20; SOUTH, September *16, 18, 21,* 25, 26, 27. *Spring migration period:* Early March through late May, with a peak during early April. Latest dates: SOUTH, May 12, 15, 16; NORTH, May 23, 26, 27.
Winter. Common to locally abundant winter visitant in the southern half of the state, decreasing in numbers northward; rare in northern third of the state.

CHIPPING SPARROW *(Spizella passerina)*

Minnesota status. Regular. Migrant and summer resident; accidental in winter.
Migration. A common spring and fall migrant

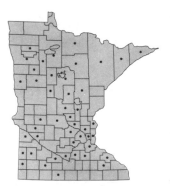

Chipping Sparrow

throughout the state; occasionally abundant, especially in northern areas in the spring. Usually encountered as individuals or in pairs, but at peak migration periods flocks of ten to 20 birds may be seen. *Spring migration period:* Late March through late May, with a peak in mid to late April. Earliest dates: SOUTH, March *10, 15*, 19, 22, 24; NORTH, April *1*, 7, 9, 12. *Fall migration period:* Early August (in the northeast) through early November, with the bulk of the migration in September. Latest dates: NORTH, October 26, 28, 29, *November 4, 8, 28*; SOUTH, October 27, 30, November 2, *10, 22-27, 30.*

Summer. A well-represented resident throughout the state; most numerous in eastern and northern regions. Found in urban and rural areas, and especially in the heavily forested areas in the north.

Winter. The first evidence that this species attempted to overwinter in the state was a bird picked up dead in Rochester, Olmsted County, on December 6, 1975 (*The Loon* 48:77). On December 21, 1980 a single bird was seen at Cottonwood, Lyon County (Christmas Bird Count). In December 1976 a single bird was seen at a feeder in St. Paul until January 4, 1977 (*The Loon* 49:51-52). The first overwintering record is of a bird seen daily at a feeder in Austin, Mower County, from November 26, 1978 to March 2, 1979 (*The Loon* 51:100); another bird overwintered at a feeder in Crosby, Crow Wing County, from November 1980 to March 1981. A single bird was seen in Minneapolis from December 1, 1984 to January 1, 1985, and one was at a Rochester, Olmsted County, feeder December 10-30, 1985.

CLAY-COLORED SPARROW *(Spizella pallida)*

Minnesota status. Regular. Migrant and summer resident; accidental in winter.

Migration. An uncommon spring and fall migrant throughout most of the state, uncommon to rare in southern regions, especially in the south-central region. Usually encountered as individuals. *Spring migration period:* Mid-April through late May, with a peak in early May. Earliest dates: SOUTH, April *2, 4, 6, 7, 8,* 13, 19, 20; NORTH, April *13,* 24, 25, 26. *Fall migration period:* Mid-August through late October, with a peak from mid to late September. Latest dates: NORTH, October 19, 22, 23; SOUTH, October 20, 27, 31.

Summer. A well-represented resident from central portions of the southeast region through the central part of the state to the South Dakota border in Lincoln County. Increases in abundance north of this line except in the most heavily forested portions of the northeast (northern Cook, Lake, and St. Louis Counties) and north-central (Itasca and Koochiching Counties) regions. It appears that it formerly bred sparingly across the southern part of the state but disappeared from many areas after the 1920s. It may be returning to some of these areas with recent observations in Pipestone County (1974, 1975, 1977 [*The Loon* 47:190-91]) and Olmsted County (1975 [*The Loon* 47:191]; nested 1976). In June 1986 it was present in northern Fillmore County.

Winter. A single bird attempted to overwinter at a feeder in Duluth from November 7, 1984 to January 20, 1985 (*The Loon* 57:104-5).

Clay-colored Sparrow

BREWER'S SPARROW *(Spizella breweri)*

Minnesota status. Accidental.
Records. There are two sight records for this species in the state: a single bird seen and heard on September 28, 1974 at Blue Mounds State Park, Rock County (*The Loon* 47:40-41), another seen and heard at Pipestone National Monument, Pipestone County, on October 10, 1975 (K. Eckert).

FIELD SPARROW *(Spizella pusilla)*

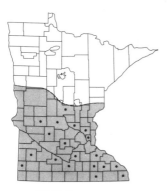

Field Sparrow

Minnesota status. Regular. Migrant and summer resident.

Migration. An uncommon to occasionally common spring migrant in the southern and central regions; most numerous in southeastern and east-central regions. Rare to absent over the northern regions. Usually encountered as individuals; at peak migration periods small groups of up to ten may occasionally be found. *Spring migration period:* Late March through early May, with a peak in mid-April. Earliest dates: SOUTH, March 9, 13, 18, 19; NORTH, April 11, 12, 17 (April 21, 1977, Duluth [*The Loon* 49:171]). There is one record on May 24, 1978 from Bemidji, Beltrami County. *Fall migration period:* September and October, with stragglers into November. Latest dates: NORTH, October 13, 16, 20; SOUTH, October 27, 29, November 1, *11, 16, 29, 30.*

Summer. Resident in the southern and central regions of the state. Best represented in southeastern and east-central regions. Decreasing in numbers to the west in the south-central and southwestern regions except in the Minnesota River Valley where it is well represented to the South Dakota border. There are casual summer observations northward into the northern region in southern St. Louis County in the east, Itasca, Aitkin, Crow Wing, Wadena, and Hubbard Counties in the north-central region and Clay County in the west. It is regular in Otter Tail County. No actual nesting evidence is available from these areas.

Winter. There are records of overwintering individuals at feeders from December through February in Hennepin (2), Scott, and Goodhue Counties. There are, in addition, December records on Christmas Bird Counts from Scott, Dakota, and Ramsey Counties. One individual was seen at a feeder in Two Harbors, Lake County, on December 18, 1983 (*The Loon* 56:135-36), and one was seen at a feeder in Grand Marais, Cook County, from November 1984 to January 14, 1985 (*The Loon* 57:61).

VESPER SPARROW *(Pooecetes gramineus)*

Minnesota status. Regular. Migrant and summer resident; accidental in early winter.
Migration. A common spring and fall migrant throughout the state, rare to casual in the northeast region in both spring and fall. Usually encountered as individuals or in pairs. *Spring migration period:* Late March through mid-May, with a peak in mid to late April. Earliest dates: SOUTH, March *2, 12, 23, 24, 26;* NORTH, April 4, 5, 6. *Fall migration period:* Late August through late October, with stragglers into November; peak in mid to late September. Latest dates: NORTH, November 1, 3, 12, *20, 21, 26;* SOUTH, October 26, 27, 28, November *15, 25.*

Vesper Sparrow

Summer. A widespread resident throughout most of the state, least numerous in the northeast and north-central regions in the heavily forested portions of these areas. Absent over most of St. Louis, Cook, and Lake Counties. They were present at Aurora, St. Louis County, in June 1984.
Winter. There are December records from Duluth (December 5, 1966) and Otter Tail (December 13, 1981) County in the north and Fillmore (December 22, 1985), Wabasha (December 3, 1983), Nobles (December 29, 1984), and Martin (December 25, 1957 [4]) Counties in the south. There are two January records: January 4, 1975, Cottonwood County, and January 11, 1923, Anoka County.

LARK SPARROW *(Chondestes grammacus)*

Minnesota status. Regular. Migrant and summer resident.
Migration. Rare spring migrant in the southeastern, east-central, and northern portions of the west-central region and the northwestern regions. Casual to absent over most of the north-central, central, south-central, southwest, and northeastern regions. In the fall less numerous, and seldom seen anywhere after August; there is a gradual exodus from breeding areas in late summer. Usually encountered as

Lark Sparrow

individuals or in pairs on breeding grounds. *Spring migration period:* Early April through mid-May, with a peak in early May. Earliest dates: SOUTH, April 4, 6, 8; NORTH, April *5, 16,* 29, May 3, 6. *Fall migration period:* August and September. Latest dates: NORTH, August 28, September 1, 3, *11,* October *22* (1985, Cook County; only dates); SOUTH, September 18, 20, 27, October *4.*

Summer. There are four somewhat separate breeding areas in the state: in the southeast corner of the state; in the east-central and central regions as far north as Washington and Sherburne Counties; in the Minnesota River Valley to Chippewa and Yellow Medicine Counties; and in the northwestern region from Clay County northward.

BLACK-THROATED SPARROW
(Amphispiza bilineata)

Minnesota status. Accidental.
Records. There are two fall records: a single immature bird seen and photographed at Stony Point, St. Louis County, September 20-23, 1974 (*The Loon* 46:100-101); another single immature bird, in Duluth Township, St. Louis County, on October 7, 1980 (*The Loon* 53:52).

LARK BUNTING *(Calamospiza melanocorys)*

Minnesota status. Regular. Migrant and summer visitant; casual summer resident; accidental in winter.
Migration. A very rare spring migrant mainly in the southwest and west-central regions along the western border of the state. Less numerous and seldom seen in the fall in these areas. Casual to accidental elsewhere in the state, with scattered records from the northeast (Cook, Lake, and St. Louis Counties), north-central (Cass, Aitkin, and Clearwater Counties), and central regions (Mille Lacs, Sherburne, and Kandiyohi Counties), and a

scattering of other counties in the southern part of the state (Ramsey, Rice, Nobles, and Fillmore). *Spring migration period:* May through early June. Earliest dates: SOUTH, *April 22*, May 6, 11, 12, 15; NORTH, May 9, 11, 12. *Fall migration period:* No defined period, a gradual exodus from breeding grounds in August and September; vagrants occur into November. Latest dates: NORTH, September 20, 30, October 10, *19, 28, 29, November 9*; SOUTH, October 2, 20 (only October dates).

Summer. A casual resident mainly in the southwestern and southern portions of the west-central region along the western border of the state from Rock County in the south to southern Traverse County in the north. The last recorded breeding took place in 1964 in Rock and Pipestone Counties. There are a scattering of summer records of vagrants in Stearns County (*The Loon* 49:229), Lake County (*The Loon* 51:200-202), Hawley, Clay County (June 14, 1983), and near MacGregor, Aitkin County (June 25, 1973, unpublished).

Winter. One bird overwintered at a feeder in Winona, Winona County, from November 12, 1976 to April 22, 1977 (*The Loon* 49:105-6).

SAVANNAH SPARROW
(Passerculus sandwichensis)

Minnesota status. Regular. Migrant and summer resident.

Migration. A common to abundant spring and fall migrant throughout the state; most numerous in the western regions, least numerous in the heavily forested portions of the northeastern region. Usually encountered in small groups of ten or fewer birds; at peak migration periods hundreds of birds can be found in close proximity, mainly in western regions. *Spring migration period:* Early April through late May, with the bulk of the migration in late April and early May. Earliest dates: SOUTH, March *21, 24, 26, 30, 31* (only March dates), April 2, 5, 6; NORTH, *March 30,* April *5*, 10, 12, 16. *Fall migration period:*

Savannah Sparrow

Mid-August through late October, with the bulk of the migration from mid-September through early October. Latest dates: NORTH, October 26, 29, 30, *November 3, 5, 6*; SOUTH, October 30, 31, November 1, *11, 17-22*.

Summer. A widespread resident throughout the state, with breeding records in all regions; well represented wherever there are low-lying grassy fields.

BAIRD'S SPARROW *(Ammodramus bairdii)*

Minnesota status. Casual. Spring migrant; former summer resident.

Records. This species has been recorded only recently in the west-central and northwestern regions, mainly in Clay County. It occurs casually in the remnant virgin prairie of the Glacial Lake Agassiz beach ridge southeast of Felton and Averill, Clay County. There are records from this area in May, June, and July in 1970, 1972, 1976, 1977, 1978, 1980, and 1986; it may have nested. Formerly a resident throughout the Red River Valley from northern Traverse to Kittson County. The only recent records outside of Clay County is one observation in Wilkin County on May 31, 1976 (*The Loon* 49:102) and in the same area on May 11, 1977 (*The Loon* 49:226). During late June and early July 1986 a singing male was present in a field just west of Deerwood, Crow Wing County. This is a most unusual occurrence for this species and represents the only record away from the northwestern part of the state. The only confirmed nesting records for the state are from western Pennington County (1930) and near Euclid, Polk County (1937).

GRASSHOPPER SPARROW
(Ammodramus savannarum)

Minnesota status. Regular. Migrant and summer resident.

Migration. An uncommon spring and fall migrant throughout most of the state; rare to casual in the north-central and northeastern regions. Most birds seen in the spring are on breeding territories. Less numerous and seldom seen in the fall. There is a gradual exodus from breeding areas. Usually encountered as individuals. *Spring migration period:* Mid-April through late May, with a peak in early May. Earliest dates: SOUTH, April 14, 17, 18; NORTH, April 22, 25, 26. *Fall migration period:* There is a gradual exodus from breeding areas during August and September. Since Minnesota lies at the northern limit of the breeding range of this species, few concentrations are seen in the state during the fall. Latest dates: NORTH, September 17, 29, *October 3* (Grand Marais, Cook County [*The Loon* 55:180]), *10, 21* (Grand Marais, Cook County); SOUTH, October 1, 3, 4.

Grasshopper Sparrow

Summer. A widespread resident throughout most of the state except in the northeast and north-central regions. It reaches the Canadian border in the northwest region in Roseau and Kittson Counties. In these latter two regions no nests have been reported, but there is evidence that it may be spreading into these regions where suitable open grassy habitat exists. There are summer observations from Cook, St. Louis (1979), and Lake of the Woods Counties.

HENSLOW'S SPARROW
(Ammodramus henslowii)

Minnesota status. Regular. Migrant and summer resident.
Migration. This species is seldom seen during migration; most birds are on breeding territories. Very rare in both spring and fall across the southern part of the state and northward along the western margin of the state as far north as Mahnomen County. There is one record as far north as Kittson County (June 6, 1898, Roberts) in the northwest and one from Beltrami County (May 22, 1982 [*The Loon*

Henslow's Sparrow

55:120-21]) in the north-central region. Best represented in the southeastern region adjacent to the Mississippi River in Winona County. *Spring migration period:* Very few data are available, but it apparently occurs from late April through late May. Earliest dates: SOUTH (only), April 19, 21, 24. *Fall migration period:* A gradual exodus from breeding areas in August and September, and seldom if ever seen during migration. Latest dates: SOUTH (only), September 27, October 2, 3, *13, 19*. **Summer.** A very local summer resident in the southeastern part of the state and casual in the western part of the state as far north as Mahnomen and Norman Counties in the northwest region. Best represented in the southeast region (O. L. Kipp State Park, Winona County). There are recent summer observations from Houston, Winona, Wabasha, Steele, Hennepin, Sherburne, Becker, Clay, and Norman Counties. The only recent nest actually found was in Hennepin County on July 9, 1982 (*The Loon* 54:192).

LE CONTE'S SPARROW
(Ammodramus leconteii)

Le Conte's Sparrow

Minnesota status. Regular. Migrant and summer resident.
Migration. Uncommon to locally common spring and fall migrant in the western regions; most numerous in the fall in the west-central region. Uncommon to rare migrant in the eastern and central regions; rare to absent in both spring and fall in the south. Usually encountered as individuals, but loose aggregations of 20 or more birds may occasionally be encountered in the fall in the west. *Spring migration period:* Mid-April through late May, with the bulk of the migration during the first half of May. Earliest dates: SOUTH, April *6, 8,* 14, 15, 18; NORTH, April 24, 26, 27. *Fall migration period:* August through late October. Latest dates: NORTH, October 11, 15, 16, *November 8*; SOUTH, October 31, November 1, 2, *9, 10*.

Summer. A common and widespread resident in the central and northern regions southward to southern Pine County (24 singing males, June 1983 [*The Loon* 56:162-65]), in the east to Sherburne and Stearns counties in the central part of the state, to Wilkin and Clay Counties in the west. Formerly (1950s and 1960s) found as far south as Lac Qui Parle County in the west and Dakota County in the east, but the only recent summer observations from this area are from Lake Benton, Lincoln County, in June 1973, Lyon County in June 1972, and one was seen on July 5, 1985 at Crow Hassan Park, Hennepin County. Most numerous in the north-western region and open areas of the north-central region. Not found in the heavily forested portions of the northeast or north-central regions.

SHARP-TAILED SPARROW
(Ammodramus caudacutus)

Minnesota status. Regular. Migrant and summer resident.
Migration. A rare spring and fall migrant in the western regions of the state; casual to absent over most of the central and eastern regions. Most often encountered on breeding areas. *Spring migration period:* Throughout May. Earliest dates: SOUTH, *April 10* (*The Loon* 56:274), *23*, May 3, 4, 7; NORTH, May 20, 21, *23*, 24 (the May 23 date is from Grand Marais, Cook County, in 1977, the only spring date from the northeast). *Fall migration period:* Late August through mid-October, with most birds seen in late September. Latest dates: NORTH, October 5, 6, 9, *26*; SOUTH, October 11, 12, 18.

Sharp-tailed Sparrow

Summer. Until 1974 this species was presumed to be a resident in the northwestern region only, from Felton, Clay County, northward to Kittson County on the Canadian border. The only report of an actual nest was one in 1929 near Twin Lakes, Kittson County; young just out of the nest were found in Marshall County in 1928 (Roberts, 1932). There were summer observations in Pennington County

(*The Loon* 52:175) and in Roseau County in 1980. During the summer of 1982 the species was seen in Roseau, Mahnomen, Becker, Marshall, and Polk Counties. There was also a summer observation in 1982 in southern Cass County in the north-central region. In 1974 a small colony was found near MacGregor, Aitkin County, and a nest was located in June 1977 (*The Loon* 50:48-49). They have been found in this area every summer since that time. Best represented in Marshall County at Agassiz National Wildlife Refuge and nearby areas.

FOX SPARROW *(Passerella iliaca)*

Minnesota status. Regular. Migrant and winter visitant.

Migration. A common spring and fall migrant throughout the state, most numerous in the eastern region. Usually encountered as individuals, but at peak migration periods loose aggregations of 10 or more birds may occasionally be seen. *Spring migration period:* Early March through late May, with a peak in early April (south) to late April (north). Earliest dates: SOUTH, March 3, 5, 6; NORTH, March 26, 28, 30. Latest dates: SOUTH, May 17, 19, 21; NORTH, May 20, 21, 27. *Fall migration period:* Early September through mid-November, with stragglers into December and the bulk of the migration in early October. Earliest dates: NORTH, *August 28*, 30, 31; SOUTH, September 4, 7, 8. Latest dates: NORTH, November 20, 21, 30; *December 8, 15, 18*; SOUTH, December 14, 16, 17.

Winter. There are numerous records of individuals at feeding stations during late December, January, and February, most of them from the eastern regions. There are early January dates from St. Louis (Duluth) and Cook Counties in the north, and one early January date from Otter Tail County in the west. Most overwintering birds have been recorded at feeders in the Twin Cities area, the east-central region, and the southeast region. One bird overwintered at St. Cloud, Stearns County, in the central region during 1984-85. One bird was seen in Brown County from December 1, 1983 to January 20, 1984.

SONG SPARROW *(Melospiza melodia)*

Minnesota status. Regular. Migrant, summer resident, and winter visitant.
Migration. A common spring and fall migrant throughout the state. Widespread and seen in all regions. Usually encountered as individuals, but at peak migration periods loose aggregations of 15 to 20 or more birds may be seen in one area. *Spring migration period:* Early March through early May, with a peak in early to mid-April. Earliest dates: SOUTH, none can be given because of wintering birds (early arrival dates are usually during the first ten days of March); NORTH, March *12*, 18, 21, 25. *Fall migration period:* Late August through late November, with the bulk of the migration in late September and early October. Latest dates: NORTH, November 8, 9, 11, *22, 29*; SOUTH, none can be given because of wintering birds.

Song Sparrow

Summer. A resident throughout the state. One of the most numerous and evenly distributed breeding species in the state; found in all regions.
Winter. Found rarely around open water and sometimes at feeding stations, mainly in the southern part of the state. Most often recorded in the Twin Cities area and the east-central and southeast region along the Mississippi River and its tributaries. There are numerous records in December and early January for the central and southern portions of the state. In the north there are December (Christmas Bird Count) records for Cook and St. Louis Counties, and birds have overwintered in Otter Tail County and as far north as Marshall County. There is a record of a single bird at Baudette, Lake of the Woods County, on December 10, 1984 in the extreme northern part of the state; this is probably an exceptionally late migrant.

LINCOLN'S SPARROW *(Melospiza lincolnii)*

Lincoln's Sparrow

Minnesota status. Regular. Migrant and summer resident; accidental in winter.

Migration. An uncommon to locally common spring and fall migrant throughout the state. Most numerous in the eastern regions. Usually encountered as individuals, but small groups of five to ten birds are occasionally seen at peak migration periods. *Spring migration period:* Mid-April through late May, with the bulk of the migration in late April and early May. Earliest dates: SOUTH, *March 30*, April 6, 7, 8; NORTH, *March 31*, April *1, 8*, 12, 14, 16. Latest dates: SOUTH, May 21, 22, 23, *June 3, 5, 26*; NORTH, none can be given because of breeding birds. *Fall migration period:* Late July through early November, with the bulk of the migration from mid-September through early October. Earliest dates: NORTH, none can be given because of breeding birds; SOUTH, *July 12*, August 12, 14, 17. Latest dates: NORTH, October 28, 31, November 2; SOUTH, November 2, 6, 7.

Summer. A resident in the northeastern region, primarily in St. Louis, Cook, and Lake Counties and south to northern Pine County. Nests have been found as far south as Kelsey in central St. Louis County. Also found sparingly in the north-central regions in Aitkin and Beltrami Counties, and in the northern part of the northwest region. A nest with two eggs was found in Roseau County on July 3, 1976 (Nero, 1982), and this species was observed in Kittson County on July 16, 1975. These records indicate that it probably breeds sparingly across the northern portions of all northern regions.

Winter. A single bird was seen on a Christmas Bird Count on December 19, 1981 in Yellow Medicine County (*The Loon* 54:66); most unusual was a single bird at a feeder near Centerville, Anoka County, from January 6 to January 29, 1983 (*The Loon* 55:86-87).

SWAMP SPARROW *(Melospiza georgiana)*

Minnesota status. Regular. Migrant and summer resident; casual in winter.

Migration. A common spring and fall migrant throughout the state. Usually encountered as individuals. *Spring migration period:* Late March through late May, with the peak of the migration in late April. Earliest dates: SOUTH, March *12*, 18, 21, 24; NORTH, April 4, 9, 10. *Fall migration period:* Early August through late November, with the bulk of the migration in late September and early October. Latest dates: NORTH, November 4, 5, 9; SOUTH, November 22, 23, 25.

Swamp Sparrow

Summer. A well-distributed and widespread summer resident throughout the state wherever suitable marsh and swamp habitat exists. Well represented in wooded swamps of the north.

Winter. There are approximately 14 records of birds wintering or attempting to overwinter at feeders or in swampy areas and along creeks where there is open water. Most of these records are in the Twin Cities area southward into the southeast and south-central regions. There is one record, December 20, 1966 from Lyon County, in the southwest region. The only northern records are one bird overwintering at Duluth from January 22 to April 14, 1970 and a bird seen in Lake County until January 18, 1981. There are no overwintering records since 1971.

WHITE-THROATED SPARROW
(Zonotrichia albicollis)

Minnesota status. Regular. Migrant, summer resident, and rare winter visitant.

Migration. A common to abundant spring and fall migrant throughout the state. Encountered in groups of anywhere from a few to hundreds of birds. Can be very abundant in local areas at peak migration periods. *Spring migration period:* Mid-March through late May, with a peak in late April

White-throated Sparrow

and early May. Earliest dates: SOUTH, March 13, 16, 20; NORTH, *March 24*, April 2, 3, 5. Latest dates: NORTH (outside of breeding area), June 1, 4, 10, *26*. *Fall migration period:* Mid-August through November, with stragglers into mid-December; the peak of the migration is in late September and early October. Earliest dates: SOUTH, *July 28, August 16, 26, 27*, September 1, 3, 4. Latest dates: NORTH, November 27, 29, 30; SOUTH, November 30, December 2, 6, *14*.

Summer. A widespread resident in the northeastern and north-central regions southward into the northern portions of the central and east-central regions; scarce along the western and southern margins of these areas. There is breeding evidence as far south as Cedar Creek, Anoka County, where it was a common breeder for the past 30 years but is now almost absent. Breeds as far west as eastern Marshall and Kittson Counties in the northwest. What was no doubt a summer vagrant was seen in Wabasha County July 5-19, 1985.

Winter. There are dozens of overwintering records of individuals remaining mainly at feeding stations, primarily in the southern part of the state. Many of the records are from the Twin Cities area where feeding stations are abundant. In recent years numbers of birds have been found wintering in the downtown areas of Minneapolis and St. Paul; up to eight to ten birds have been found in one area. The most birds found in winter were 25 on the Mountain Lake, Cottonwood County Christmas Count on January 1, 1972. In the north, wintering birds have been recorded in Duluth and Lake, Cook, Crow Wing, Clay, Beltrami, Roseau, Pennington, and Otter Tail Counties. Many of these birds disappear after late January. One bird overwintered at International Falls, Koochiching County, during the winter of 1984-85.

WHITE-CROWNED SPARROW
(Zonotrichia leucophrys)

Minnesota status. Regular. Migrant; casual in winter; accidental in summer.

Migration. Uncommon to locally common spring migrant and common to abundant fall migrant throughout the state. Encountered in groups of from a few up to tens of birds. *Spring migration period:* Mid-April through early June, with a peak in mid-May. Earliest dates: SOUTH, *March 29, 30,* April 9, 14, 16; NORTH, April 13, 14, 15. Latest dates: SOUTH, May 23, 26, 30; NORTH, June 3, 6-9, 7-13. *Fall migration period:* Early September through late November, with stragglers in December; the bulk of the migration occurs from late September through mid-October. Earliest dates: NORTH, September 3, 5, 6; SOUTH, September 11, 12, 13. Latest dates: NORTH, October 24, 27, 28, *November 1-3, 13, 24, 25, 29* (only November dates); SOUTH, November 6, 7, 15, *25, 30.*

Winter. Overwintering birds have been recorded in the north, mainly at feeders, in Pine and Otter Tail Counties, and in the south in Benton, Hennepin, Cottonwood, Murray, and Olmsted Counties. In addition, there are records in December from as far north as Duluth, Marshall, and Cook Counties, a number of records in Hennepin County, and individual records from Ramsey, Redwood, Dakota, Scott, and Olmsted Counties. There are individual February records from Winona and Anoka Counties, and, most unusual, two birds on March 7, 1964 in Hennepin County.

Summer. Most unusual is the record of one bird at Pipestone National Monument, Pipestone County, on July 30, 1981 (*The Loon* 53:226).

HARRIS' SPARROW *(Zonotrichia querula)*

Minnesota status. Regular. Migrant and winter visitant.

Migration. Common to locally abundant spring and

fall migrant in the western regions, and uncommon to locally common spring and fall migrant in central and eastern regions. Encountered in groups of from a few to tens of birds. *Spring migration period:* Mid-March through early June, with a peak in mid-May. Earliest dates: SOUTH, March *1, 5, 10* (these could be wintering birds), 18, 19, 20; NORTH, April 17, 20, 22. Latest dates; SOUTH, May 19, 23, 26, *June 16, 19*; NORTH, May 30, 31, June 2, *7. Fall migration period:* Mid-September through late November, with the bulk of the migration in October. Earliest dates: NORTH, September *3*, 8, 10, 11; SOUTH, *August 30*, September *3*, 17, 18, 22. Latest dates: NORTH, November 11, 13, 16, *30*; *December 5*; SOUTH, November 27, 29, 30.

Winter. Regular but rare in the winter in the southwestern region. This species was not known to winter in the state until the mid-1950s; in the 1960s it began to appear regularly in the southwest. There are records throughout the winter (December to February) in more than ten counties throughout the southwest, west-central, and south-central regions (from Watonwan to Pope and Big Stone Counties). Most reports are of individual birds seen at feeders, but a few small groups have been seen in Rock and Jackson Counties. Elsewhere in the state it is casual, with overwintering records from several counties—in the north, Clay, Pennington, and Crow Wing Counties, plus Duluth. There are December and January records in the north from Clearwater, Polk, Wilkin, Carlton, Cook, and St. Louis (Hibbing) Counties. In the central and southern (outside the southwest) regions there are overwintering records from Benton, Olmsted, and Le Sueur Counties. There are other winter records from Mower, Freeborn, Rice, Carver, Ramsey, Dakota, and Hennepin Counties.

DARK-EYED JUNCO *(Junco hyemalis)*

Minnesota status. Regular. Migrant and summer resident; regular in winter.

Migration. An abundant spring and fall migrant throughout the state. Occurs in flocks numbering from a few birds into the hundreds. Often occurs with American Tree Sparrows. *Spring migration period:* Early March through late May, with a peak from late March through mid-April. Earliest dates: None can be given because of wintering birds. Latest dates: SOUTH, May 27, 29, 31; NORTH, none can be given because of breeding birds. *Fall migration period:* Late August through early December, with the bulk of the migration in October. Earliest dates: SOUTH (only), August *4, 18, 25* (only August dates), September 6, 7, 15. Latest dates: None can be given because of wintering birds.

Summer. A resident primarily in the coniferous forests of the northeast and north-central regions as far south as northern Carlton and Crow Wing Counties. Very scarce along the southern and western margins of this range. May occasionally breed as far south as Pine and Chisago Counties in the east-central region. There is one summer record from June 2 to July 12, 1977 at Fergus Falls, Otter Tail County.

Winter. Most often found in the southern and central parts of the state; rare or absent in northern regions, with only a few birds found around feeding stations in the southern part of the state.

Taxonomic note. The Oregon Junco, *J. h. oreganus*, occurs as a spring and fall migrant and winter visitant. The Gray-headed Junco, *J. h. caniceps*, is accidental in the state, with one fall record and three winter records. The fall record is from Tofte, Cook County, from October 27-29, 1968 (*The Loon* 41:10). The winter records are from Duluth (*The Loon* 42:116); Boyd, Lac Qui Parle County (*The Loon* 45:26); and Richardson Nature Center, Hennepin County (*The Loon* 56:70).

Dark-eyed Junco

McCOWN'S LONGSPUR *(Calcarius mccownii)*

Minnesota status. Accidental. This species occurred as a migrant and summer resident in the nineteenth century.

Records. There are two twentieth-century records. One bird was seen and photographed at Grand Marais, Cook County (*The Loon* 54:195), and another individual was seen in Duluth on October 19-20, 1986 (*The Loon* 58:198-99).

Former status. In the nineteenth century this species bred on the high prairie along the extreme western margin of the state from Pipestone County north to Big Stone County and occasionally northward into the Red River Valley. It disappeared from the state about 1900. Roberts (1932) mentioned breeding records from Pipestone, Lincoln, and Lac Qui Parle Counties and an average spring arrival date of May 8 in this area.

LAPLAND LONGSPUR *(Calcarius lapponicus)*

Minnesota status. Regular. Migrant and winter visitant; accidental in summer.

Migration. Common to locally abundant spring and fall migrant in the more open areas of the state; avoids the heavily wooded areas. Most numerous in western regions, where flocks numbering in the thousands are seen at peak migration periods in both spring and fall. Numbers vary from year to year; it may be absent from a given area one year and abundant the next. Least numerous in eastern regions. *Fall migration period:* Early September through mid-November, with peak periods from late September through early October in the north and from late October through early November in the south. Earliest dates: NORTH, September 4, 6, 8; SOUTH, September 8, 10, 13. Latest dates: NORTH, November 19, 21, 29, *December 6*; SOUTH, none can be given because of wintering birds. *Spring migration period:* Late February through late May, with a peak from late March through early April in the south and late April and early May in the north. Earliest dates: SOUTH, none can be given because of wintering birds; NORTH, February 24, March 1, 2. Latest dates: SOUTH, May 5, 6, 8, *30*; NORTH, May 28, 29, 31, *June 4.*

Winter. A common to uncommon winter visitant in the southern and central regions. Flocks numbering up to 500 birds or more may occasionally be encountered. Until recently there were only a few scattered records in northern regions, mainly in mid-December and early January, indicating that they may have been late fall stragglers. During the winters of 1981-82 and 1982-83 many were seen in January and February from the west-central (Wilkin County) region to the northwest (Pennington County) region. During January 1986 flocks were seen in the northwest in Kittson and Marshall Counties.
Summer. A single individual was seen on June 26, 1983 at Rice Lake National Wildlife Refuge, Aitkin County (*The Loon* 55:178).

SMITH'S LONGSPUR *(Calcarius pictus)*

Minnesota status. Regular. Migrant.
Migration. A very rare spring and fall migrant in the west-central and southwest regions. Accidental elsewhere in the state. There are a number of records from Duluth, most of them in the fall, and from Stearns, Blue Earth, Aitkin, Hennepin, and Martin Counties, and in the northwest from Marshall and Kittson Counties. Usually encountered in small groups of fewer than ten birds in conjunction with flocks of Lapland Longspurs. On October 15, 1977 between 250 and 300 were seen in one loose flock at the Rothsay Wildlife Management Area, Wilkin County (*The Loon* 49:242). *Spring migration period:* Early April through mid-May. Earliest dates: SOUTH, March *12, 13* (Lyon County), April *1*, 10, 13, 18; NORTH, no data. Latest dates: SOUTH, May 8, 9, 10; NORTH, May 6, 17 (only dates). *Fall migration period:* Mid-September through mid-November. Earliest dates: NORTH, September 9, 15, 16; SOUTH, October 10, 15, 19. Latest dates: NORTH, October 28, 20, November 6; SOUTH, November 11, 15, 17.

CHESTNUT-COLLARED LONGSPUR
(Calcarius ornatus)

Chestnut-collared Longspur

Minnesota status. Regular. Migrant and summer resident.

Migration. A rare to casual spring and fall migrant in western regions from Rock to Kittson Counties. Accidental elsewhere in the state, with records only from St. Louis (Duluth) and Wadena Counties. In spring most birds seen are on breeding territories. A flock of 15 was seen on September 30, 1973 in Rock County and 150+ were seen on October 27, 1978 in Grant County. *Spring migration period:* Late April through mid-May. Earliest dates: SOUTH, April *12*, 25, 26, 27; NORTH, April 12, 14, 17. *Fall migration period:* Probably mid-August through mid-October; there are very few fall dates. Latest dates: NORTH, September 20, 28, October 11, *27*; SOUTH, October 12, 19, *November 17.*

Summer. At present there are only two breeding locations known in the state. The largest and best known is near Felton, Clay County, in Keene and Flowing Townships. This colony was intensively studied in 1985; an estimated 250 birds were present and breeding. The colony has been known since the late 1950s and probably existed for many years before that time. In July 1984 a second and much smaller breeding colony consisting of approximately 30 birds was discovered in Clifton Township, Traverse County. In addition to these colonies, there are recent June records from Big Stone County (1980) and July records from Yellow Medicine County (1975), indicating that breeding may occur sporadically in other western areas. There is one summer vagrant record at Duluth from June 15-18, 1974. The species formerly bred throughout the western regions from Jackson County to the Canadian border. It disappeared from the southern part of this range about 1900 and gradually disappeared from other portions of this range by the 1950s. It was last recorded in summer in Murray County in the southwest in 1955 and in Grant County in the west-central region also in 1955.

SNOW BUNTING *(Plectrophenax nivalis)*

Minnesota status. Regular. Migrant and winter visitant.

Migration. A common to locally abundant spring and fall migrant throughout the state. Most numerous in northern regions but erratic and sporadic in occurrence, some years very abundant, other years only local in occurrence. Least numerous in the southeast region and heavily wooded portions of the state. Numbers vary from year to year. Encountered in flocks that can number into the hundreds of birds (700 +, April 7, 1978, Lockhart, Norman County). *Fall migration period:* Occasionally mid-September, but usually early October through late November, with the bulk of the migration in early November. Earliest dates: NORTH, *September 1, 3, 6, 8, 10, 14, 18, 29* (only September dates), October 3, 10, 11; SOUTH, *September 26*, October 6, 7, 9, 14, 15, 16. *Spring migration period:* Mid-February through late May, with a peak in late March and early April. Latest dates: SOUTH, May 5, 12, 14, *29* (injured bird); NORTH, May 23, 25, 26.

Winter. Common to abundant winter visitant throughout most of the state. Uncommon to absent in heavily wooded areas of the north-central and northeastern regions. Most numerous in early winter (late December and January). Flocks numbering in the thousands are occasionally encountered: 2,500, late December 1977, Big Stone County; 1,500, January 26, 1982, Aitkin County; and 3,100 + on the 1975 Mountain Lake, Cottonwood County Christmas Count.

BOBOLINK *(Dolichonyx oryzivorus)*

Minnesota status. Regular. Migrant and summer resident.

Migration. A common to locally abundant spring and fall migrant throughout most of the state. Uncommon in the heavily wooded portions of the north-central and northeastern regions. Locally

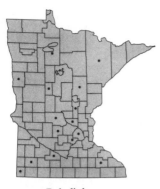

Bobolink

abundant, mainly in the fall when flocking occurs. At that time flocks numbering up to 100 or more birds may be seen. *Spring migration period:* Late April through late May, with a peak in mid-May. Earliest dates: SOUTH, April *15*, 20, 21, 23; NORTH, April *19*, 29, May 4, 6. *Fall migration period:* Late July through early October, with stragglers into November; peak migration period is from late August to early September. Latest dates: NORTH, September 24, 29, October 5, *November 3, 10*; SOUTH, September 30, October 4, 5, *12, 15, 21*.
Summer. A widespread resident throughout most of the state wherever suitable prairie and lowland grassy type habitat is available. Most numerous in the west-central and northwestern regions; least numerous in the heavily wooded portions of the north-central and northeastern regions, where it is found only in the larger more open grassy portions.

RED-WINGED BLACKBIRD
(Agelaius phoeniceus)

Red-winged Blackbird

Minnesota status. Regular. Migrant, summer resident, and winter visitant.
Migration. An abundant spring and fall migrant throughout the state. Occurs in flocks numbering anywhere from a few birds into the thousands, In the spring concentrations of up to 250,000 birds have been seen (March 28, 1964, Black Dog Lake, Dakota County), and in the fall large flocks numbering in the many thousands are common (100,000, October 20, 1979, Anoka County). *Spring migration period:* Late February (south) through early May, with the bulk of the migration from mid-March through mid-April. Earliest dates: SOUTH, mid to late February; NORTH, mid-March. No exact dates can be given because of the presence of wintering birds in both areas. *Fall migration period:* Early August through mid-December, with the bulk of the migration from early October through mid-November. Latest dates: Difficult to determine because of the presence of wintering birds in all

regions of the state; the vast majority of birds have left the state by late November.

Summer. A widespread and numerous resident throughout the state. One of the most common and evenly distributed breeding species in the state.

Winter. Regular in the southern half of the state, occurring from small groups of a few birds around feeding stations and farms to flocks numbering up to 100 birds. Large concentrations have occurred in early winter in the Mississippi River Valley in the southeast region; 25,000 were estimated on December 21, 1980 at LaCrescent, Houston County. Rare in the northern half of the state, but individuals and small groups of ten or fewer have been reported as far north as Marshall County. Most often seen in the north in early winter, although there are February dates from Becker, Hubbard, and Beltrami Counties.

EASTERN MEADOWLARK *(Sturnella magna)*

Minnesota status. Regular. Migrant and summer resident.

Migration. A common spring and fall migrant in eastern regions, except in Lake and Cook Counties where it is rare; decreasing in numbers westward in central regions until it becomes rare to absent over most of the western regions. Ranges as far west as eastern Marshall County, Clearwater and eastern Becker Counties in the northwest to eastern Ottertail County in the west-central region. Ranges only to Stearns, Wright, and Renville Counties in the central region, but reaches the South Dakota border (Rock County) in the southwest region. *Spring migration period:* Early March through early May, with a peak in early April. Earliest dates: SOUTH, difficult to determine because of wintering birds, but most early arrival dates are in early to mid-March; NORTH, March 6, 8, 9. *Fall migration period:* September through late November, with a peak in early and mid-October. Latest dates: NORTH, November 22, 23, 28; SOUTH, none can be given

Eastern Meadowlark

because of wintering birds, but most birds have left the state by late November.

Summer. A resident eastward from eastern Lake of the Woods County, Clearwater, and eastern Otter Tail County in the north; southward through the center of the central region in Nicollet County to Blue Earth and Freeborn Counties in the south.

Winter. Because this species is difficult to distinguish from the Western Meadowlark except by song, the differentiation of winter records for the two species may be unreliable. Meadowlarks occur rarely to casually throughout the winter in the southern half of the state. No doubt some of these birds, especially in the east-central and southeastern regions, are Eastern Meadowlarks.

WESTERN MEADOWLARK *(Sturnella neglecta)*

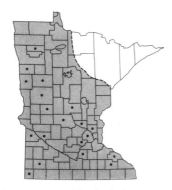

Western Meadowlark

Minnesota status. Regular. Migrant, summer resident, and winter visitant.

Migration. A common to abundant spring and fall migrant throughout most of the state; rare in the north-central and northeastern regions. Usually encountered as individuals, but during migration peaks, especially in the fall, loose aggregations of ten or more birds are occasionally encountered. *Spring migration period:* Early March through early May, with a peak in late March and early April. Earliest dates: SOUTH, difficult to determine because of wintering birds; NORTH, March 2, 6, 10, 11. *Fall migration period:* September through mid-November, with a peak in mid to late October and stragglers into December in the north. Latest dates: NORTH, November 23, 29, 30, *December 8, 9, 10, 17, 18, 22, 23*; SOUTH, difficult to determine because of wintering birds, but most birds have departed by late November.

Summer. A numerous and widespread resident throughout the state except in Lake and Cook Counties in the northeast region, where it is casual to absent. Least numerous in the north-central region and adjoining St. Louis County, where it is rare to casual.

Winter. Both Eastern and Western Meadowlarks occur rarely but regularly across the southern half of the state as far north as Sherburne County in the east and Swift County in the west. There is one overwintering record from Marshall County in the northwest during the winter of 1982-83, a January 1, 1983 record from Aitkin County, February dates from Becker and Hubbard Counties in 1983, and a November 1984 to early January 1985 record from Duluth. These records may indicate that the species is attempting to winter farther north in the state. Because the two species are difficult to separate, especially in the winter, no exact data are available on which species occurs where and when. It is assumed that the Western Meadowlark is the more numerous of the two in winter. It is interesting to note that this species has been heard singing as early as February 18 (in 1978) in Le Sueur County.

YELLOW-HEADED BLACKBIRD
(Xanthocephalus xanthocephalus)

Minnesota status. Regular. Migrant and summer resident; accidental in winter.
Migration. A common to abundant spring and fall migrant throughout most of the state; rare to absent over most of Koochiching and Itasca Counties and most of the northeast region except at Duluth; it is casual along the North Shore of Lake Superior. Usually encountered in flocks, especially in late summer and early fall when up to 200 or more birds may be seen in one flock. *Spring migration period:* Early April through mid-May, with a peak in late April. Earliest dates: SOUTH, March *14,* 19, 21, 25; NORTH, *March 29, 30,* April 7, 8, 9. *Fall migration period:* Mid-August through mid-November, with a peak in late August; unusual after early October. Latest dates: NORTH, October 24, 25, 28, *November 2, 5, 6, December 5*; SOUTH, November 11, 15, 17, *25* (30 in Kandiyohi County), *29.*
Summer. A resident throughout most of the state wherever suitable cattail-marsh habitat exists. Absent over most of the northeast region, but appears

Yellow-headed Blackbird

to be expanding into this area. There are June records for Cook County, but these are probably summer vagrants.

Winter. One bird was seen on December 20, 1980, at Fergus Falls, Otter Tail County, for the only record in the north. In the south there are December and early January records from Hennepin (several years), Dakota, Carver, Big Stone, Lyon, and Houston (20 on December 21, 1981) Counties. There are two records of overwintering birds, one in Nicollet County from December 1980 to February 1981 and the other in Hennepin County from November 1981 to February 1982 (*The Loon* 54:135). There are two other February records, both in Cottonwood County: 25 birds on February 26, 1943 and a single bird on February 24, 1983. These two records could be of exceptionally early migrants.

RUSTY BLACKBIRD *(Euphagus carolinus)*

Rusty Blackbird

Minnesota status. Regular. Migrant and summer resident; casual in winter.

Migration. A common spring and abundant fall migrant throughout the state. Usually encountered in small flocks; in fall flocks containing 100 or more birds are often seen. *Spring migration period:* Early March through early May, with a peak in early to mid-April. Earliest dates: SOUTH, *February 27, 28*, March 6, 9, 16 (often difficult to determine because of wintering birds); NORTH, *February 27*, March 6, 16, 21, 22. Latest dates: SOUTH, May 17, 18, 22; NORTH, away from known breeding areas, May 24, 25, 29. *Fall migration period:* Early September through early December, with the bulk of the migration in October. Earliest dates: NORTH, away from known breeding areas. *August 20*, September 2, 4, 6; SOUTH, *August 26*, September 8, 12, 13. Latest dates: NORTH, November 27, 29, 30, *December 6, 19*; SOUTH, December 5, 7, 12 (often difficult to determine because of wintering birds).

Summer. This species breeds regularly in the

Quetico-Superior area of Ontario just north of the border from the northeastern region of Minnesota. It was not until the late 1960s that this species began to be recorded during June and July in Cook County. Records increased during the 1970s, when it was recorded in Cook, Lake, and northern St. Louis Counties (*The Loon* 47:192). It was not until May 1982 that the first nest was discovered along the South Brule River, Cook County (*The Loon* 54: 141-42). There are recent records in mid-June from Lake County (*The Loon* 54:246-47) and from Cook County in June 1983 and 1984 (carrying food). Because of the inaccessibility of much of the area that this species uses for breeding, it is difficult to confirm nesting, but it is presumed, based on breeding-season sightings, that this species breeds rather regularly in the more remote areas of northern Cook, Lake, and St. Louis Counties.

Winter. There are numerous winter records for this species in the southern half of the state, mainly about farm-feed lots and open-water areas from Hennepin County in the east to Big Stone County in the west. During the winter of 1976-1977 this species was reported north to Wilkin, Otter Tail (also winter 1985-86), and Grant Counties in the west and Todd and Crow Wing Counties in the central part of the state. One bird was seen at Grand Marais, Cook County, on December 26, 1983, possibly a very late migrant.

BREWER'S BLACKBIRD
(Euphagus cyanocephalus)

Minnesota status. Regular. Migrant and summer resident; accidental in winter.

Migration. A common spring and an abundant fall migrant in the central and northern regions; uncommon to casual in all southern regions; and uncommon in the heavily wooded portions of the northern regions. This species expanded its range into Minnesota from the Red River Valley to the east-central

Brewer's Blackbird

region between 1914 and 1918, and into the north-eastern region in 1928 (Roberts, 1932). Usually encountered in small flocks of ten or fewer birds in the spring; in fall flocks numbering in the hundreds are seen (500+ near Campbell Lake, Carver County, on October 3, 1980. *Spring migration period:* Mid-March through early May, with a peak in mid-April. Earliest dates: SOUTH, *February 26*, March *1*, 6, 9, 10; NORTH, March *16, 17*, 21, 22, 23. *Fall migration period:* Mid-August through late November, with the bulk of the migration from late September through mid-October. Latest dates: NORTH, November 9, 11, 13, *24;* SOUTH, November 16, 17, 23, *December 4, 9.*

Summer. A resident in the central and northern regions; very scarce or absent in southern regions south of the Minnesota River except in Lac Qui Parle and Dakota Counties. One was recorded on July 28, 1984 in Houston County, probably a summer vagrant. Only sporadic breeding occurs in these southern regions. Also avoids the heavily wooded portions of the northern regions. Common in the Duluth area, and breeding evidence has been reported as far north as Tofte, Cook County, Hibbing, St. Louis County in the northeast, and Kittson County in the northwest.

Winter. A few stragglers occasionally linger into early winter (December to mid-January) mainly in the southern part of the state. On December 17, 1983, 51 were recorded in Mankato, Blue Earth County. Winter records of this species may be erroneous because of confusion with Rusty Blackbirds and Common Grackles. Few birds remain into February. There are a few early winter records from northern regions: St. Louis County (Hibbing and Duluth, one until January 10, 1987), Marshall, Polk, Otter Tail, and Beltrami Counties. Most unusual was the presence of a single bird at a feeder in Isabella, Lake County, throughout the winter of 1986-87. There is a record of one bird on February 25, 1983 in Clay County, a most unusual date and location, probably an extremely early migrant.

GREAT-TAILED GRACKLE
(Quiscalus mexicanus)

Minnesota status. Accidental.
Records. One bird was seen at Black Dog Lake,
Dakota County on June 19, 1982 (*The Loon* 55:83).
Because the possibility of this bird being a Boat-
tailed Grackle was not completely eliminated, this
species is listed as Great-tailed/Boat-tailed Grackle
(*Quiscalus mexicanus/major*) on the Minnesota
Checklist.

COMMON GRACKLE *(Quiscalus quiscula)*

Minnesota status. Regular. Migrant, summer resident, and winter visitant.
Migration. An abundant spring and fall migrant
throughout the state; least numerous in the heavily
wooded areas of the north-central and northeastern
regions. Usually encountered in flocks, the largest
occurring in fall. Large roasts occasionally occur;
the incredible number of 400,000 were estimated in
Anoka County on October 20, 1970, and 800,000
to 1,000,000 birds during the fall of 1974 at Palmer
Lake Slough, Hennepin County. The population of
this species may have peaked in the mid-1970s; it

Common Grackle

appeared to be leveling off or possibly declining in
1984. *Spring migration period:* Late February
through early May, with a peak in late March and
early April. Earliest dates: SOUTH, difficult to determine because of wintering birds, but obvious migrants begin to show up in late February and early
March; NORTH, March 2, 6, 10, 11, 12. *Fall migration period:* Postbreeding flocking begins in late
July, migration from late August through late November, with a peak from mid-October through early November; stragglers frequently remain until mid
or late December. Latest dates: Very difficult to
determine because of the presence of stragglers in
any area of the state into early winter; the bulk of
the population has left the state by mid-November.
Summer. A widespread and numerous resident

throughout the state, especially numerous in rural areas around windbreaks and in urban areas where plantings of evergreen trees are numerous. Less numerous in the heavily wooded areas of the north-central and northeastern regions.

Winter. Individuals or small flocks can be found throughout the winter at feeding stations in urban areas or around cattle feedlots in rural areas. Most often seen in southern areas, with records from numerous counties. Numbers dwindle by late winter. In the north it is rare; there are a few records of individuals as far north as Pennington, Lake of the Woods, Koochiching, and Cook Counties in early winter.

BROWN-HEADED COWBIRD *(Molothrus ater)*

Brown-headed Cowbird

Minnesota status. Regular. Migrant and summer resident; casual in winter.

Migration. A common to abundant spring migrant and an uncommon to common fall migrant throughout the state. Usually encountered in small flocks numbering anywhere from a few birds to 100 or more. *Spring migration period:* Early March through early May, with a peak in mid-April. Earliest dates: SOUTH, *February 28, March 1, 3,* 6, 7, 9; NORTH, March 30, 31, April 1. *Fall migration period:* Very poorly defined; it appears that most resident birds leave in late June and July after the normal breeding season is over. Some migration is then noted sporadically throughout the fall. Latest dates: NORTH, November 1, 4, 6; SOUTH, November 23, 24, 25.

Summer. The species parasitizes nests of host species throughout the state, most numerous in the wooded areas of the state where nesting songbirds are abundant.

Winter. Casual in early winter in the southern half of the state, southward from Hennepin County in the east to Big Stone County in the west. Most often seen in early winter (December and January). Usually seen in conjunction with other wintering blackbird species around feeding stations in urban areas and cattle feedlots in rural areas. On the 1975 Winona, Winona County Christmas Bird Count held in late December, a total of 74 cowbirds were counted and from February 2-10, 1974, 25 were present in Winona. Up to ten individuals were present at a feeder in Mankato, Blue Earth County, during the winter of 1983-84.

ORCHARD ORIOLE *(Icterus spurius)*

Minnesota status. Regular. Migrant and summer resident.

Migration. A rare spring migrant in southern and western regions and into the southern portions of the east-central and central regions as far north as Washington, Anoka, Sherburne, and Stearns Counties. In the west it ranges regularly as far north as Clay County and occasionally all the way to the Canadian border in Kittson County. Accidental north of the above areas in the east with records from Pine (Finlayson, May 25, 1981) and St. Louis (Stony Point, May 21, 1979) Counties. Little is known about its movements in the fall. Most often seen on breeding territories, and usually encountered as individuals or in pairs. *Spring migration period:* May. Earliest dates: SOUTH, *April 28, 30,* May 2, 3, 4; NORTH, May 5, 11, 12, 15. *Fall migration period:* A gradual exodus from the state from late July through early September. Latest dates: NORTH, August 27, September 6 (only dates); SOUTH, August 28, September 3, 4.

Summer. A resident in the same areas as given under migration: the southern and western regions, and the southern portions of the east-central and central regions. In the west, regular as far north as Red Lake County; there are no recent records farther north. There are two early June records from other north areas; June 2-5, 1974, Duluth; and June 2, 1984, Ponemah, Beltrami County. Best represented and most numerous in the southeastern region in Houston, Winona, and Wabasha Counties, and along the Minnesota River Valley from

Orchard Oriole

Nicollet and Blue Earth Counties westward and also in the far southwest corner of the state in Rock and Pipestone Counties.

NORTHERN ORIOLE *(Icterus galbula)*

Northern Oriole

Minnesota status. Regular. Migrant and summer resident; accidental in winter.
Migration. A common spring and fall migrant throughout most of the state; uncommon to rare in Cook and Lake Counties in the northeast region in both seasons. Usually encountered as individuals or pairs in spring; in fall loose aggregations of family groups and migrants consisting of ten or more birds may occasionally be seen. *Spring migration period:* late April through early June, with a peak in mid-May. Earliest dates: SOUTH, April 24, 26, 27; NORTH, *April 11, 25,* May 2, 3, 4. *Fall migration period:* August through late September. Latest dates: NORTH, September 14, 15, 17, *October 26, November 1, 13;* SOUTH, September 30, October 1, 4, *8, November 9, 10.*
Summer. A widespread and numerous resident throughout most of the state, rare and local in the extreme northeast (Lake and Cook Counties).
Winter. A number of individuals have attempted to overwinter in the Twin Cities area and in Winona. These birds appear at feeding stations in mid-November and usually disappear or perish by early January. The latest dates of survival in the Twin Cities area are January 12, 15, 29. A single bird is reported to have survived over the winter of 1982-83 in Winona, Winona County. One bird was present at a feeder from November 13 to December 15, 1984 at Hoyt Lakes, St. Louis County.
Taxonomic note. An immature male Bullock's Oriole (*I. g. bullockii*) was banded and photographed at a feeding station in Duluth from mid-October to December 13, 1968 (*The Loon* 41:41-42).

SCOTT'S ORIOLE *(Icterus parisorum)*

Minnesota status. Accidental.
Records. An immature male was seen and banded at Duluth from May 23 to mid-June 1974 (*The Loon* 47:22-24, 48:34).

BRAMBLING *(Fringilla montifringilla)*

Minnesota status. Accidental.
Records. A single individual appeared at a feeder in Owatonna, Steele County, in mid-January 1984 and remained at the feeder or in the area until March 24, 1984 (*The Loon* 56:79-80).

ROSY FINCH *(Leucosticte arctoa)*

Minnesota status. Casual. Migrant and winter visitant.
Records. There are nine records for this species in the state from late fall to early spring. October 28, 1972, Grand Rapids, Itasca County (*The Loon* 45:20); on January 3, 1889 a male was shot from a flock of Snow Buntings near Minneapolis (Roberts, 1932); from late December 1967 to March 1968, two birds visited a feeder at Bagley, Clearwater County (*The Loon* 40:99); a single bird visited a feeder in Minnetonka, Hennepin County, from December 26, 1980 to January 23, 1981 (*The Loon* 53:116-17); one bird visited a feeder from January 25 to February 16, 1972 at Little Marais, Lake County (*The Loon* 44:117-18); from December 1977 to March 2, 1978, one, possibly two birds were seen at two different feeders in Menagha, Wadena County (*The Loon* 50:213). The spring records of single birds are: March 11, 1978, Hoyt Lakes, St. Louis County (*The Loon* 50:171-72); March 31, 1976, Bemidji, Beltrami County (*The Loon* 48:185-86); March 27 to April 6, 1974, Pokegama Lake, Pine County (*The Loon* 46:82).

PINE GROSBEAK *(Pinicola enucleator)*

Minnesota status. Regular. Migrant and winter visitant; accidental in summer.

Migration. A common to uncommon fall migrant into the northeastern and north-central regions; uncommon to rare in northwestern, central, and east-central regions; accidental elsewhere. Numbers fluctuate from year to year, especially outside the northeastern region. Usually does not reach southern regions until late winter, and this usually occurs only in invasion years. Much less numerous in spring, except in invasion years. Most birds withdraw northward by late winter and early spring. Usually encountered in loose flocks or groups of ten to 100 birds. *Fall migration period:* Mid-October through late November and into December depending on the availability of food. Earliest dates: NORTH, *September 15, 29, 30*, October *3, 6*, 16, 18, 19; SOUTH, *September 22, October 15, 25*, November 1, 7, 11. *Spring migration period:* A gradual exodus, with most birds departing from the south by late February to early March and from the north by late March or early April. Latest dates: SOUTH, April 1, 10, 12, *16*; NORTH, April 22, 26, 30, *May 5*, 6.

Winter. Usually a common visitant in the northeastern and north-central regions; numbers vary from uncommon to abundant, the latter during invasion years. In the northern part of the northwestern, the central, east-central, and southeastern regions, the species is usually rare to uncommon and in some years totally absent. It is occasionally common in these regions during invasion years. During the winter of 1977-78, which was the largest invasion on record, the species was common to the Iowa border in the southeast region (Houston and Fillmore Counties [*The Loon* 50:164]). It is accidental in any year in the south-central and southwestern regions. Several birds were present in Austin, Mower County, from January 13 to February 2, 1985, and they were present in Mountain Lake, Cottonwood County in the same period. During the winter of 1985-86 birds ranged southward into the southeastern part of the state; several birds were present in Rochester, Olmsted County, during December 1985 and January and February 1986, and they were also seen in Waseca and Cottonwood Counties. The availability of its winter food, such as cones and berries, does much to determine the distribution of this species, especially during invasion years.

Summer. The only summer record is of a single bird at Burntside Lake, St. Louis County, from June 16 to 24, 1971. There are two August records: August 20, 1930, Itasca County (Roberts, 1932) and August 27, 1979, Duluth Township, St. Louis County. These records are difficult to categorize; they are either nonbreeding summer vagrants or exceptionally early fall migrants.

PURPLE FINCH *(Carpodacus purpureus)*

Minnesota status. Regular. Migrant, summer resident, and winter visitant.

Migration. A common fall and spring migrant in the eastern and central regions; uncommon in the western regions during both seasons. May occasionally be abundant at peak spring migration periods in the eastern region. Usually encountered in small groups from a few birds to 10 or more; occasionally 50 or more birds are seen in one area. *Fall migration period:* Mid-July (north) through late November; most birds have left the north by early November. Earliest dates: NORTH, none can be given because of breeding birds; SOUTH, away from breeding areas, September 1, 3, 4. *Spring migration period:* Late February through late May, with a peak from late March to mid-April. Latest dates: SOUTH, away from breeding areas, May 22, 24, 25; NORTH, none can be given because of breeding birds.

Summer. A resident throughout the northeastern and north-central regions southward into the northern portions of the central and east-central regions. Occurs regularly south to Isanti and Stearns Counties, and occasionally west to eastern Otter Tail,

Purple Finch

Becker, Marshall, and Kittson Counties. There are a few summer records for the Twin Cities region and southward into the southeastern region, and there is a record from Brown County in the south-central region on July 28-August 2, 1985. These are presumed to be nonbreeding summer wanderers since there is no breeding evidence from these regions.

Winter. A widespread visitant in the state. Numbers vary considerably from year to year; invasions occur erratically in both north and south, usually in late winter or early spring; usually rare or absent over most of the northern regions in mid-winter, uncommon in the west-central, southwestern, and south-central regions. Best represented in the central, east-central, and southeastern regions.

HOUSE FINCH *(Carpodacus mexicanus)*

Minnesota status. Accidental.
Records. A specimen of this species was taken in Minneapolis during the spring of 1876, thought to be an escaped bird. During the 1960s and 1970s this species began expanding westward from an introduced population on the east coast of the United States. At this time the wild population in the western United States was expanding eastward. It was not until 1980 that the first positive identification of this species was made in the state; a single male was seen at a feeder in Minnetonka, Hennepin County, on November 21 and December 15, 1980 (*The Loon* 53:109). There were no positive records in 1981 or 1982, but in 1983 single individuals were seen on December 9 in Hennepin County (*The Loon* 56:64) and December 3, 4, 6, and 8 in Mankato, Blue Earth County (*The Loon* 56:130-31). In 1984 a single male was seen on March 18 at a feeder in St. Cloud, Stearns County (*The Loon* 56:194), and an immature male was seen on April 25, 1984 at Austin, Mower County (*The Loon* 56:198-99) and another male was seen from mid-May to mid-June at a feeder on Ripple Lake, Aitkin County (*The*

Loon 56:189-90). In 1985 a single bird was seen at Lewiston, Winona County, on May 12 (*The Loon* 57:137) and another bird was seen at Le Sueur, Le Sueur County, on July 6 and 7 (*The Loon* 57:134). On September 2, 1985 a single bird was seen at Pipestone, Pipestone County. In 1986 records for this species began to increase. On April 7 and 8 a single male was seen at St. Cloud, Stearns County (*The Loon* 59:204); on May 6 another male was seen at Fergus Falls, Otter Tail County; from December 22 to 28 a single female was at a feeder in Marshall, Lyon County; most interesting was the presence of a pair of birds at a feeder in north Minneapolis from mid-November through late December.

RED CROSSBILL *(Loxia curvirostra)*

Minnesota status. Regular. Migrant, erratic summer resident, and winter visitant.
Migration. An erratic migrant in many parts of the state in both seasons. Best represented in the northeast and north-central regions. When present the species is usually uncommon, but it may be locally common in the north at peak migration periods. Unpredictable in distribution and numbers vary from season to season and from year to year. Unrecorded in many areas in the central, west-central, and southwest regions. Because of the erratic occurrence of this species, no exact migration periods

Red Crossbill

can be delineated. In the spring, winter invasion flocks usually have left the state by mid-April. A few birds may remain to breed. Usually encountered in flocks numbering from a few birds to 50 or more. The years of major invasions are as follows: 1961 (February to May); 1972-1973 (June, all over the state); 1974; minor influx in the fall of 1975; 1982 (January through November); 1984-1985 (November to May) biggest invasion on record, found in many areas of the state, including south and southwest regions.
Summer. In the summer flocks may invade mainly in the north, but they can occur in other areas from

mid-June through August, no later in the fall. The only positive nesting record for this erratic species is of a nest found in 1967 (*The Auk* 86:352-53) from Clay County. There are records of juveniles just out of the nest from St. Louis, Clearwater, Cook, Washington, Pennington, and Ramsey Counties. These records indicate erratic nesting mainly in northern regions. There are summer records as far south as Cottonwood County in the southwest region and Rice County in the south-central region. There are scattered records from localities in the central regions. These summer occurrences in the central and southern regions may be mainly non-breeding visitants, but sporadic nesting may occur.

Winter. Erratic visitant in many parts of the state. Completely absent in some years, uncommon to locally common in other years. Most often seen in the northeastern and north-central regions, but during invasion years flocks may wander all the way to the Iowa border. The numbers and areas of occurrence are dependent on the availability of coniferous cones, this species' primary food supply in winter. During the winter of 1984-85 there was a large invasion of this species in most areas of the state, with records occurring south to the Iowa border.

WHITE-WINGED CROSSBILL *(Loxia leucoptera)*

Minnesota status. Regular. Migrant, erratic summer visitant, and winter visitant.

Migration. An erratic migrant in many parts of the state during both spring and fall. Usually best represented in the northeastern and north-central regions. Numbers, which are sporadic, vary from rare to abundant, abundant in invasion years only. It is usually rare in central and southern regions, but varies from uncommon to locally common during invasion years. Unrecorded in many areas in the central, west-central, and southwest regions. Like the Red Crossbill, it is unpredictable in distribution and numbers vary from season to season and from year to year. Usually less common than the Red Crossbill and less widespread, although larger flocks of this species do occur and this species appears to be more subject to invasions than does the Red Crossbill. Because of its erratic occurrence, no exact migration periods can be accurately described. An invasion peak may occur at any season, but most often it occurs in late fall in northern regions. There is a gradual exodus of these invasion flocks by the end of April. Late dates in the south are May 14, 17, 18. Usually occurs in flocks of from a few birds up to 50 or more. On July 31 and August 1, 1977 flocks numbering 200+ birds were seen in Cook County.

Summer. This species is probably a very scarce and sporadic resident in the coniferous forests of the northeast and north-central regions. No actual nests have been found, but fledged juvenile birds being fed by adults have been observed in Cook, St. Louis (Duluth), and Clearwater (Itasca State Park) Counties. Birds were seen in Lake County from June 26 to July 29, 1984 and in Cook County on July 27, 1984. Flocks of juveniles and adults may be seen in northern areas from late June through August. Most unusual even for this erratic species was the observation of a flock of ten birds at Luverne, Rock County, on July 5, 1975. This is the only summer record in the southern part of the state.

Winter. An uncommon to common visitant mainly in northern regions, abundant in invasion years. During invasion years such as 1981-82 this species was recorded as far south as Blue Earth, Mower, and Martin Counties in the south-central region, and in 1984-85 it occurred in many areas of the southern regions south to the Iowa border. However, in most years it is rare to uncommon in the central regions and rare to totally absent over most of the south.

COMMON REDPOLL *(Carduelis flammea)*

Minnesota status. Regular. Migrant and winter visitant.

Migration. A common to uncommon spring and fall migrant, abundant during invasion years in northern and central regions; rare in southern regions except during invasion years when it can be uncommon to common. Usually rare to absent in southwest regions. Usually encountered in flocks of from a few birds to hundreds; flocks in excess of 1,000 birds are occasionally recorded in peak invasion years. *Fall migration period:* Early October through late November. Earliest dates: NORTH, October 4, 5, 8; SOUTH, October 14, 16, 17, 18. *Spring migration period:* Early February through late May, with the bulk of the migration from mid-March through mid-April. Latest dates: SOUTH, April 20, 22, 28, *May 1, 5, 15*; NORTH, May 19, 20, 26.

Winter. Normally a common visitant in northern and central regions, uncommon to rare in southern regions, especially in the southwest where it is normally absent. Numbers vary from year to year; an example of an invasion winter was 1981-82 when birds reached the Iowa border and were even seen in the southwestern region where they had not been reported since 1974. During invasion years large flocks of thousands of birds are occasionally seen, especially in the north.

HOARY REDPOLL *(Carduelis hornemanni)*

Minnesota status. Regular. Migrant and winter visitant.

Migration. A rare fall migrant in northern regions, rare to casual in central regions, and accidental in the southern regions. In the spring rare to uncommon in northern regions, rare in central regions, and accidental across the south. Absent from many portions of the above range. Usually encountered as individuals in flocks of Common Redpolls; the larger the flocks of the latter, the more likely the occurrence of this species. Up to ten or more individuals have been recorded in large flocks of Common Redpolls. Like the Common Redpoll, numbers vary from year to year. *Fall migration* *period:* Late October into December. Earliest dates: NORTH, October *18*, 24, 27, 28; SOUTH, October 21, November 3 (only dates), usually does not occur until late December. *Spring migration period:* Probably February through April. Latest dates: SOUTH, April 6, 12, 15; NORTH, April 20, 22, 23, *May 11*, Duluth (*The Loon* 54:191).

Winter. A rare visitant mainly into northern regions; occasionally uncommon during invasion years. Years of recent winter invasions are 1973-74, 1975-76 (reported from 15 counties), 1977-78, and major invasions in 1981-82 and 1984-85. Rare to casual in central regions and accidental in southern regions. During invasion years individuals have occurred as far south as the Iowa border in the southeastern region, Blue Earth County in the south-central region, and Lincoln (January 25, 1985) County in the southwest. Most often found with Common Redpolls.

PINE SISKIN *(Carduelis pinus)*

Minnesota status. Regular. Migrant, summer resident, and winter visitant.

Migration. A common to at times abundant (during invasion years) spring and fall migrant in the eastern and central regions; uncommon to rare in western regions; absent in many years in the southwest region. Numbers are variable from one year to the next. Usually encountered in flocks ranging in size from a few birds to 50 or more. Because of the erratic pattern of movements of this species, no exact migration periods can be given. In the fall birds begin to show up in the south by late September or early October. In the spring, migration takes place primarily in April and most birds have left the south by mid-May.

Pine Siskin

Summer. A sporadic resident primarily in the northeastern and north-central regions, with occasional breeding in the central region (Stearns County). After fall and winter invasions individuals and pairs remain in the south. There are nesting records as far south as Hennepin, Ramsey, Rice, Blue Earth, and Winona (*The Loon* 56:197-98, 57:141) Counties in the east and central areas, and a sight observation of adults and young in June in Lac Qui Parle County in the west. There is also one sight observation in Houston County in the southeast corner of the state on June 20, 1980. During the summer of 1984 nesting occurred in Lake, Stearns, and Ramsey Counties, and there were observations in Hennepin and Brown Counties.

Winter. An erratic visitant throughout the state, most numerous in eastern and central regions, especially in the Twin Cities area and other urban areas around feeding stations. Least numerous in the west, seen only in the southwest during invasion years. Distribution and numbers vary sharply from one year to another. During invasion years the species may be abundant in many areas of the east and central regions. May be absent in the north during one year and abundant the next. More regular in numbers in east-central and central regions, with some birds present every winter.

AMERICAN GOLDFINCH *(Carduelis tristis)*

Minnesota status. Regular. Migrant, summer resident, and winter visitant.

Migration. A common to abundant spring and fall migrant throughout the state; most numerous in southern and central regions. Usually encountered in small flocks consisting of a few birds up to 30 or sometimes more individuals. *Spring migration period:* Early April (south) through early June (north), with the bulk of the migration in mid to late April. Earliest dates: SOUTH, none can be given because of wintering birds; NORTH, April 1, 3, 8. *Fall migration period:* Early September through late November, with the bulk of the migration in October. Latest dates: NORTH, most birds have departed by early November, but stragglers remain into early winter; SOUTH, none can be given because of wintering birds.

American Goldfinch

Summer. A widespread and numerous resident throughout most of the state. Most numerous in the southern half; also well represented in the north, but avoids the heavily wooded areas of the northeast and north-central regions.

Winter. Winter flocking begins in late November and December as wintering birds congregate around food supplies such as feeding stations in urban areas. Winter numbers are variable, fluctuating in abundance from one year to the next. It is usually common in southern and central regions. In the north it is generally absent after November, since most individuals have retreated southward. In 1979 good numbers were recorded in late December on the Itasca State Park (Clearwater County), Walker (Cass County), and Warren (Marshall County) Christmas Bird Counts. During the winter of 1982-83 for the first time on record this species was found commonly in many northern areas. Whether this northern invasion phenomenon will continue or is of sporadic occurrence is not known at the present time.

EVENING GROSBEAK
(Coccothraustes vespertinus)

Minnesota status. Regular. Migrant, summer resident, and winter visitant.

Migration. A common but erratic spring and fall migrant in the more heavily wooded portions of northern regions southward in the northern portions of the central region. Uncommon in the open areas of the northwest and west-central region, and uncommon in the east-central and southern portions of the central regions. Rare to absent over most of the southern regions except in the southeast where it is occasionally uncommon. Usually encountered in small flocks of fewer than ten birds, but occasionally larger flocks of up to 100 or more birds are seen. *Fall migration period:* Late July (north) through early December, with the bulk of the migration in late October and all through November. Earliest dates: NORTH, none can be given because

Evening Grosbeak

of breeding birds; SOUTH, *August 20, 24, 30, September 4, 6, 15, October 5*, 15, 16, 17. *Spring migration period:* March through early June (north), with the bulk of the migration from mid-April through mid-May. Latest dates: SOUTH, May 19, 23, 24, *38;* NORTH, none can be given because of breeding birds.

Summer. A sporadic resident in the northeastern and north-central regions as far west as eastern Becker County and Clearwater County and as far south as northeastern Morrison County (*The Loon* 46:91). Sporadic in occurrence, but indications are that it is increasing as a breeding species in the above areas and may be expanding westward and southward.

Winter. A visitant throughout most of the northern half of the state, usually in flocks at feeding stations in urban areas, but occasionally in the coniferous forest where there is an adequate food supply. Erratic in distribution and variable in numbers from year to year. Normally common to abundant in the north, decreasing in numbers southward to where it is uncommon to rare in the southern one-third of the state. Absent over much of the southwest and south-central regions. During the winter of 1984-85 a minor invasion took place in the southern part of the state with birds ranging as far south as Rochester, Olmsted County, in the east and Ortonville, Big Stone County, and Marshall, Lyon County, in the west. The winter of 1985-86 saw a major invasion into southern regions, with small flocks being reported south to the Iowa border especially in the east and in Brown and Watonwan Counties in the south-central region; scattered individuals were reported in the southwest as far as Jackson County.

HOUSE SPARROW *(Passer domesticus)*

Minnesota status. Regular, introduced. Permanent resident.

Distribution. Permanent resident throughout the

state; does not occur in heavily wooded areas. This Old World species was introduced into the Twin Cities area in 1875 and became established as a breeding bird two years later. Roberts (1932) described its acclimatization in Minnesota as follows: "From this time (1877) it spread steadily throughout the state, following the lines of railroads and establishing itself first in cities and towns. It took some years to develop a breed hardy enough to endure the long cold winters, and for a time many perished when conditions were especially severe. It reached Lanesboro, Fillmore County, in the south-eastern part of the state in the fall of 1886; Duluth in 1887; Tower, on the Iron Range in St. Louis County, in 1892; and about the same time the Red River Valley in the northwestern corner of the state."

House Sparrow

Migration. Although this species is not thought to migrate, flocks that are perhaps migrants have been reported in the fall along the North Shore of Lake Superior. Since most people ignore this bird, the information available on it is not sufficient to permit a description of its migration movements.

APPENDIX

Garganey—Waseca County; April 29, 1987.
Golden-crowned Sparrow—Chippewa County; April 29, 1987.
Magnificent Hummingbird—Boyd, Lac Qui Parle County; July 3, 5, 1987.
Cassin's Finch—Duluth, St. Louis County; November 11, 12, 1987.

Species Referred to in the Literature but not on Official List

These species have been referred to in *The Flicker* and *The Loon* (unless otherwise noted). They are not on the official list of Minnesota birds for the reasons stated. Also, since 1981, a few species have been listed in *The Loon* in articles titled "Proceedings of the Minnesota Ornithological Records Committee"; these have not been accepted on the state list. Readers may consult the articles for information on why the records were not accepted.

Glossy Ibis. (*The Wilson Bulletin* 51:183; *Minnesota Birds*, p. 40.) The details of this sighting do not rule out the possibility of its being a White-faced Ibis. The record is referred to under White-faced Ibis.

American Flamingo. (*The Loon* 47:43-44.) This individual seen at Agassiz National Wildlife Refuge, Marshall County, was found to be an escapee from the Winnipeg, Manitoba Zoo.

Black-shouldered Kite (White-tailed Kite). (*The Loon* 48:180-82 and 57:120.) The description of the bird provided by the observer contained numerous discrepancies, and the record was found unacceptable by the Minnesota Ornithological Records Committee.

Common Black-Hawk. (*The Loon* 50:31-34.) Because this species is not known to wander from its range in the southwestern part of the United States and because the source of the specimen taken in Beltrami County could not be determined, the species was dropped from the Minnesota list.

Chukar. (*Minnesota Birds*, p. 74.) This species became established in the state from numerous releases of captive birds from 1937 to 1947. After that time no releases were made and it declined in numbers until only a few birds remained in the northeastern part of the state. The last remnant flock resided in Ely, St. Louis County, and was maintained with human assistance until the early 1970s. The Minnesota Ornithological Records Committee decided to drop the species from the state list because it was an introduced species that maintained only a semi-wild population for a very short time and then died out.

Slaty-backed Gull. The sight record of a gull with a dark mantle on January 4, 1968 at Knife River, Lake County, most closely fits this species (*The Loon* 41:55-56); *American Birds* 40:215). However, because no photographs were obtained and the bird was seen and described by a single observer, the level of certainty is not great enough to include this species on the state list.

Common Ground-Dove. (*The Loon* 40:18–19.) Because the origin of the specimen could not be determined, it was not added to the state list.

Monk Parakeet. (*The Loon* 48:80, 49:238, and 52:187.) It is presumed that these individuals were escapees from captivity.

Curlew Sandpiper. (*The Flicker* 24:160.) The description provided by the observer does not rule out the possibility of another shorebird species such as Dunlin or White-rumped Sandpipers.

Smooth-billed Ani. (*The Loon* 46:34.) The bird described did not have grooves in the bill, thus it was identified as a probable escaped Smooth-billed Ani. However, the bird was no doubt an immature Groove-billed Ani, which is much more likely in the state. The observer was not aware that in some immature Groove-billed Anis the grooves on the bill are not always prominent.

European Goldfinch. (*The Loon* 39:105; *Minnesota Birds*, p. 177.) This record was thought to be that of a released or escaped cage bird.

INDEX

A lifelong resident of Minnesota and a birder, **Robert B. Janssen** received his B.A. in geography from the University of Minnesota in 1954. He has been the editor of *The Loon* magazine, published by the Minnesota Ornithologists Union, since 1959. Janssen is co-author of *Minnesota Birds: Where, When and How Many* (University of Minnesota Press, 1975).